SHONEN JUMP MANGA EDITION

NARUTO

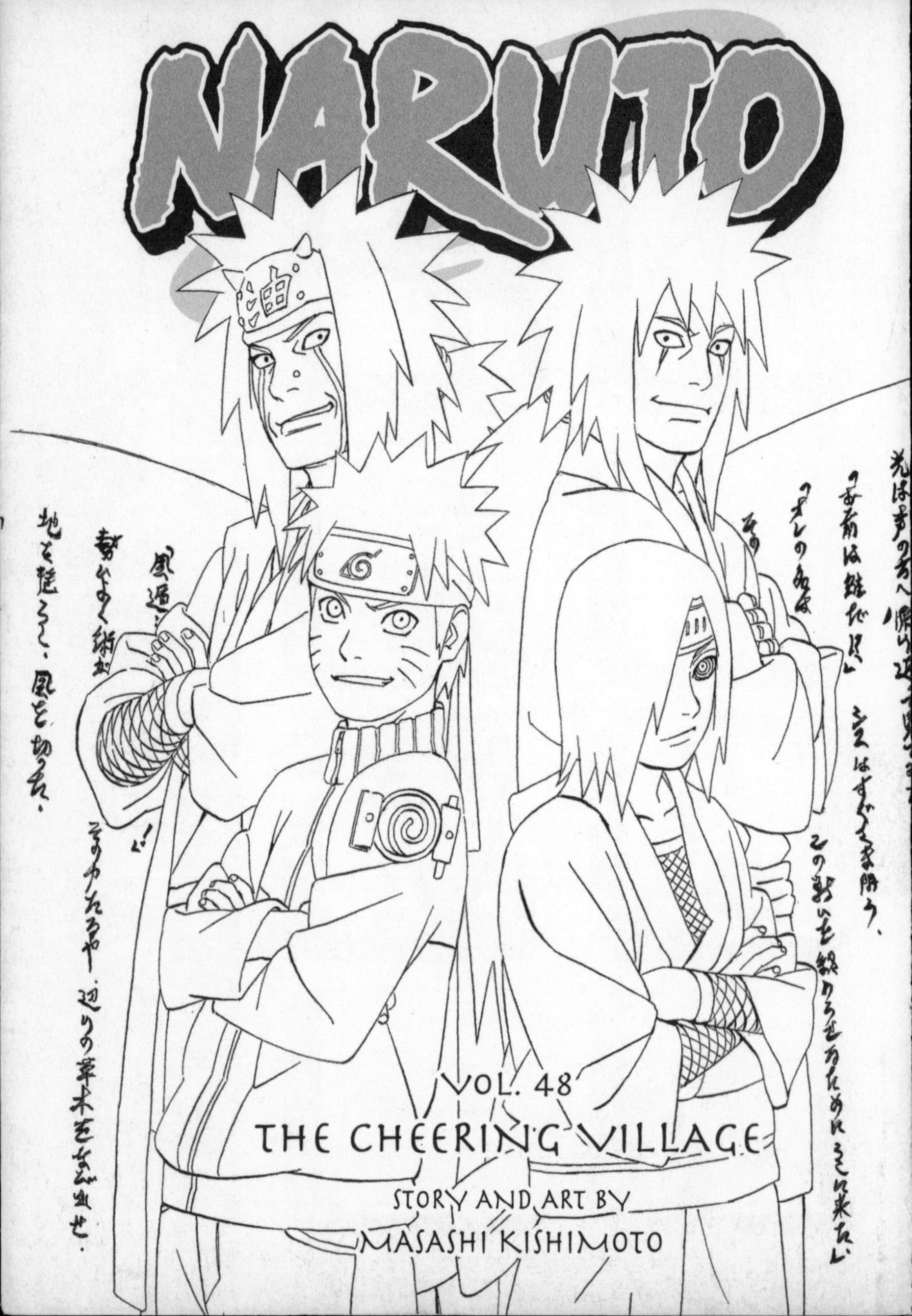

VOL. 48

THE CHEERING VILLAGE

STORY AND ART BY
MASASHI KISHIMOTO

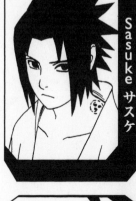

Sasuke サスケ

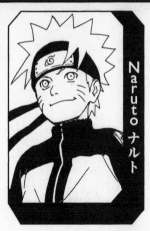

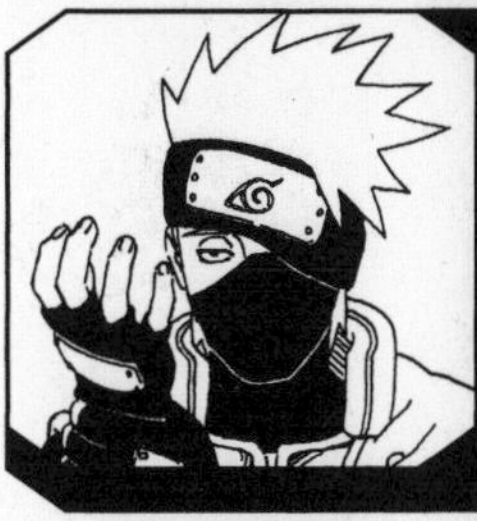

Naruto ナルト

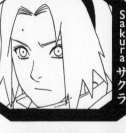

Sakura サクラ

Kakashi カカシ

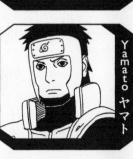

Yamato ヤマト

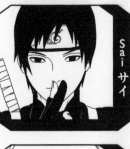

Sai サイ

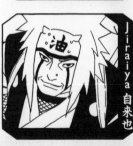

Jiraiya 自来也

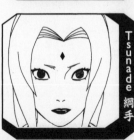

Tsunade 綱手

CHARACTERS

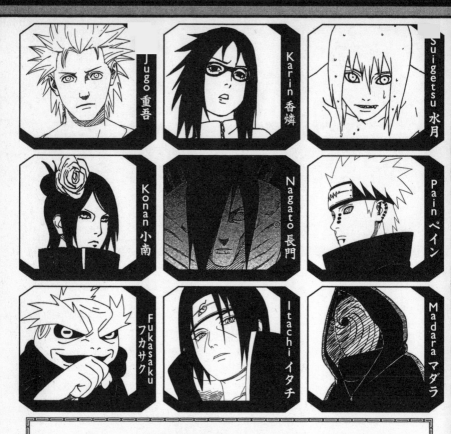

Jugo 重吾

Karin 香燐

Suigetsu 水月

Konan 小南

Nagato 長門

Pain ペイン

Fukasaku フカサク

Itachi イタチ

Madara マダラ

———— THE STORY SO FAR... ————

Naruto, the biggest troublemaker at the Ninja Academy in the Village of Konohagakure, finally becomes a ninja along with his classmates Sasuke and Sakura. They grow and mature through countless trials and battles. However, Sasuke, unable to give up his quest for vengeance, leaves Konohagakure to seek Orochimaru and his power...

Two years pass. Naruto grows up and engages in fierce battles against the Tailed Beast-targeting Akatsuki. Elsewhere, after winning the heroic battle against Itachi and learning his older brother's true intentions, Sasuke allies with Akatsuki and sets out to destroy Konoha!

During his battle against Pain, Naruto releases the Nine Tails' power... But when Naruto has a conversation with the Fourth Hokage, he regains control over himself and heads toward Pain's mastermind to end it all!!

NARUTO

VOL. 48
THE CHEERING VILLAGE

CONTENTS

Number 443: The Interview!!

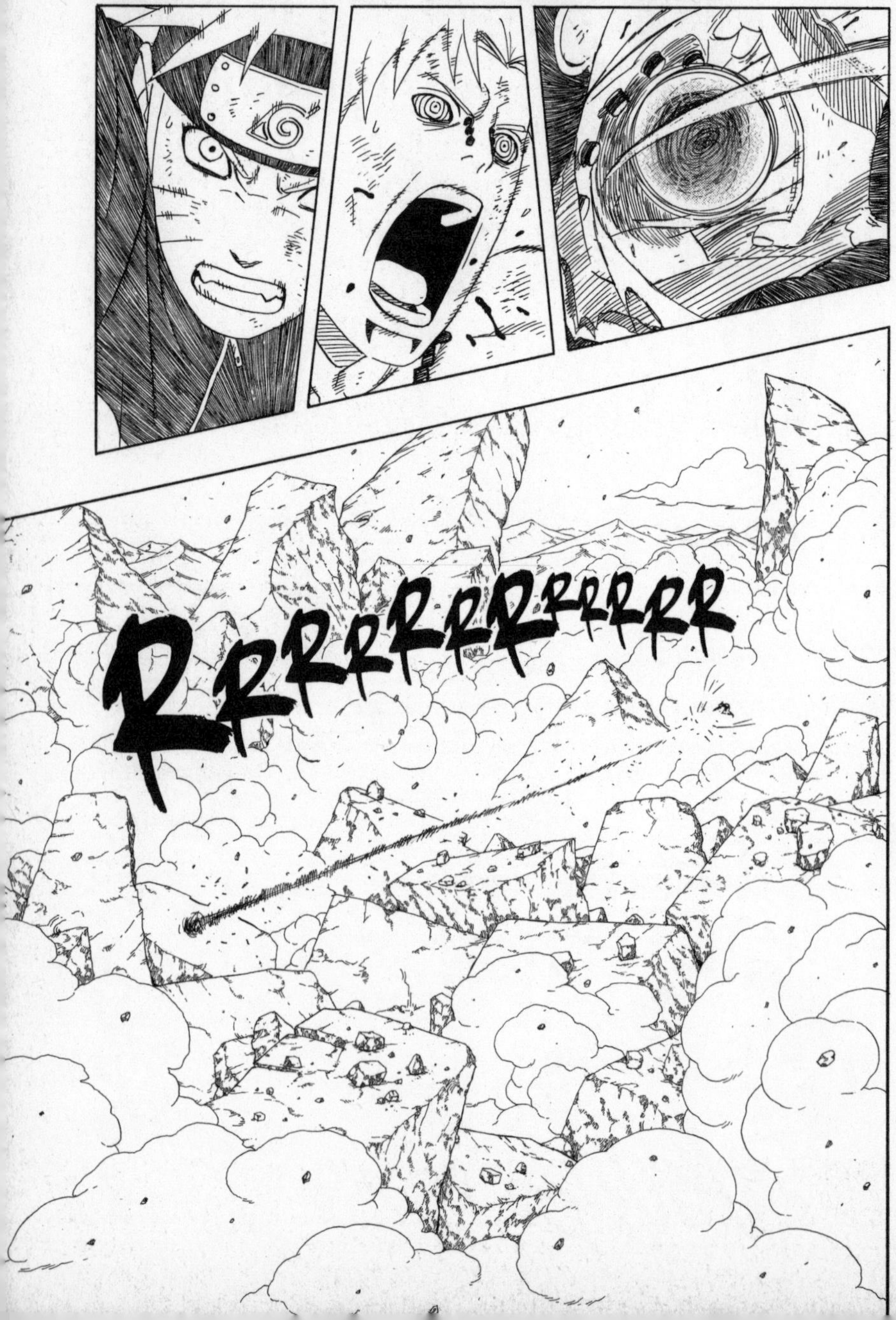
RRRRRRRRRRRRR

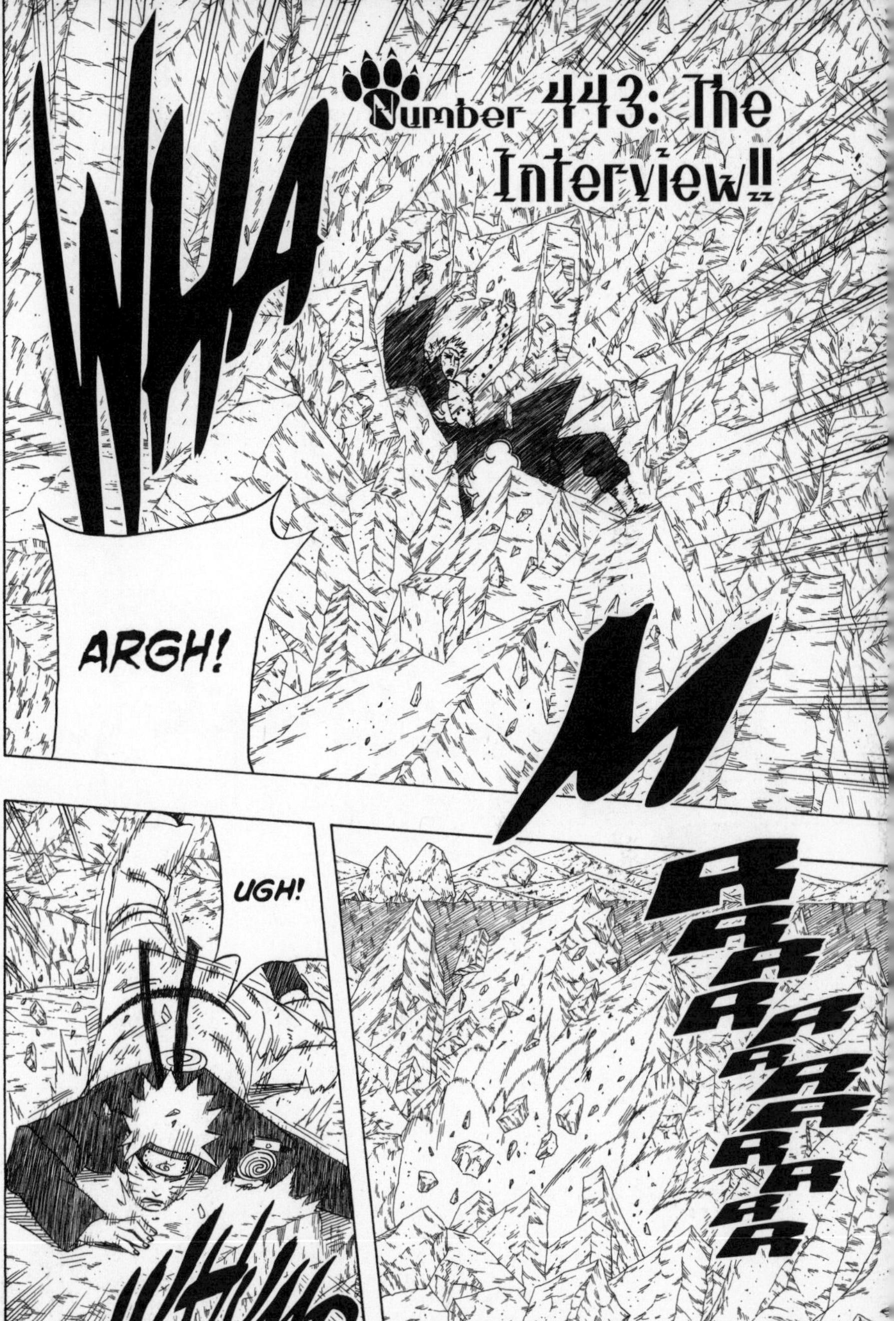
Number 443: The Interview!!
WHA
ARGH!
M
UGH!
WHUMP

READ THIS WAY

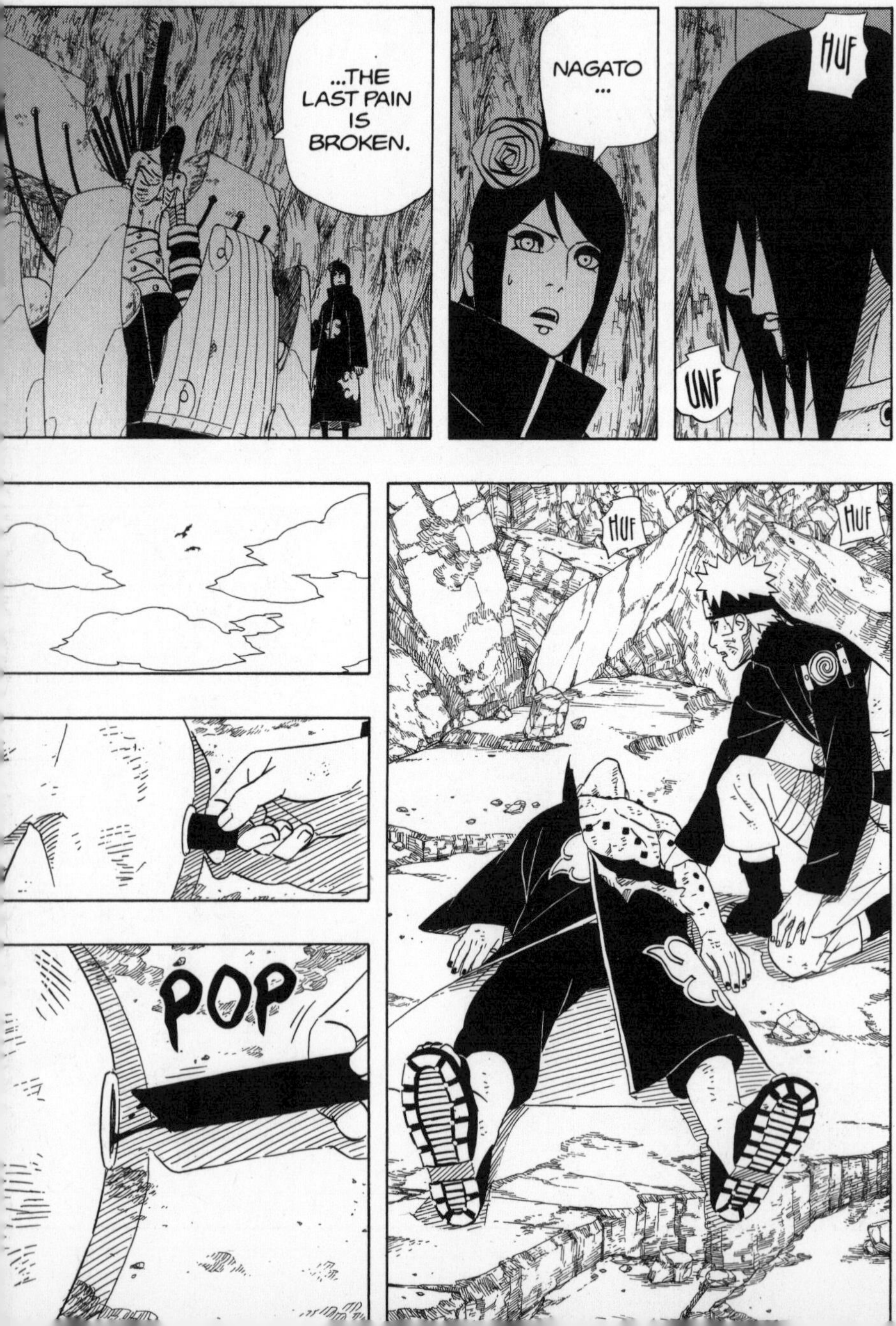
HUF
UNF
NAGATO ...
...THE LAST PAIN IS BROKEN.
HUF
HUF
POP

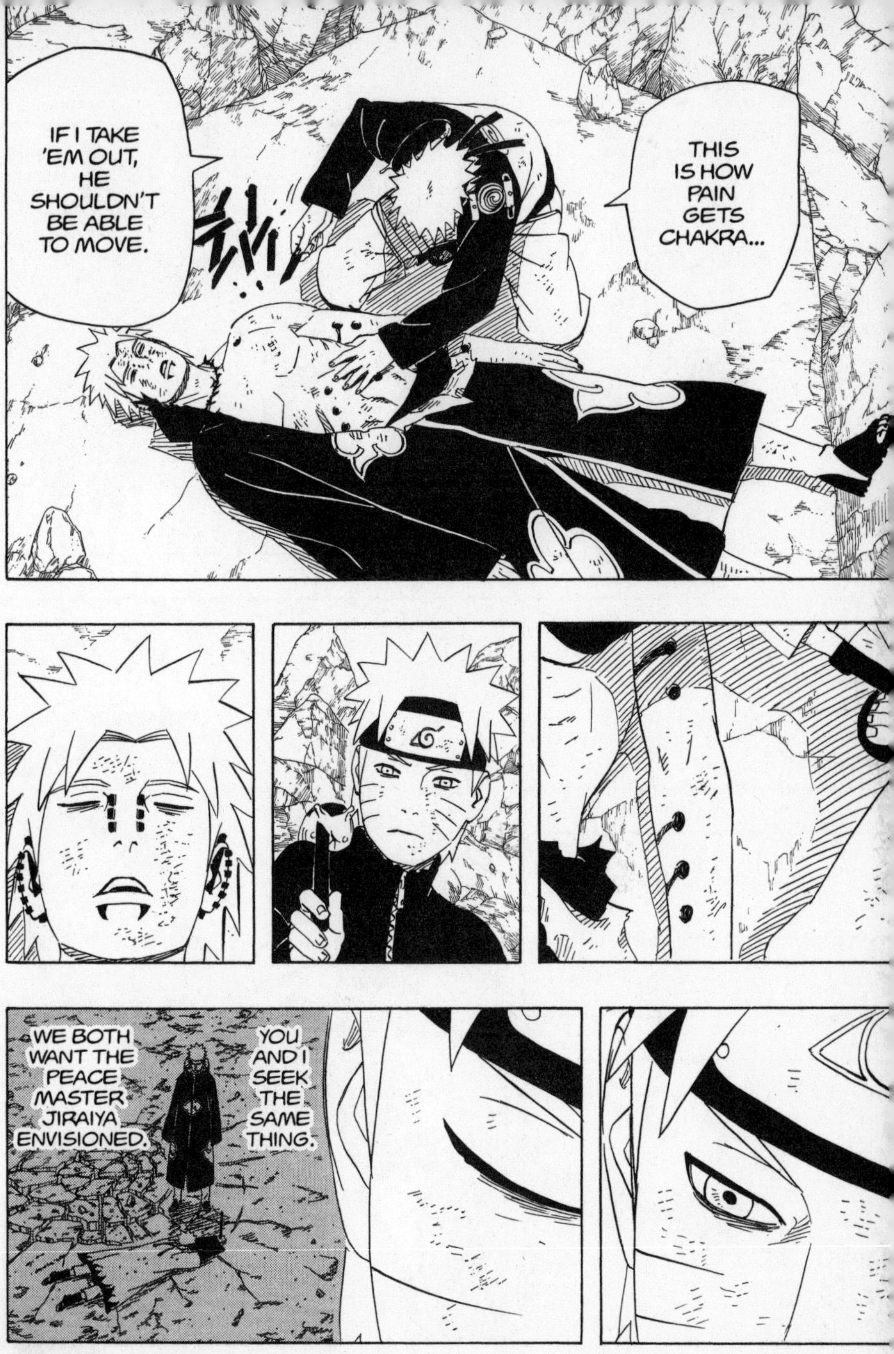
THIS IS HOW PAIN GETS CHAKRA...
IF I TAKE 'EM OUT, HE SHOULDN'T BE ABLE TO MOVE.
YOU AND I SEEK THE SAME THING.
WE BOTH WANT THE PEACE MASTER JIRAIYA ENVISIONED.

READ THIS WAY

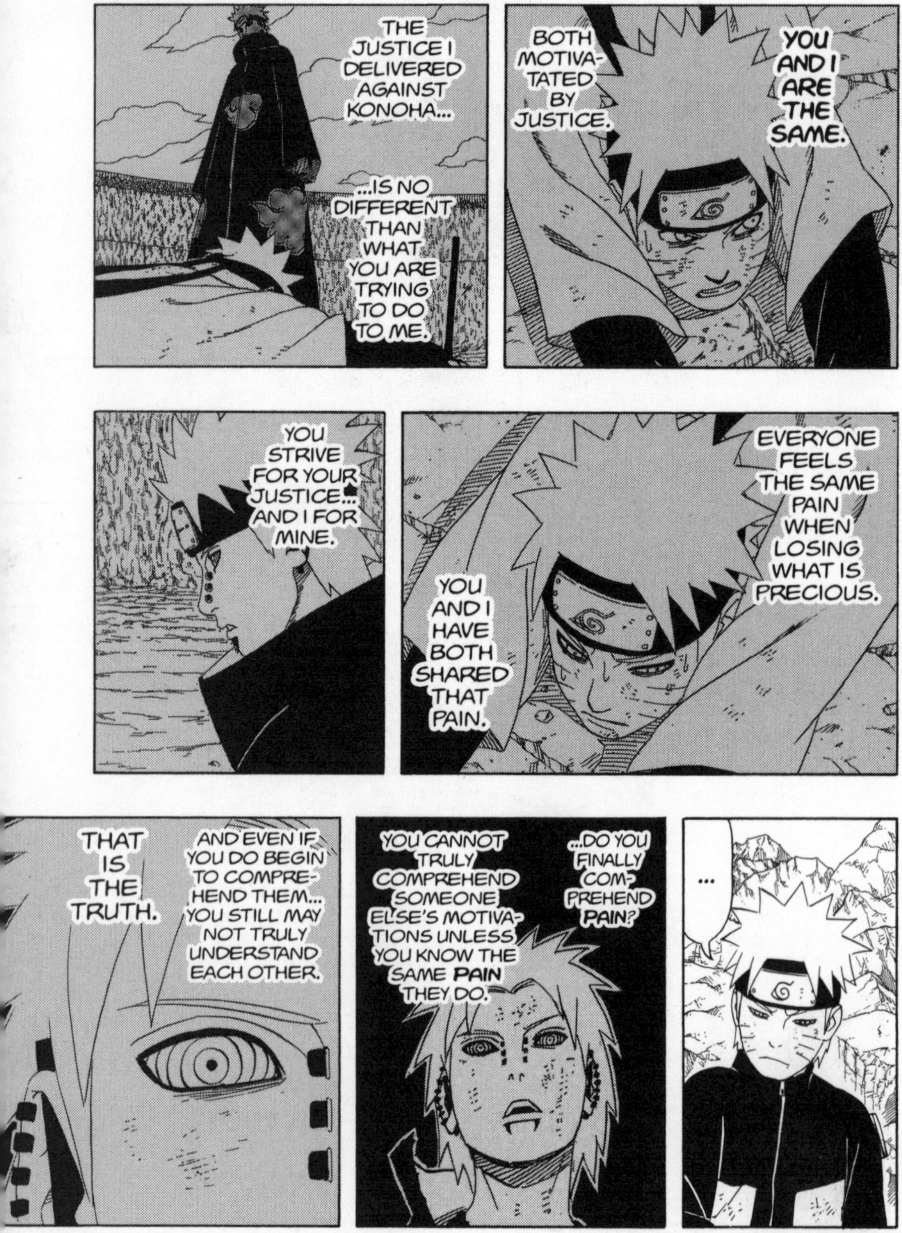
YOU AND I ARE THE SAME.
BOTH MOTIVA-TATED BY JUSTICE.
THE JUSTICE I DELIVERED AGAINST KONOHA...
...IS NO DIFFERENT THAN WHAT YOU ARE TRYING TO DO TO ME.
EVERYONE FEELS THE SAME PAIN WHEN LOSING WHAT IS PRECIOUS.
YOU AND I HAVE BOTH SHARED THAT PAIN.
YOU STRIVE FOR YOUR JUSTICE... AND I FOR MINE.
...
...DO YOU FINALLY COM-PREHEND **PAIN**?
YOU CANNOT TRULY COMPREHEND SOMEONE ELSE'S MOTIVA-TIONS UNLESS YOU KNOW THE SAME **PAIN** THEY DO.
AND EVEN IF YOU DO BEGIN TO COMPRE-HEND THEM... YOU STILL MAY NOT TRULY UNDERSTAND EACH OTHER.
THAT IS THE TRUTH.

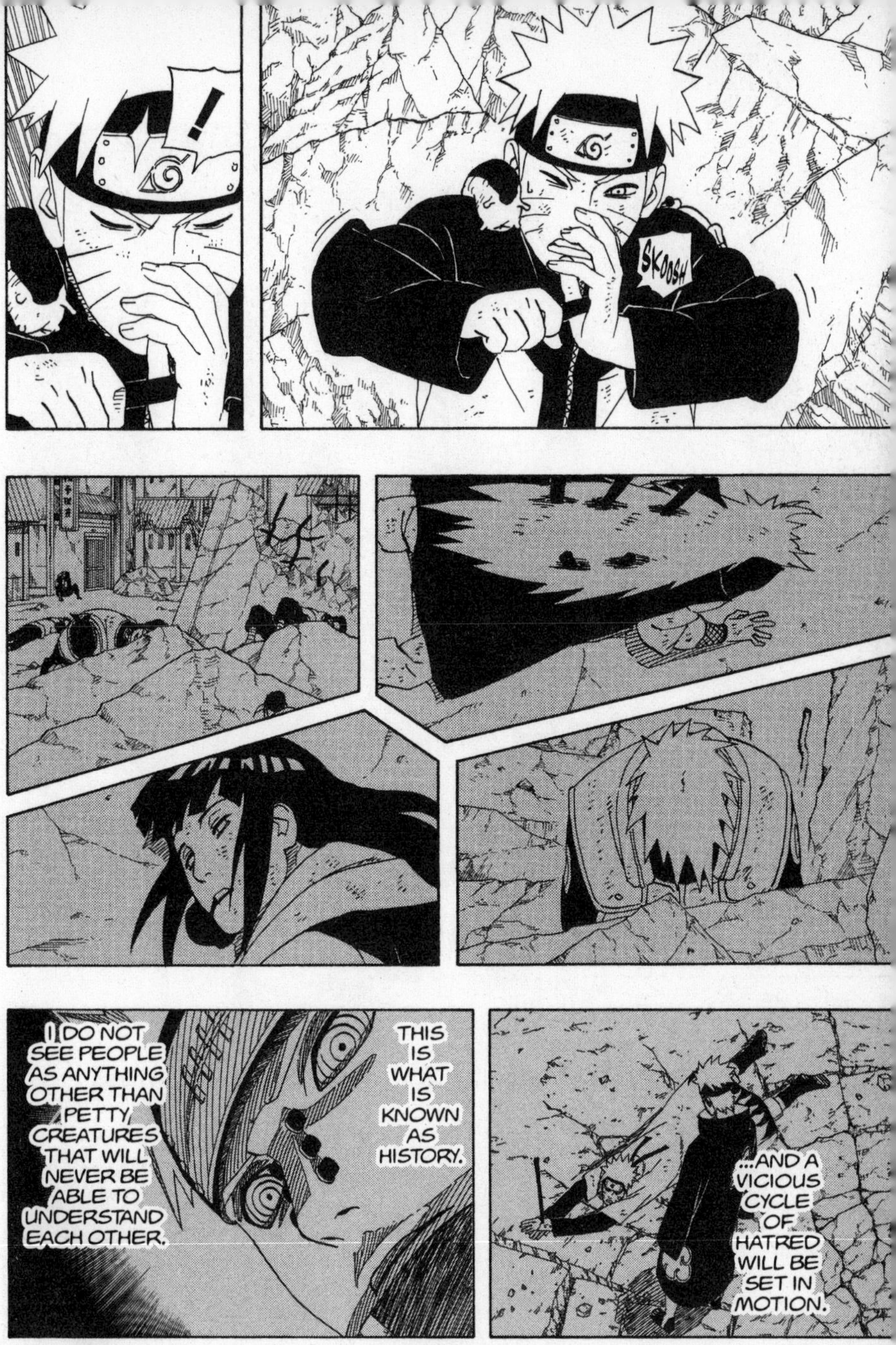
SKOOSH
!
...AND A VICIOUS CYCLE OF HATRED WILL BE SET IN MOTION.
THIS IS WHAT IS KNOWN AS HISTORY.
I DO NOT SEE PEOPLE AS ANYTHING OTHER THAN PETTY CREATURES THAT WILL NEVER BE ABLE TO UNDERSTAND EACH OTHER.

READ THIS WAY

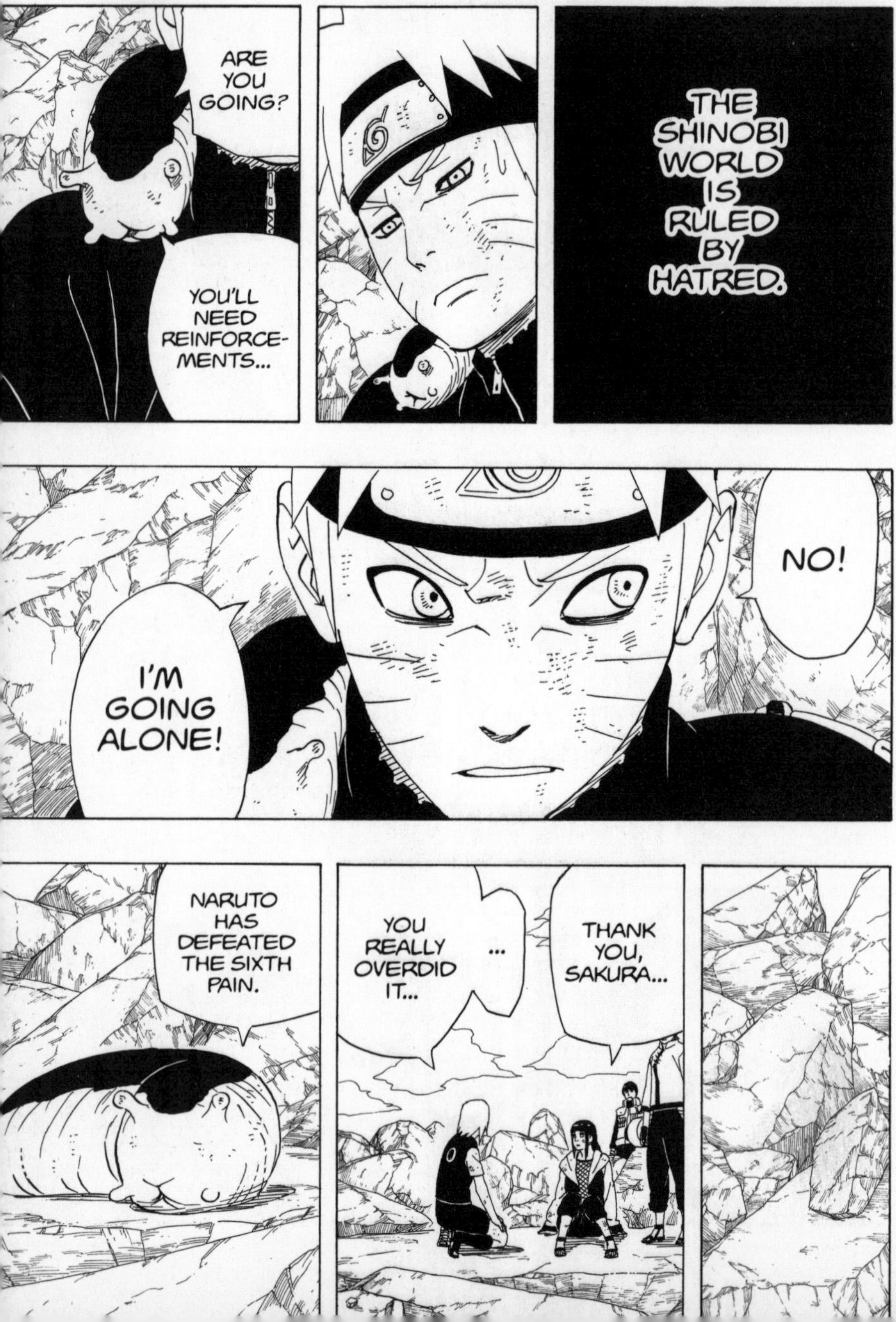
THE SHINOBI WORLD IS RULED BY HATRED.
ARE YOU GOING?
YOU'LL NEED REINFORCEMENTS...
NO!
I'M GOING ALONE!
THANK YOU, SAKURA...
...
YOU REALLY OVERDID IT...
NARUTO HAS DEFEATED THE SIXTH PAIN.

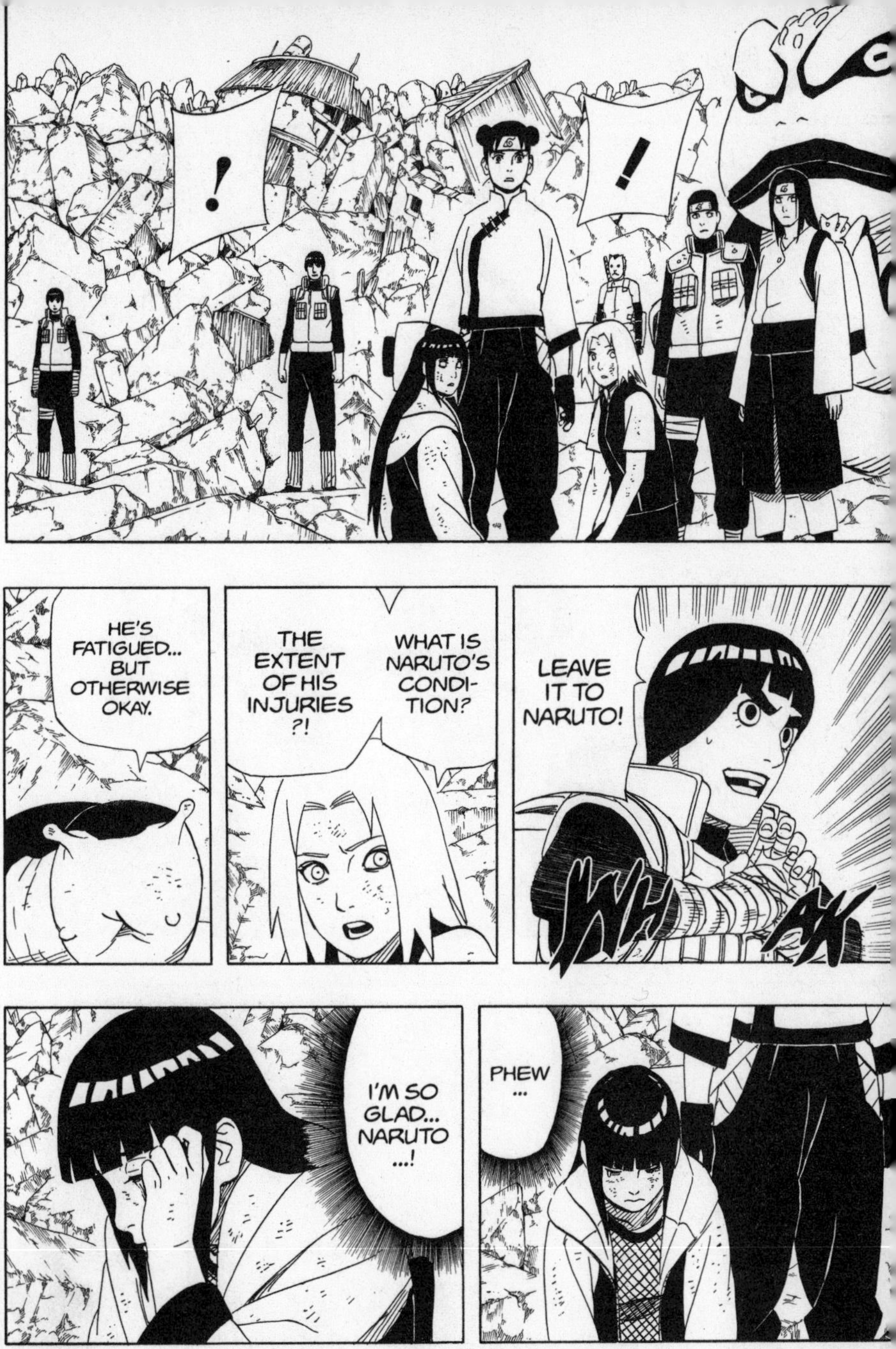
!
!
LEAVE IT TO NARUTO!
WHAK
WHAT IS NARUTO'S CONDITION?
THE EXTENT OF HIS INJURIES ?!
HE'S FATIGUED... BUT OTHERWISE OKAY.
PHEW ...
I'M SO GLAD... NARUTO ...!

READ THIS WAY

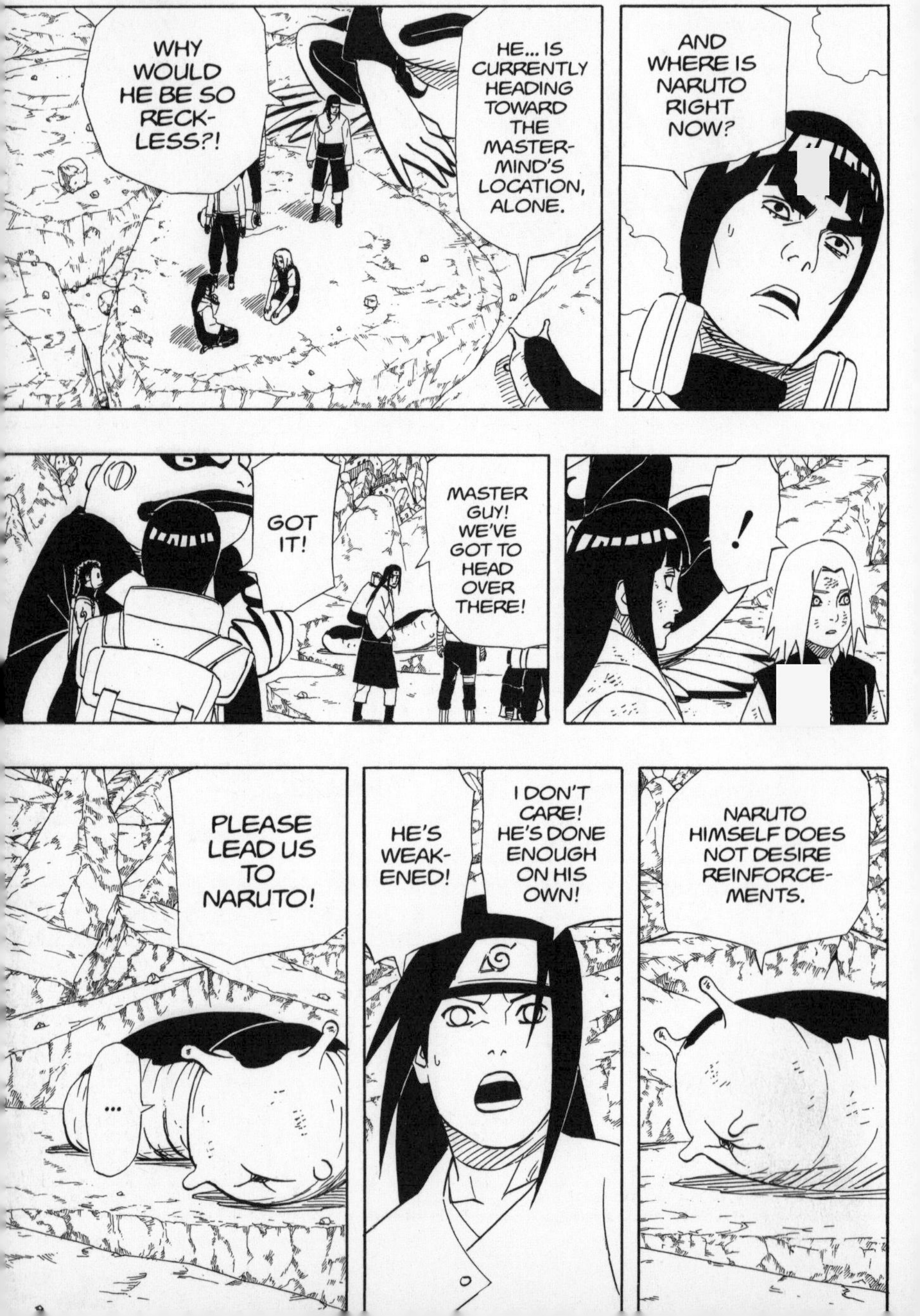
AND WHERE IS NARUTO RIGHT NOW?
HE... IS CURRENTLY HEADING TOWARD THE MASTERMIND'S LOCATION, ALONE.
WHY WOULD HE BE SO RECKLESS?!
!
MASTER GUY! WE'VE GOT TO HEAD OVER THERE!
GOT IT!
NARUTO HIMSELF DOES NOT DESIRE REINFORCEMENTS.
I DON'T CARE! HE'S DONE ENOUGH ON HIS OWN!
HE'S WEAKENED!
PLEASE LEAD US TO NARUTO!
...

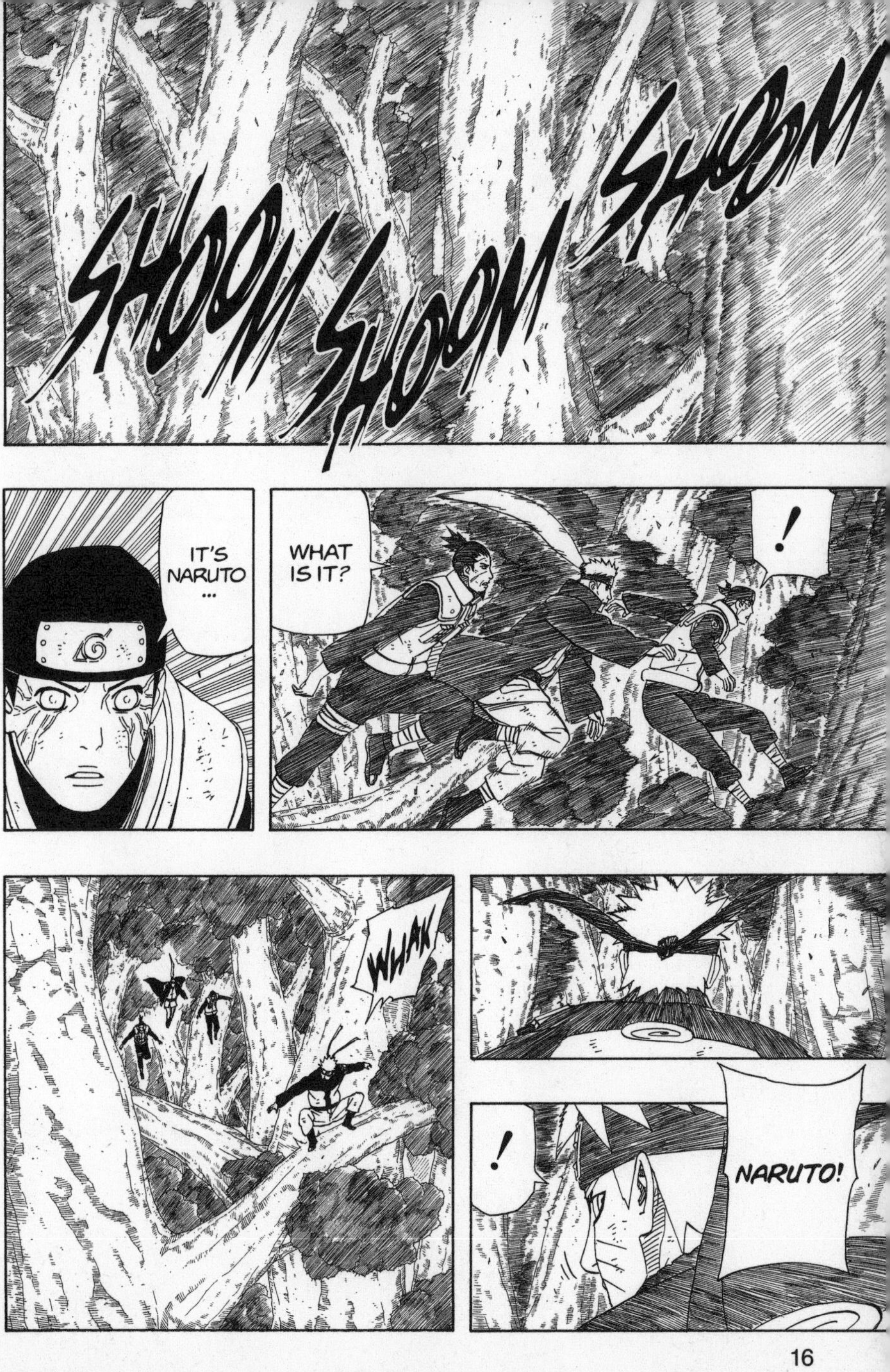
SHOOM SHOOM SHOOM
!
WHAT IS IT?
IT'S NARUTO ...
NARUTO!
!
WHAK

READ THIS WAY

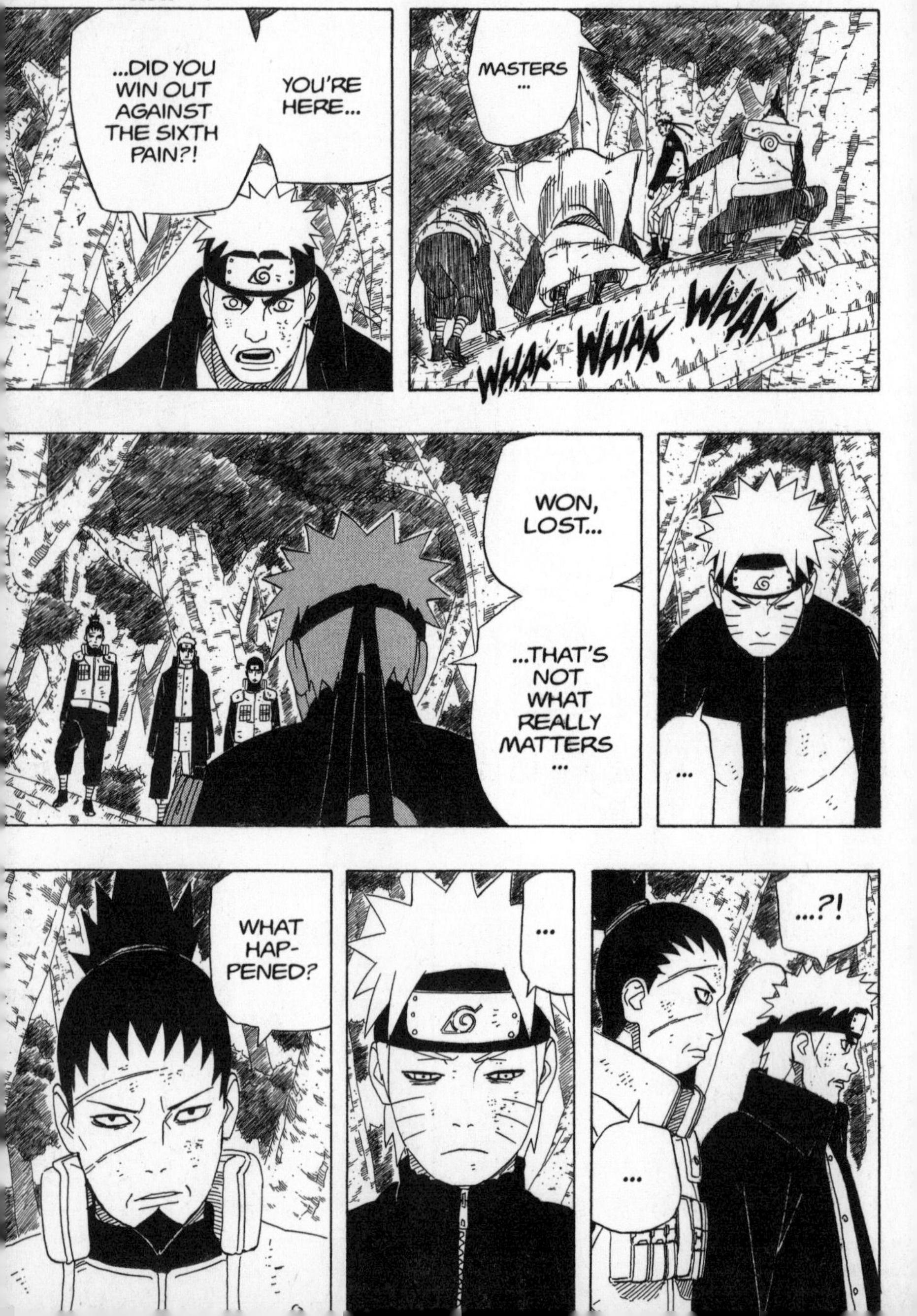
MASTERS ...
WHAK WHAK WHAK
YOU'RE HERE...
...DID YOU WIN OUT AGAINST THE SIXTH PAIN?!
...
WON, LOST...
...THAT'S NOT WHAT REALLY MATTERS ...
...?!
...
...
WHAT HAP- PENED?

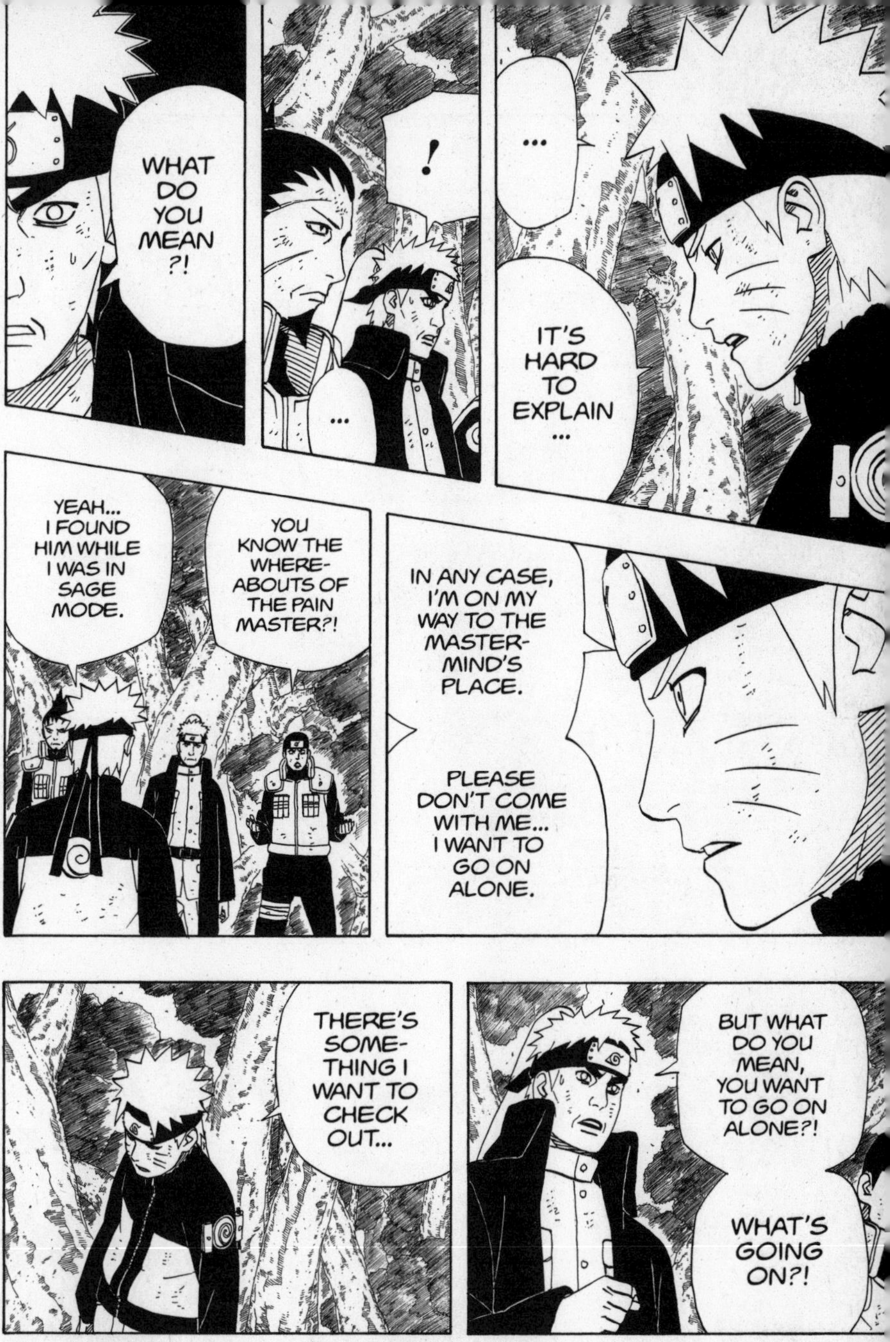
...
IT'S HARD TO EXPLAIN ...
!
...
WHAT DO YOU MEAN ?!
IN ANY CASE, I'M ON MY WAY TO THE MASTER-MIND'S PLACE.
PLEASE DON'T COME WITH ME... I WANT TO GO ON ALONE.
YOU KNOW THE WHERE-ABOUTS OF THE PAIN MASTER?!
YEAH... I FOUND HIM WHILE I WAS IN SAGE MODE.
BUT WHAT DO YOU MEAN, YOU WANT TO GO ON ALONE?!
WHAT'S GOING ON?!
THERE'S SOME-THING I WANT TO CHECK OUT...

READ THIS WAY

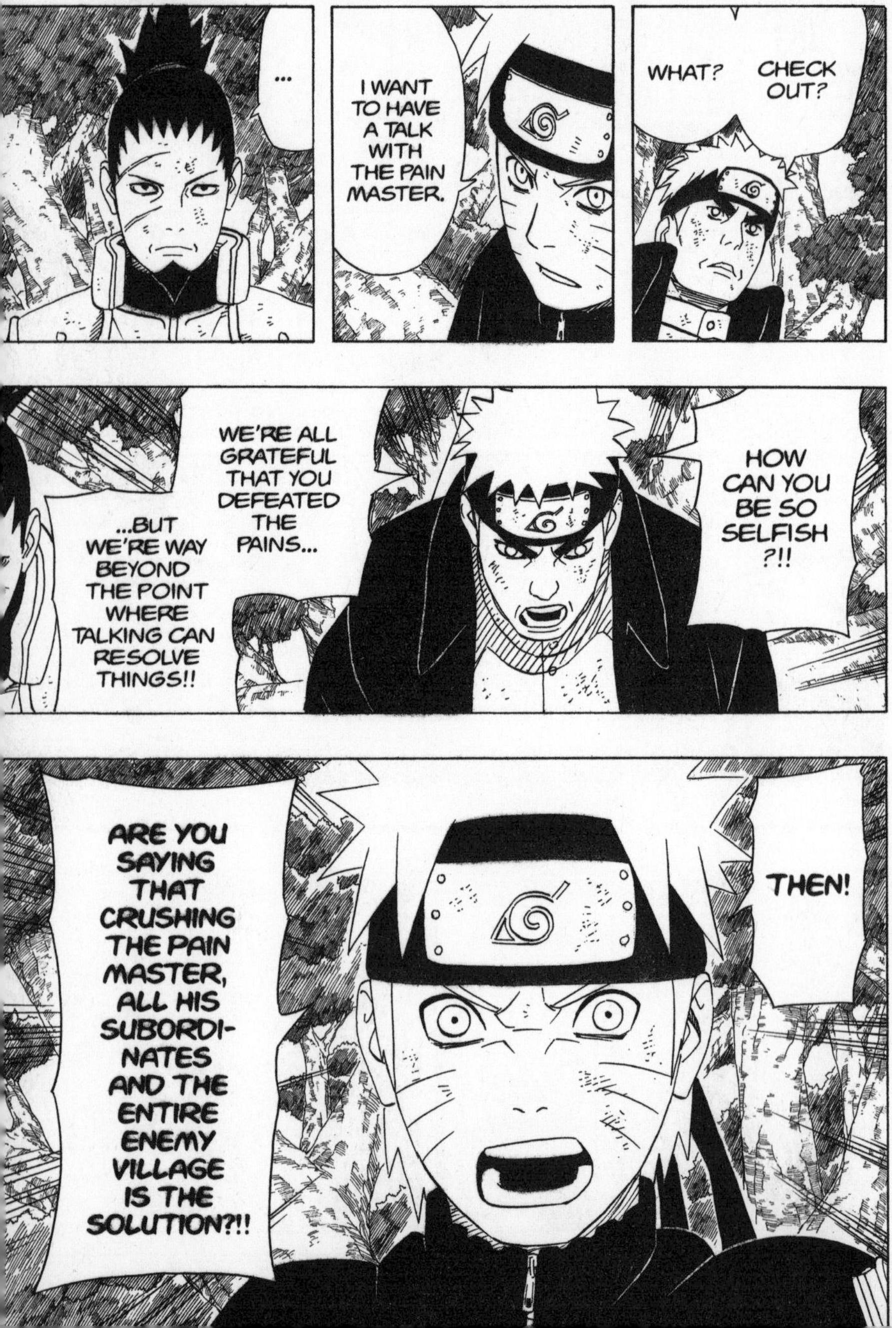
WHAT?
CHECK OUT?
I WANT TO HAVE A TALK WITH THE PAIN MASTER.
...
HOW CAN YOU BE SO SELFISH?!!
WE'RE ALL GRATEFUL THAT YOU DEFEATED THE PAINS...
...BUT WE'RE WAY BEYOND THE POINT WHERE TALKING CAN RESOLVE THINGS!!
THEN!
ARE YOU SAYING THAT CRUSHING THE PAIN MASTER, ALL HIS SUBORDINATES AND THE ENTIRE ENEMY VILLAGE IS THE SOLUTION?!!

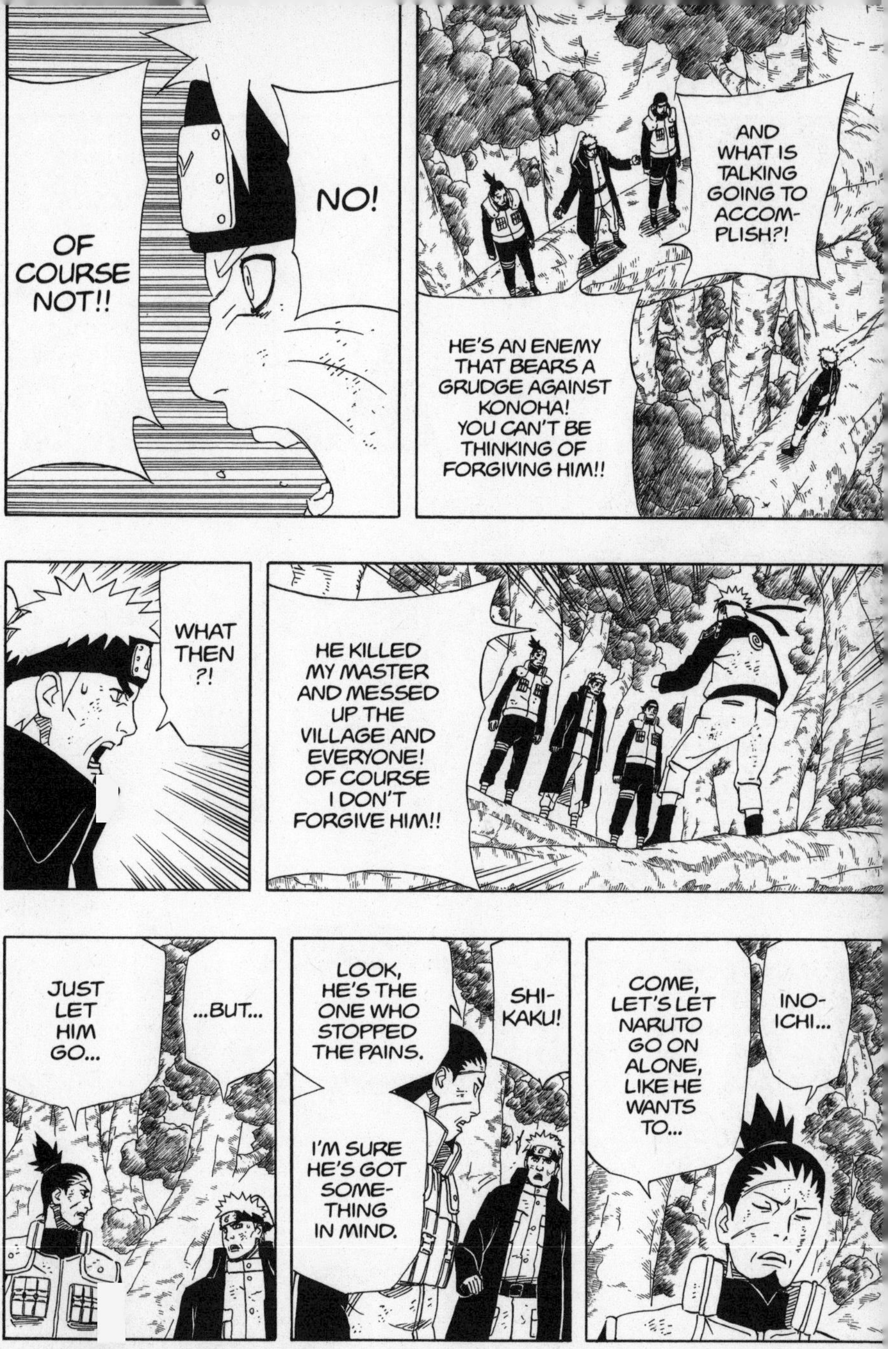
AND WHAT IS TALKING GOING TO ACCOMPLISH?!
HE'S AN ENEMY THAT BEARS A GRUDGE AGAINST KONOHA! YOU CAN'T BE THINKING OF FORGIVING HIM!!
NO!
OF COURSE NOT!!
HE KILLED MY MASTER AND MESSED UP THE VILLAGE AND EVERYONE! OF COURSE I DON'T FORGIVE HIM!!
WHAT THEN ?!
INO-ICHI...
COME, LET'S LET NARUTO GO ON ALONE, LIKE HE WANTS TO...
SHI-KAKU!
LOOK, HE'S THE ONE WHO STOPPED THE PAINS.
I'M SURE HE'S GOT SOMETHING IN MIND.
...BUT...
JUST LET HIM GO...

READ THIS WAY

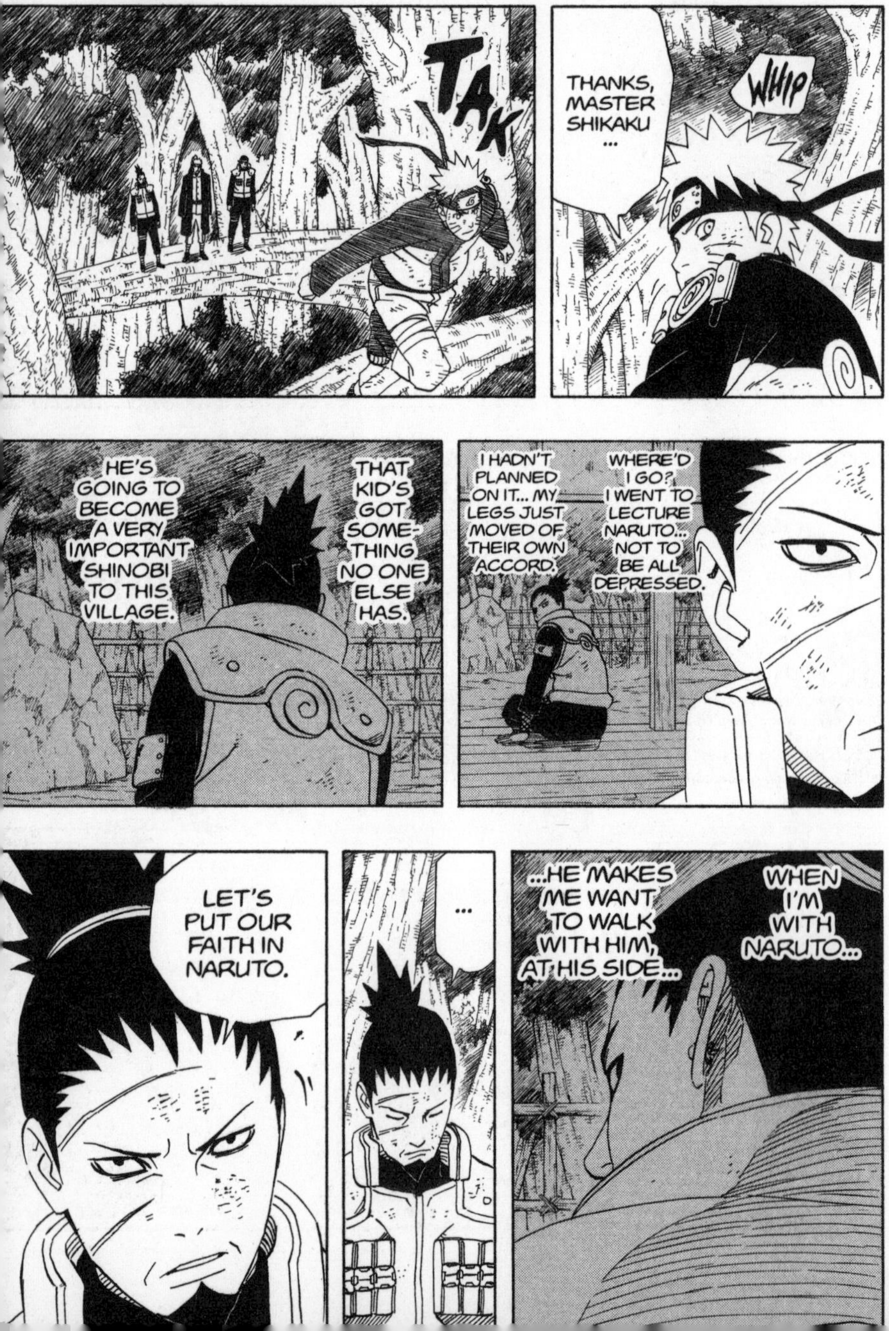
THANKS, MASTER SHIKAKU ...
WHIP
TAK
WHERE'D I GO? I WENT TO LECTURE NARUTO... NOT TO BE ALL DEPRESSED.
I HADN'T PLANNED ON IT... MY LEGS JUST MOVED OF THEIR OWN ACCORD.
THAT KID'S GOT SOME-THING NO ONE ELSE HAS.
HE'S GOING TO BECOME A VERY IMPORTANT SHINOBI TO THIS VILLAGE.
WHEN I'M WITH NARUTO...
...HE MAKES ME WANT TO WALK WITH HIM, AT HIS SIDE...
...
LET'S PUT OUR FAITH IN NARUTO.

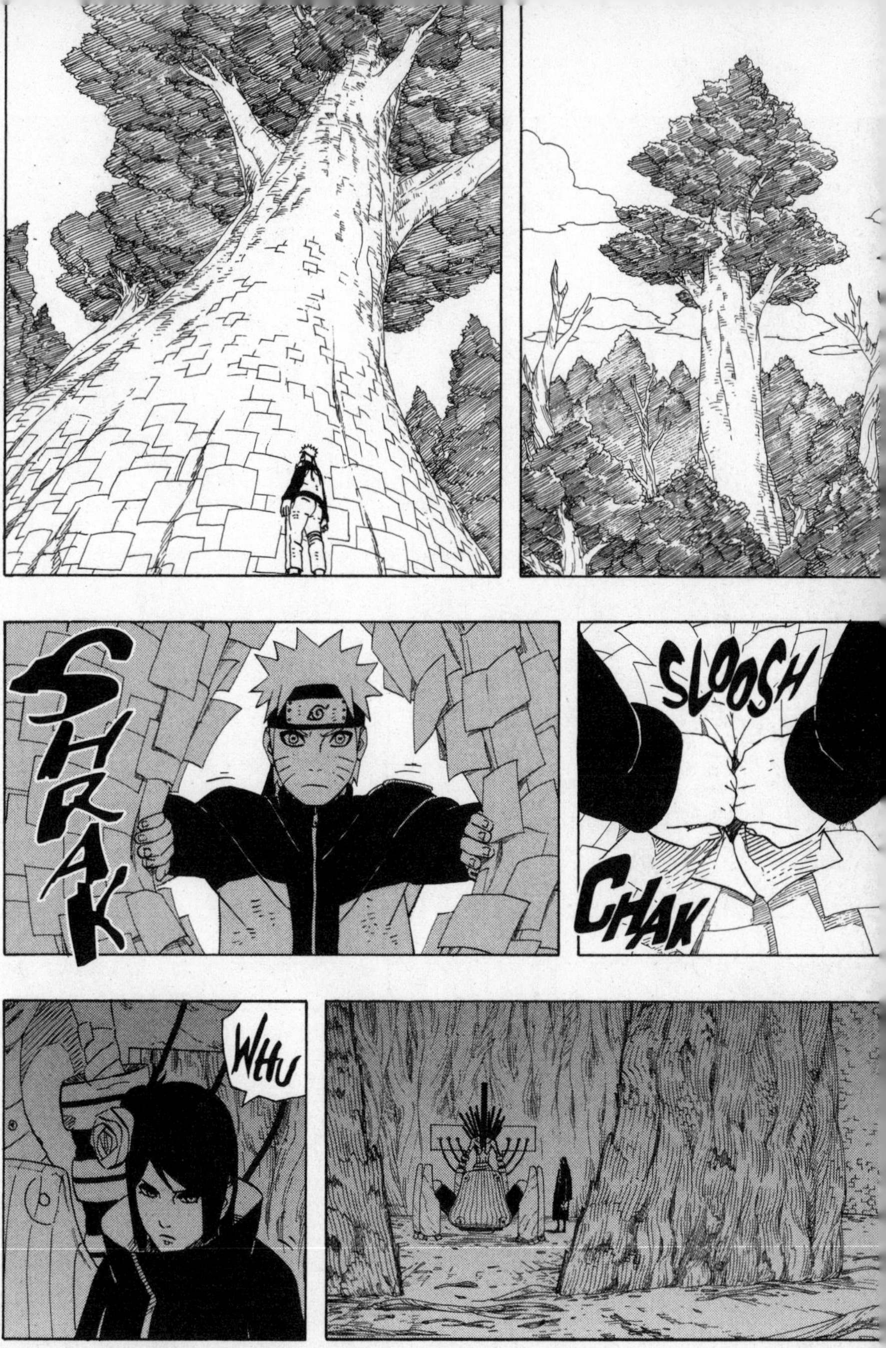
SLOOSH
CHAK
SHRAK
WHU

READ THIS WAY

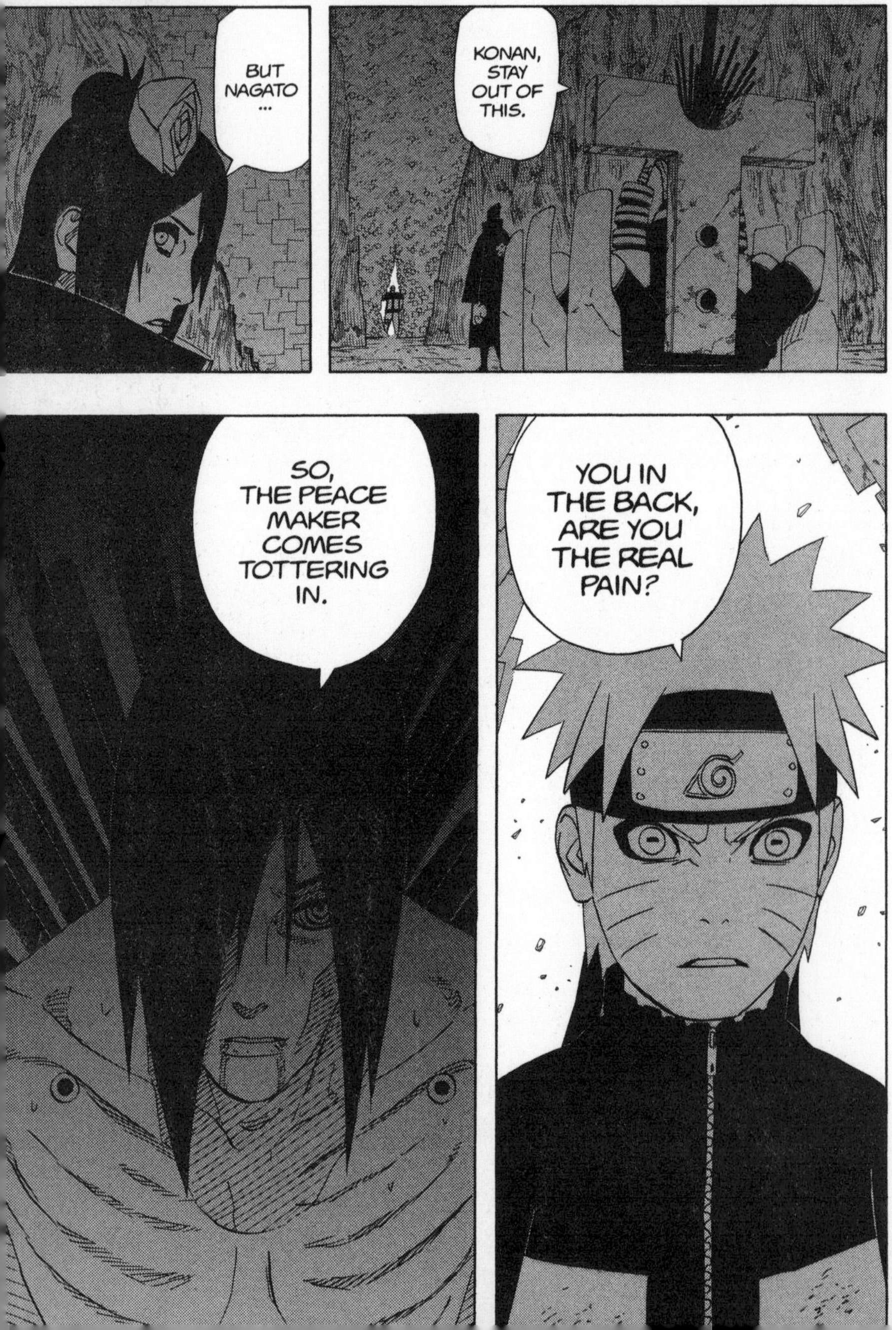
KONAN, STAY OUT OF THIS.
BUT NAGATO...
YOU IN THE BACK, ARE YOU THE REAL PAIN?
SO, THE PEACE MAKER COMES TOTTERING IN.

NARUTO

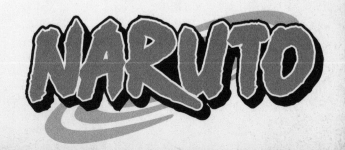

Number 444: The Response

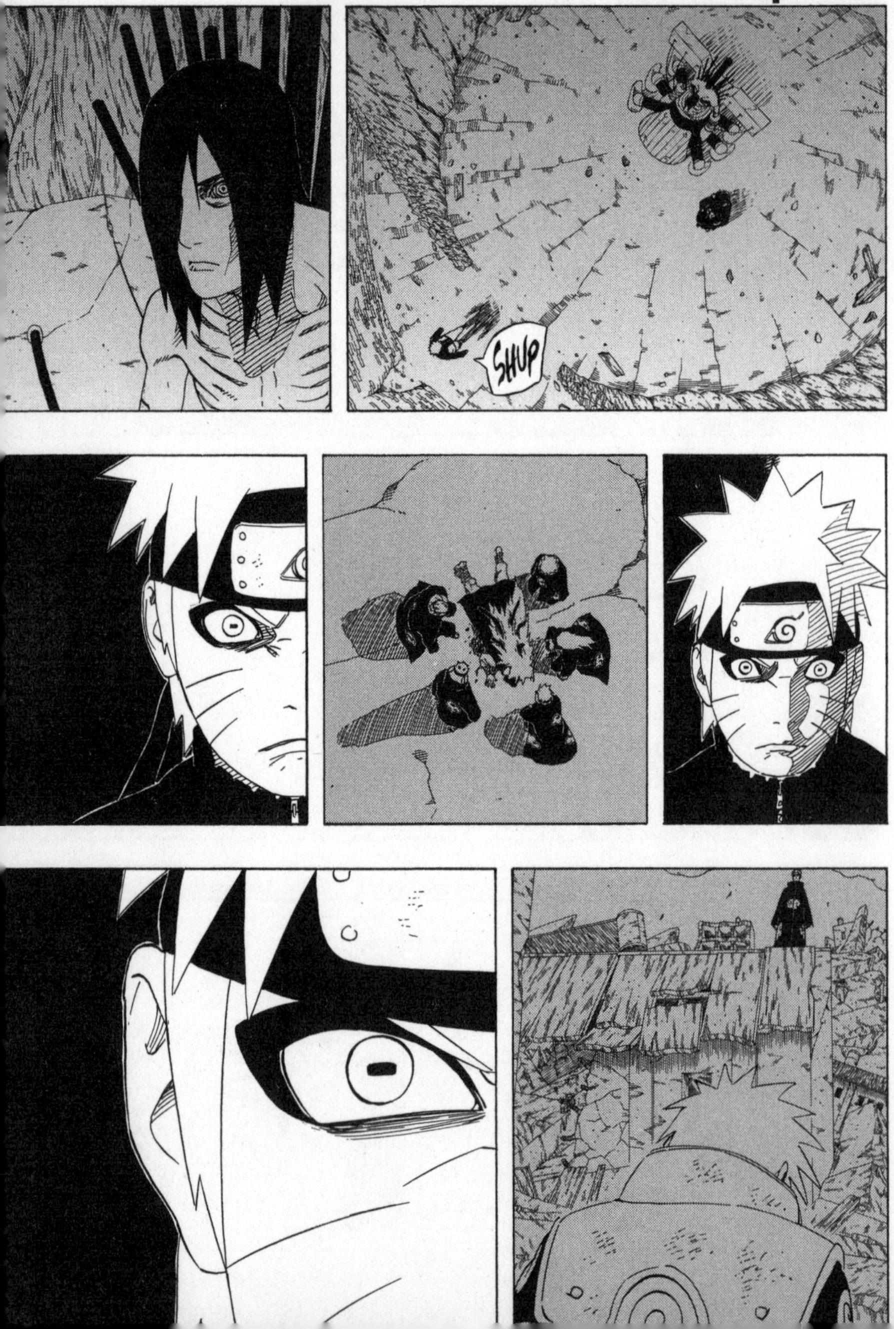
SHUP

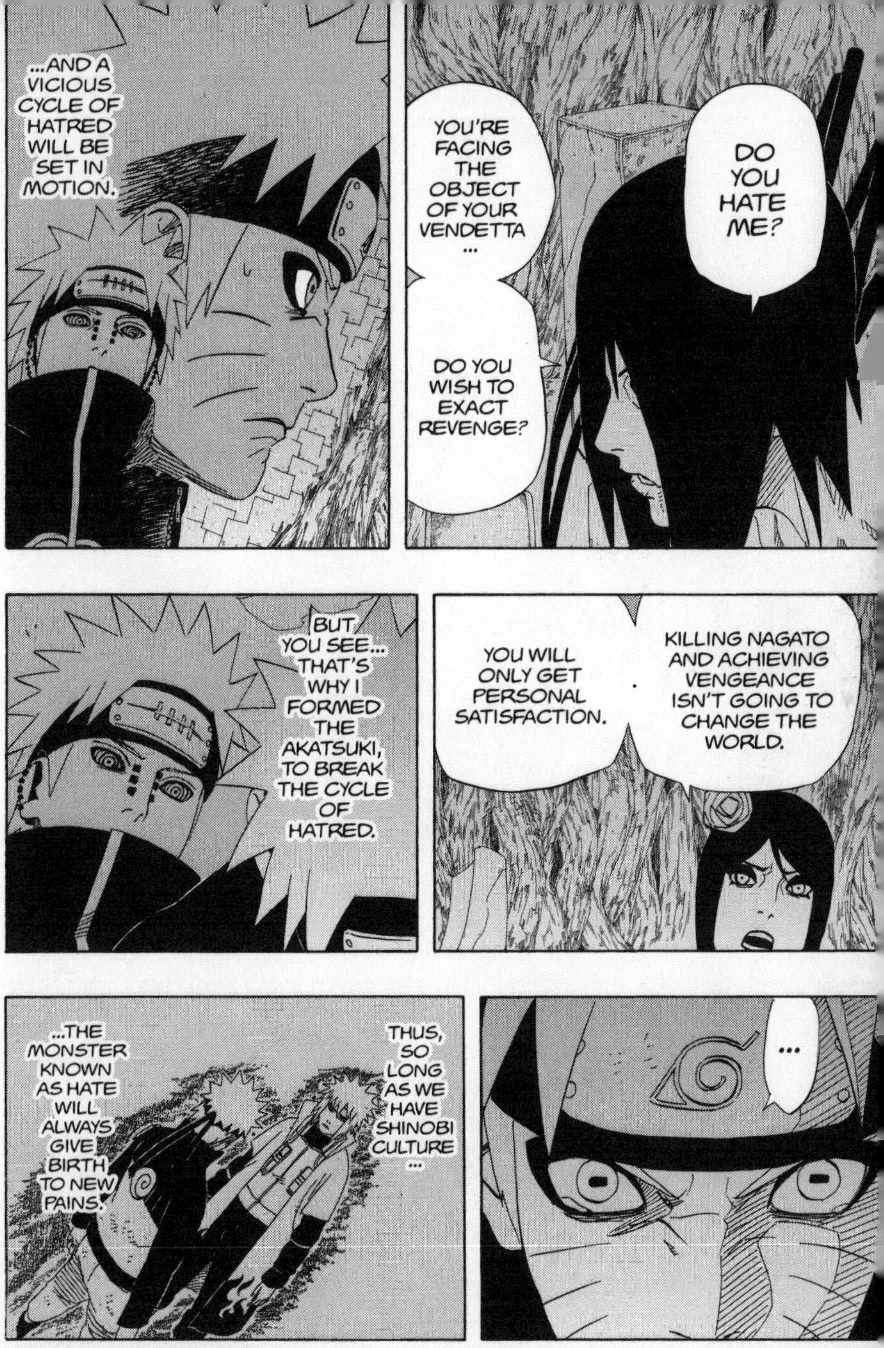
DO YOU HATE ME?
YOU'RE FACING THE OBJECT OF YOUR VENDETTA ...
DO YOU WISH TO EXACT REVENGE?
...AND A VICIOUS CYCLE OF HATRED WILL BE SET IN MOTION.
KILLING NAGATO AND ACHIEVING VENGEANCE ISN'T GOING TO CHANGE THE WORLD.
YOU WILL ONLY GET PERSONAL SATISFACTION.
BUT YOU SEE... THAT'S WHY I FORMED THE AKATSUKI, TO BREAK THE CYCLE OF HATRED.
...
THUS, SO LONG AS WE HAVE SHINOBI CULTURE ...
...THE MONSTER KNOWN AS HATE WILL ALWAYS GIVE BIRTH TO NEW PAINS.

READ THIS WAY

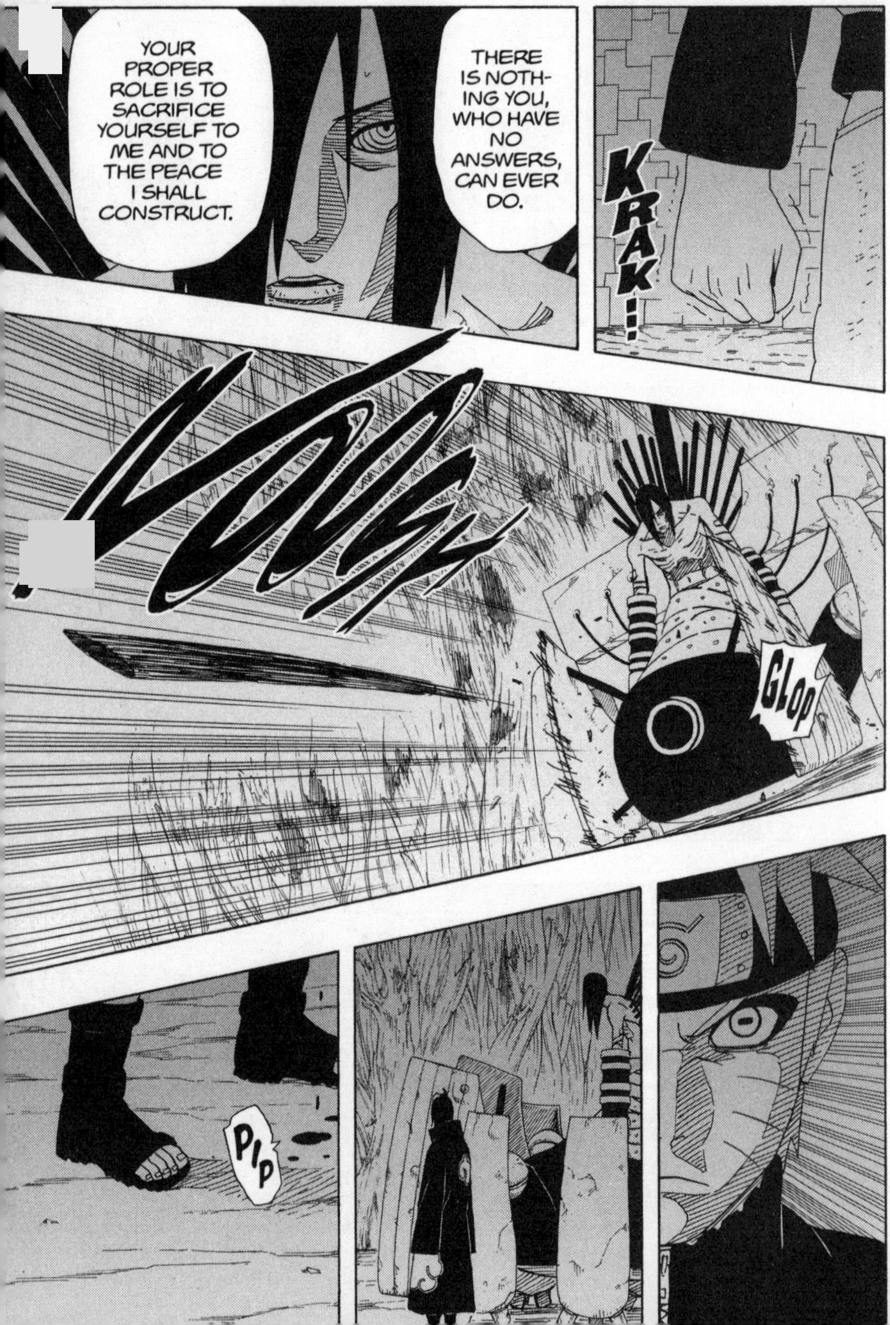
KRAK!!
THERE IS NOTHING YOU, WHO HAVE NO ANSWERS, CAN EVER DO.
YOUR PROPER ROLE IS TO SACRIFICE YOURSELF TO ME AND TO THE PEACE I SHALL CONSTRUCT.
GLOP
PIP

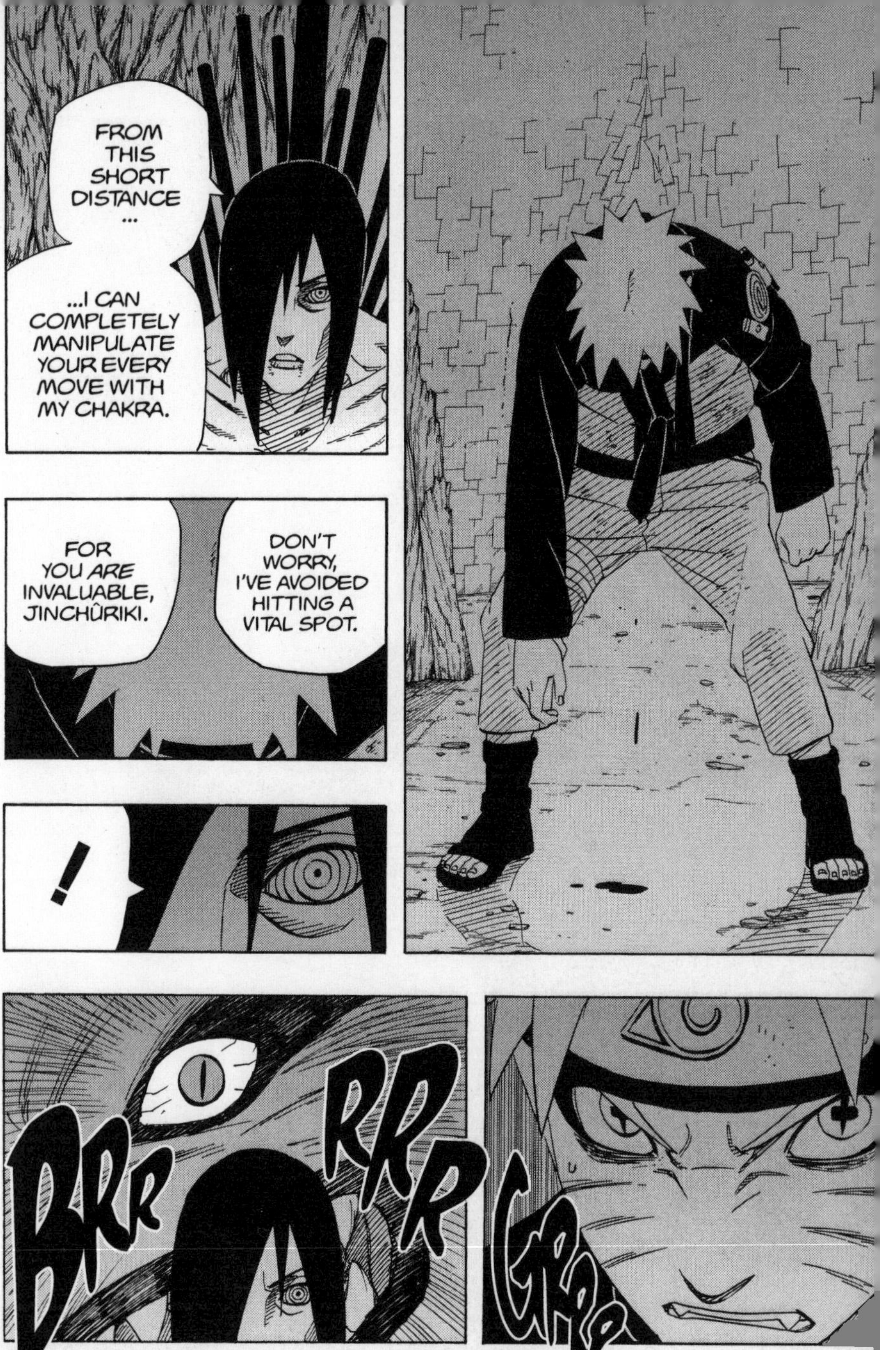
FROM THIS SHORT DISTANCE...
...I CAN COMPLETELY MANIPULATE YOUR EVERY MOVE WITH MY CHAKRA.
DON'T WORRY, I'VE AVOIDED HITTING A VITAL SPOT.
FOR YOU *ARE* INVALUABLE, JINCHÛRIKI.
!
GRRRR
BRR
RRR

READ THIS WAY

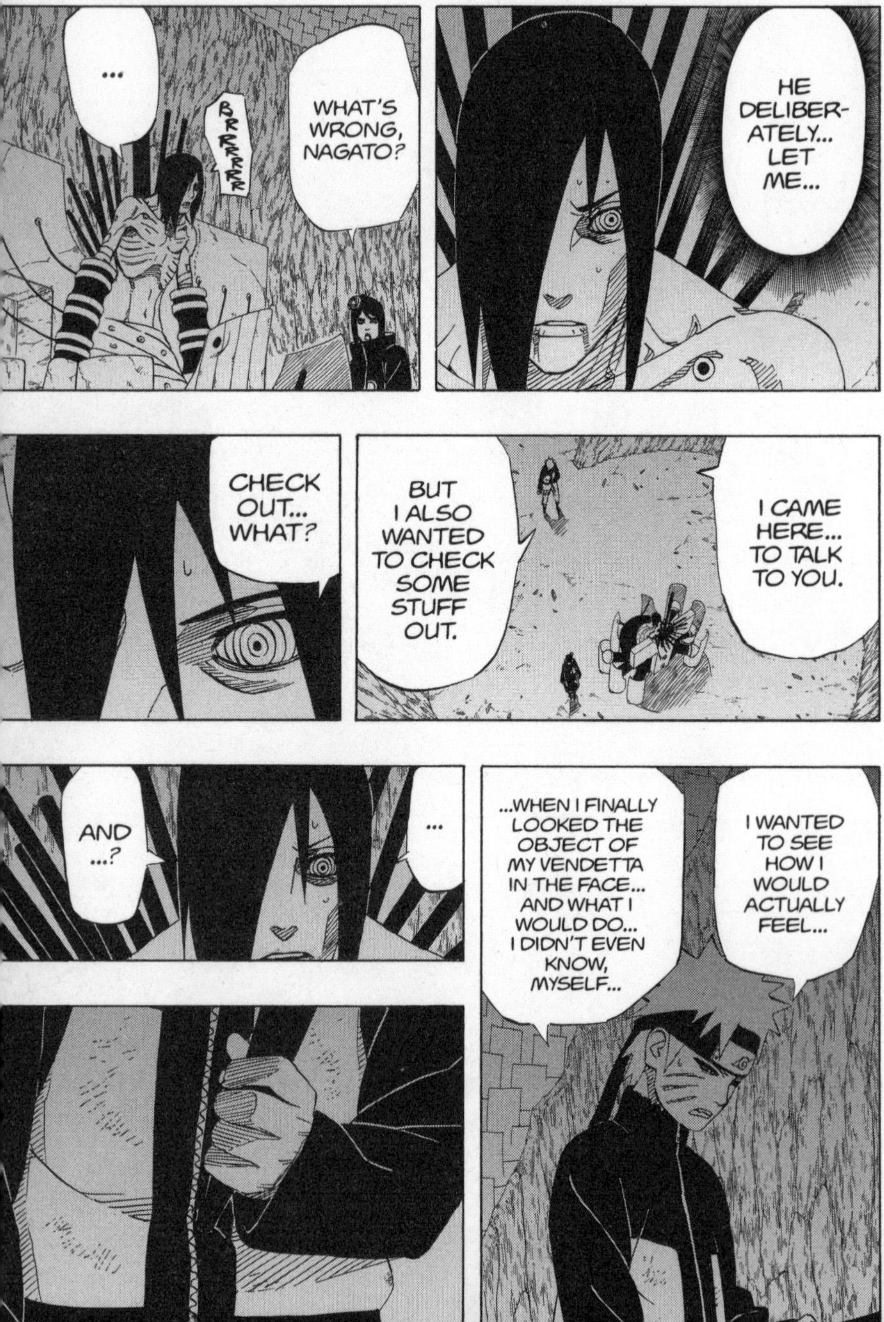
HE DELIBER-ATELY... LET ME...
WHAT'S WRONG, NAGATO?
BRRRRRR
...
I CAME HERE... TO TALK TO YOU.
BUT I ALSO WANTED TO CHECK SOME STUFF OUT.
CHECK OUT... WHAT?
I WANTED TO SEE HOW I WOULD ACTUALLY FEEL...
...WHEN I FINALLY LOOKED THE OBJECT OF MY VENDETTA IN THE FACE... AND WHAT I WOULD DO... I DIDN'T EVEN KNOW, MYSELF...
...
AND ...?

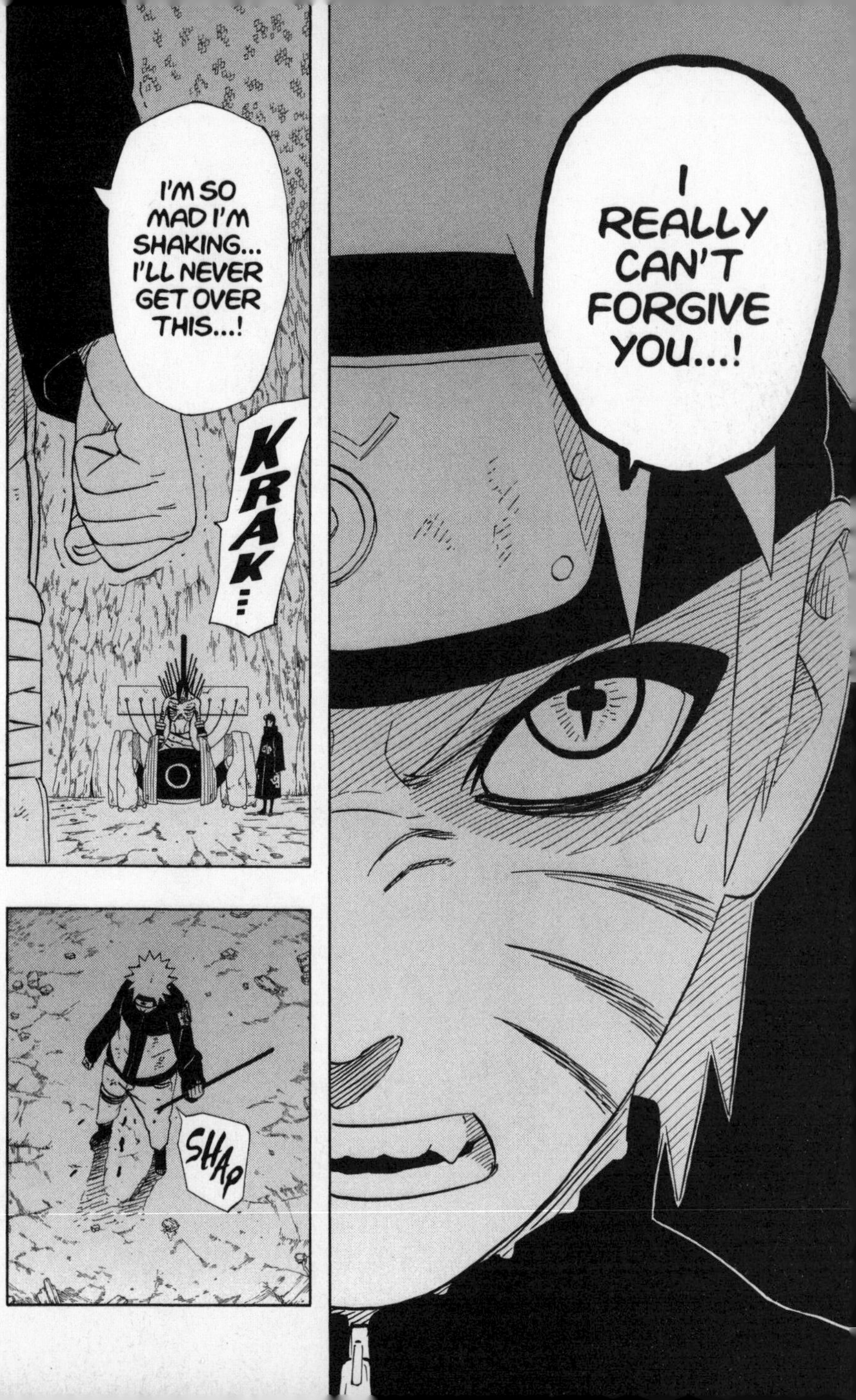
I REALLY CAN'T FORGIVE YOU...!
I'M SO MAD I'M SHAKING... I'LL NEVER GET OVER THIS...!
KRAK..
SHAP

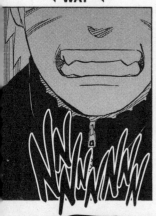

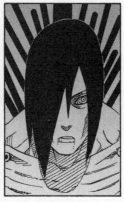

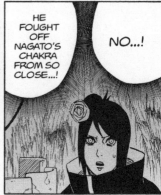

HE FOUGHT OFF NAGATO'S CHAKRA FROM SO CLOSE...!

NO...!

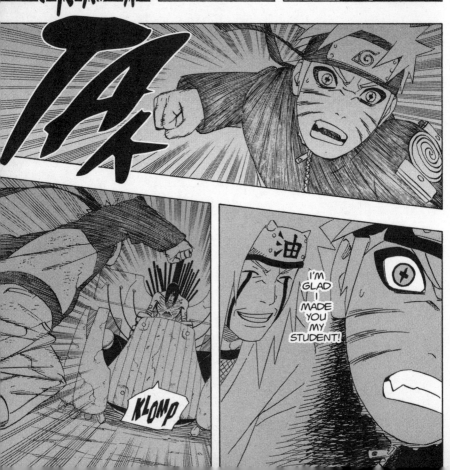

TAK

KLOMP

I'M GLAD I MADE YOU MY STUDENT!

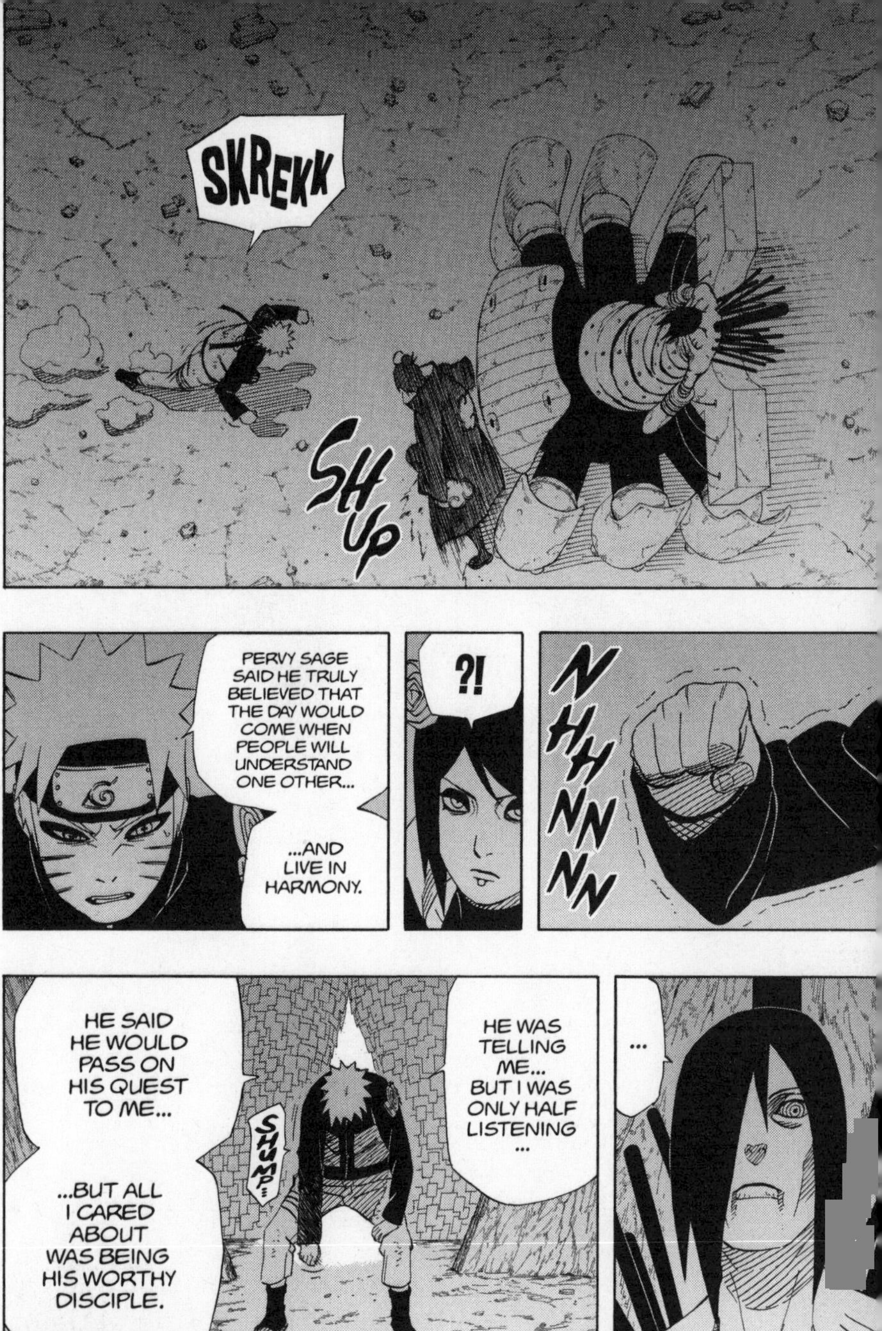
SKREKK
SHUP
NHHNNNN
?!
PERVY SAGE SAID HE TRULY BELIEVED THAT THE DAY WOULD COME WHEN PEOPLE WILL UNDERSTAND ONE OTHER...
...AND LIVE IN HARMONY.
...
HE WAS TELLING ME... BUT I WAS ONLY HALF LISTENING ...
HE SAID HE WOULD PASS ON HIS QUEST TO ME...
SHUMP
...BUT ALL I CARED ABOUT WAS BEING HIS WORTHY DISCIPLE.

READ THIS WAY

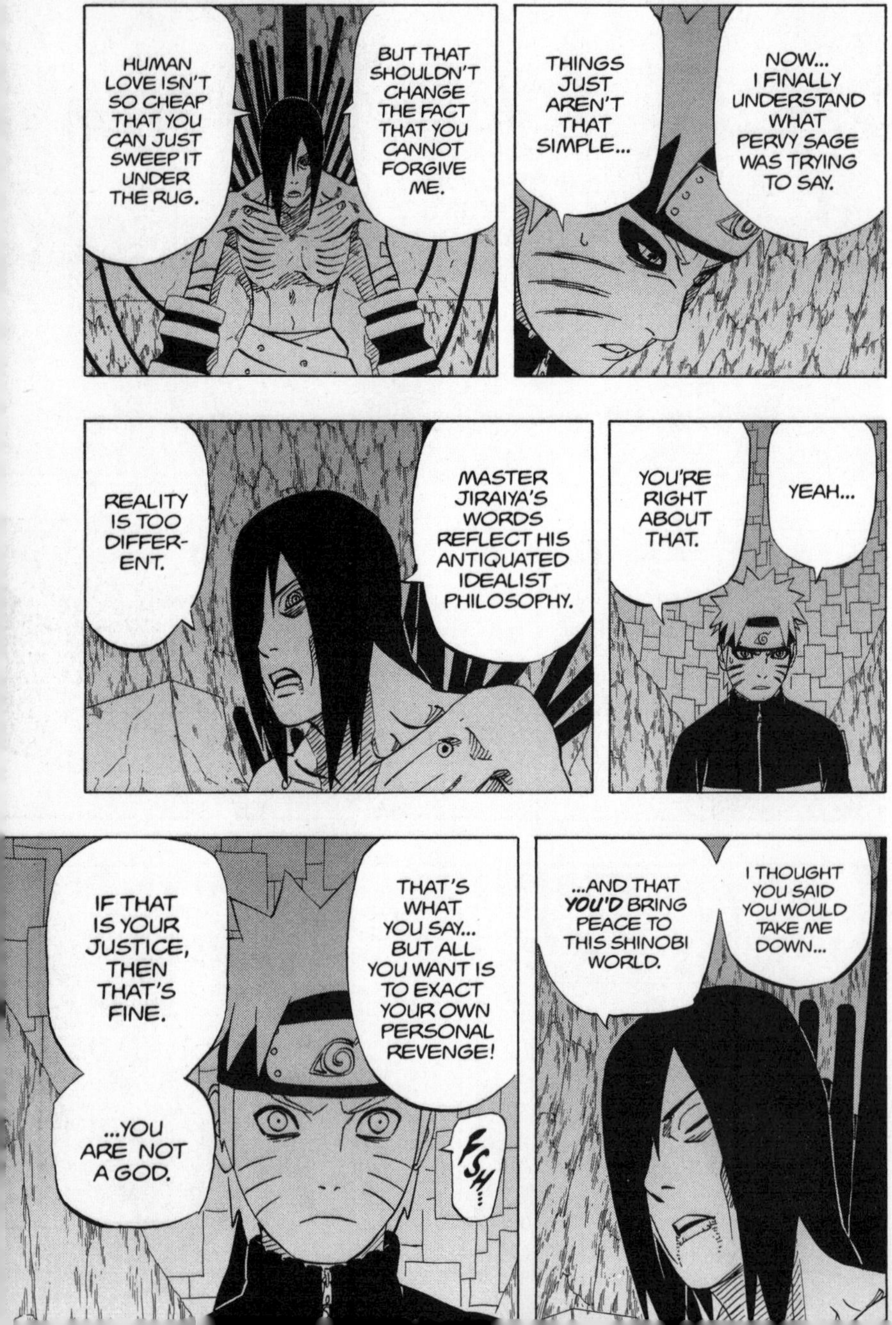
NOW... I FINALLY UNDERSTAND WHAT PERVY SAGE WAS TRYING TO SAY.
THINGS JUST AREN'T THAT SIMPLE...
BUT THAT SHOULDN'T CHANGE THE FACT THAT YOU CANNOT FORGIVE ME.
HUMAN LOVE ISN'T SO CHEAP THAT YOU CAN JUST SWEEP IT UNDER THE RUG.
YEAH...
YOU'RE RIGHT ABOUT THAT.
MASTER JIRAIYA'S WORDS REFLECT HIS ANTIQUATED IDEALIST PHILOSOPHY.
REALITY IS TOO DIFFER-ENT.
I THOUGHT YOU SAID YOU WOULD TAKE ME DOWN...
...AND THAT ***YOU'D*** BRING PEACE TO THIS SHINOBI WORLD.
THAT'S WHAT YOU SAY... BUT ALL YOU WANT IS TO EXACT YOUR OWN PERSONAL REVENGE!
FSH...
IF THAT IS YOUR JUSTICE, THEN THAT'S FINE.
...YOU ARE NOT A GOD.

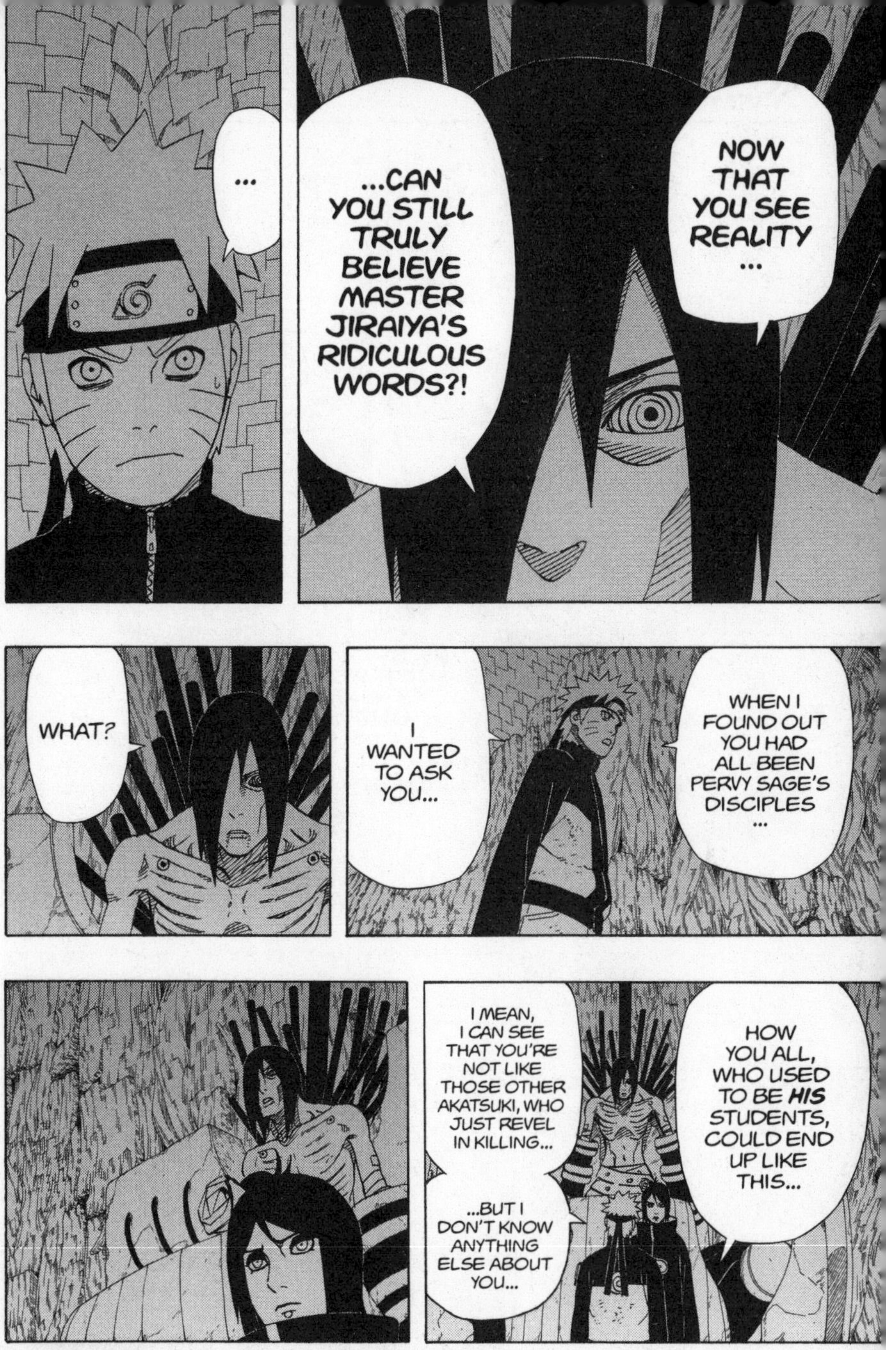
NOW THAT YOU SEE REALITY...
...CAN YOU STILL TRULY BELIEVE MASTER JIRAIYA'S RIDICULOUS WORDS?!
...
WHEN I FOUND OUT YOU HAD ALL BEEN PERVY SAGE'S DISCIPLES...
I WANTED TO ASK YOU...
WHAT?
HOW YOU ALL, WHO USED TO BE ***HIS*** STUDENTS, COULD END UP LIKE THIS...
I MEAN, I CAN SEE THAT YOU'RE NOT LIKE THOSE OTHER AKATSUKI, WHO JUST REVEL IN KILLING...
...BUT I DON'T KNOW ANYTHING ELSE ABOUT YOU...

READ THIS WAY

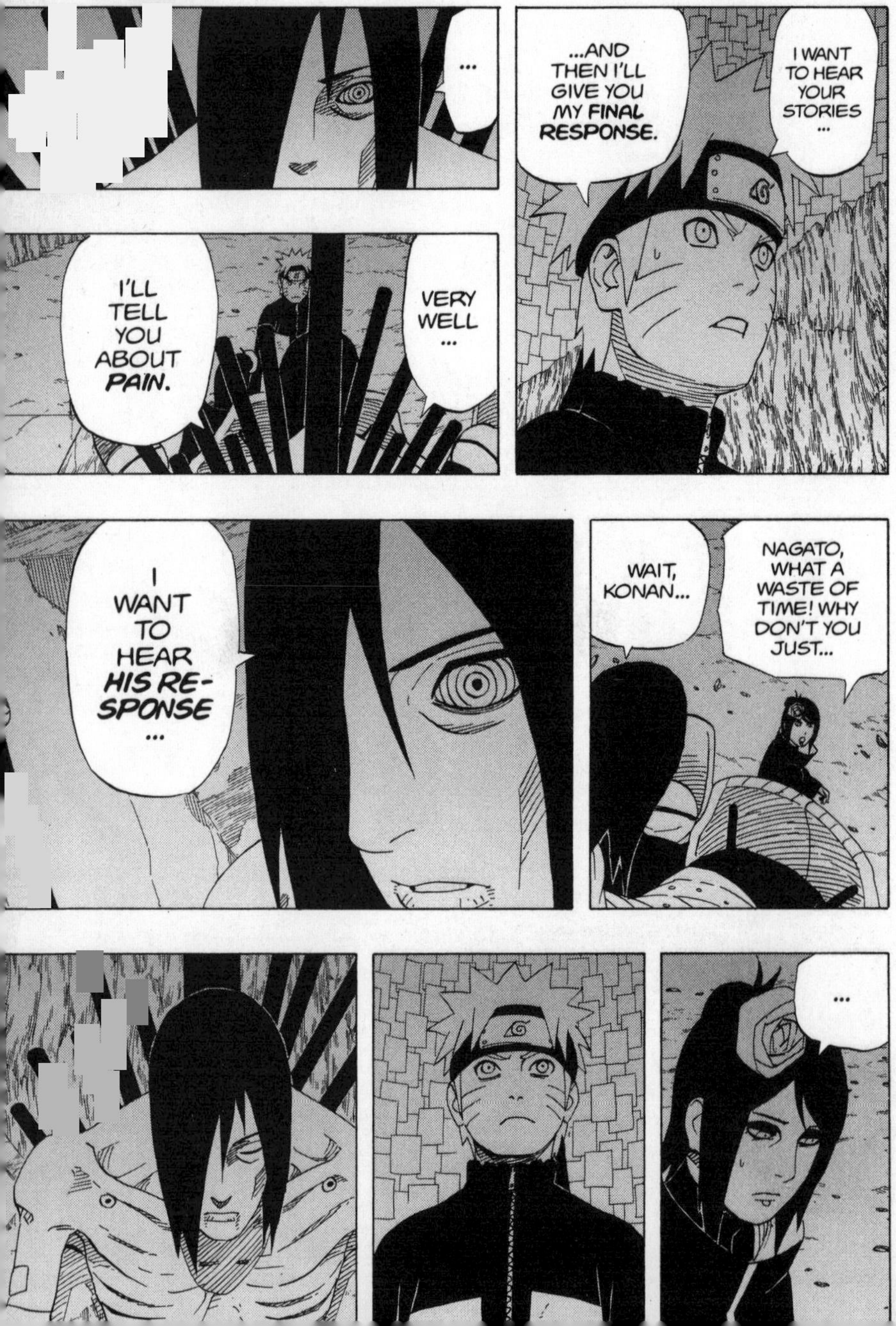
I WANT TO HEAR YOUR STORIES...
...AND THEN I'LL GIVE YOU MY **FINAL RESPONSE.**
...
VERY WELL...
I'LL TELL YOU ABOUT ***PAIN.***
NAGATO, WHAT A WASTE OF TIME! WHY DON'T YOU JUST...
WAIT, KONAN...
I WANT TO HEAR ***HIS RESPONSE***...
...

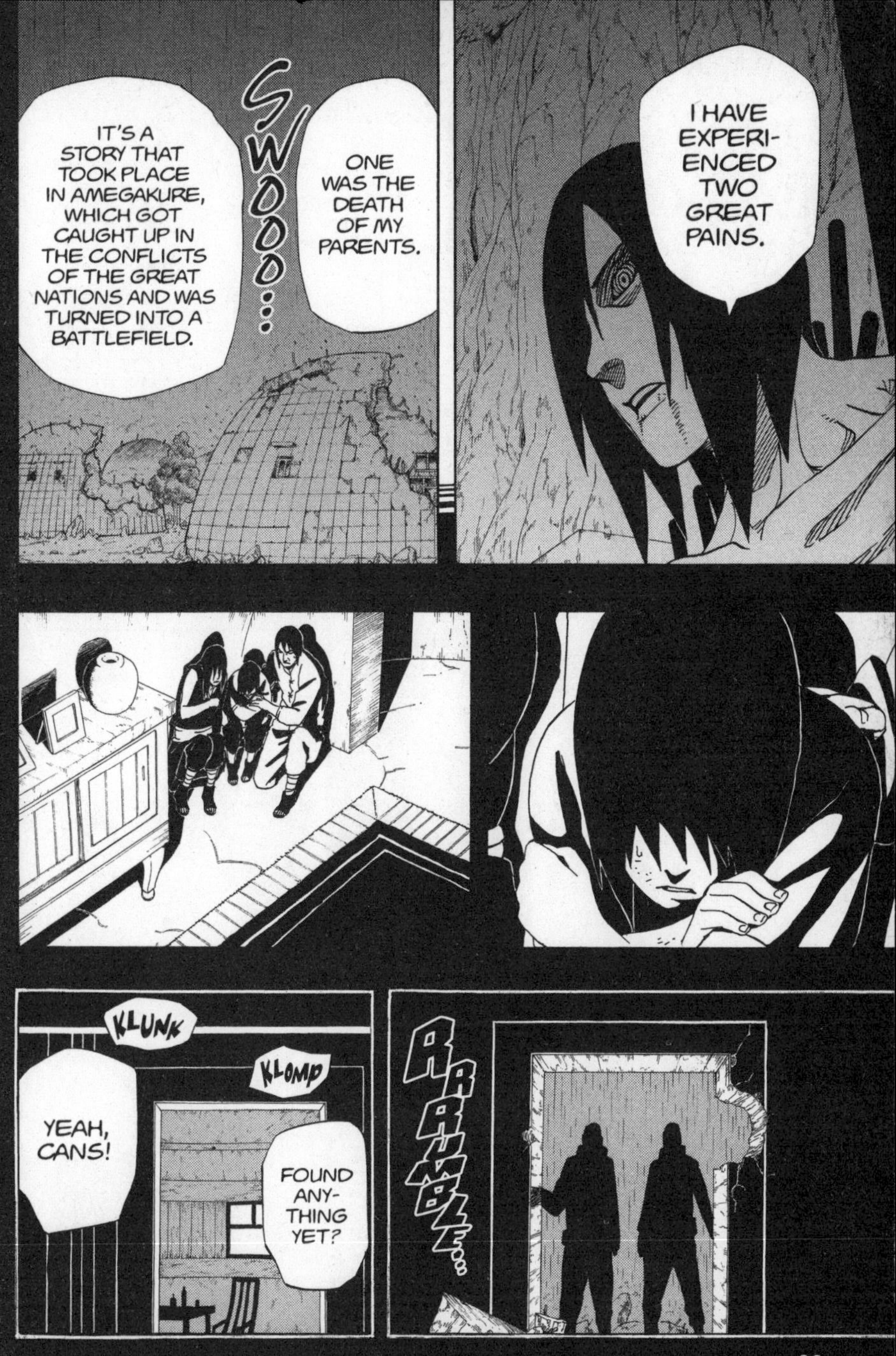
I HAVE EXPERI-ENCED TWO GREAT PAINS.
SWOOO...
ONE WAS THE DEATH OF MY PARENTS.
IT'S A STORY THAT TOOK PLACE IN AMEGAKURE, WHICH GOT CAUGHT UP IN THE CONFLICTS OF THE GREAT NATIONS AND WAS TURNED INTO A BATTLEFIELD.
RRRUMBLE...
KLUNK
KLOMP
FOUND ANY-THING YET?
YEAH, CANS!

READ THIS WAY

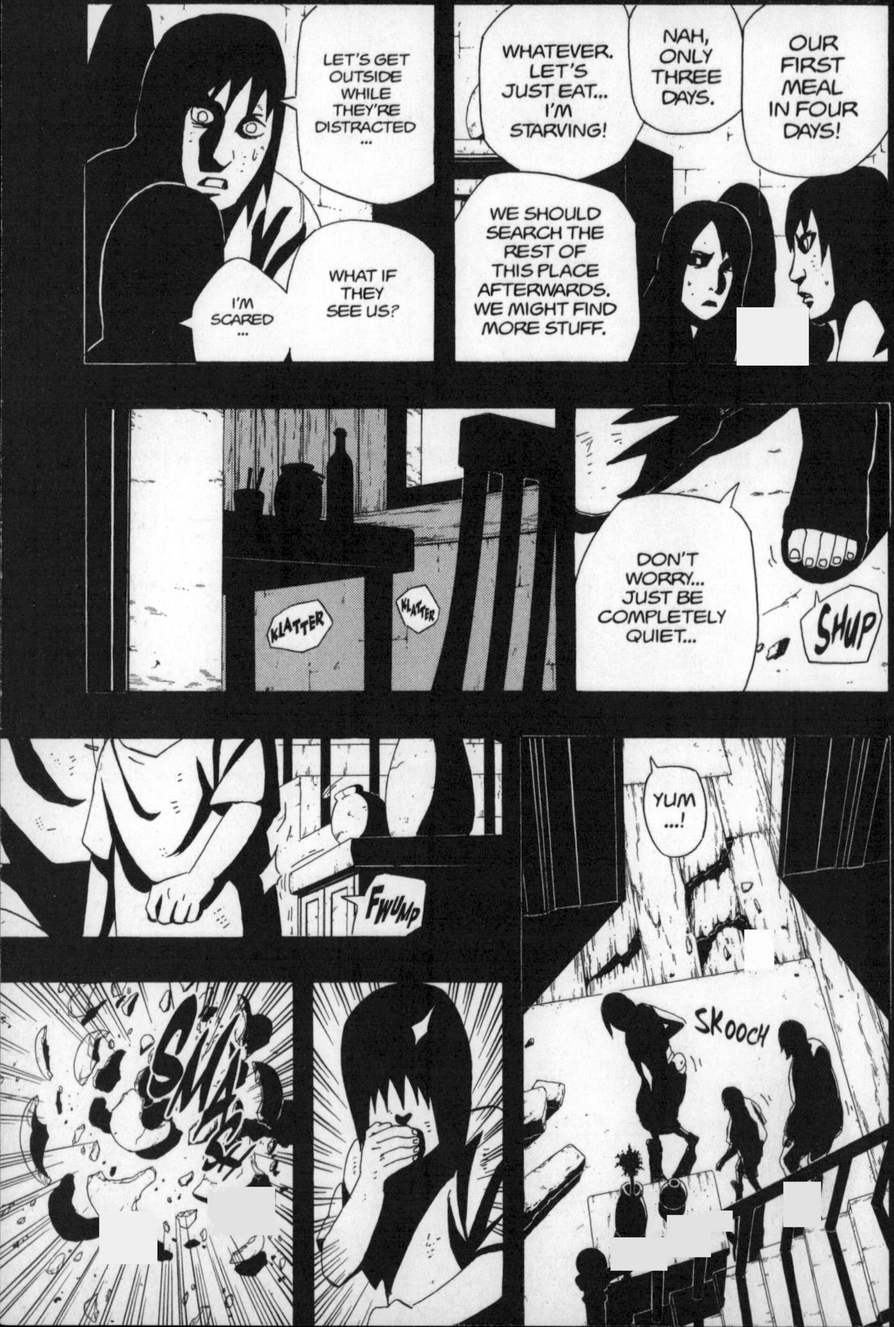

OUR FIRST MEAL IN FOUR DAYS!
NAH, ONLY THREE DAYS.
WHATEVER. LET'S JUST EAT... I'M STARVING!
WE SHOULD SEARCH THE REST OF THIS PLACE AFTERWARDS. WE MIGHT FIND MORE STUFF.
LET'S GET OUTSIDE WHILE THEY'RE DISTRACTED ...
WHAT IF THEY SEE US?
I'M SCARED ...
DON'T WORRY... JUST BE COMPLETELY QUIET...
SHUP
KLATTER
KLATTER
YUM ...!
SKOOCH
FWUMP

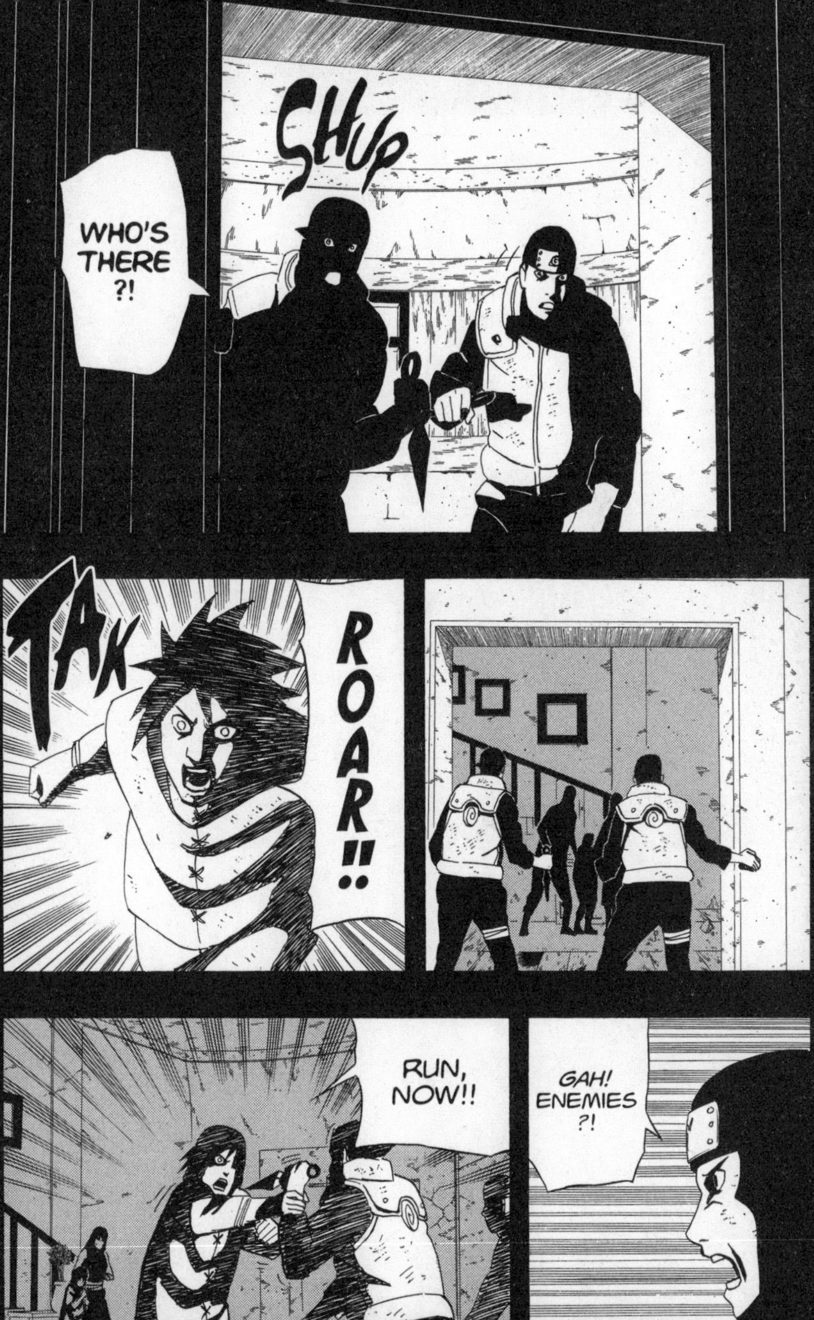
SHUP
WHO'S THERE ?!
ROAR!!
TAK
GAH! ENEMIES ?!
RUN, NOW!!

READ THIS WAY

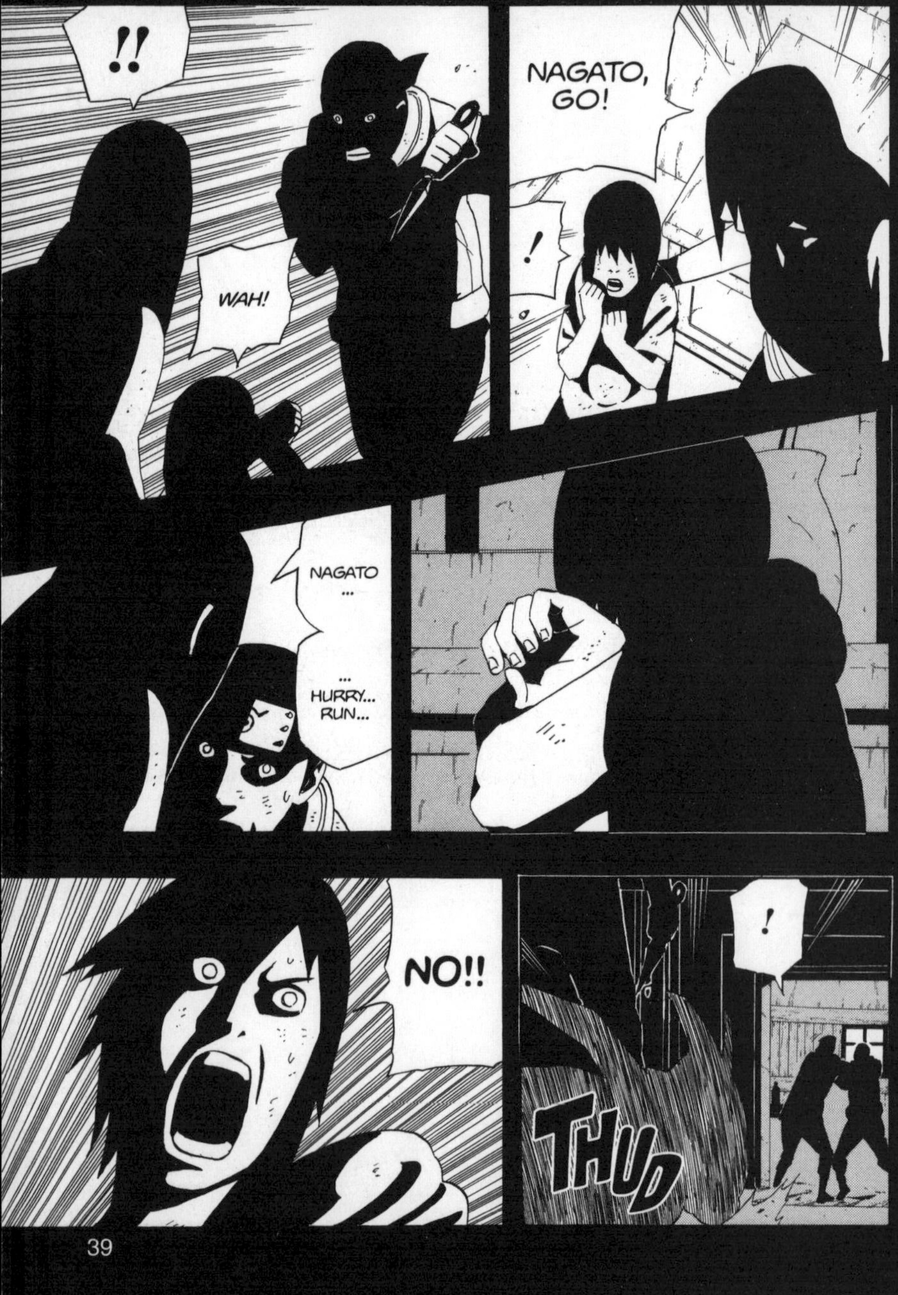
NAGATO, GO!
!
!!
WAH!
NAGATO ...
... HURRY... RUN...
!
THUD
NO!!

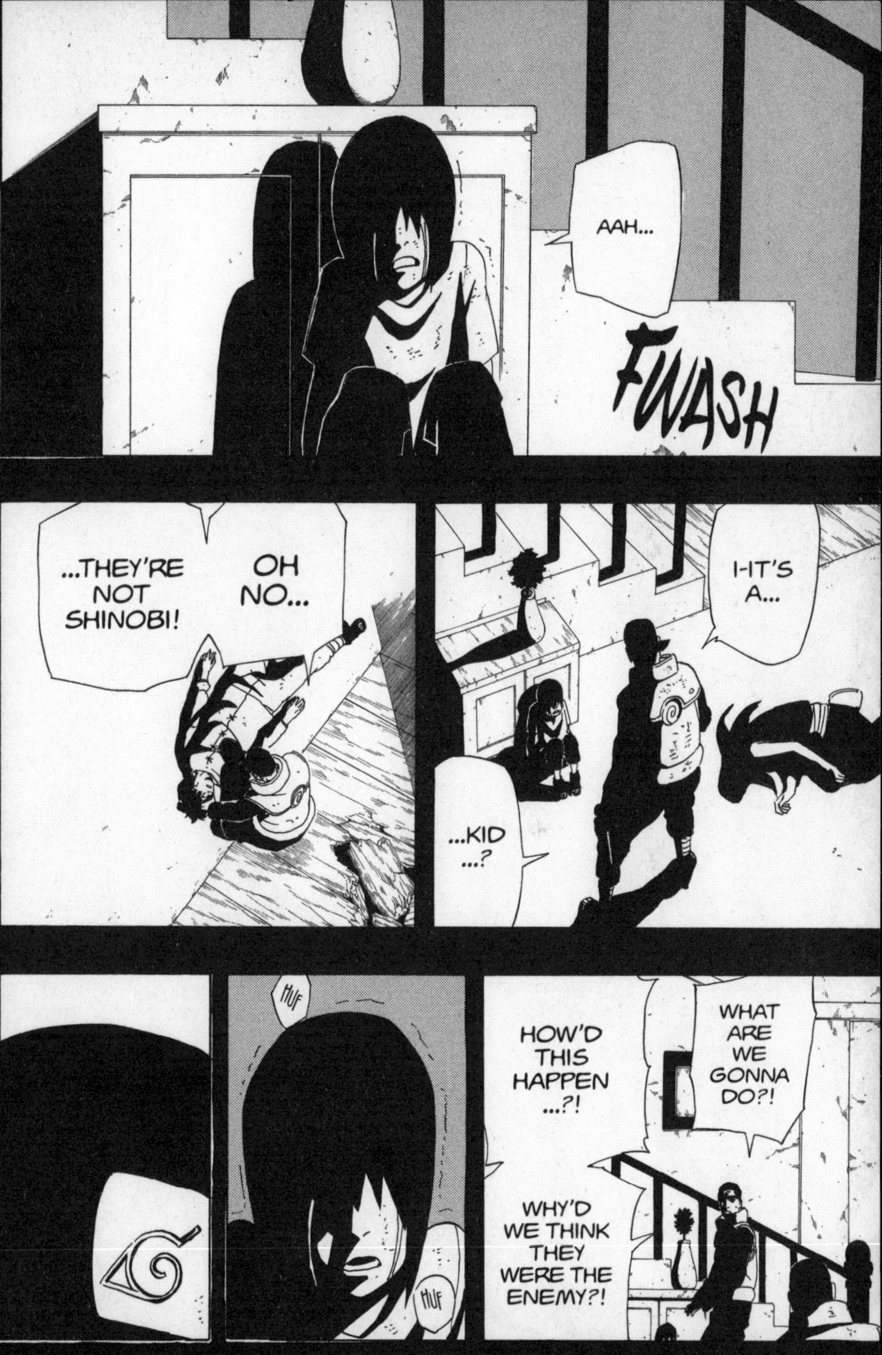
AAH...
FWASH
I-IT'S A...
...KID ...?
OH NO...
...THEY'RE NOT SHINOBI!
WHAT ARE WE GONNA DO?!
HOW'D THIS HAPPEN ...?!
WHY'D WE THINK THEY WERE THE ENEMY?!
HUF
HUF

READ THIS WAY

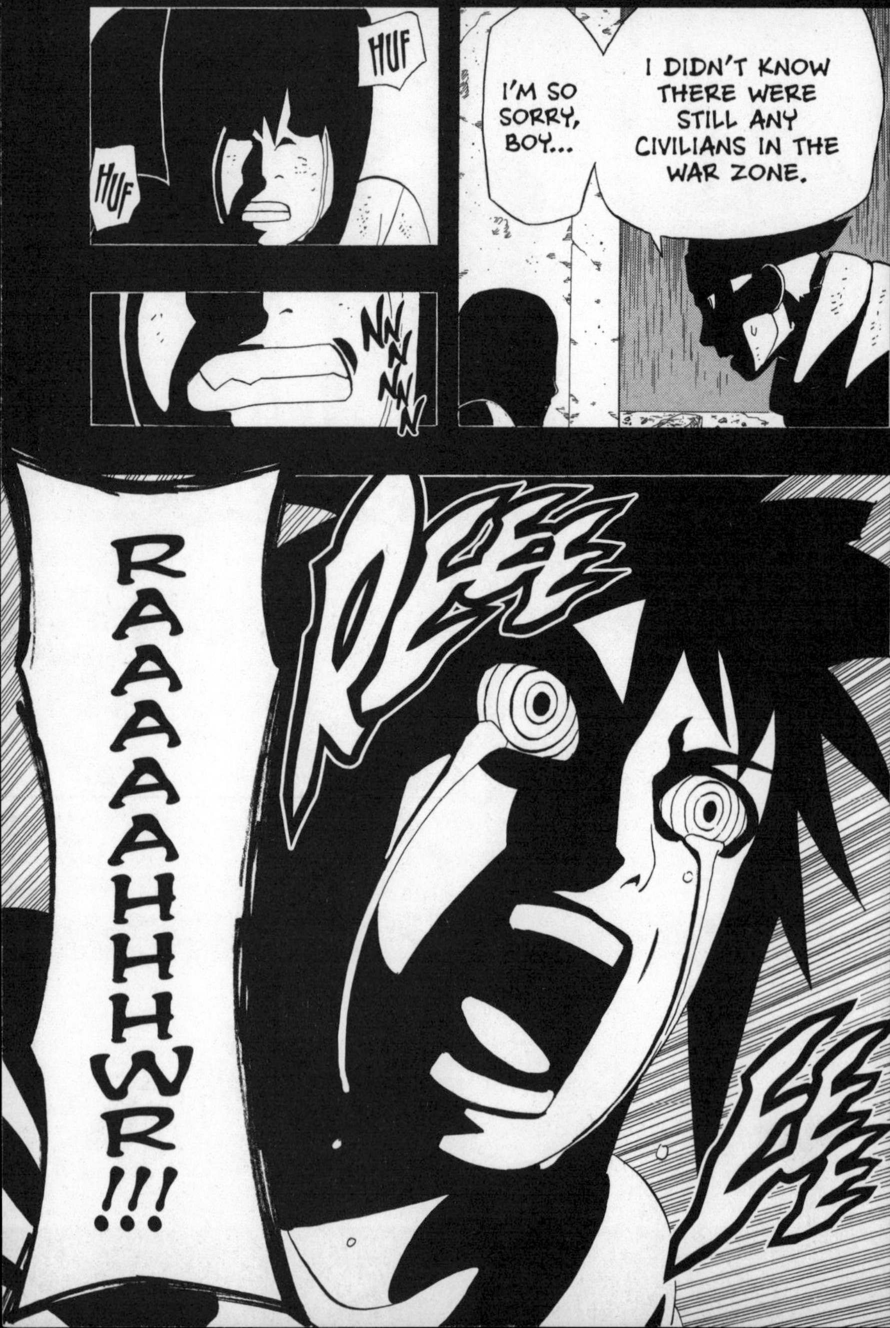
I DIDN'T KNOW THERE WERE STILL ANY CIVILIANS IN THE WAR ZONE.
I'M SO SORRY, BOY...
HUF
HUF
NNNNNNN
RAAAAHHWR!!!

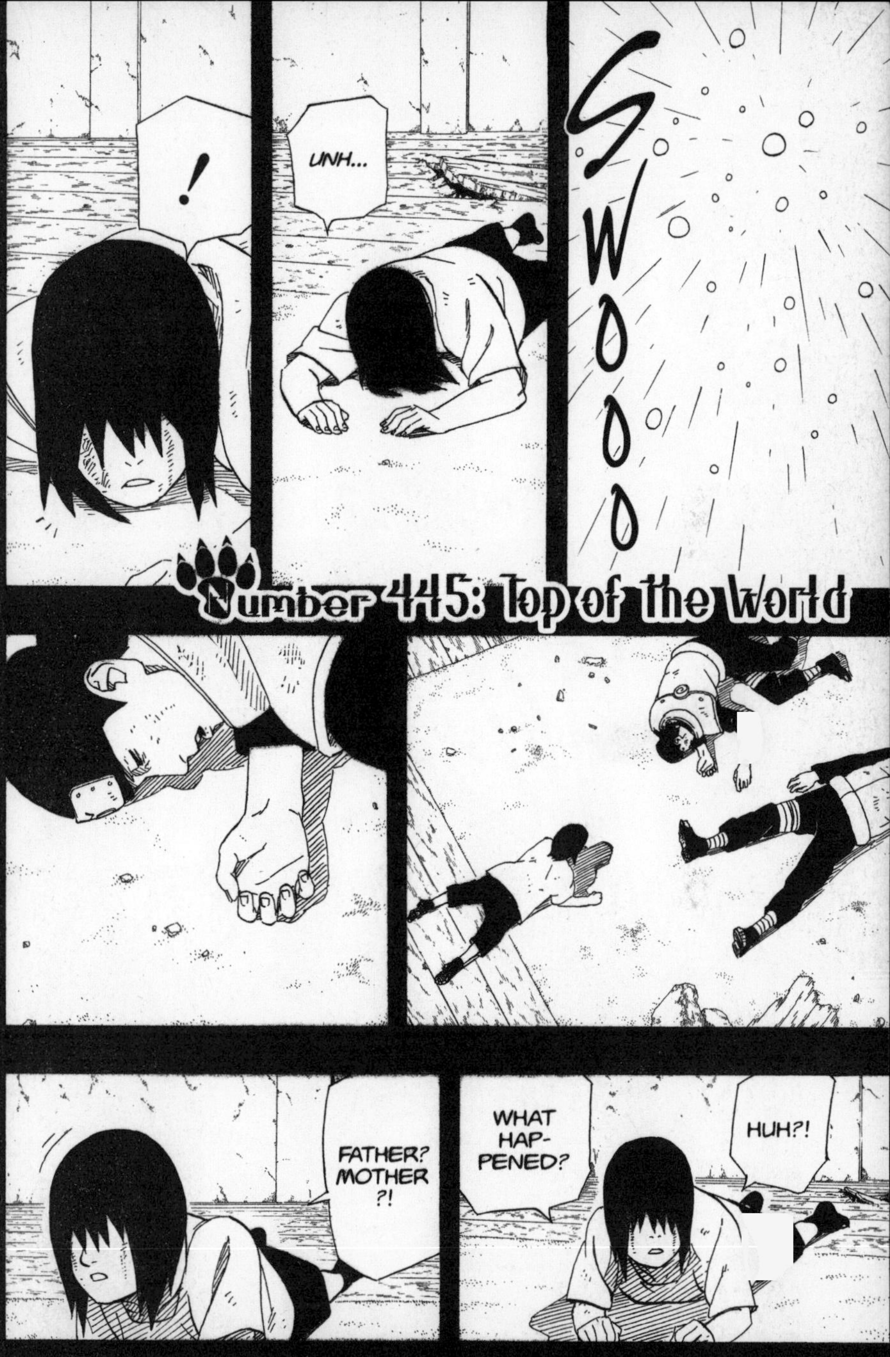
SWOOO
UNH...
!
Number 445: Top of the World
HUH?!
WHAT HAP-PENED?
FATHER? MOTHER ?!

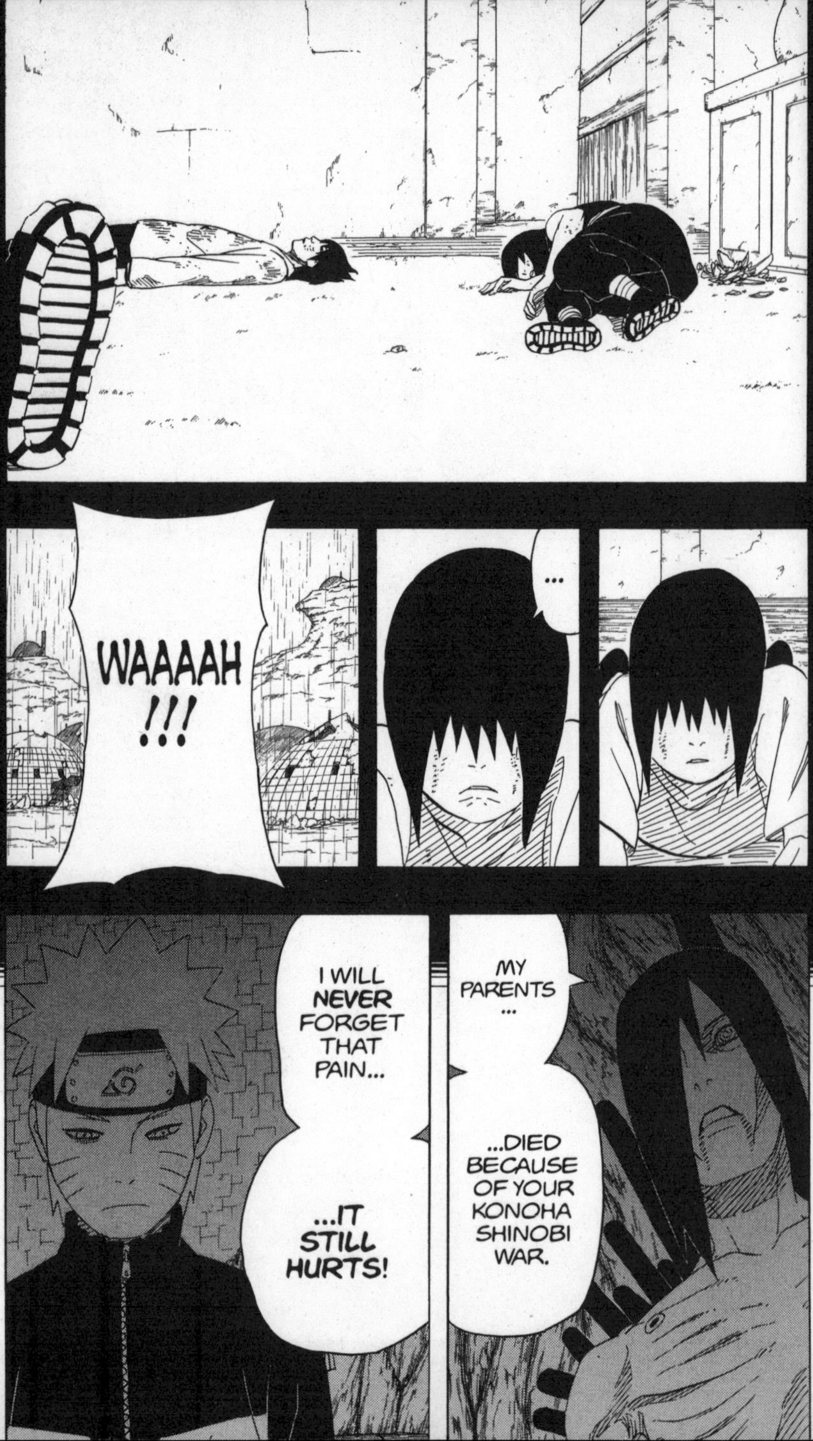
...
WAAAAH!!!
MY PARENTS...
...DIED BECAUSE OF YOUR KONOHA SHINOBI WAR.
I WILL NEVER FORGET THAT PAIN...
...IT STILL HURTS!

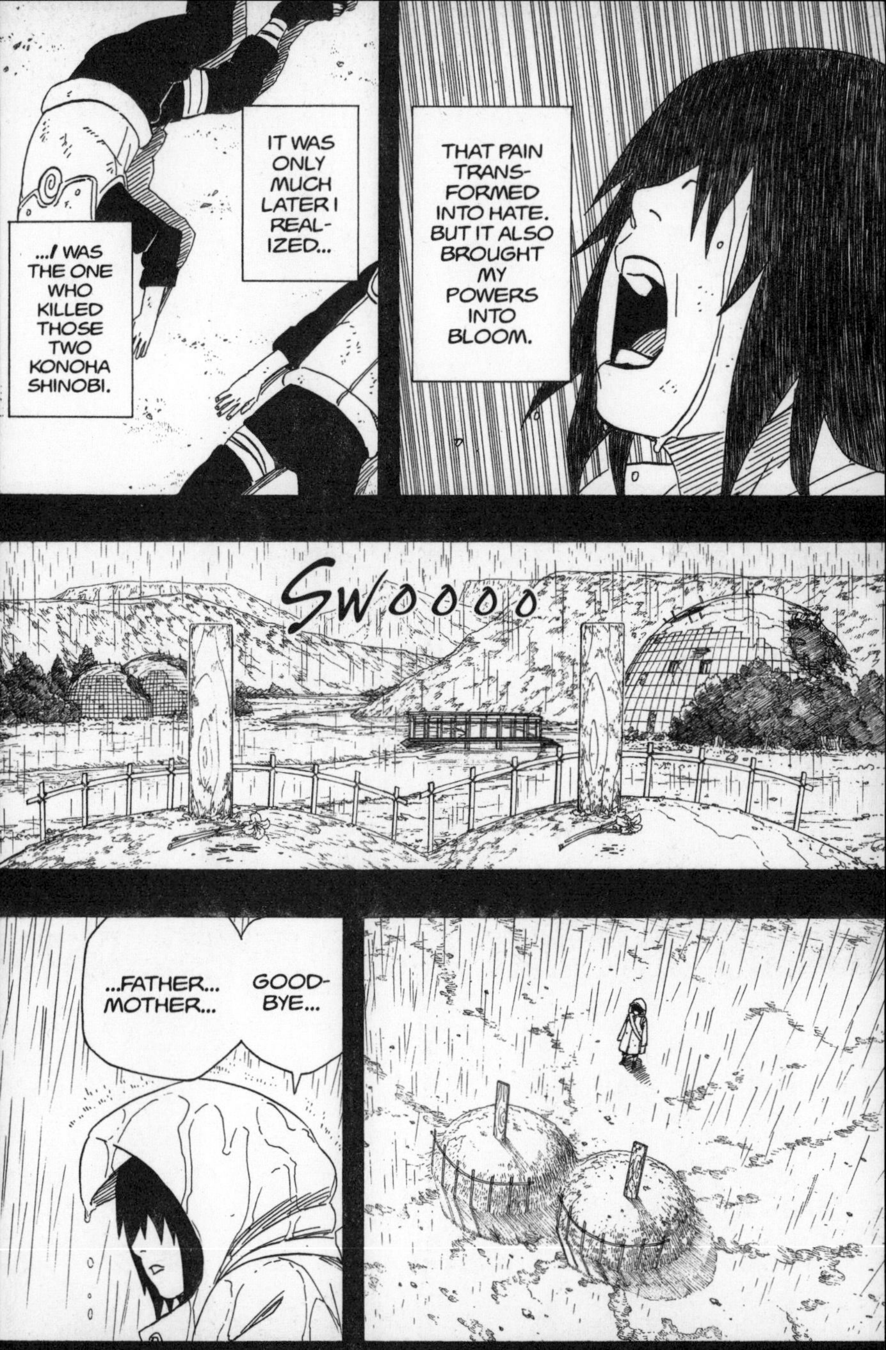
THAT PAIN TRANSFORMED INTO HATE. BUT IT ALSO BROUGHT MY POWERS INTO BLOOM.
IT WAS ONLY MUCH LATER I REALIZED...
...I WAS THE ONE WHO KILLED THOSE TWO KONOHA SHINOBI.
SWOOOO
...FATHER... MOTHER... GOOD-BYE...

READ THIS WAY

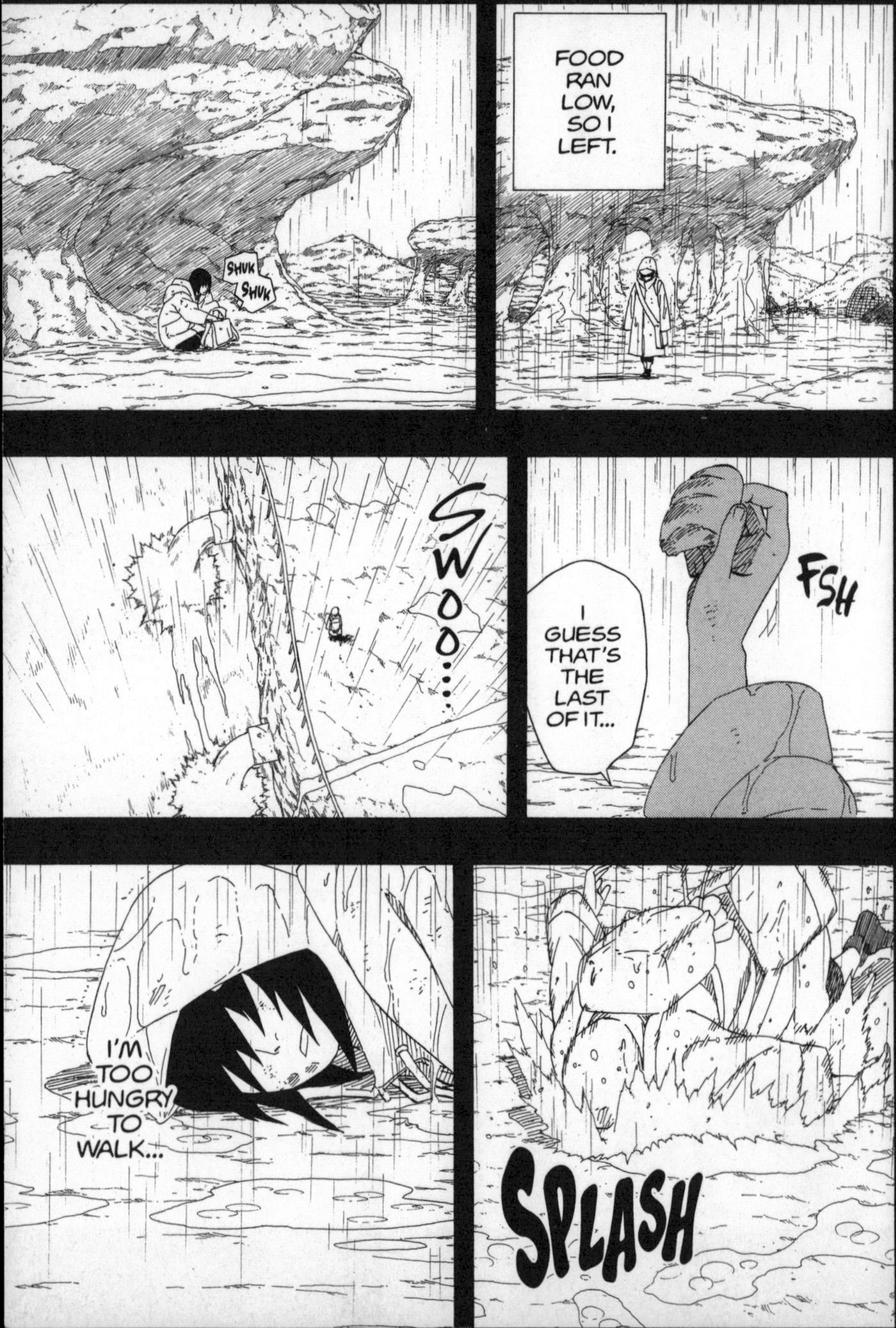
FOOD RAN LOW, SO I LEFT.
SHUK SHUK
FSH
I GUESS THAT'S THE LAST OF IT...
SWOO...
SPLASH
I'M TOO HUNGRY TO WALK...

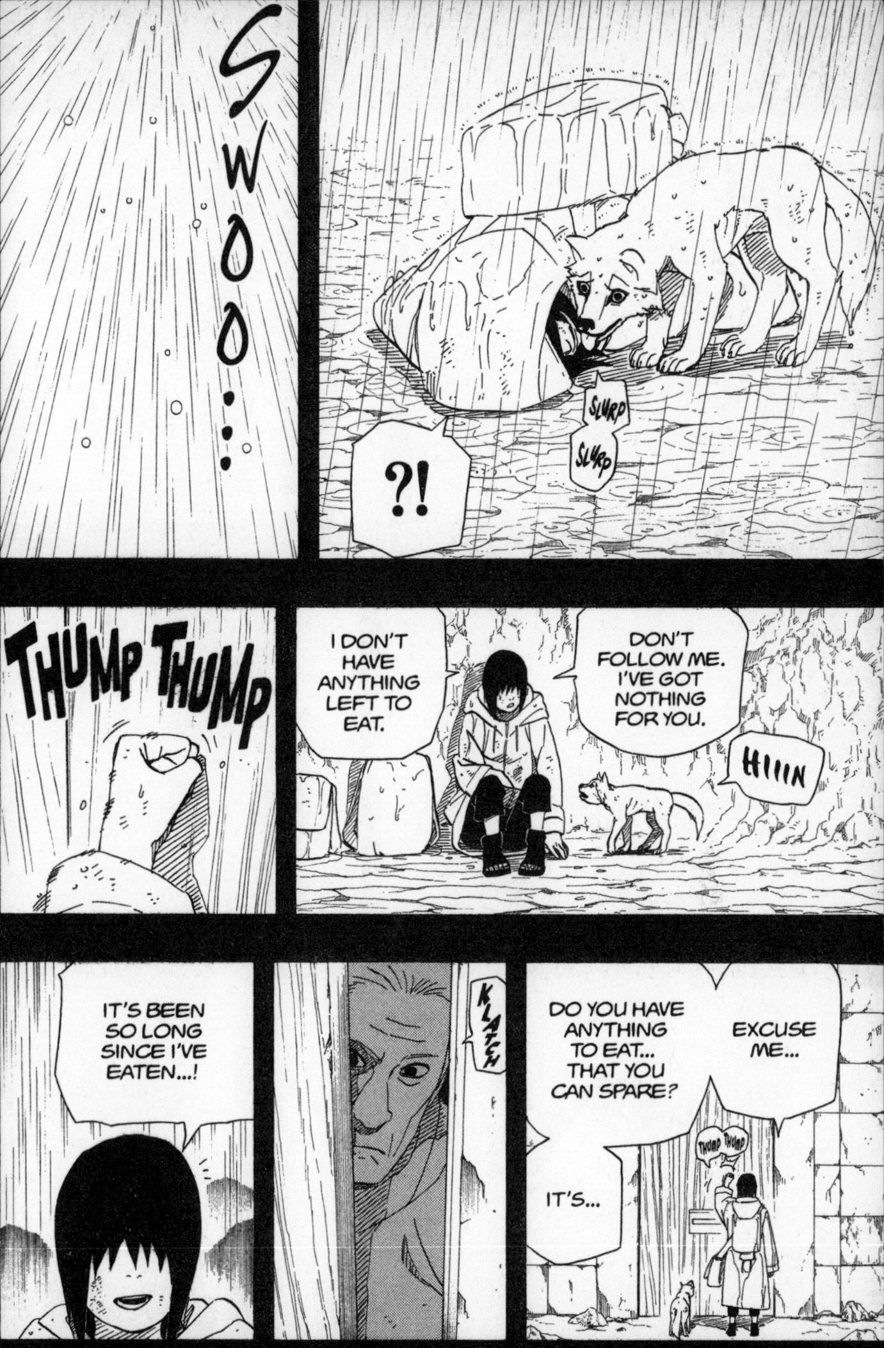
SLURP
SLURP
?!
SWOO...
DON'T FOLLOW ME. I'VE GOT NOTHING FOR YOU.
I DON'T HAVE ANYTHING LEFT TO EAT.
HIIIN
THUMP THUMP
EXCUSE ME...
DO YOU HAVE ANYTHING TO EAT... THAT YOU CAN SPARE?
THUMP THUMP
IT'S...
KLATCH
IT'S BEEN SO LONG SINCE I'VE EATEN...!

READ THIS WAY

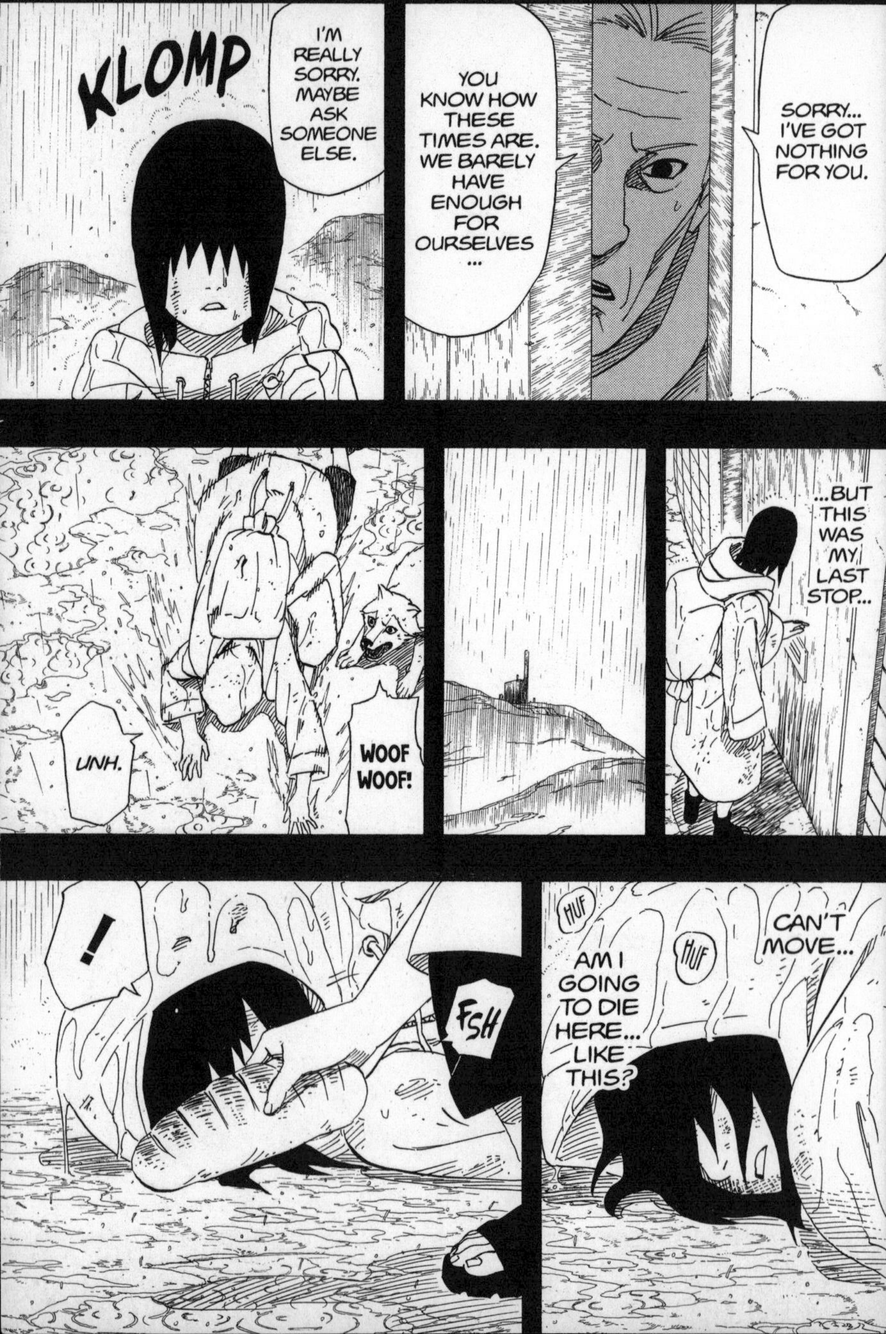
SORRY... I'VE GOT NOTHING FOR YOU.
YOU KNOW HOW THESE TIMES ARE. WE BARELY HAVE ENOUGH FOR OURSELVES ...
I'M REALLY SORRY. MAYBE ASK SOMEONE ELSE.
KLOMP
...BUT THIS WAS MY LAST STOP...
WOOF WOOF!
UNH.
CAN'T MOVE...
HUF
HUF
AM I GOING TO DIE HERE... LIKE THIS?
FSH
!

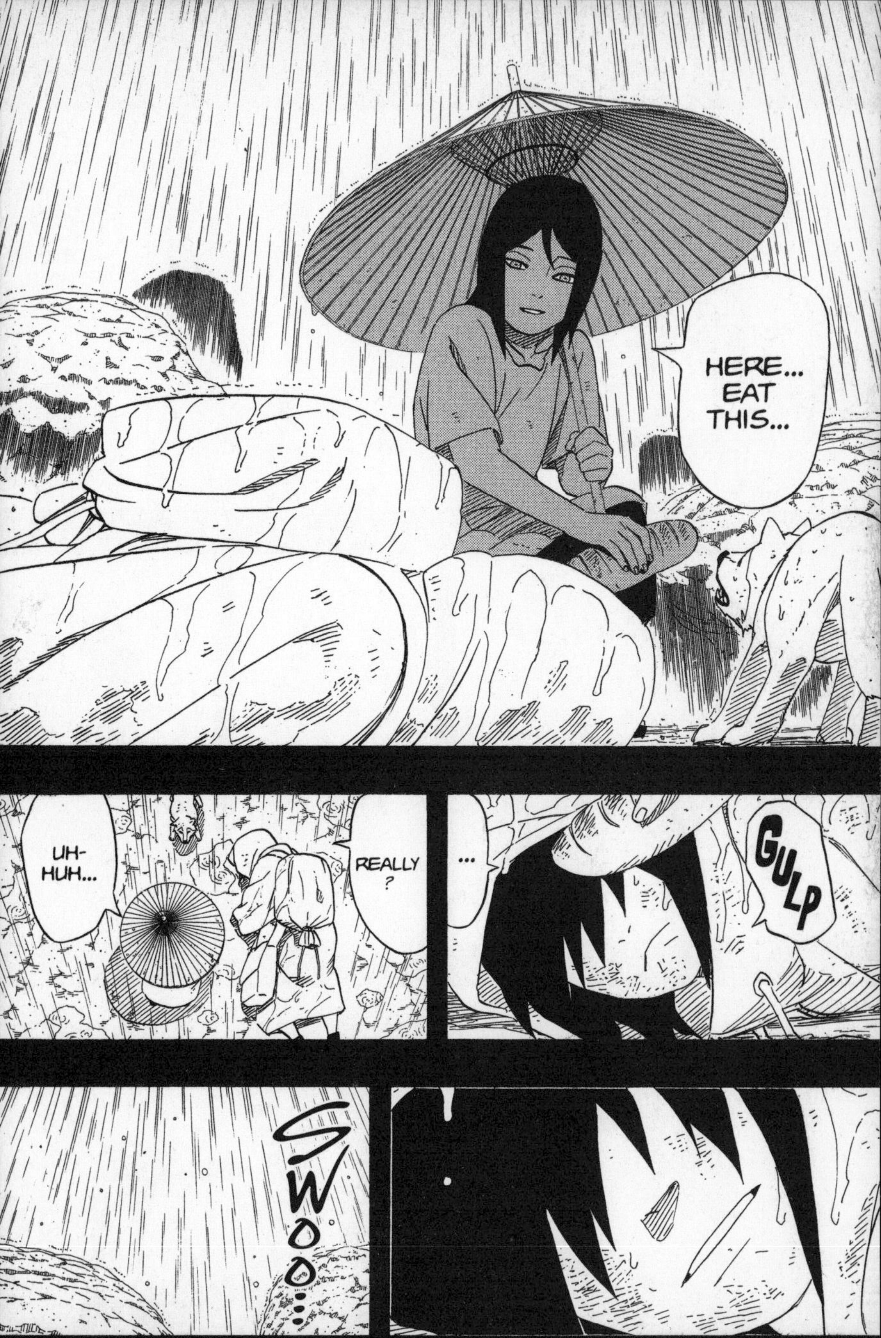
HERE... EAT THIS...
GULP
...
REALLY?
UH-HUH...
SWOO...

READ THIS WAY

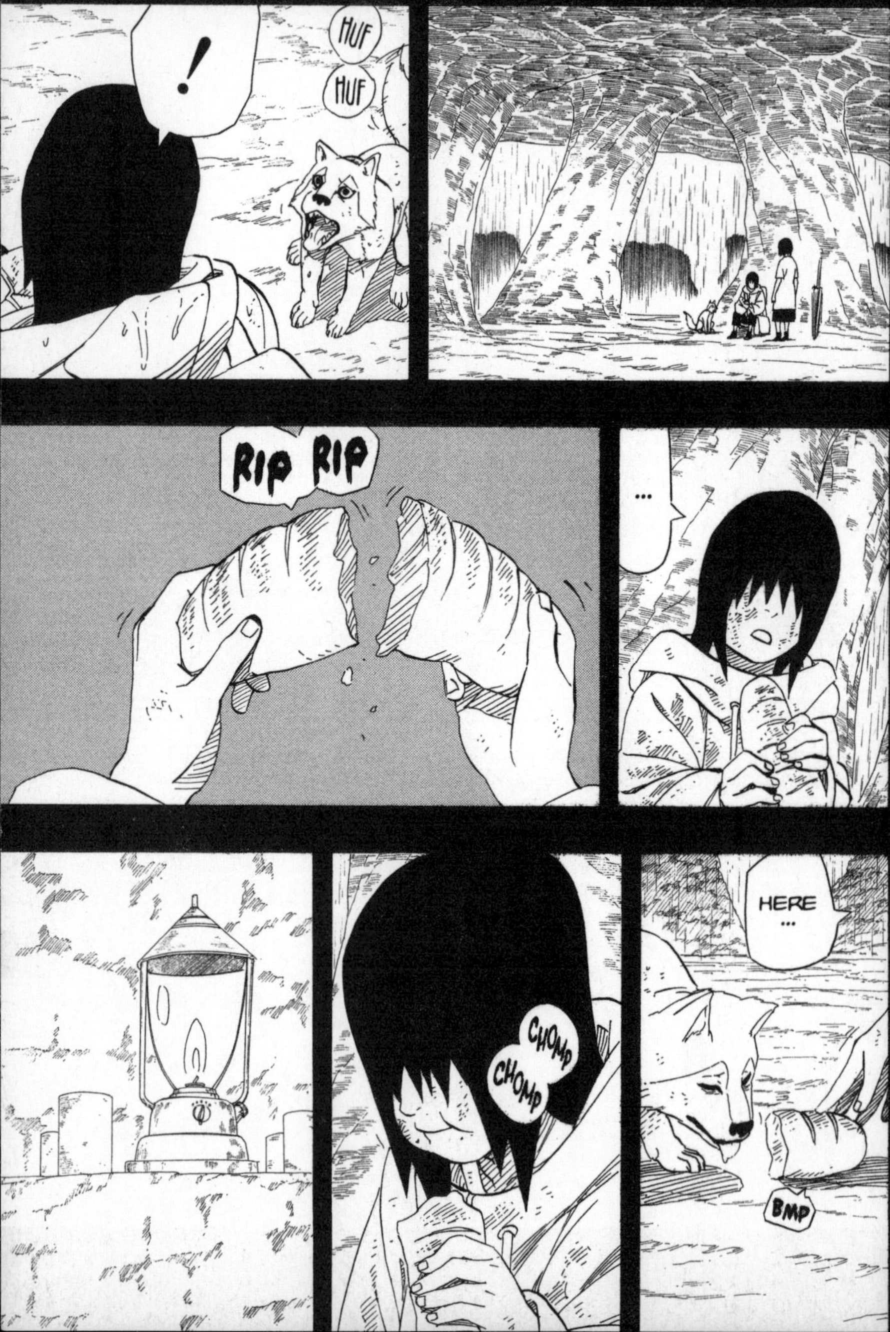
!
HUF
HUF
...
RIP RIP
HERE
...
BMP
CHOMP
CHOMP

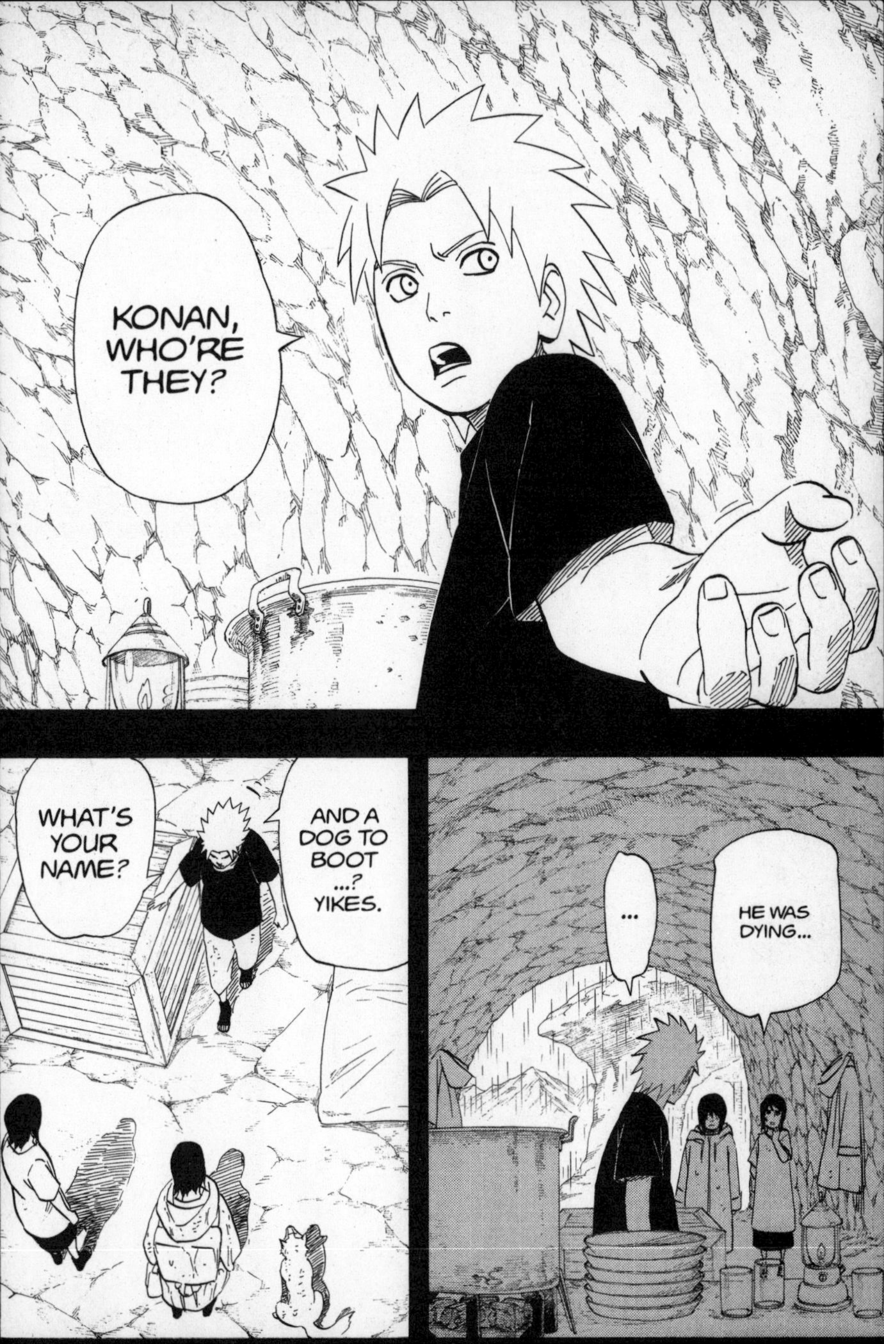
KONAN, WHO'RE THEY?
HE WAS DYING...
...
AND A DOG TO BOOT ...? YIKES.
WHAT'S YOUR NAME?

READ THIS WAY

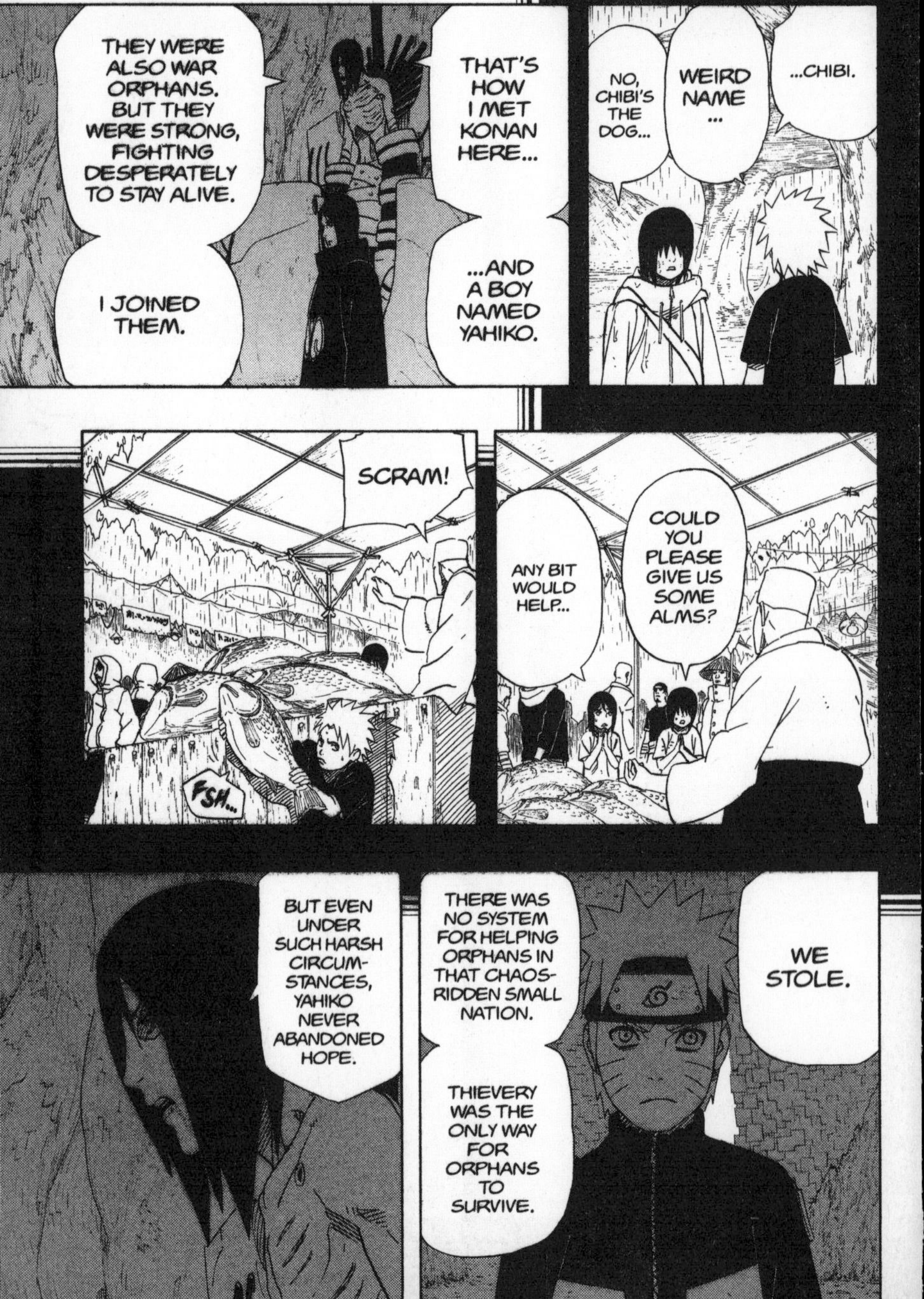
...CHIBI.
WEIRD NAME ...
NO, CHIBI'S THE DOG...
THAT'S HOW I MET KONAN HERE...
...AND A BOY NAMED YAHIKO.
THEY WERE ALSO WAR ORPHANS. BUT THEY WERE STRONG, FIGHTING DESPERATELY TO STAY ALIVE.
I JOINED THEM.
COULD YOU PLEASE GIVE US SOME ALMS?
ANY BIT WOULD HELP...
SCRAM!
FSH...
WE STOLE.
THERE WAS NO SYSTEM FOR HELPING ORPHANS IN THAT CHAOS-RIDDEN SMALL NATION.
THIEVERY WAS THE ONLY WAY FOR ORPHANS TO SURVIVE.
BUT EVEN UNDER SUCH HARSH CIRCUM-STANCES, YAHIKO NEVER ABANDONED HOPE.

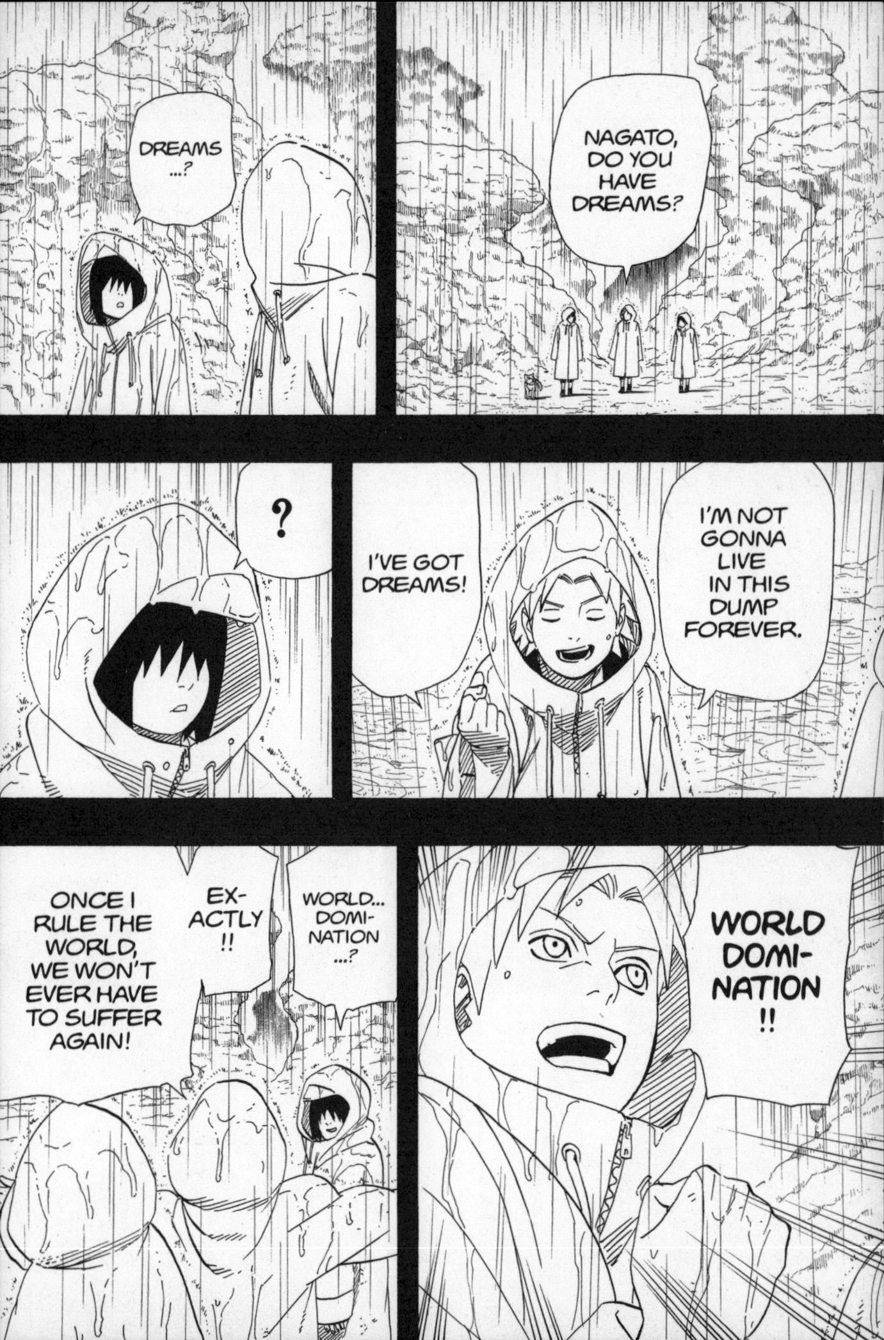
NAGATO, DO YOU HAVE DREAMS?
DREAMS ...?
I'M NOT GONNA LIVE IN THIS DUMP FOREVER.
I'VE GOT DREAMS!
?
WORLD DOMINATION !!
WORLD... DOMINATION ...?
EXACTLY !!
ONCE I RULE THE WORLD, WE WON'T EVER HAVE TO SUFFER AGAIN!

READ THIS WAY

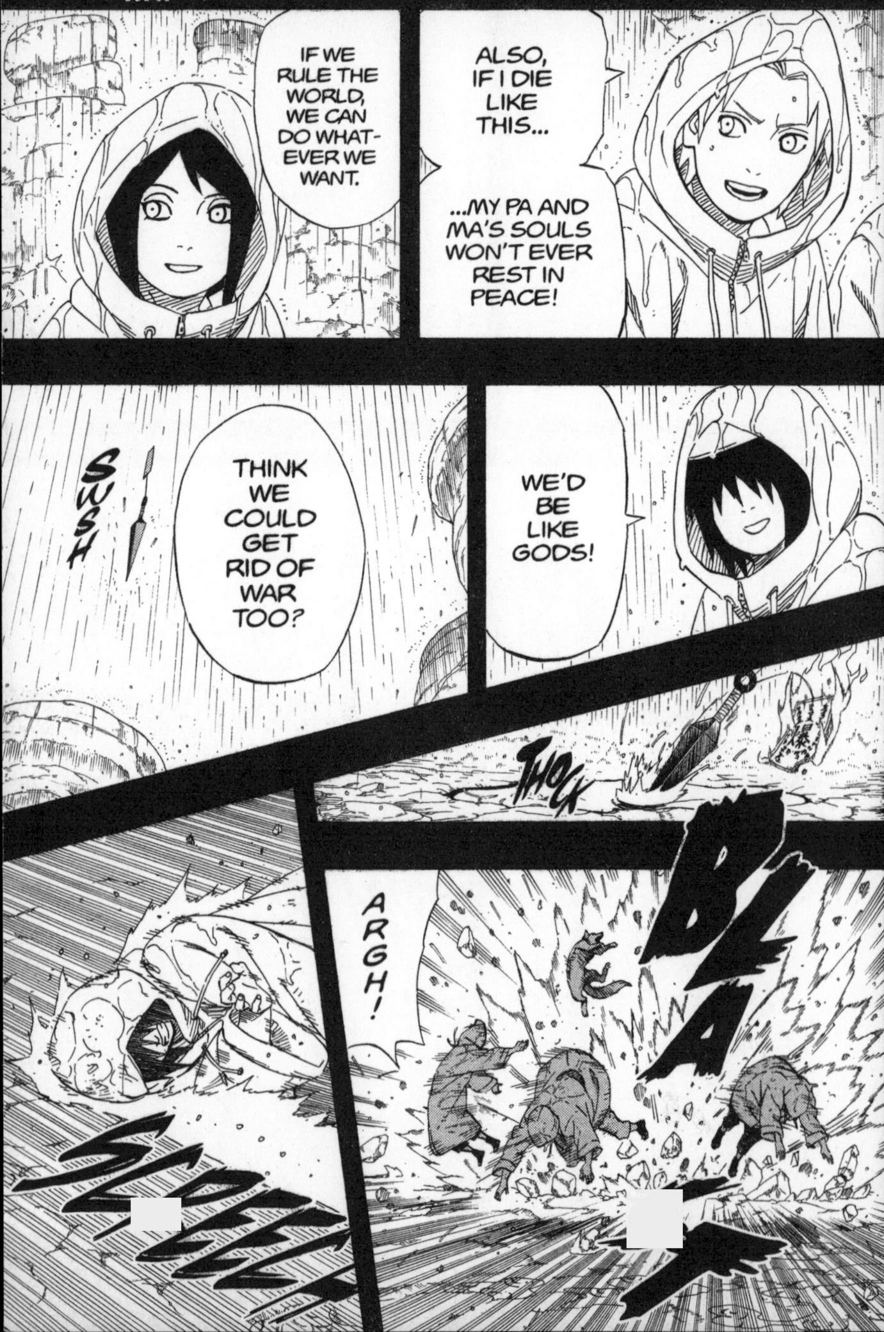

ALSO, IF I DIE LIKE THIS...
...MY PA AND MA'S SOULS WON'T EVER REST IN PEACE!
IF WE RULE THE WORLD, WE CAN DO WHAT-EVER WE WANT.
WE'D BE LIKE GODS!
THINK WE COULD GET RID OF WAR TOO?
SWSH
THOCK
ARGH!

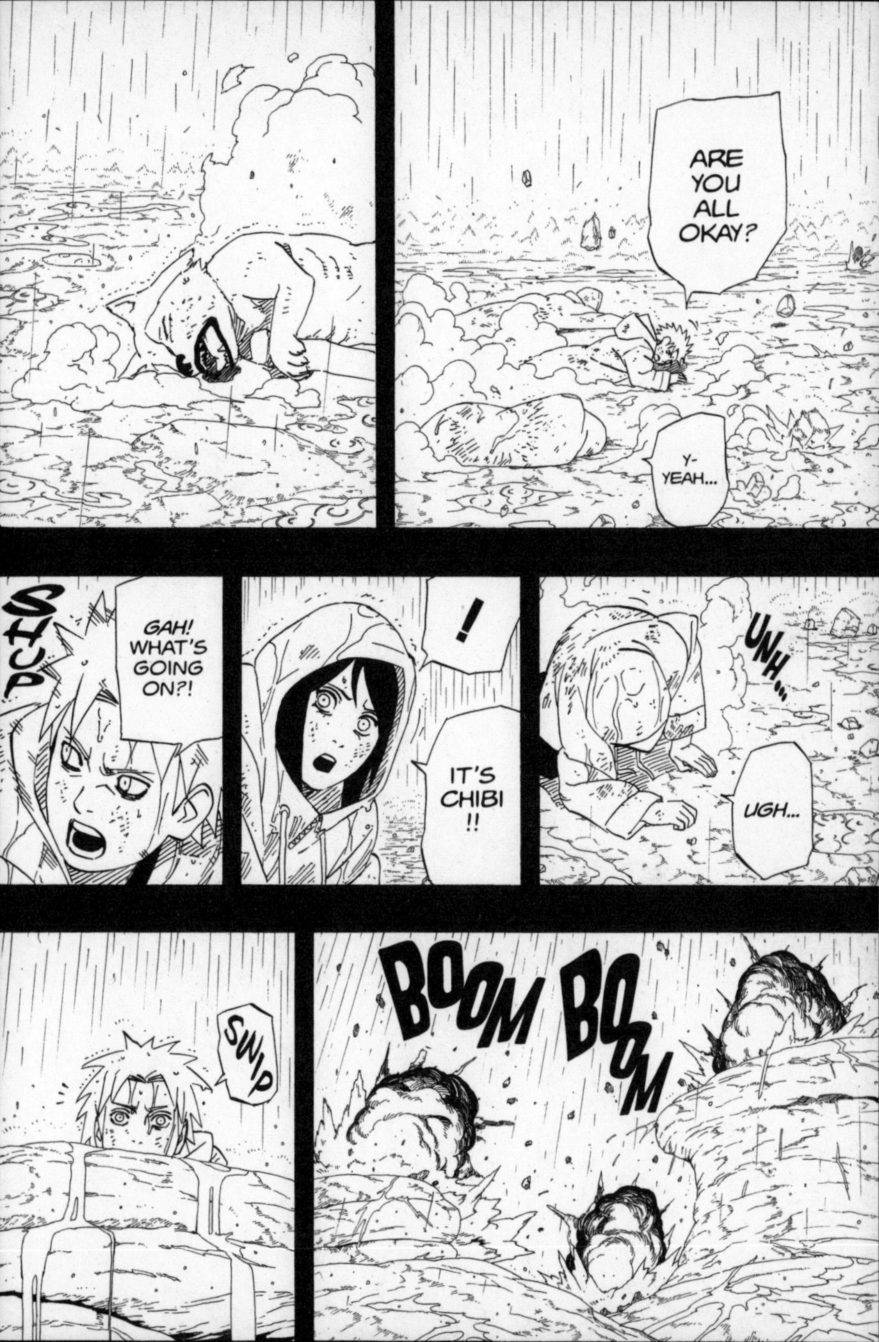
ARE YOU ALL OKAY?
Y-YEAH...
UNH...
UGH...
!
IT'S CHIBI !!
SHUP
GAH! WHAT'S GOING ON?!
BOOM BOOM
SWIP

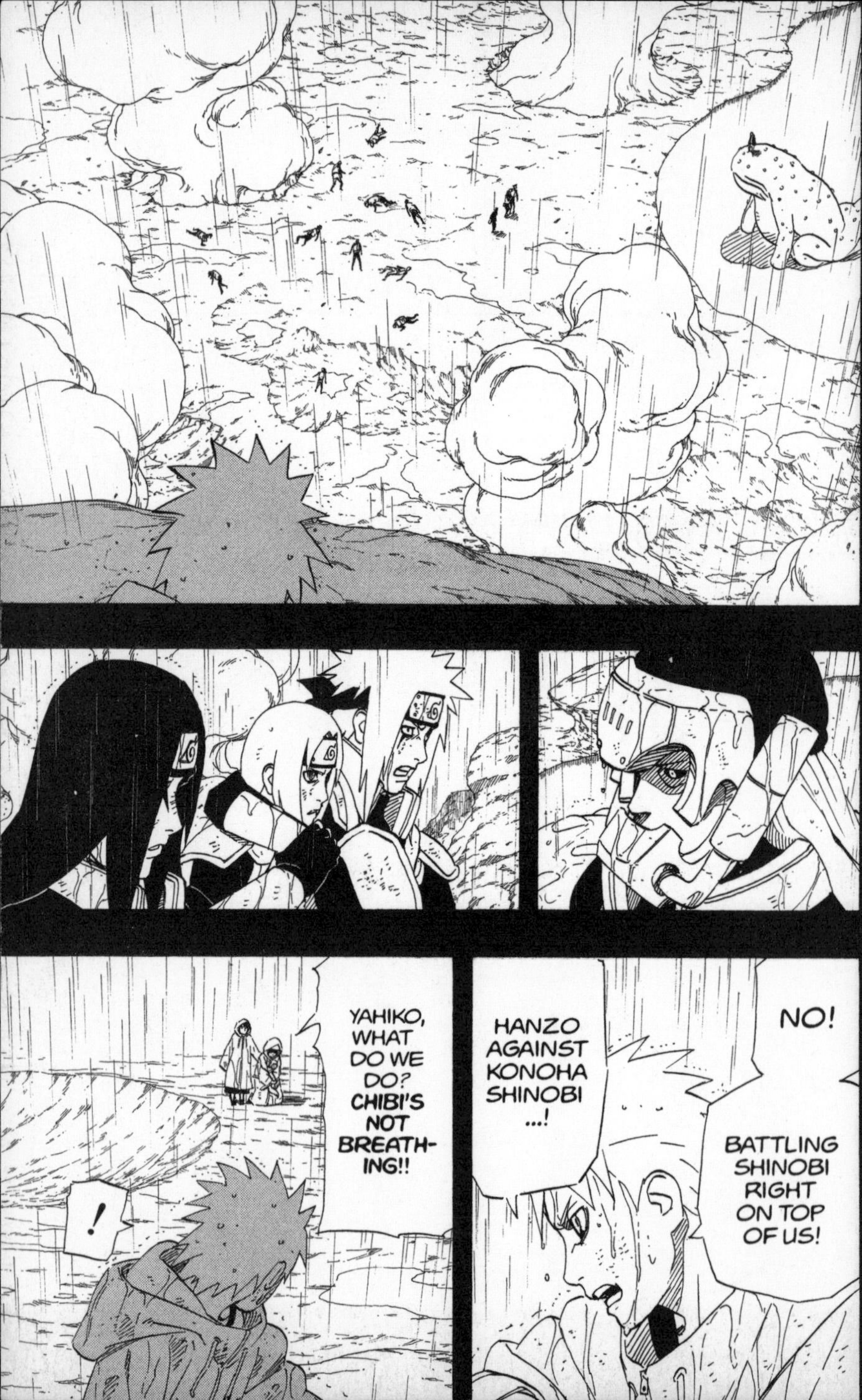
NO!
HANZO AGAINST KONOHA SHINOBI ...!
BATTLING SHINOBI RIGHT ON TOP OF US!
YAHIKO, WHAT DO WE DO? CHIBI'S NOT BREATHING!!
!

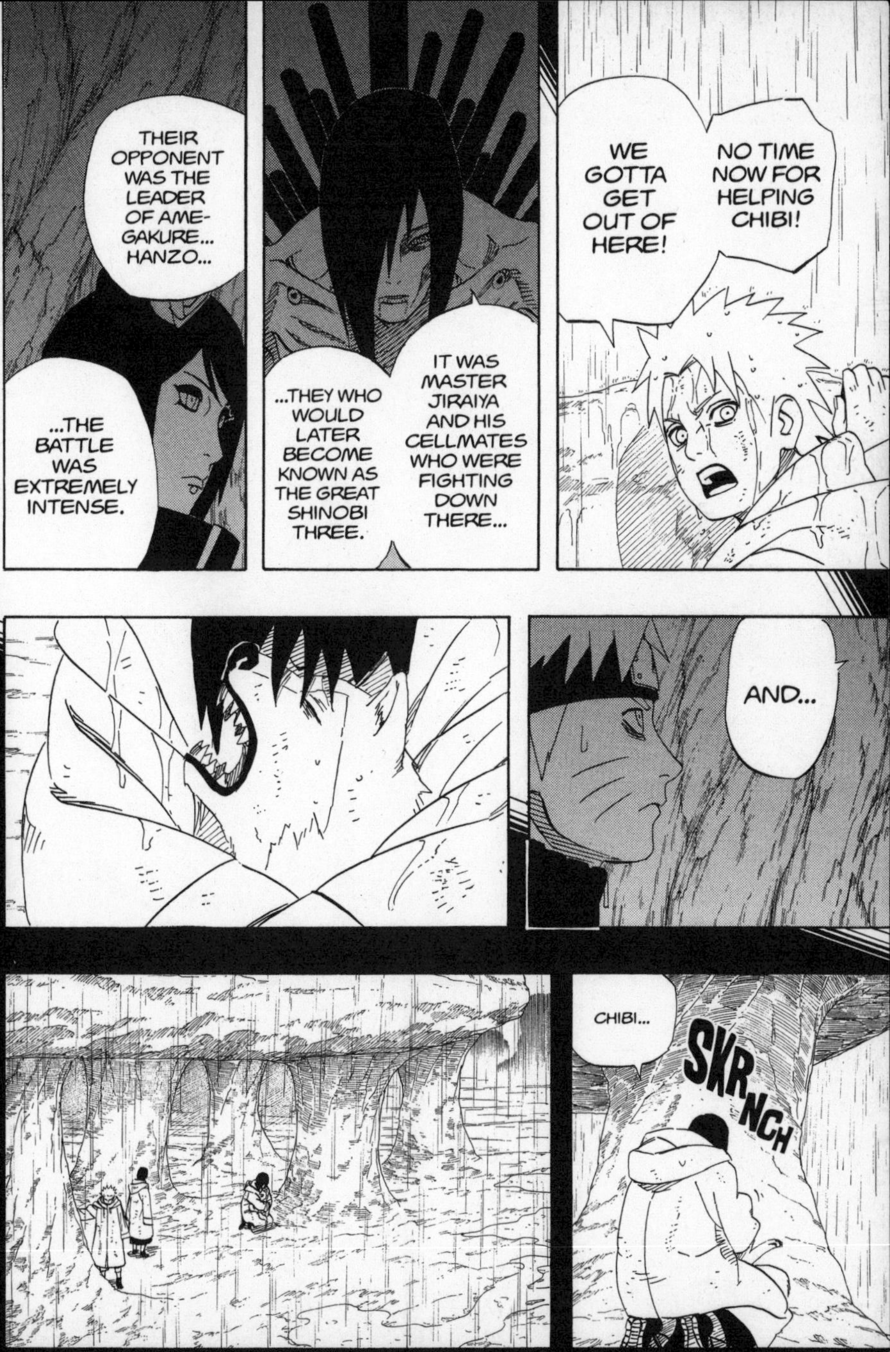
NO TIME NOW FOR HELPING CHIBI!
WE GOTTA GET OUT OF HERE!
IT WAS MASTER JIRAIYA AND HIS CELLMATES WHO WERE FIGHTING DOWN THERE...
...THEY WHO WOULD LATER BECOME KNOWN AS THE GREAT SHINOBI THREE.
THEIR OPPONENT WAS THE LEADER OF AME-GAKURE... HANZO...
...THE BATTLE WAS EXTREMELY INTENSE.
AND...
CHIBI...
SKRNCH

READ THIS WAY

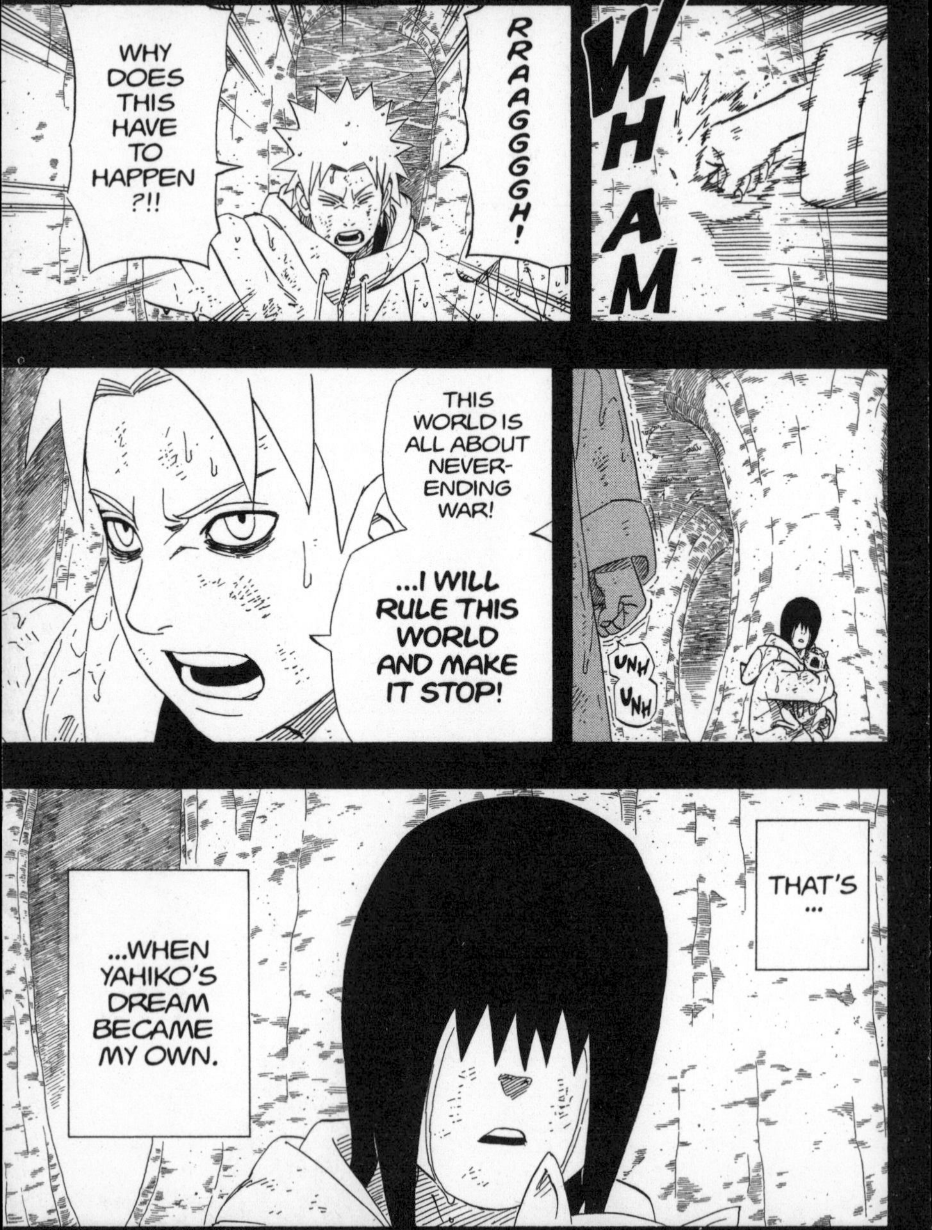

WHAM
RRAAGGGGH!
WHY DOES THIS HAVE TO HAPPEN ?!!
UNH UNH
THIS WORLD IS ALL ABOUT NEVER-ENDING WAR!
...I WILL RULE THIS WORLD AND MAKE IT STOP!
THAT'S ...
...WHEN YAHIKO'S DREAM BECAME MY OWN.

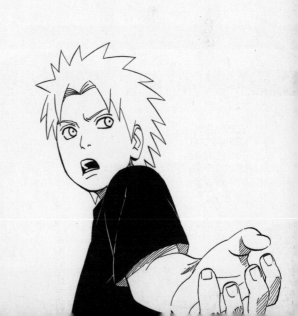

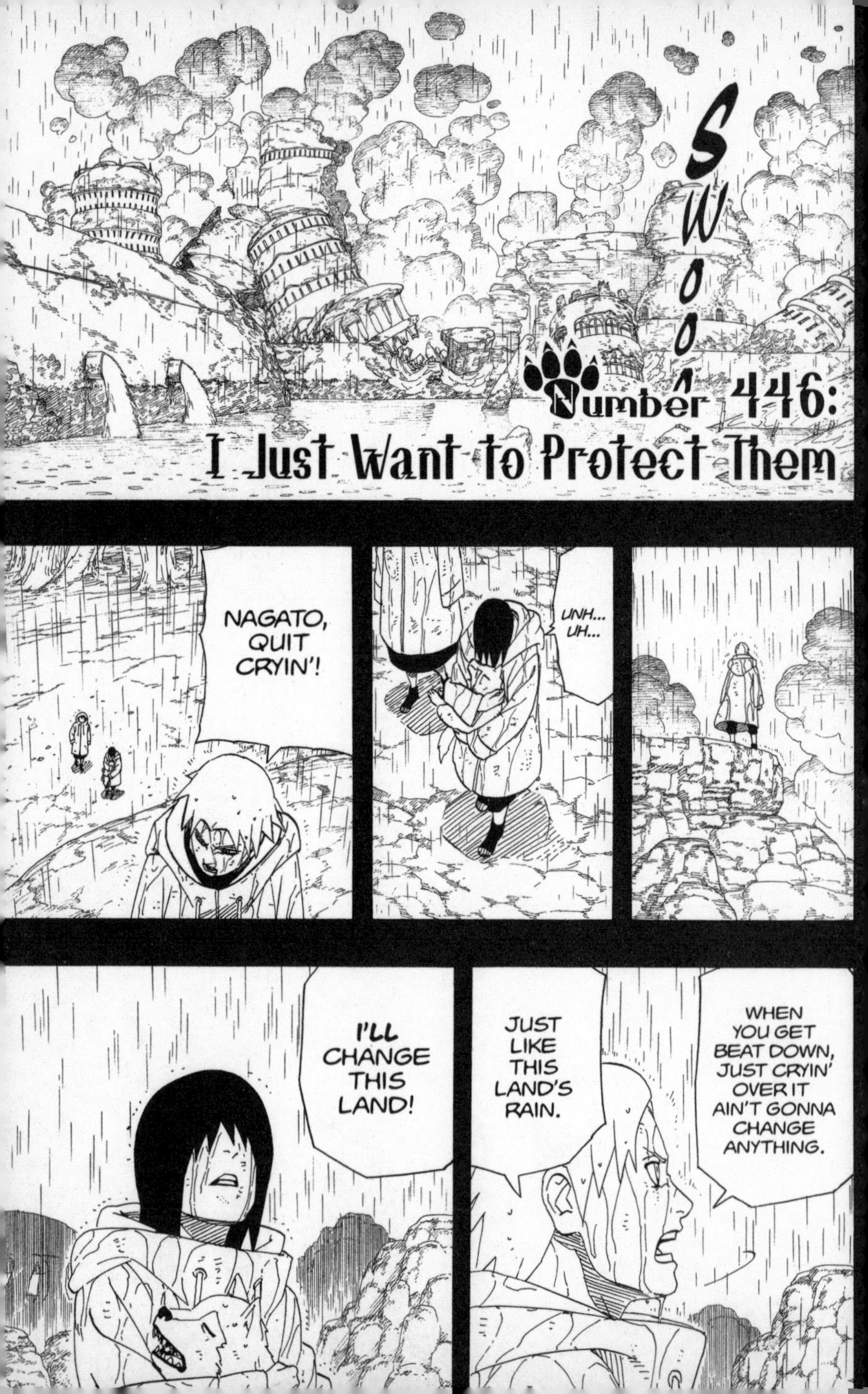
SWOOSH
Number 446: I Just Want to Protect Them
UNH... UH...
NAGATO, QUIT CRYIN'!
WHEN YOU GET BEAT DOWN, JUST CRYIN' OVER IT AIN'T GONNA CHANGE ANYTHING.
JUST LIKE THIS LAND'S RAIN.
I'LL CHANGE THIS LAND!

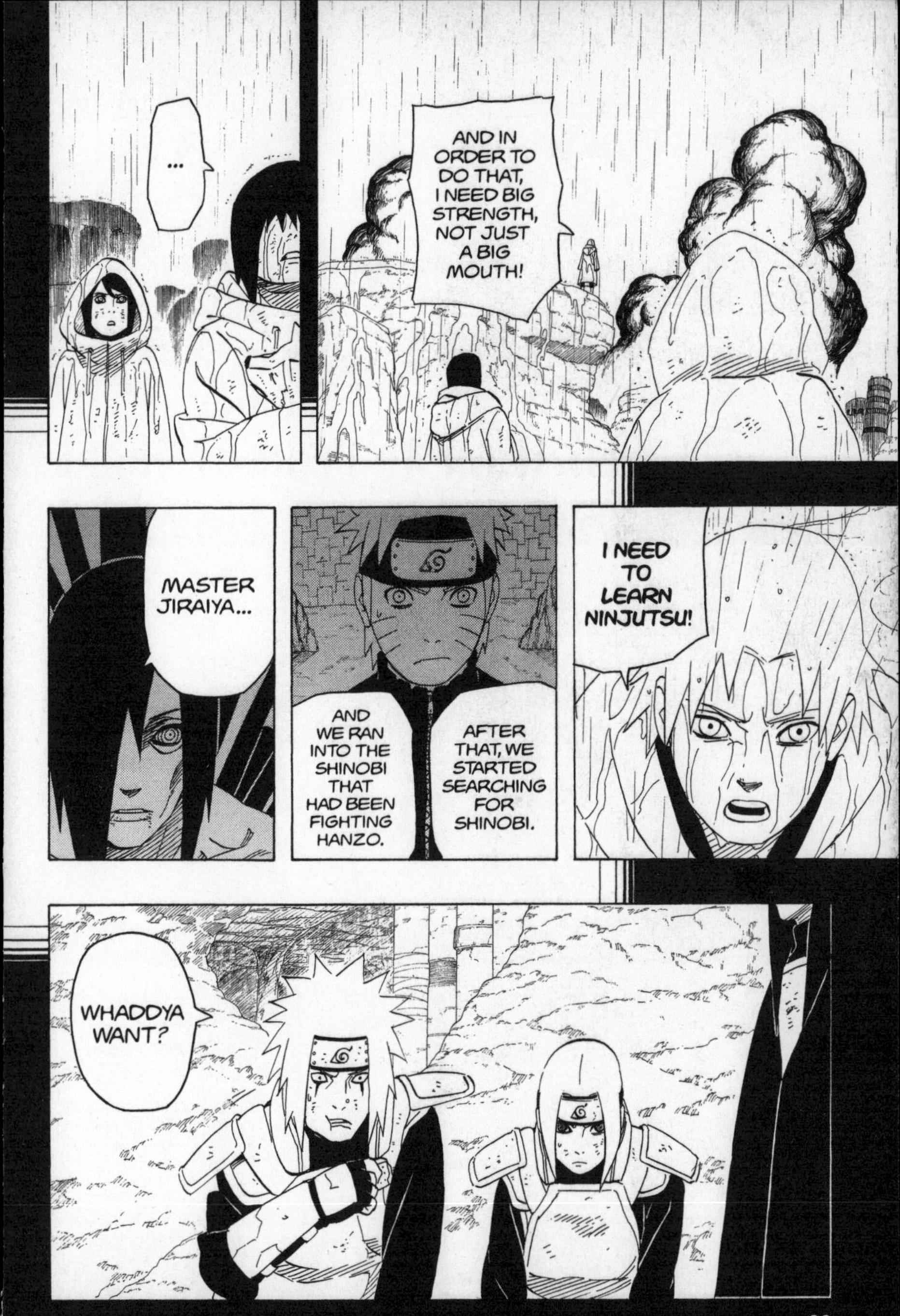
AND IN ORDER TO DO THAT, I NEED BIG STRENGTH, NOT JUST A BIG MOUTH!
...
I NEED TO LEARN NINJUTSU!
AFTER THAT, WE STARTED SEARCHING FOR SHINOBI.
AND WE RAN INTO THE SHINOBI THAT HAD BEEN FIGHTING HANZO.
MASTER JIRAIYA...
WHADDYA WANT?

READ THIS WAY

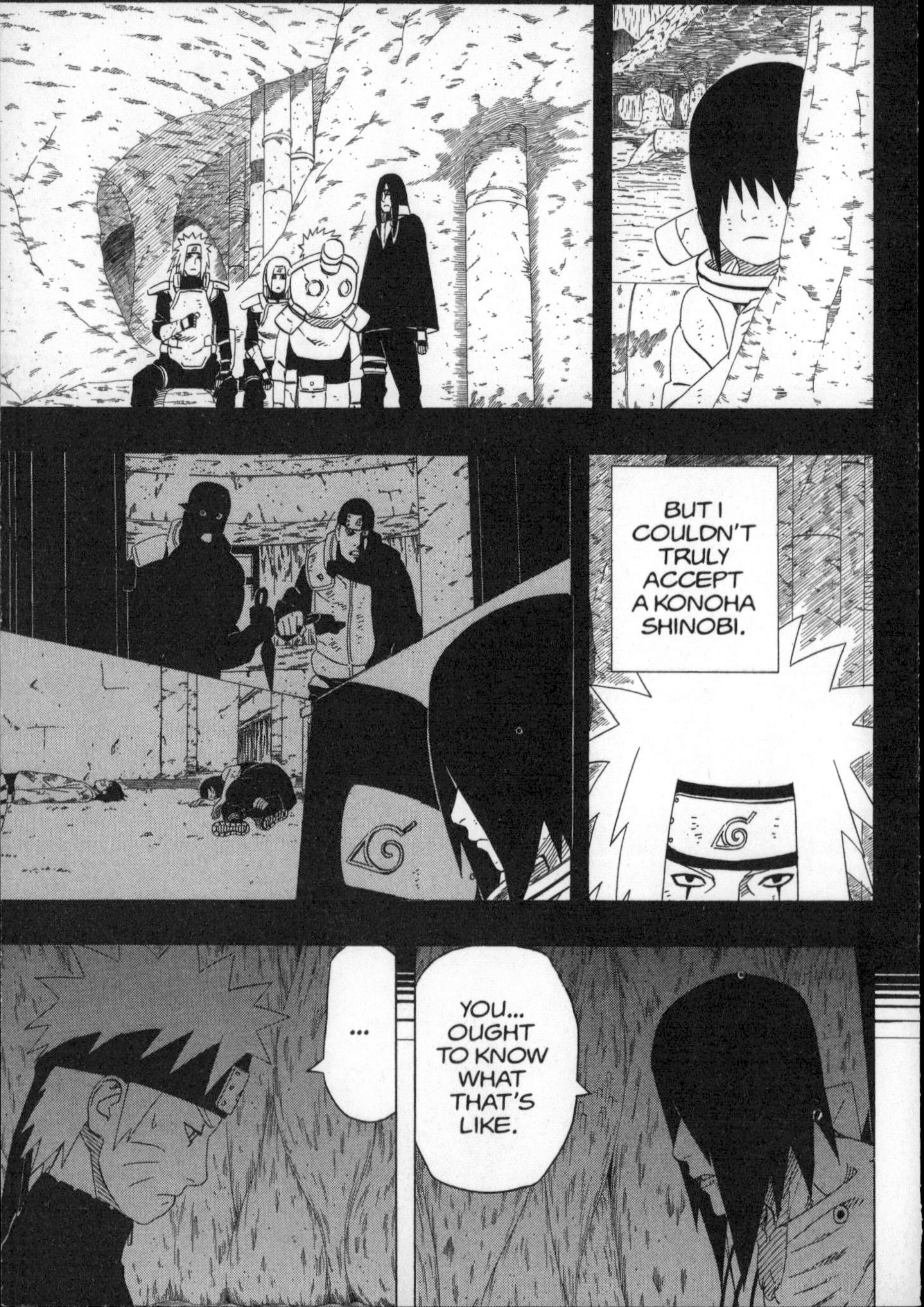
BUT I COULDN'T TRULY ACCEPT A KONOHA SHINOBI.
YOU... OUGHT TO KNOW WHAT THAT'S LIKE.
...

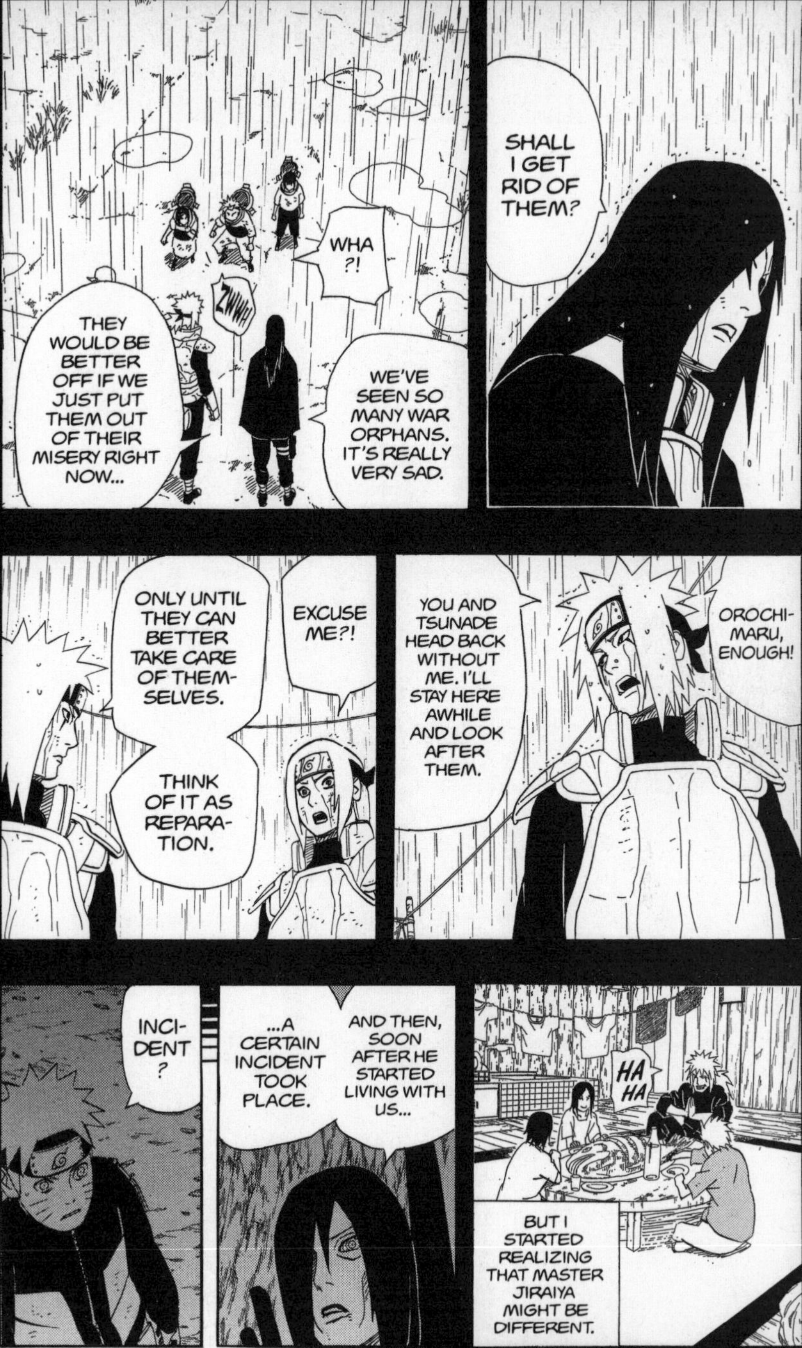
SHALL I GET RID OF THEM?
WHA?!
WE'VE SEEN SO MANY WAR ORPHANS. IT'S REALLY VERY SAD.
THEY WOULD BE BETTER OFF IF WE JUST PUT THEM OUT OF THEIR MISERY RIGHT NOW...
OROCHI-MARU, ENOUGH!
YOU AND TSUNADE HEAD BACK WITHOUT ME. I'LL STAY HERE AWHILE AND LOOK AFTER THEM.
EXCUSE ME?!
ONLY UNTIL THEY CAN BETTER TAKE CARE OF THEM-SELVES.
THINK OF IT AS REPARA-TION.
HA HA
BUT I STARTED REALIZING THAT MASTER JIRAIYA MIGHT BE DIFFERENT.
AND THEN, SOON AFTER HE STARTED LIVING WITH US...
...A CERTAIN INCIDENT TOOK PLACE.
INCI-DENT?

READ THIS WAY

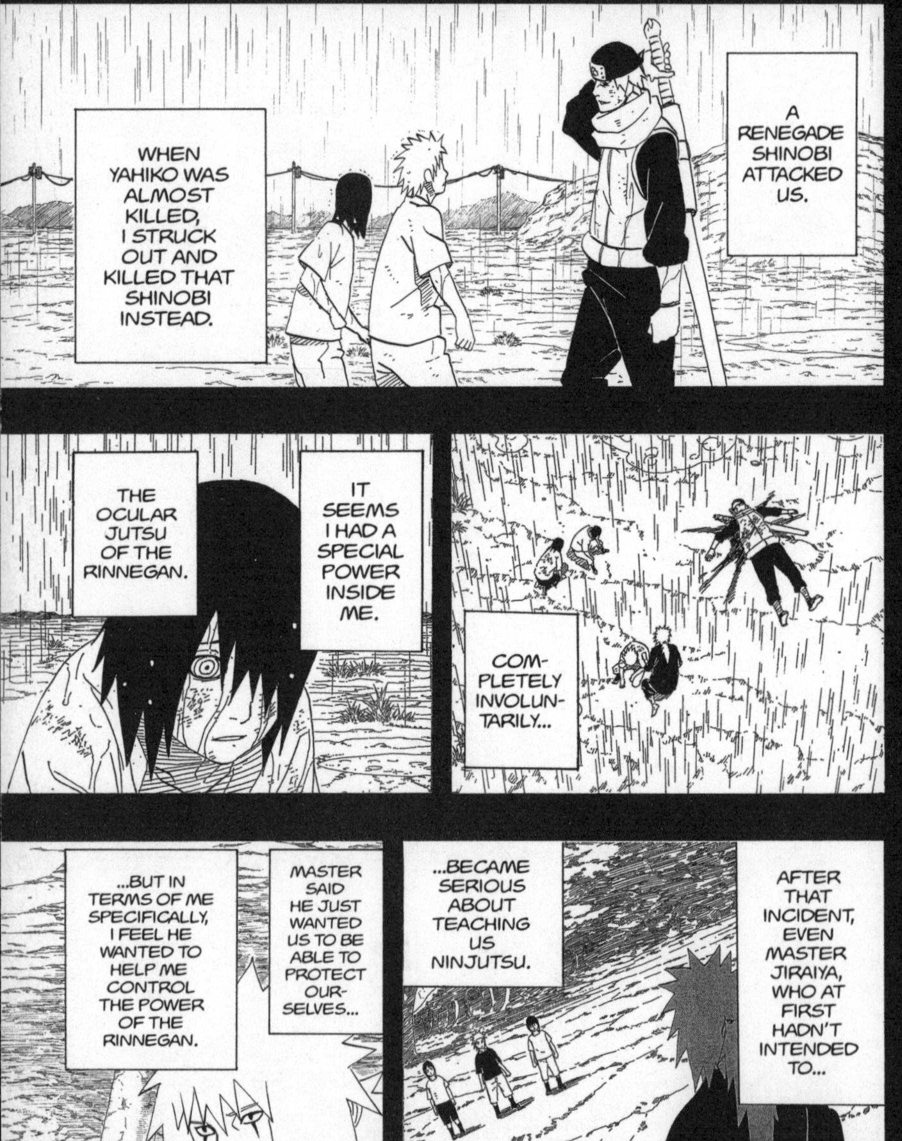
A RENEGADE SHINOBI ATTACKED US.
WHEN YAHIKO WAS ALMOST KILLED, I STRUCK OUT AND KILLED THAT SHINOBI INSTEAD.
COMPLETELY INVOLUNTARILY...
IT SEEMS I HAD A SPECIAL POWER INSIDE ME.
THE OCULAR JUTSU OF THE RINNEGAN.
AFTER THAT INCIDENT, EVEN MASTER JIRAIYA, WHO AT FIRST HADN'T INTENDED TO...
...BECAME SERIOUS ABOUT TEACHING US NINJUTSU.
MASTER SAID HE JUST WANTED US TO BE ABLE TO PROTECT OUR-SELVES...
...BUT IN TERMS OF ME SPECIFICALLY, I FEEL HE WANTED TO HELP ME CONTROL THE POWER OF THE RINNEGAN.

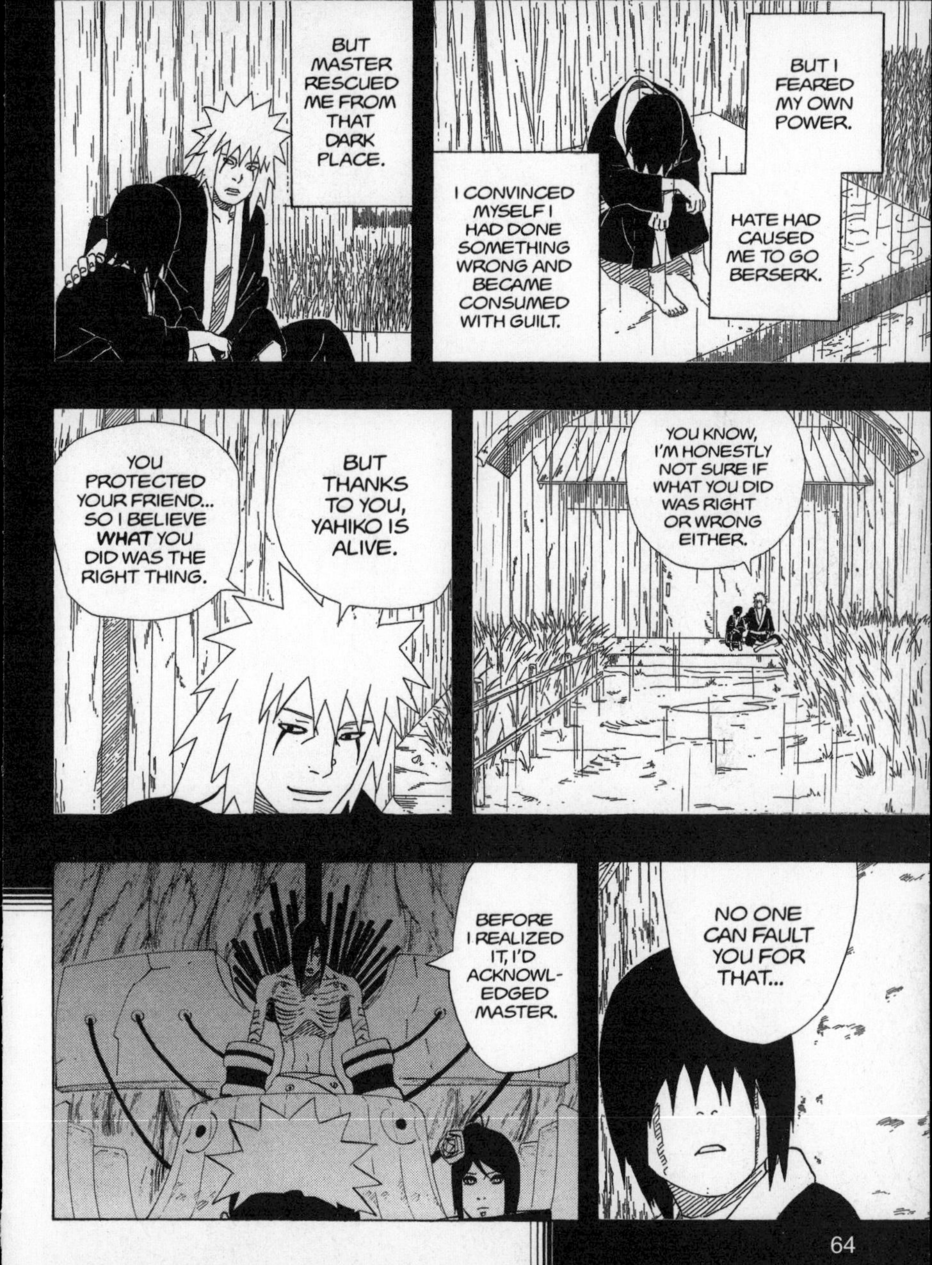
BUT I FEARED MY OWN POWER.
HATE HAD CAUSED ME TO GO BERSERK.
I CONVINCED MYSELF I HAD DONE SOMETHING WRONG AND BECAME CONSUMED WITH GUILT.
BUT MASTER RESCUED ME FROM THAT DARK PLACE.
YOU KNOW, I'M HONESTLY NOT SURE IF WHAT YOU DID WAS RIGHT OR WRONG EITHER.
BUT THANKS TO YOU, YAHIKO IS ALIVE.
YOU PROTECTED YOUR FRIEND... SO I BELIEVE **WHAT** YOU DID WAS THE RIGHT THING.
NO ONE CAN FAULT YOU FOR THAT...
BEFORE I REALIZED IT, I'D ACKNOWL-EDGED MASTER.

READ THIS WAY

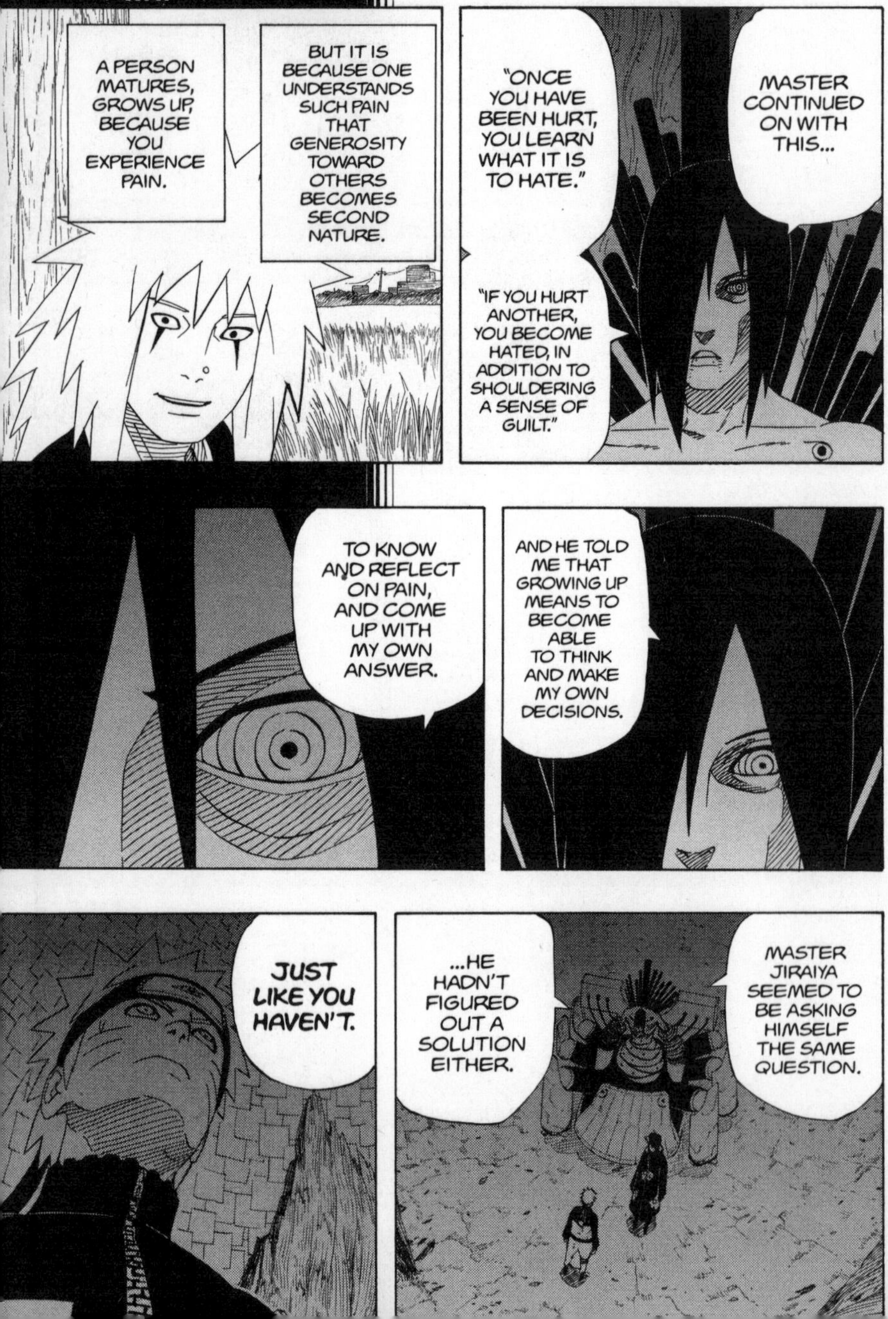
MASTER CONTINUED ON WITH THIS...
"ONCE YOU HAVE BEEN HURT, YOU LEARN WHAT IT IS TO HATE."
"IF YOU HURT ANOTHER, YOU BECOME HATED, IN ADDITION TO SHOULDERING A SENSE OF GUILT."
A PERSON MATURES, GROWS UP, BECAUSE YOU EXPERIENCE PAIN.
BUT IT IS BECAUSE ONE UNDERSTANDS SUCH PAIN THAT GENEROSITY TOWARD OTHERS BECOMES SECOND NATURE.
AND HE TOLD ME THAT GROWING UP MEANS TO BECOME ABLE TO THINK AND MAKE MY OWN DECISIONS.
TO KNOW AND REFLECT ON PAIN, AND COME UP WITH MY OWN ANSWER.
MASTER JIRAIYA SEEMED TO BE ASKING HIMSELF THE SAME QUESTION.
...HE HADN'T FIGURED OUT A SOLUTION EITHER.
JUST LIKE YOU HAVEN'T.

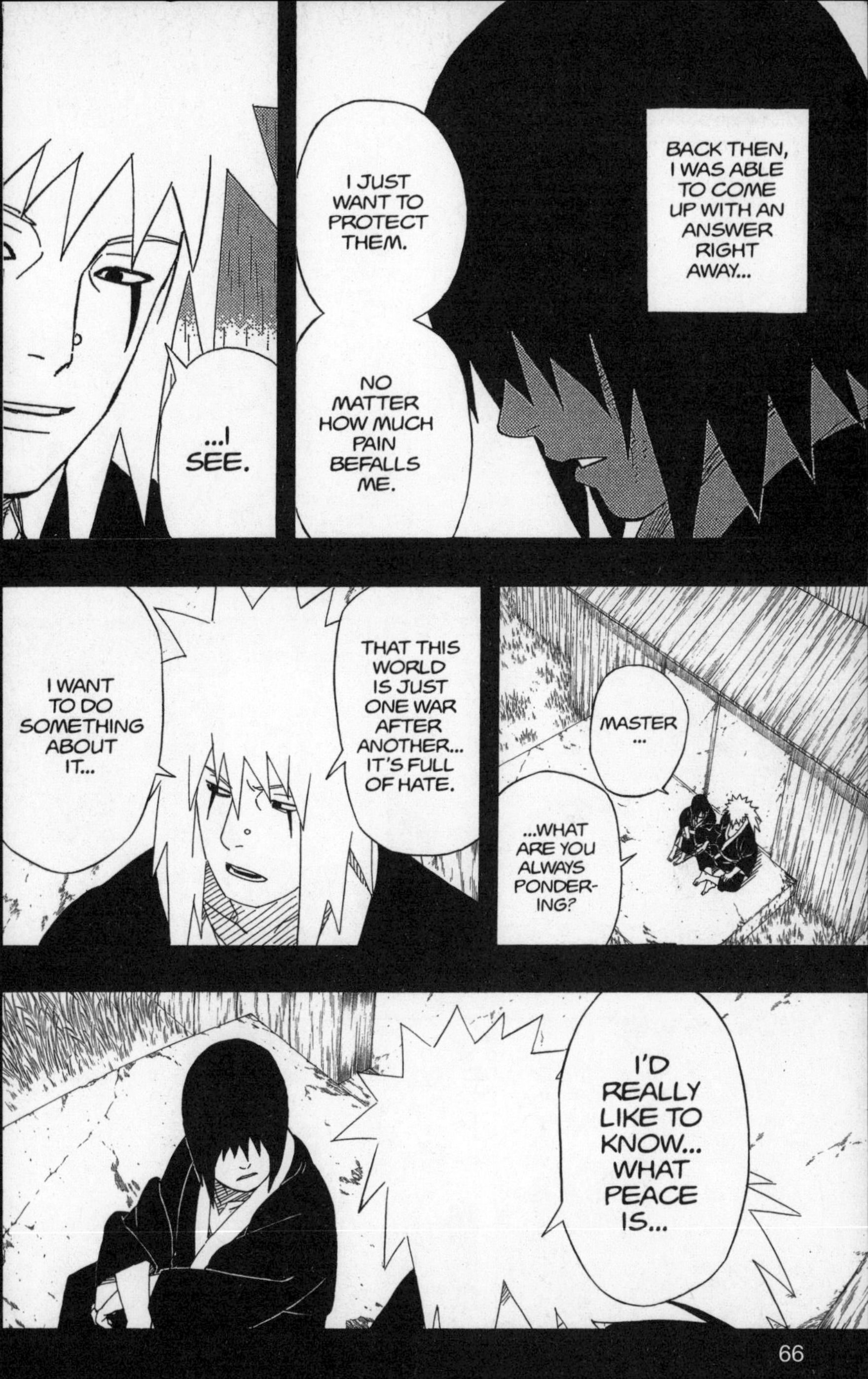
BACK THEN, I WAS ABLE TO COME UP WITH AN ANSWER RIGHT AWAY...
I JUST WANT TO PROTECT THEM.
NO MATTER HOW MUCH PAIN BEFALLS ME.
...I SEE.
MASTER...
...WHAT ARE YOU ALWAYS PONDER-ING?
THAT THIS WORLD IS JUST ONE WAR AFTER ANOTHER... IT'S FULL OF HATE.
I WANT TO DO SOMETHING ABOUT IT...
I'D REALLY LIKE TO KNOW... WHAT PEACE IS...

READ THIS WAY

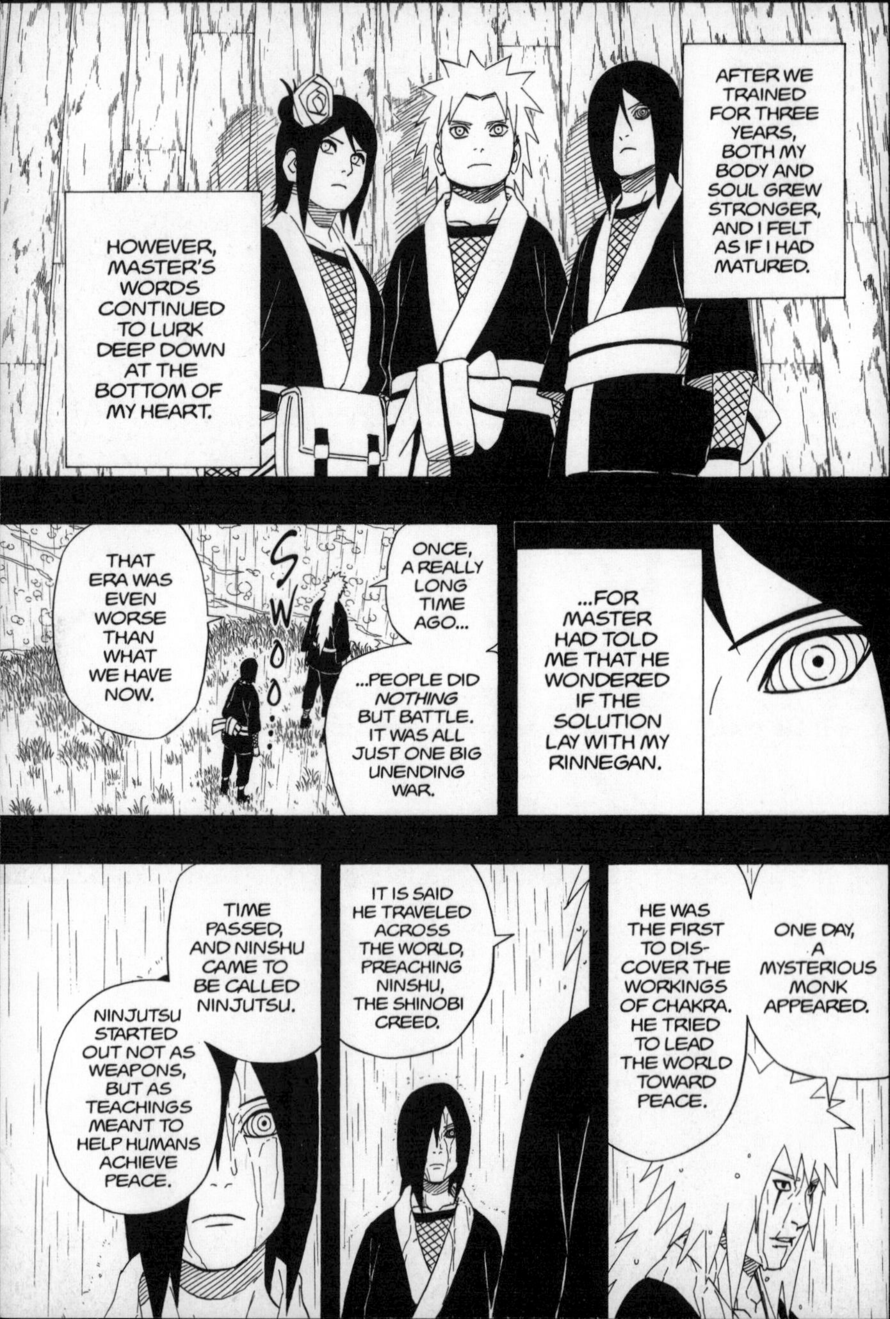
AFTER WE TRAINED FOR THREE YEARS, BOTH MY BODY AND SOUL GREW STRONGER, AND I FELT AS IF I HAD MATURED.
HOWEVER, MASTER'S WORDS CONTINUED TO LURK DEEP DOWN AT THE BOTTOM OF MY HEART.
...FOR MASTER HAD TOLD ME THAT HE WONDERED IF THE SOLUTION LAY WITH MY RINNEGAN.
ONCE, A REALLY LONG TIME AGO...
...PEOPLE DID *NOTHING* BUT BATTLE. IT WAS ALL JUST ONE BIG UNENDING WAR.
SWOO...
THAT ERA WAS EVEN WORSE THAN WHAT WE HAVE NOW.
ONE DAY, A MYSTERIOUS MONK APPEARED.
HE WAS THE FIRST TO DIS-COVER THE WORKINGS OF CHAKRA. HE TRIED TO LEAD THE WORLD TOWARD PEACE.
IT IS SAID HE TRAVELED ACROSS THE WORLD, PREACHING NINSHU, THE SHINOBI CREED.
TIME PASSED, AND NINSHU CAME TO BE CALLED NINJUTSU.
NINJUTSU STARTED OUT NOT AS WEAPONS, BUT AS TEACHINGS MEANT TO HELP HUMANS ACHIEVE PEACE.

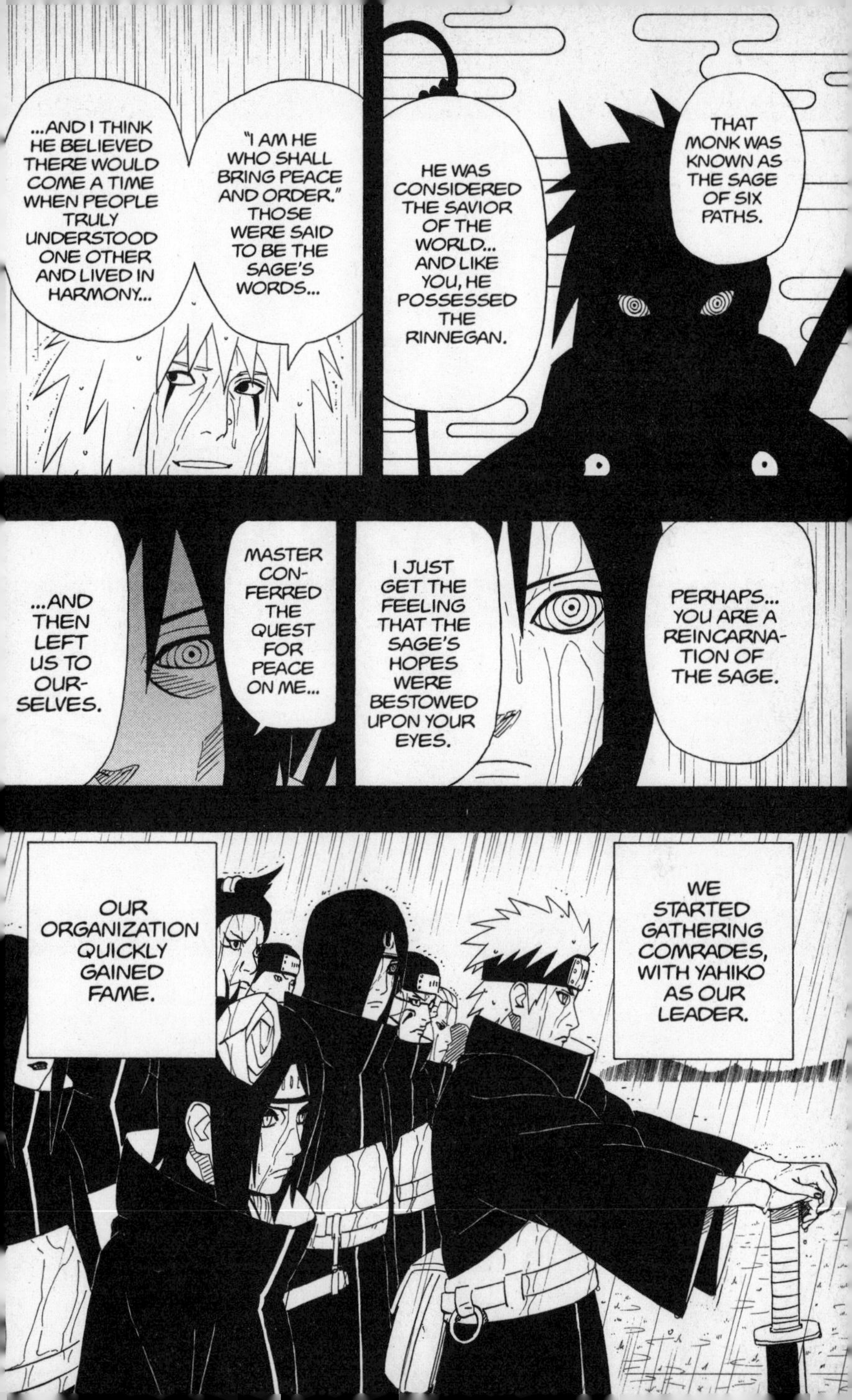
THAT MONK WAS KNOWN AS THE SAGE OF SIX PATHS.
HE WAS CONSIDERED THE SAVIOR OF THE WORLD... AND LIKE YOU, HE POSSESSED THE RINNEGAN.
"I AM HE WHO SHALL BRING PEACE AND ORDER." THOSE WERE SAID TO BE THE SAGE'S WORDS...
...AND I THINK HE BELIEVED THERE WOULD COME A TIME WHEN PEOPLE TRULY UNDERSTOOD ONE OTHER AND LIVED IN HARMONY...
PERHAPS... YOU ARE A REINCARNA-TION OF THE SAGE.
I JUST GET THE FEELING THAT THE SAGE'S HOPES WERE BESTOWED UPON YOUR EYES.
MASTER CON-FERRED THE QUEST FOR PEACE ON ME...
...AND THEN LEFT US TO OUR-SELVES.
WE STARTED GATHERING COMRADES, WITH YAHIKO AS OUR LEADER.
OUR ORGANIZATION QUICKLY GAINED FAME.

READ THIS WAY

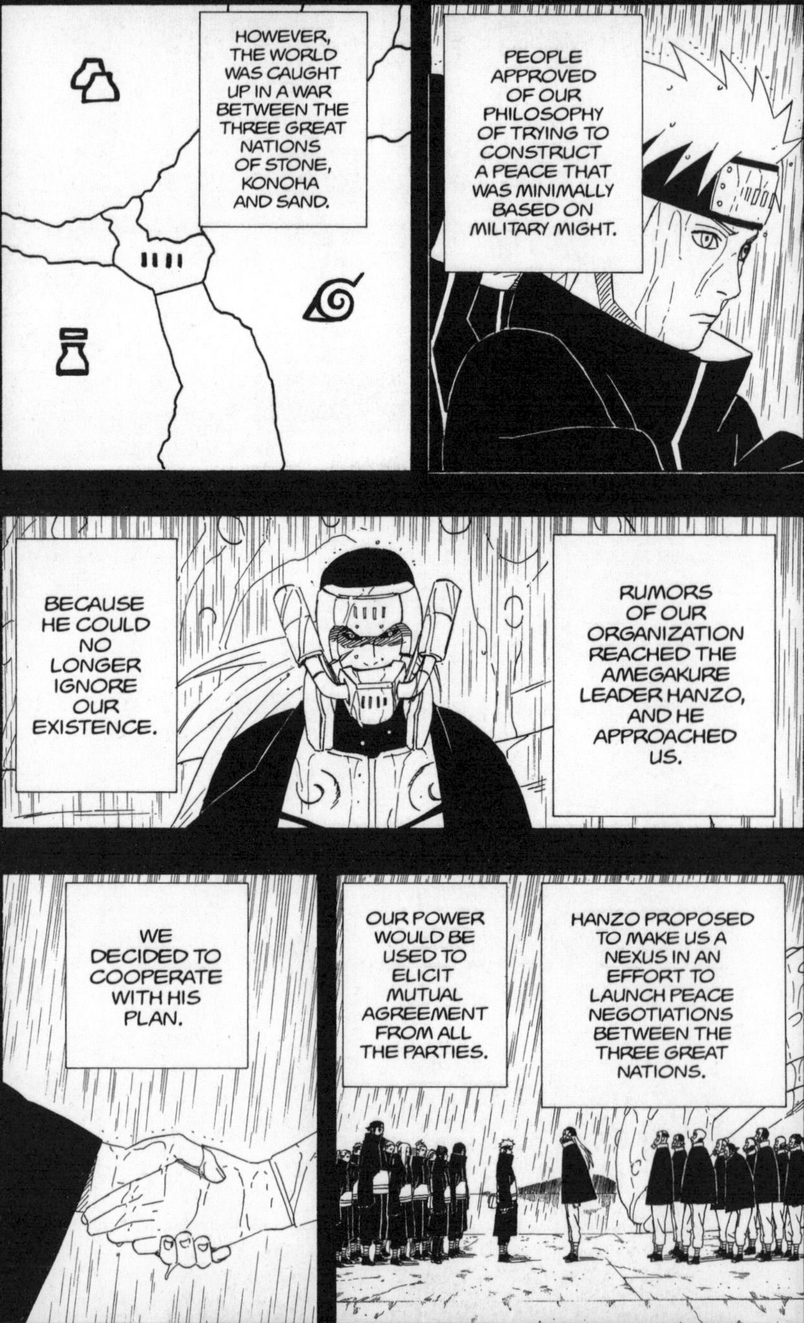
PEOPLE APPROVED OF OUR PHILOSOPHY OF TRYING TO CONSTRUCT A PEACE THAT WAS MINIMALLY BASED ON MILITARY MIGHT.
HOWEVER, THE WORLD WAS CAUGHT UP IN A WAR BETWEEN THE THREE GREAT NATIONS OF STONE, KONOHA AND SAND.
RUMORS OF OUR ORGANIZATION REACHED THE AMEGAKURE LEADER HANZO, AND HE APPROACHED US.
BECAUSE HE COULD NO LONGER IGNORE OUR EXISTENCE.
HANZO PROPOSED TO MAKE US A NEXUS IN AN EFFORT TO LAUNCH PEACE NEGOTIATIONS BETWEEN THE THREE GREAT NATIONS.
OUR POWER WOULD BE USED TO ELICIT MUTUAL AGREEMENT FROM ALL THE PARTIES.
WE DECIDED TO COOPERATE WITH HIS PLAN.

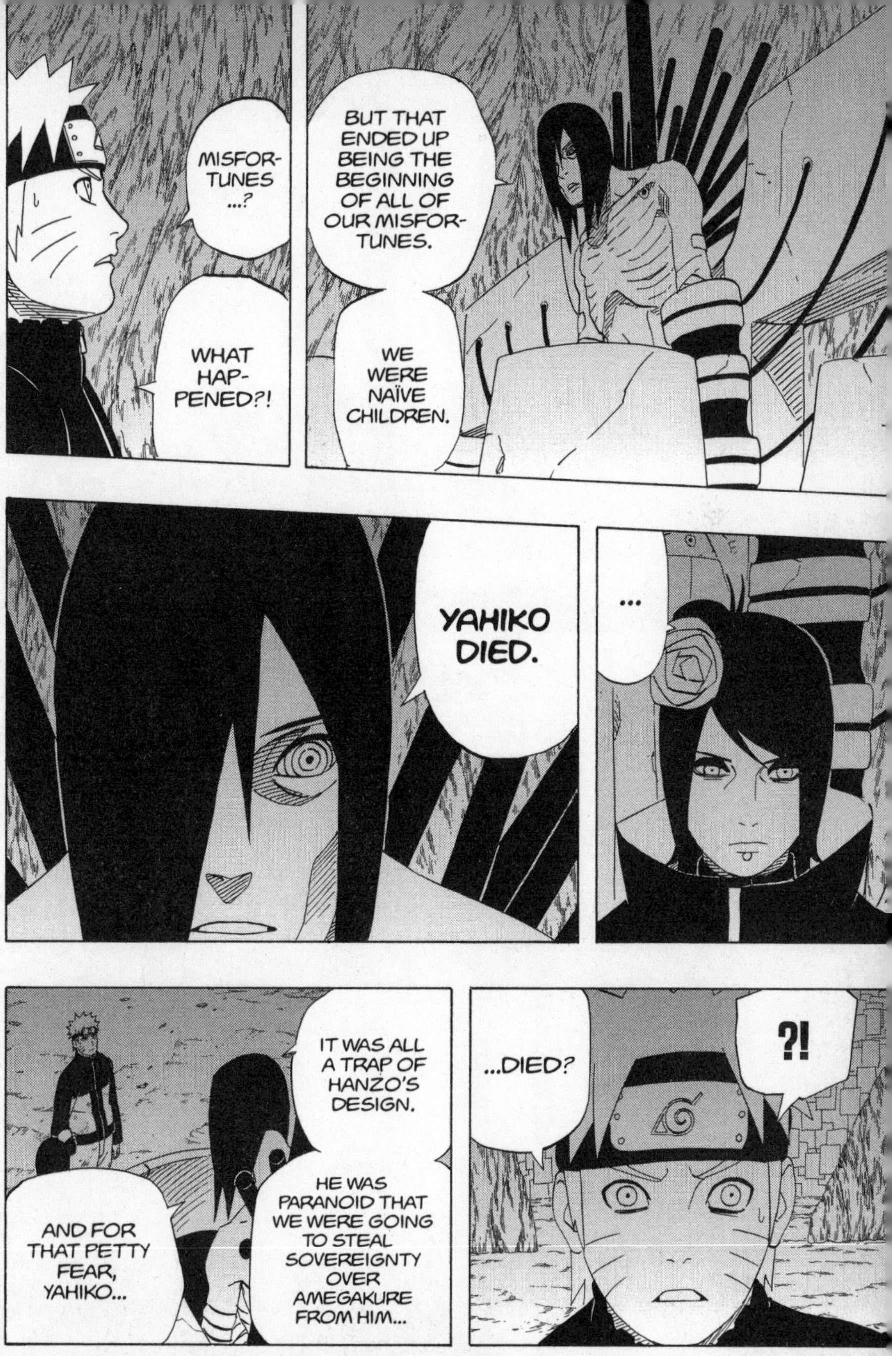
BUT THAT ENDED UP BEING THE BEGINNING OF ALL OF OUR MISFORTUNES.
WE WERE NAÏVE CHILDREN.
MISFORTUNES ...?
WHAT HAPPENED?!
...
YAHIKO DIED.
?!
...DIED?
IT WAS ALL A TRAP OF HANZO'S DESIGN.
HE WAS PARANOID THAT WE WERE GOING TO STEAL SOVEREIGNTY OVER AMEGAKURE FROM HIM...
AND FOR THAT PETTY FEAR, YAHIKO...

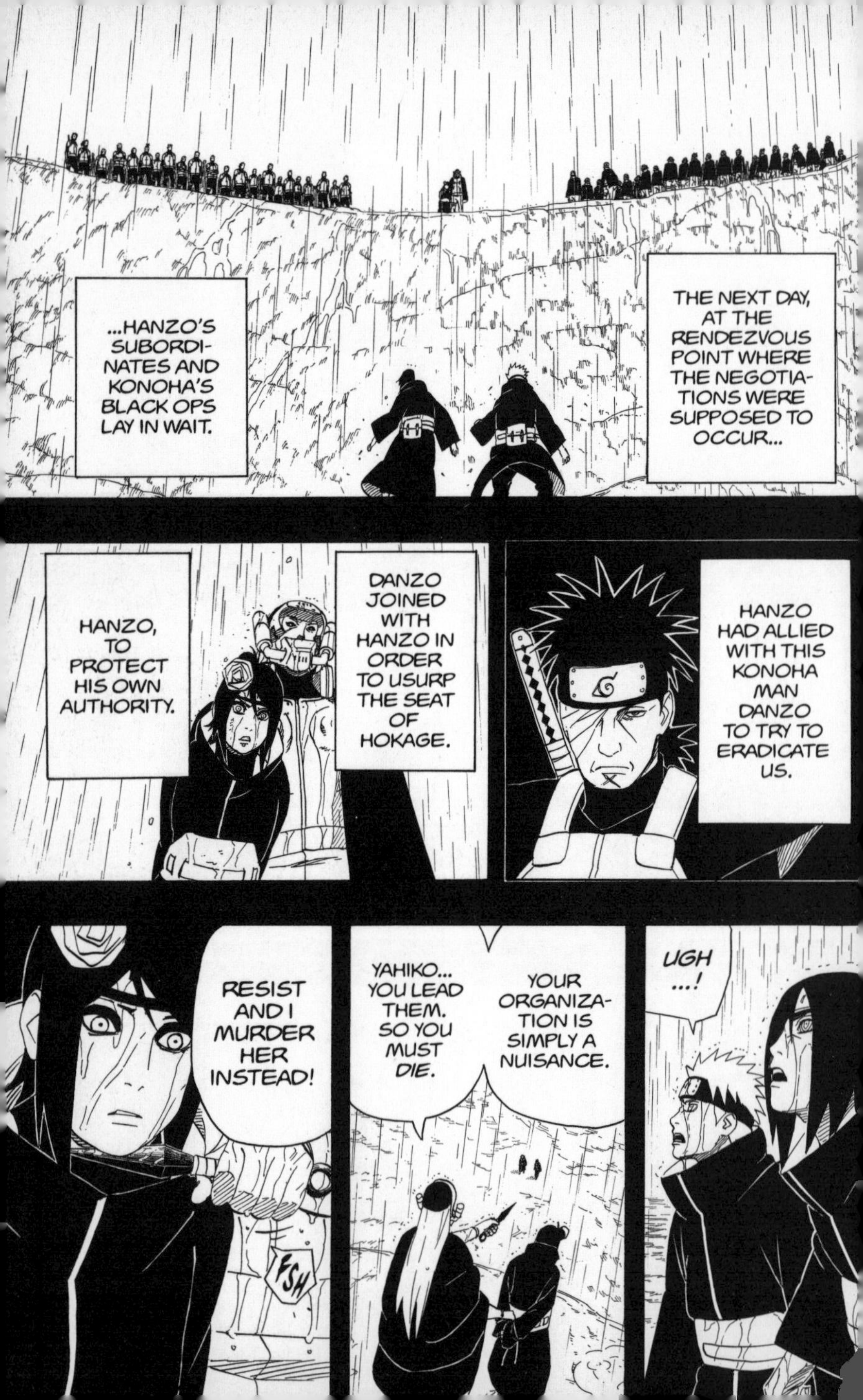
THE NEXT DAY, AT THE RENDEZVOUS POINT WHERE THE NEGOTIATIONS WERE SUPPOSED TO OCCUR...
...HANZO'S SUBORDINATES AND KONOHA'S BLACK OPS LAY IN WAIT.
HANZO HAD ALLIED WITH THIS KONOHA MAN DANZO TO TRY TO ERADICATE US.
DANZO JOINED WITH HANZO IN ORDER TO USURP THE SEAT OF HOKAGE.
HANZO, TO PROTECT HIS OWN AUTHORITY.
UGH ...!
YOUR ORGANIZATION IS SIMPLY A NUISANCE.
YAHIKO... YOU LEAD THEM. SO YOU MUST DIE.
RESIST AND I MURDER HER INSTEAD!
FSH

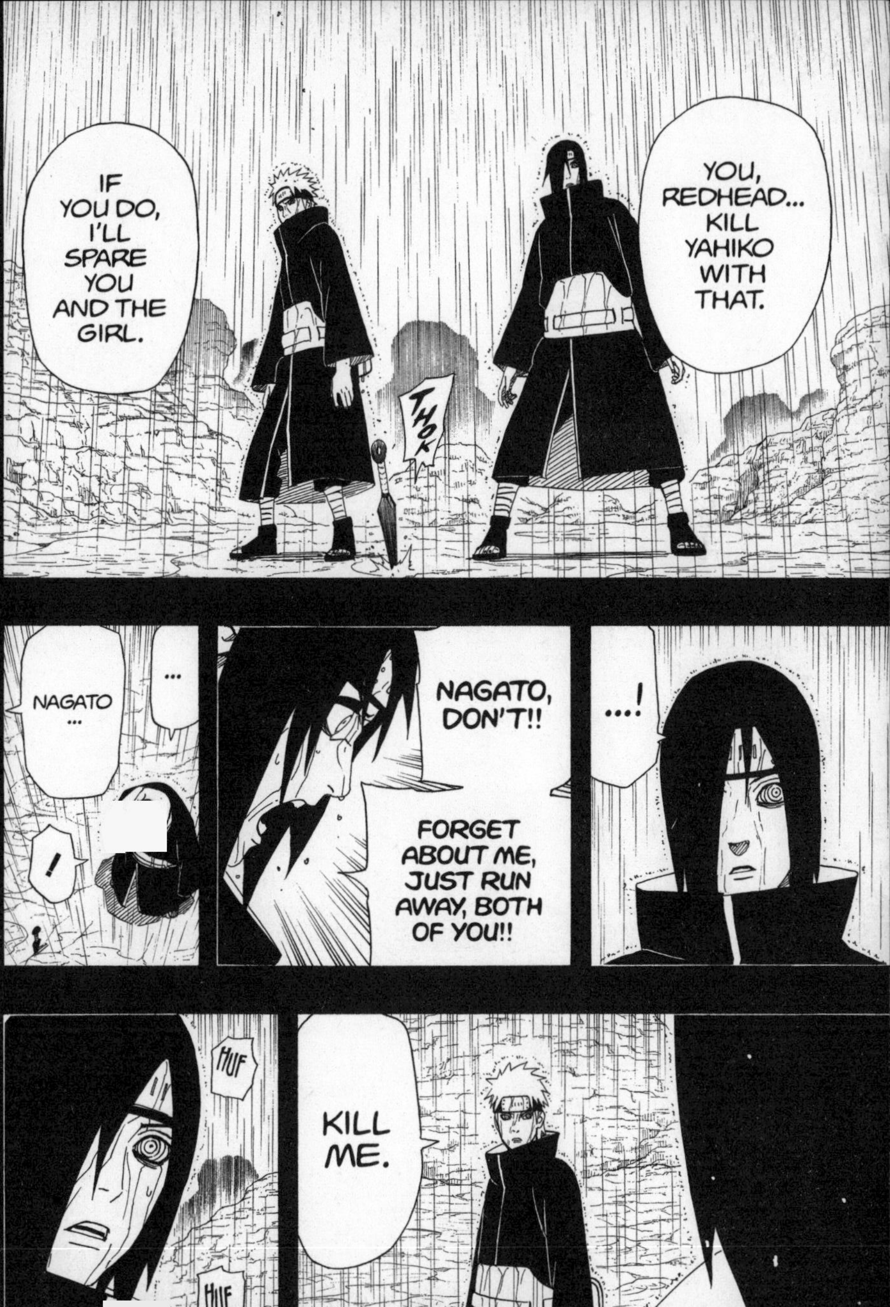
YOU, REDHEAD... KILL YAHIKO WITH THAT.
THOK
IF YOU DO, I'LL SPARE YOU AND THE GIRL.
...!
NAGATO, DON'T!!
FORGET ABOUT ME, JUST RUN AWAY, BOTH OF YOU!!
...
NAGATO ...
!
KILL ME.
HUF
HUF

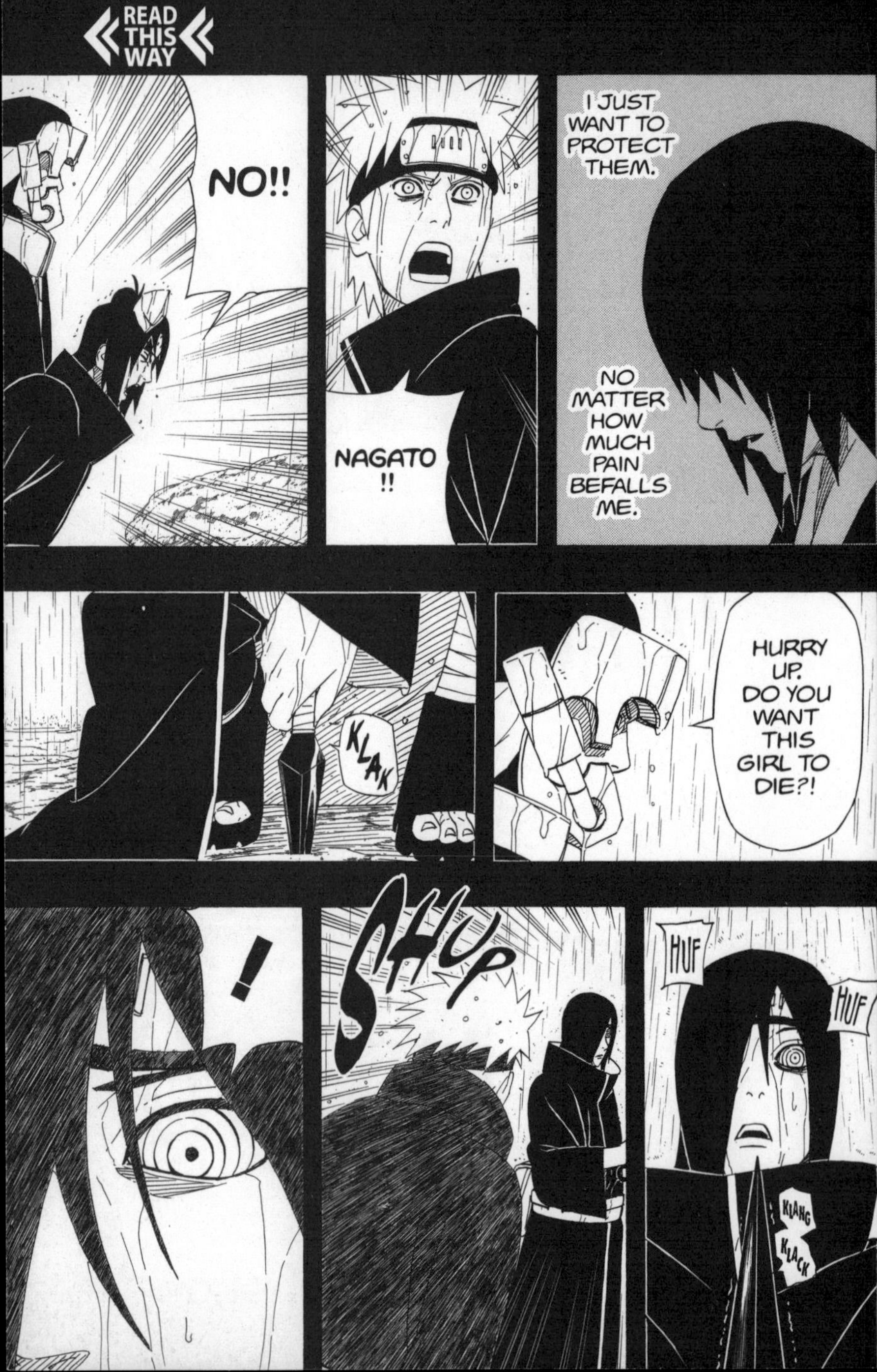
READ THIS WAY
I JUST WANT TO PROTECT THEM.
NO MATTER HOW MUCH PAIN BEFALLS ME.
NAGATO !!
NO!!
HURRY UP. DO YOU WANT THIS GIRL TO DIE?!
KLAK
HUF
HUF
KLANG
KLACK
SHUP
!

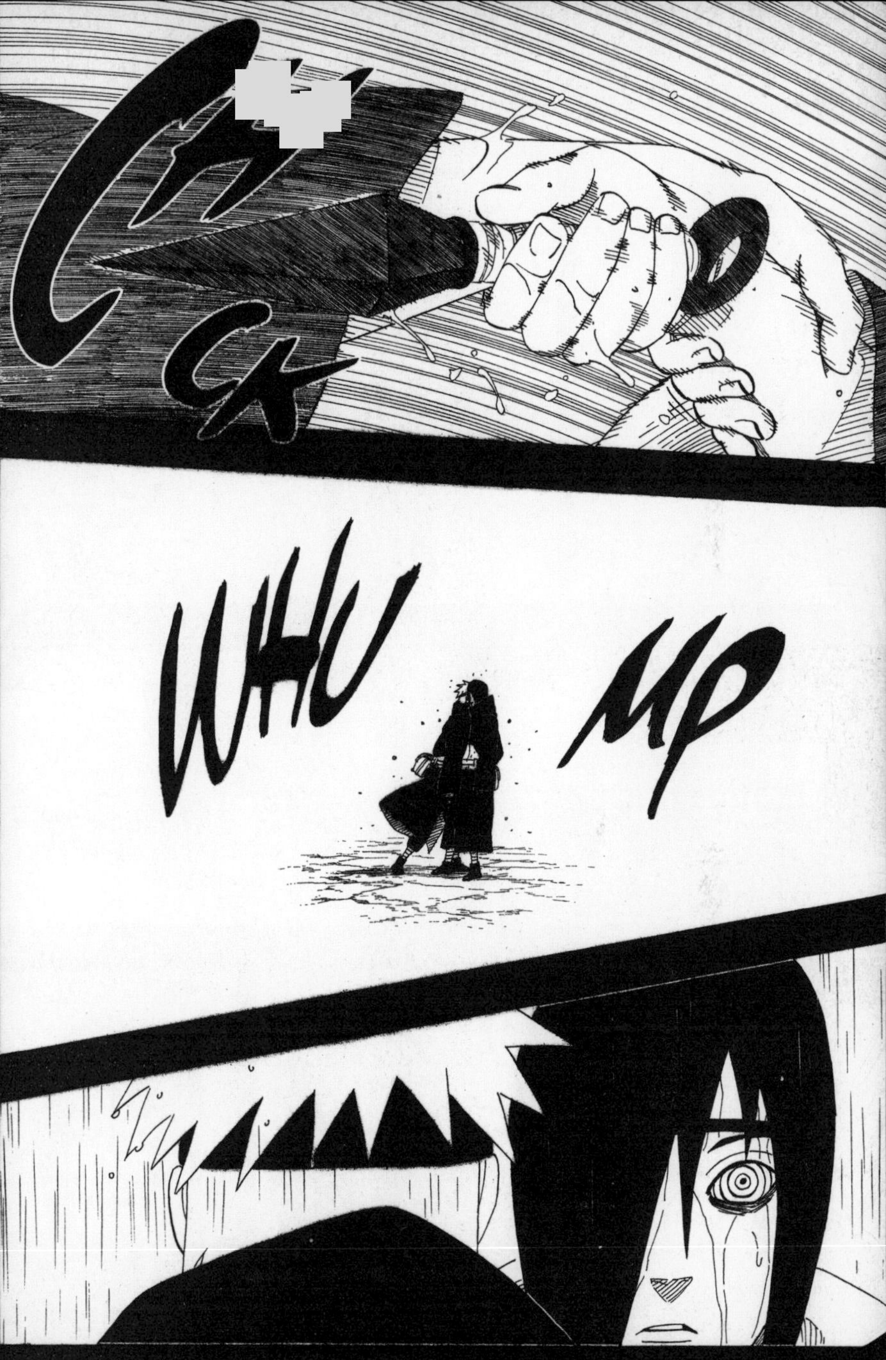
WHUMP

READ THIS WAY

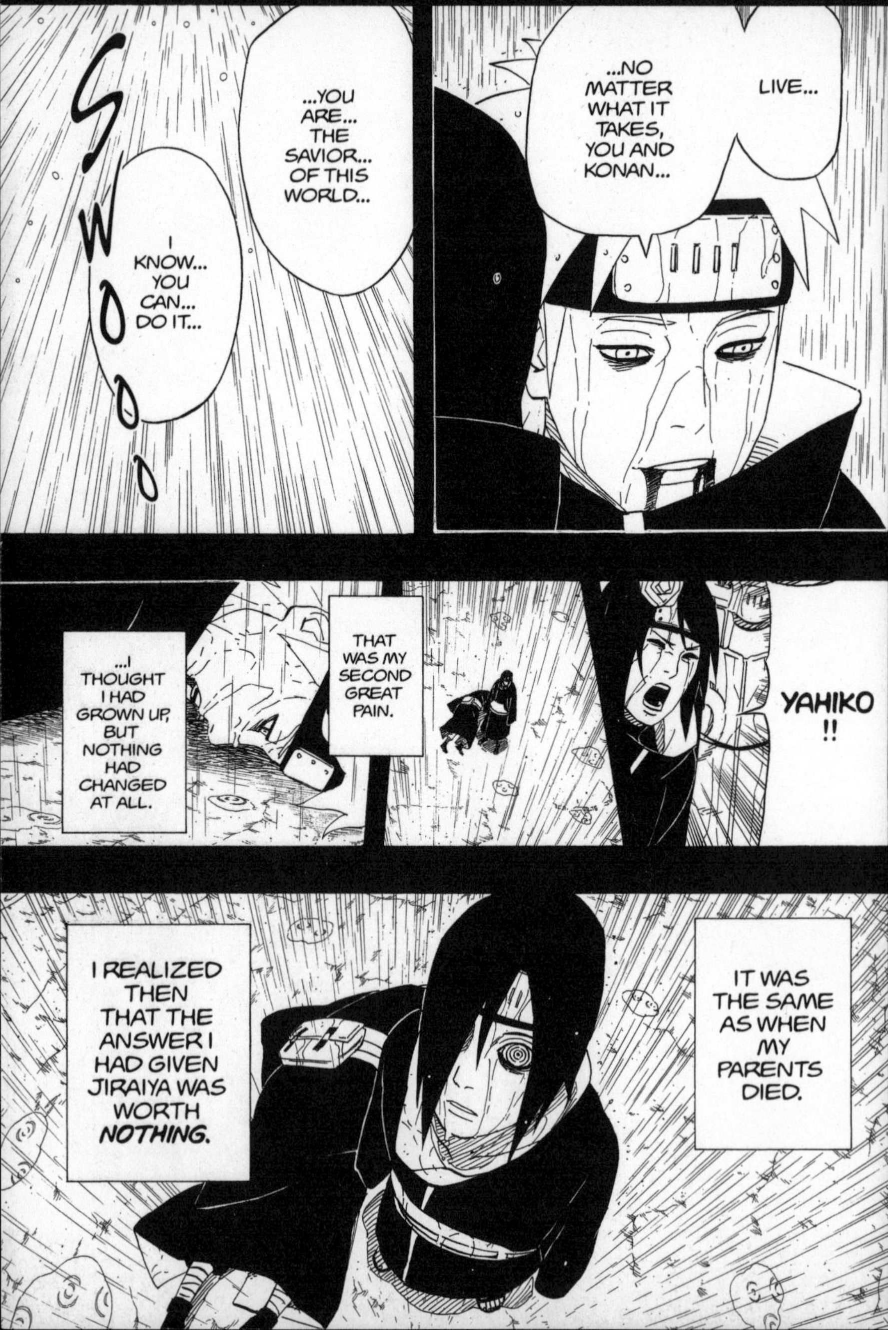
LIVE...
...NO MATTER WHAT IT TAKES, YOU AND KONAN...
...YOU ARE... THE SAVIOR... OF THIS WORLD...
I KNOW... YOU CAN... DO IT...
YAHIKO !!
THAT WAS MY SECOND GREAT PAIN.
...I THOUGHT I HAD GROWN UP, BUT NOTHING HAD CHANGED AT ALL.
IT WAS THE SAME AS WHEN MY PARENTS DIED.
I REALIZED THEN THAT THE ANSWER I HAD GIVEN JIRAIYA WAS WORTH ***NOTHING.***

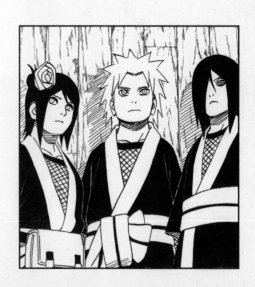

Number 447: I Believe

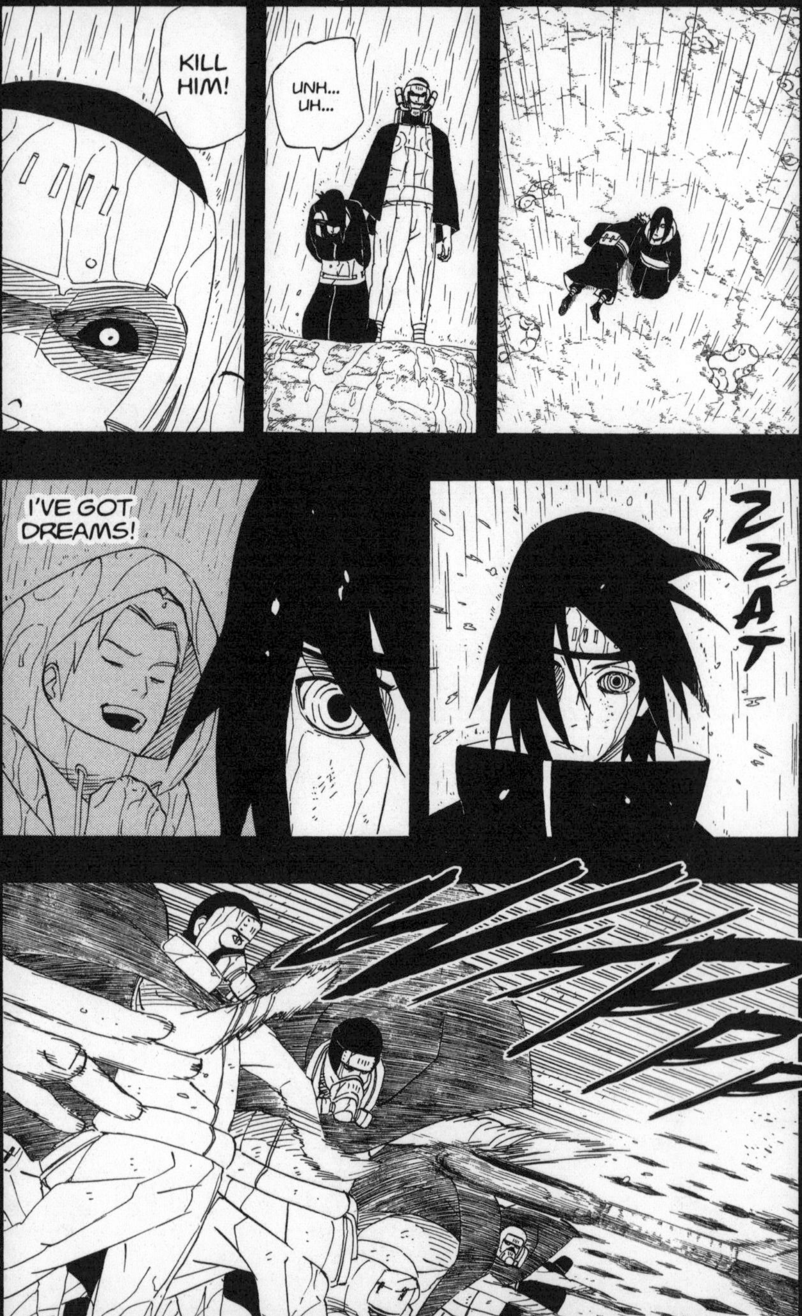
UNH... UH...
KILL HIM!
ZZAT
I'VE GOT DREAMS!

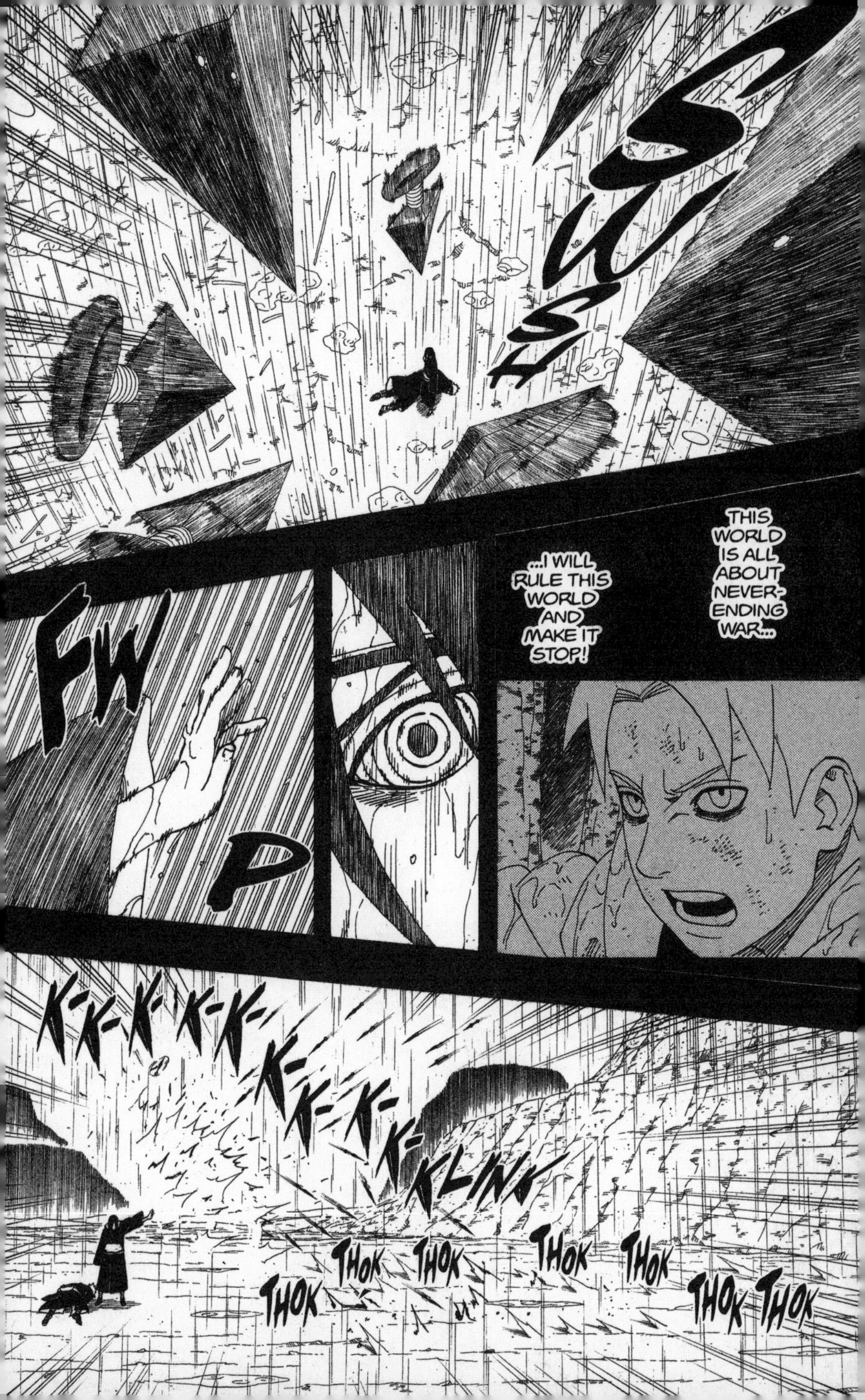
SWISH
THIS WORLD IS ALL ABOUT NEVER-ENDING WAR...
...I WILL RULE THIS WORLD AND MAKE IT STOP!
FWP
K-K-K-K-K-K-K-K-K-KLING
THOK THOK THOK THOK THOK THOK THOK THOK

READ THIS WAY

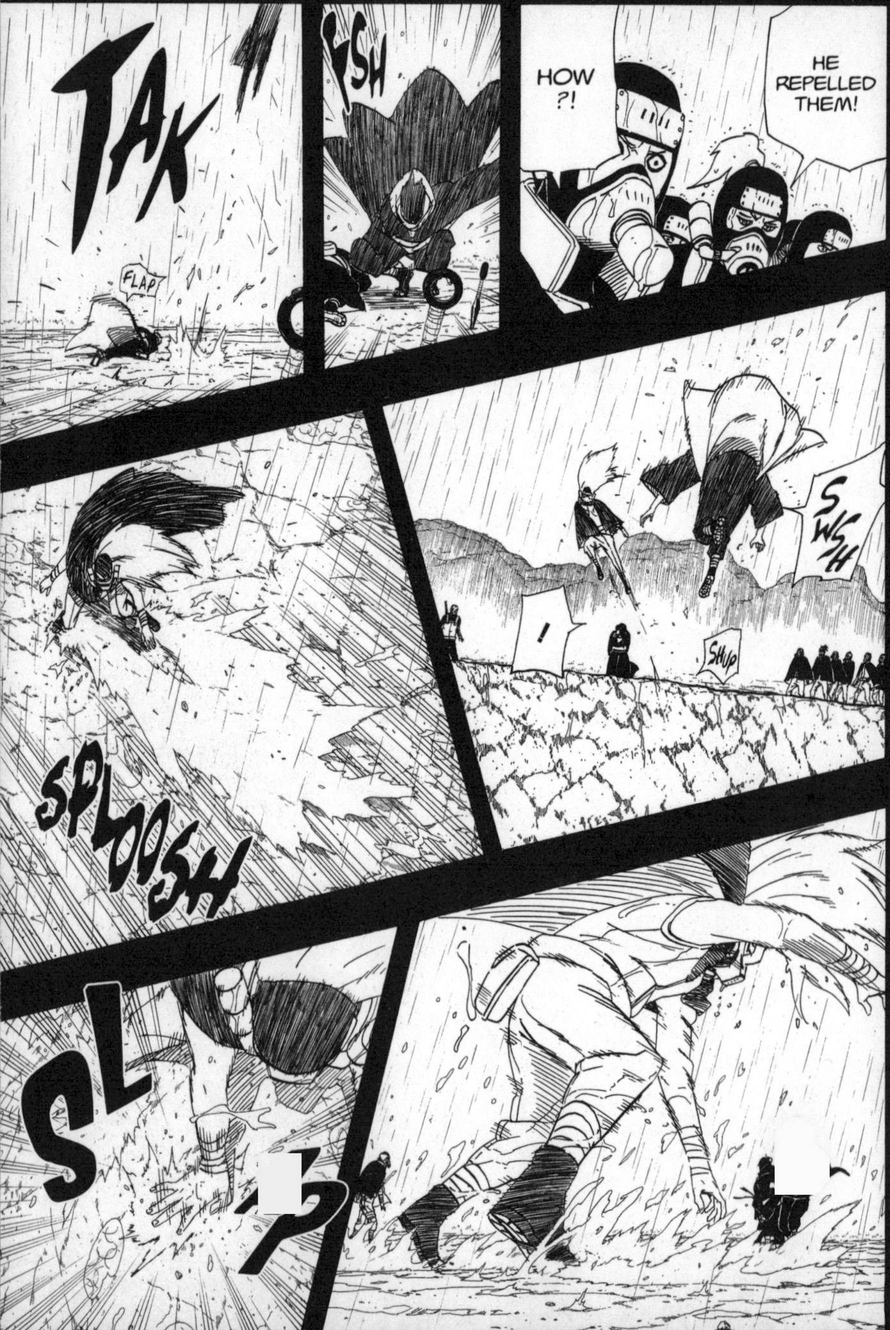
HE REPELLED THEM!
HOW ?!
SH
TAK
FLAP
SWSH
!
SHUP
SPLOOSH
SL
P

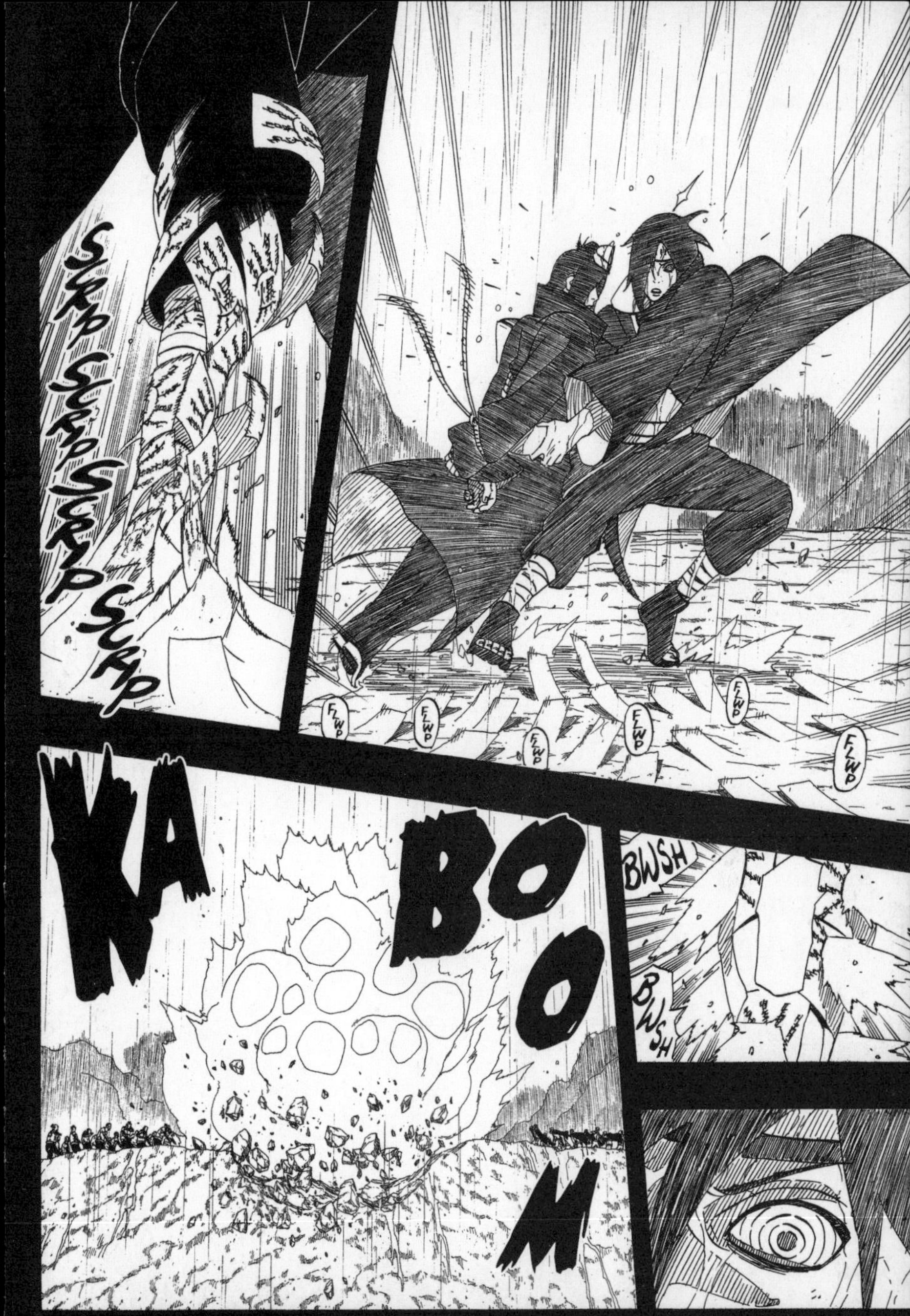
FLWP
FLWP
FLWP
FLWP
FLWP
FLWP
FLWP
SCRP SCRP SCRP SCRP
SCRP
BWSH
BWSH
KA BOOM

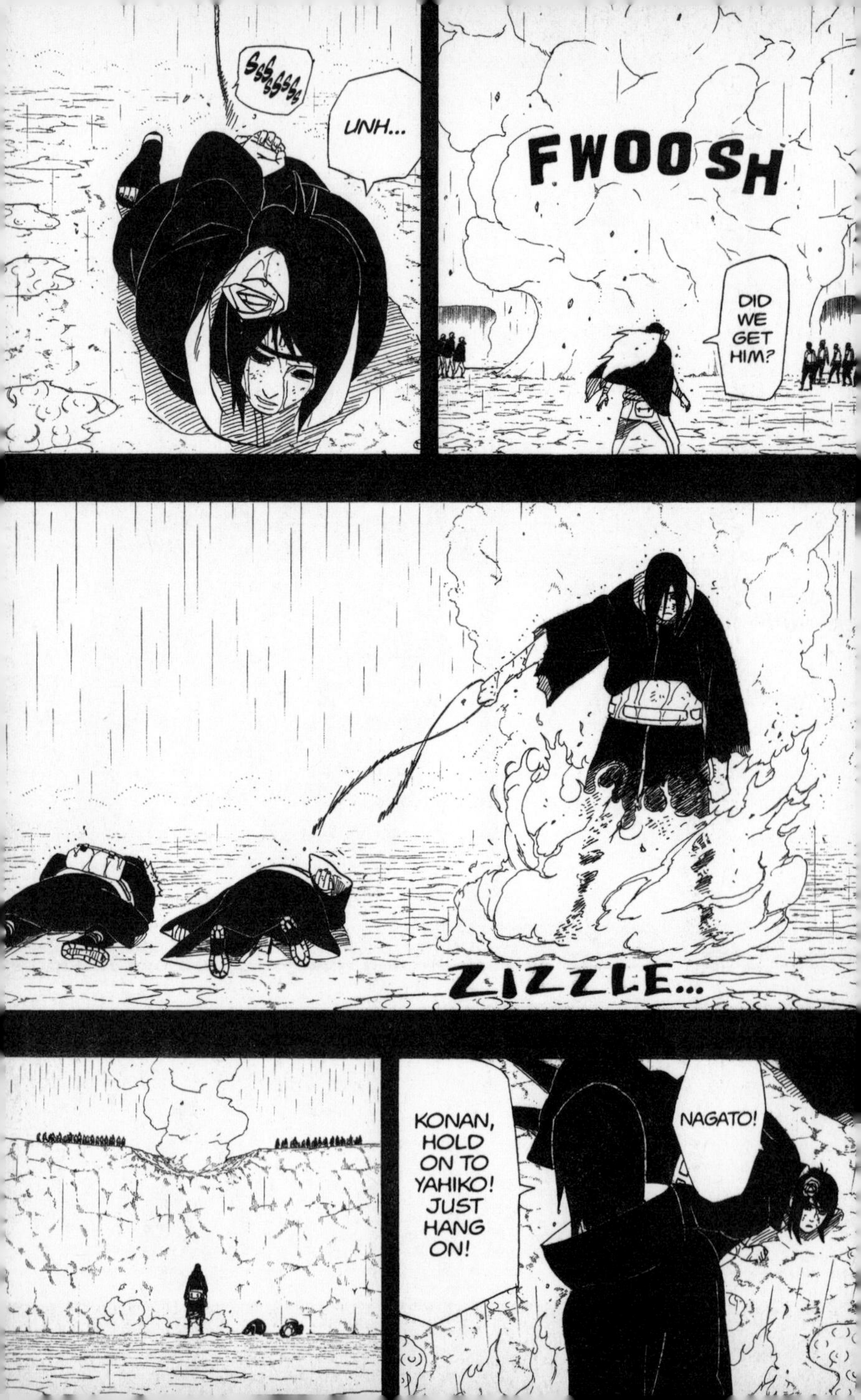
FWOOSH
DID WE GET HIM?
SSSSSSS
UNH...
ZIZZLE...
NAGATO!
KONAN, HOLD ON TO YAHIKO! JUST HANG ON!

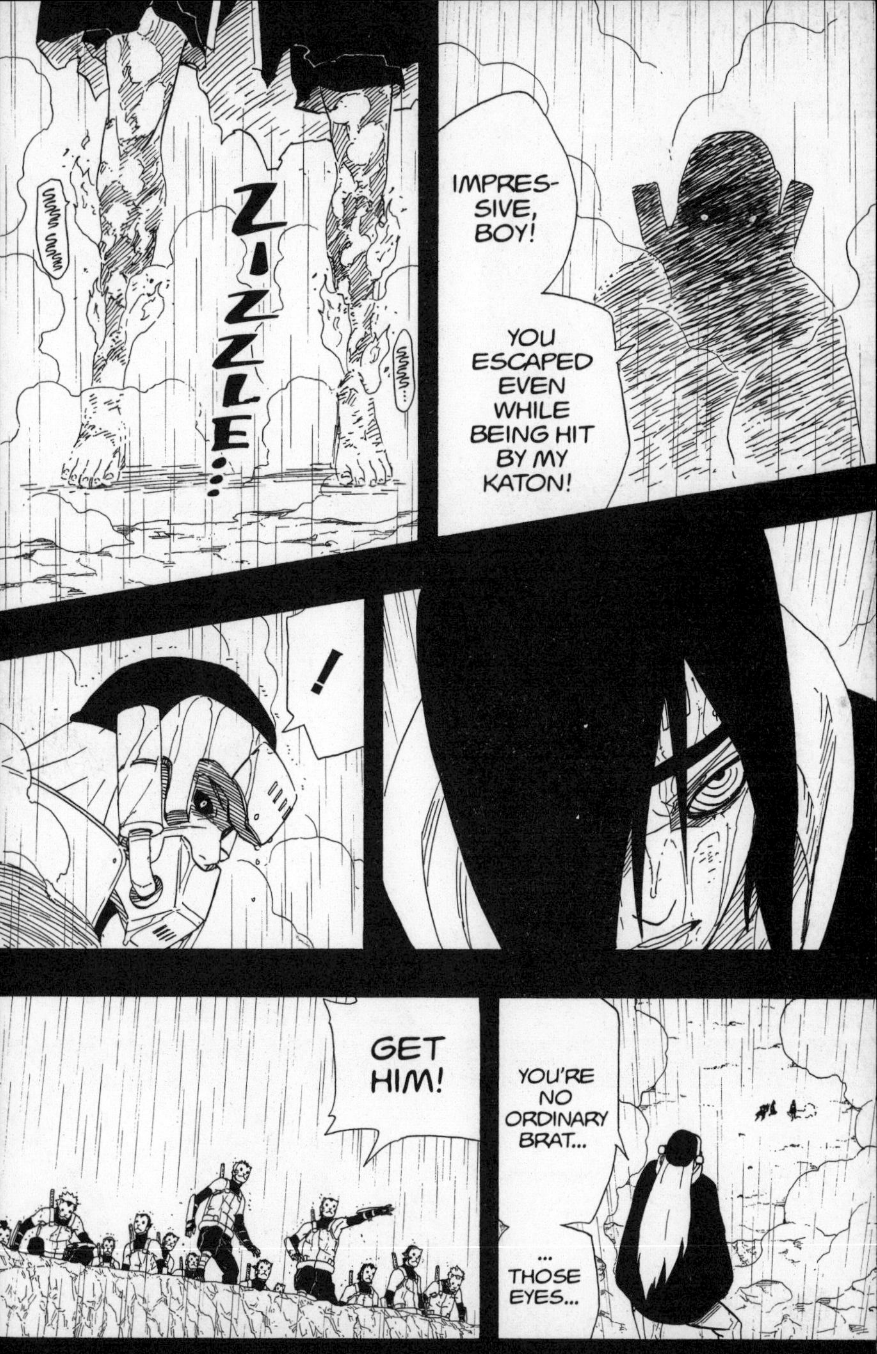
IMPRES-
SIVE,
BOY!
YOU
ESCAPED
EVEN
WHILE
BEING HIT
BY MY
KATON!
ZIZZLE...
!
YOU'RE
NO
ORDINARY
BRAT...
...
THOSE
EYES...
GET
HIM!

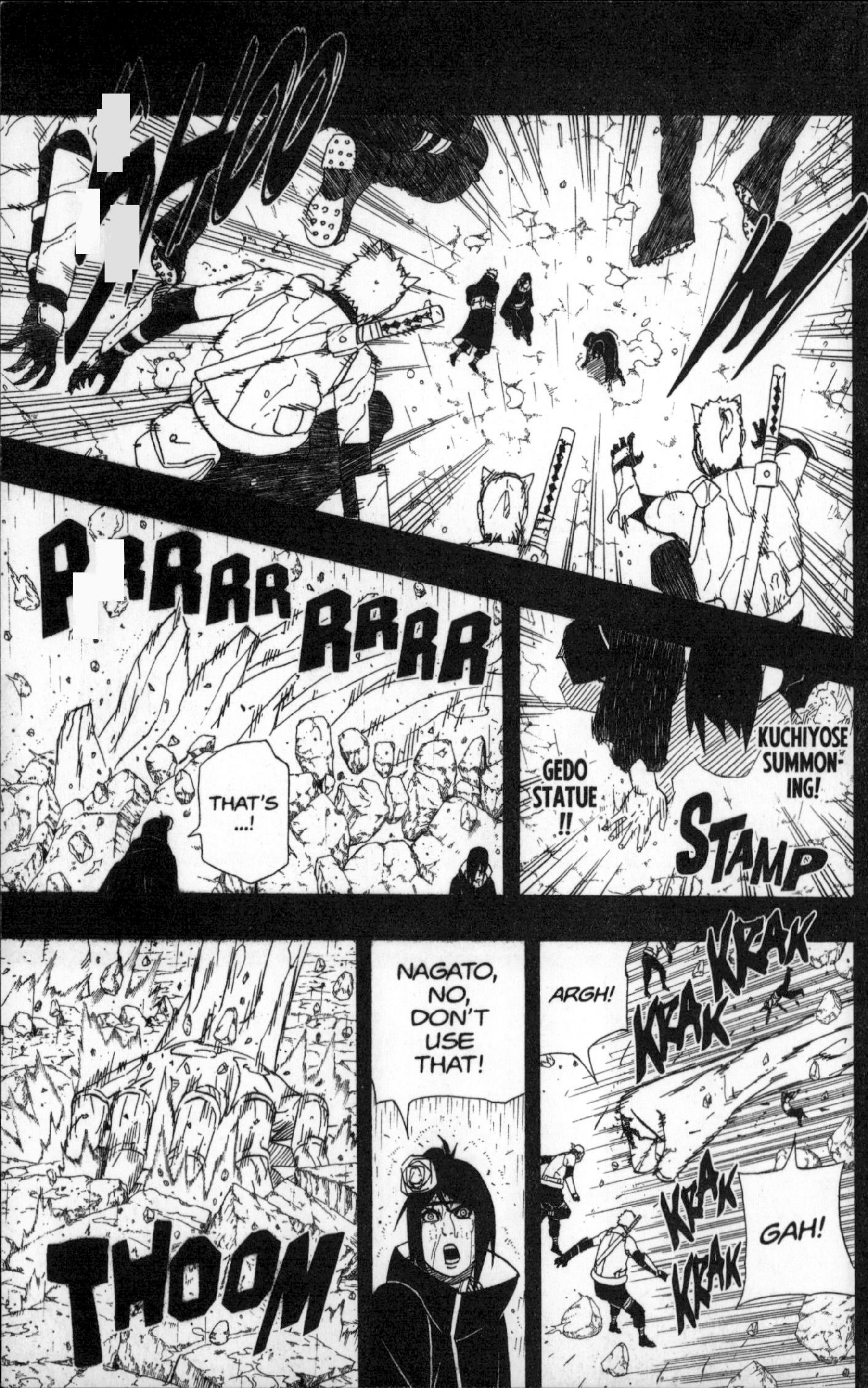
KUCHIYOSE SUMMONING!
GEDO STATUE!!
STAMP
THAT'S ...!
ARGH!
KRAK KRAK KRAK
KRAK KRAK KRAK
GAH!
NAGATO, NO, DON'T USE THAT!
THOOM

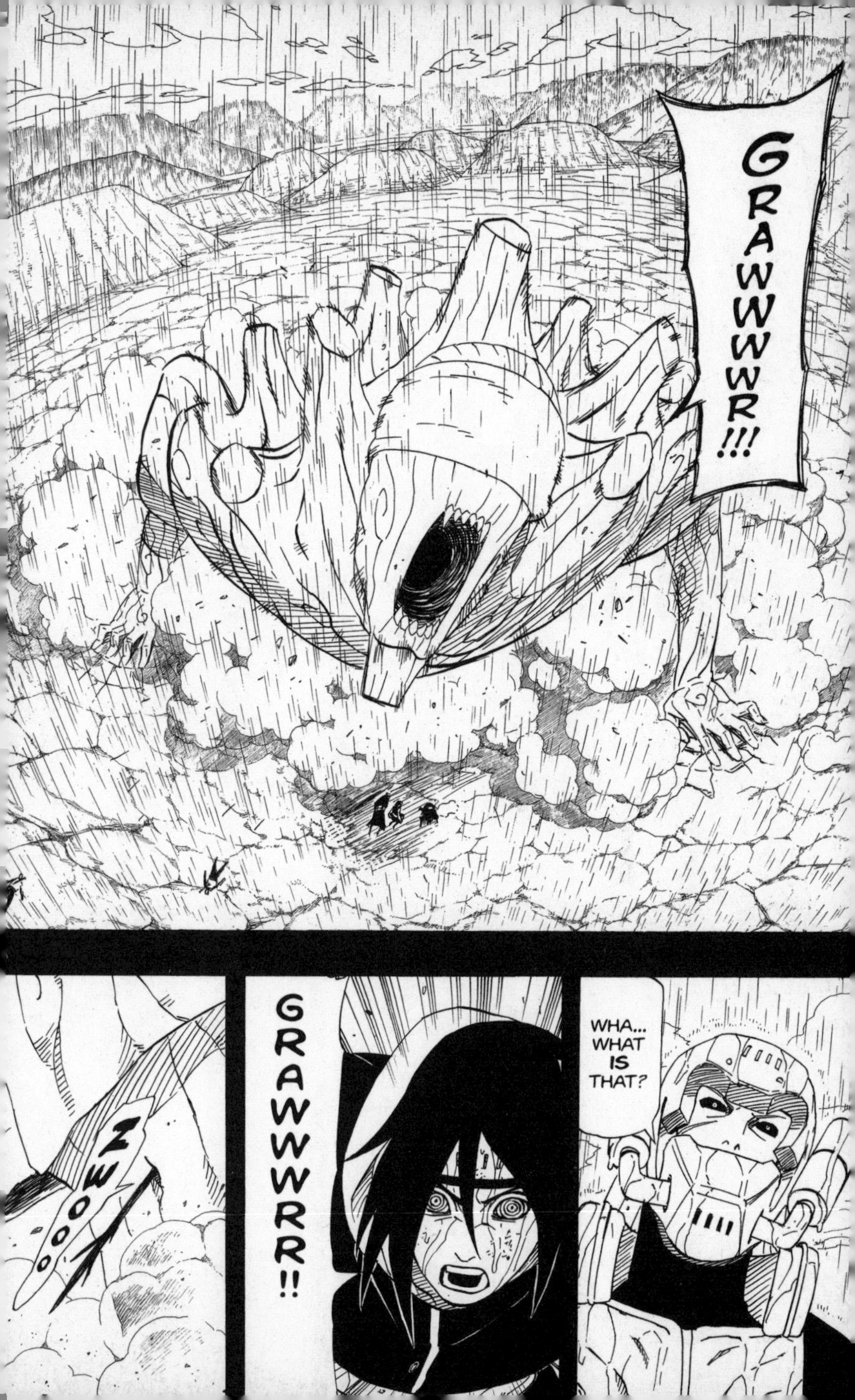
GRAWWWWWR!!!
WHA... WHAT IS THAT?
GRAWWWRR!!
FWOOO

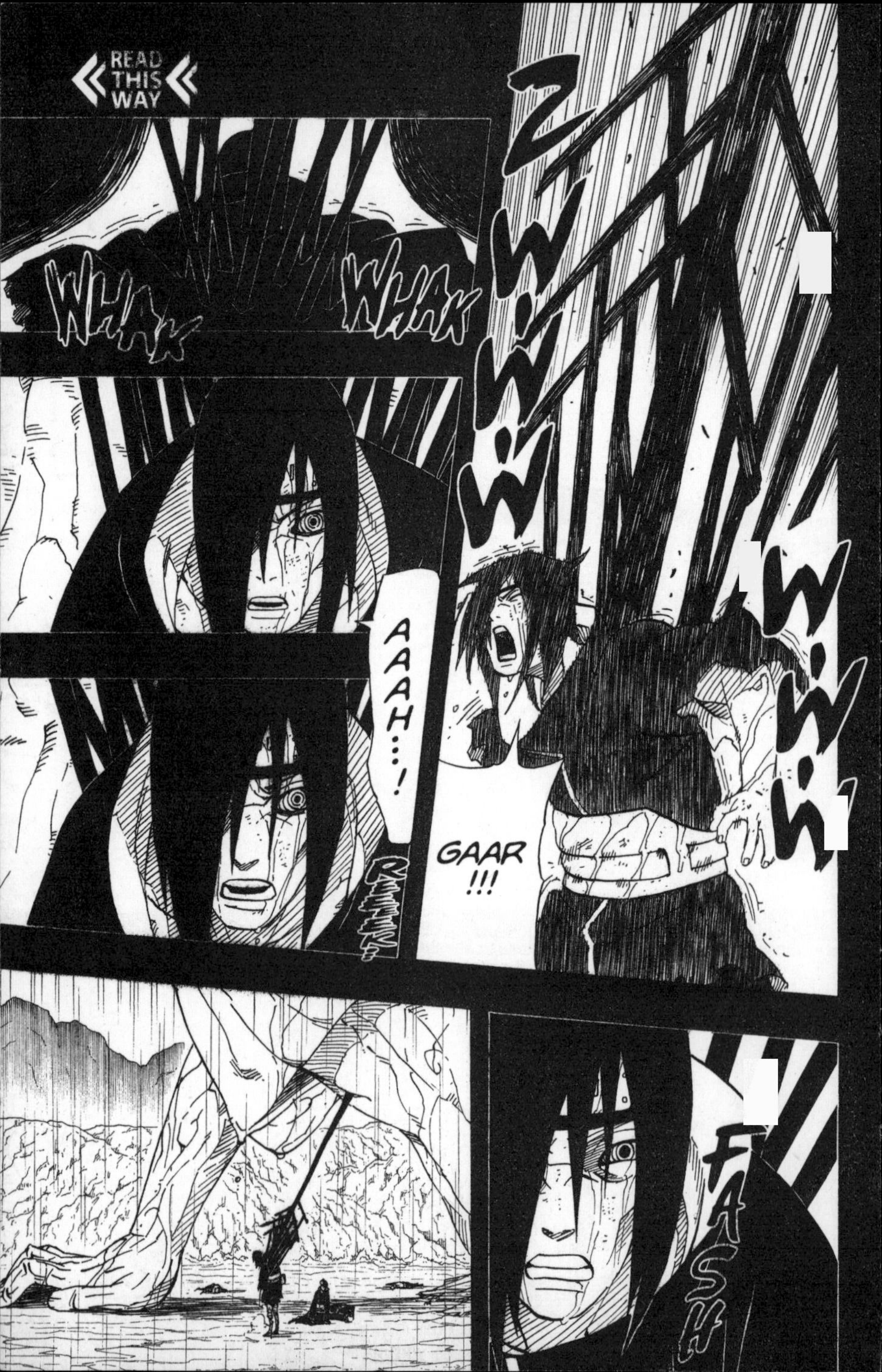
READ THIS WAY
WHAK
WHAK
AAAAH...!
GAAR !!!
FASH

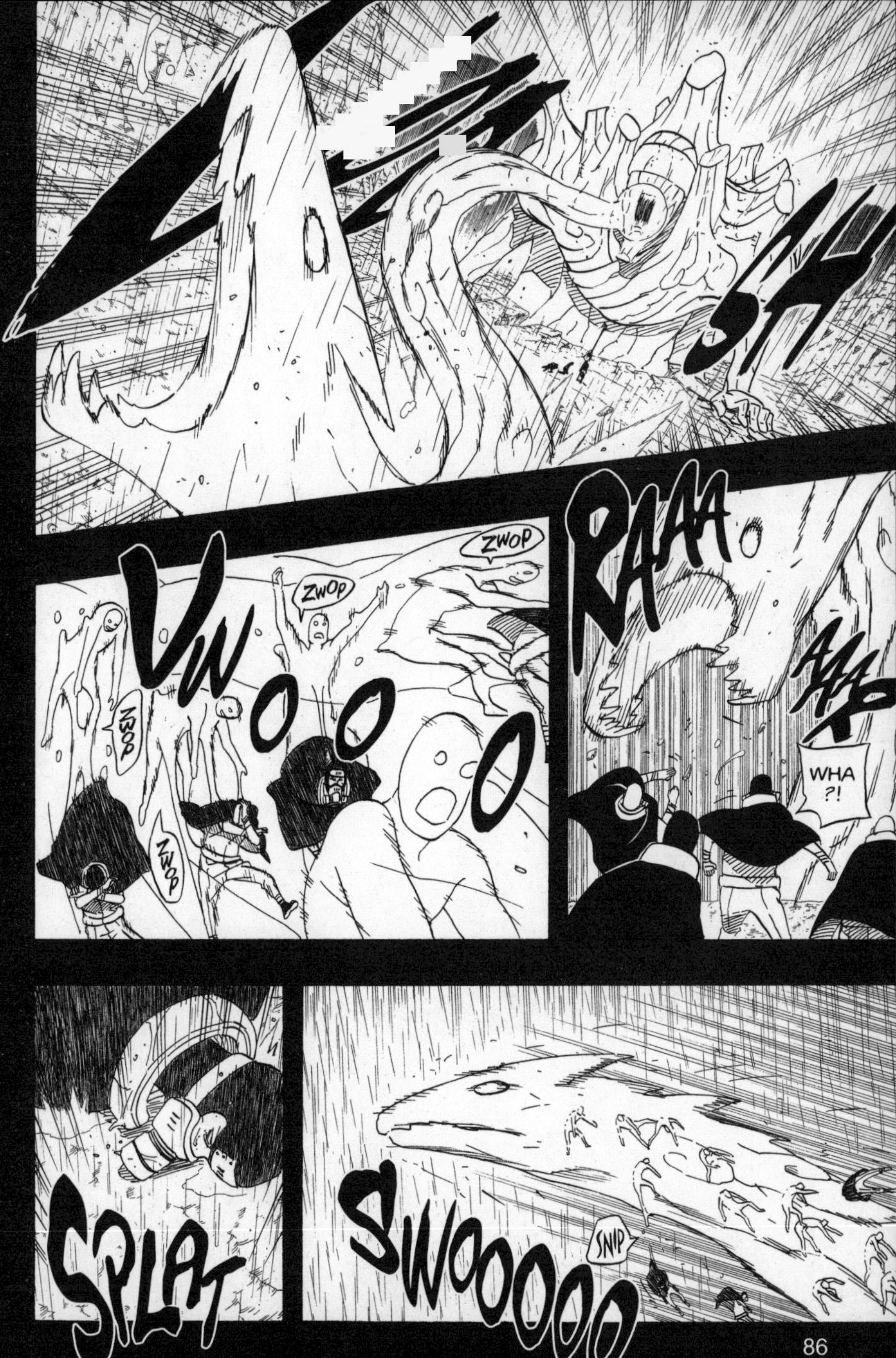
SHH
RAAAAAA
WHA ?!
VWOOOO
ZWOP
ZWOP
ZWOP
ZWOP
SWOOOOOO
SNIP
SPLAT

READ THIS WAY

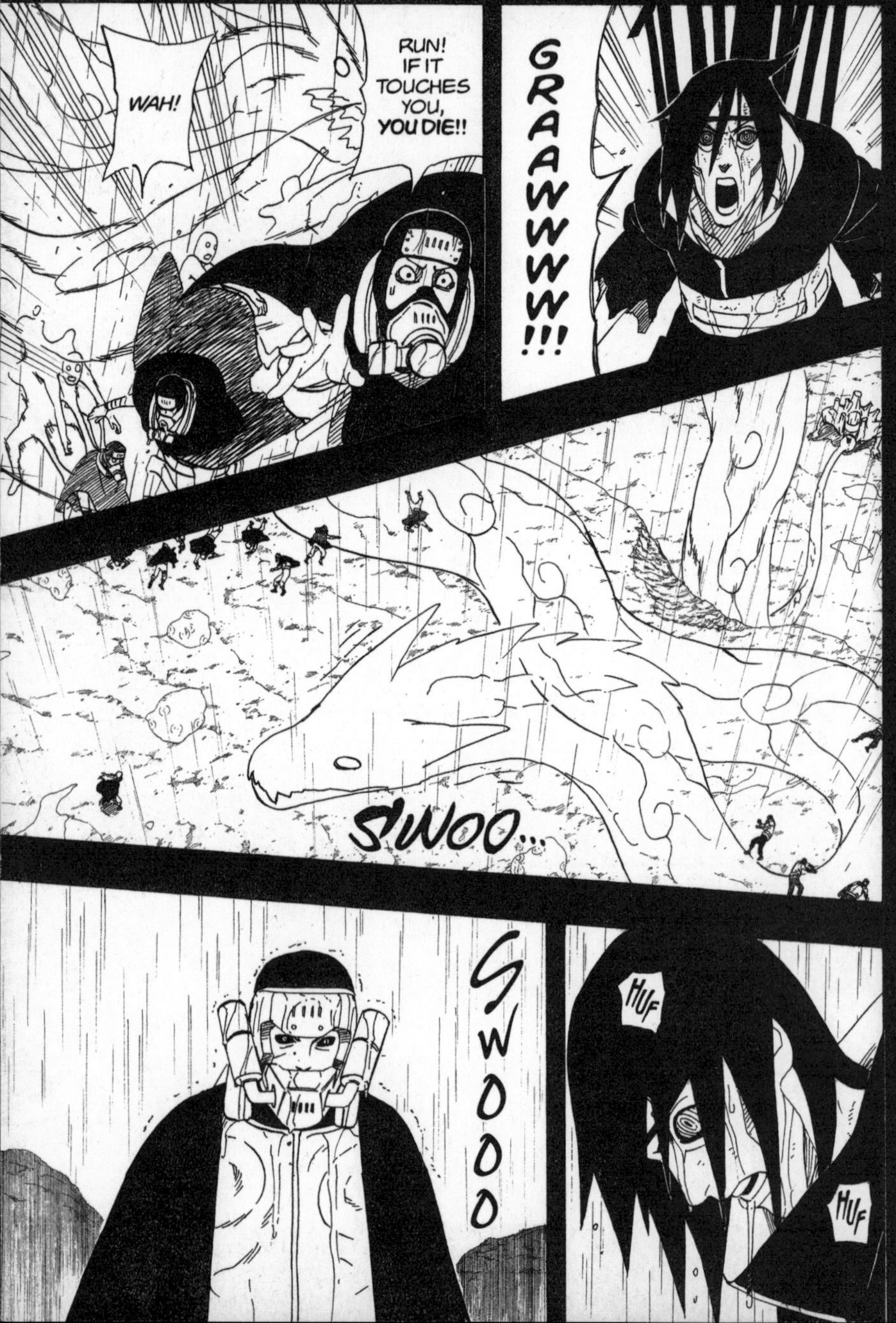
GRAAWWWWW!!!
RUN! IF IT TOUCHES YOU, YOU DIE!!
WAH!
SWOO...
HUF
HUF
SWOOO

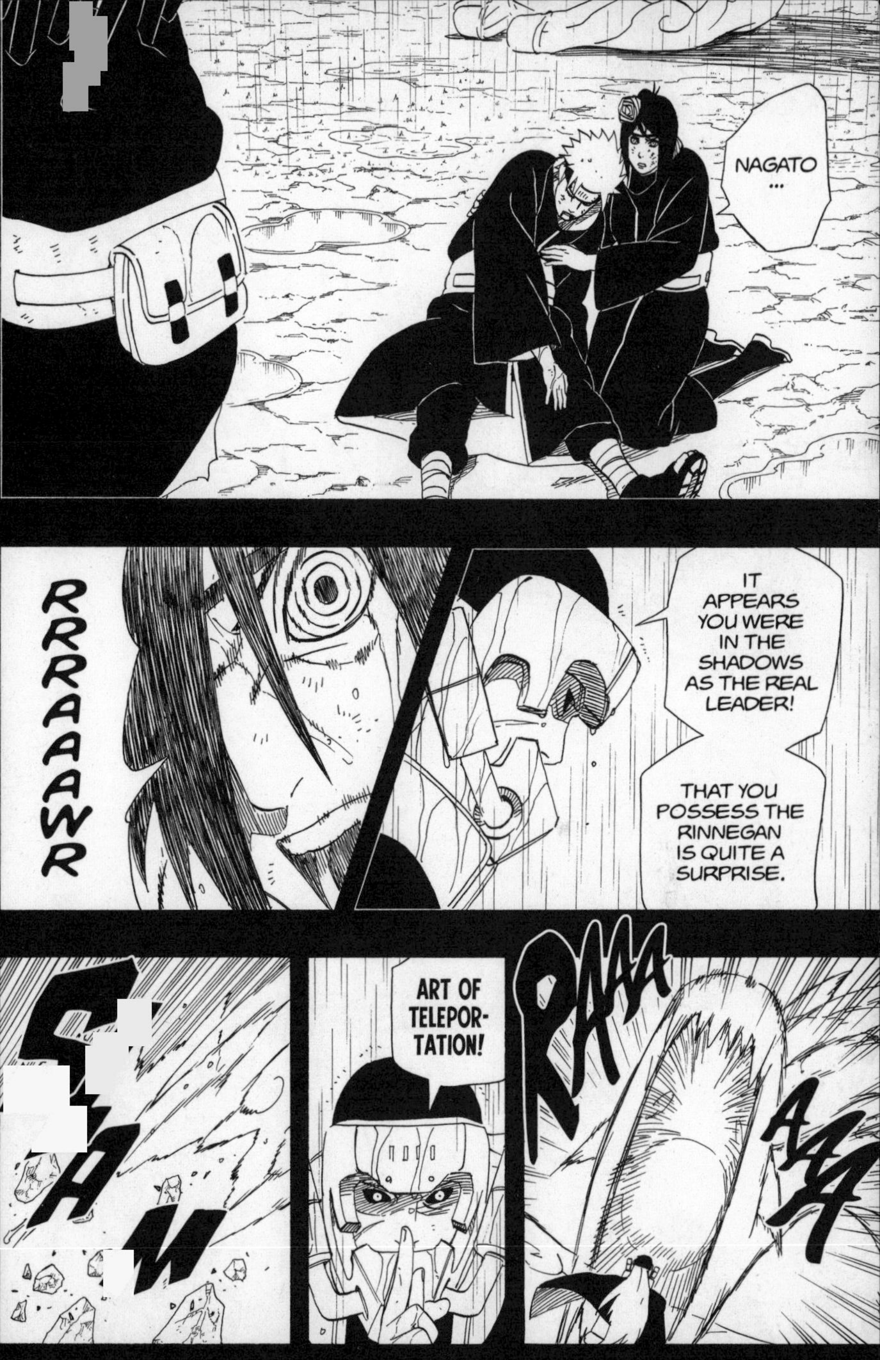
NAGATO...
IT APPEARS YOU WERE IN THE SHADOWS AS THE REAL LEADER!
THAT YOU POSSESS THE RINNEGAN IS QUITE A SURPRISE.
RRRAAAAWR
RAAAAAA
ART OF TELEPOR-TATION!

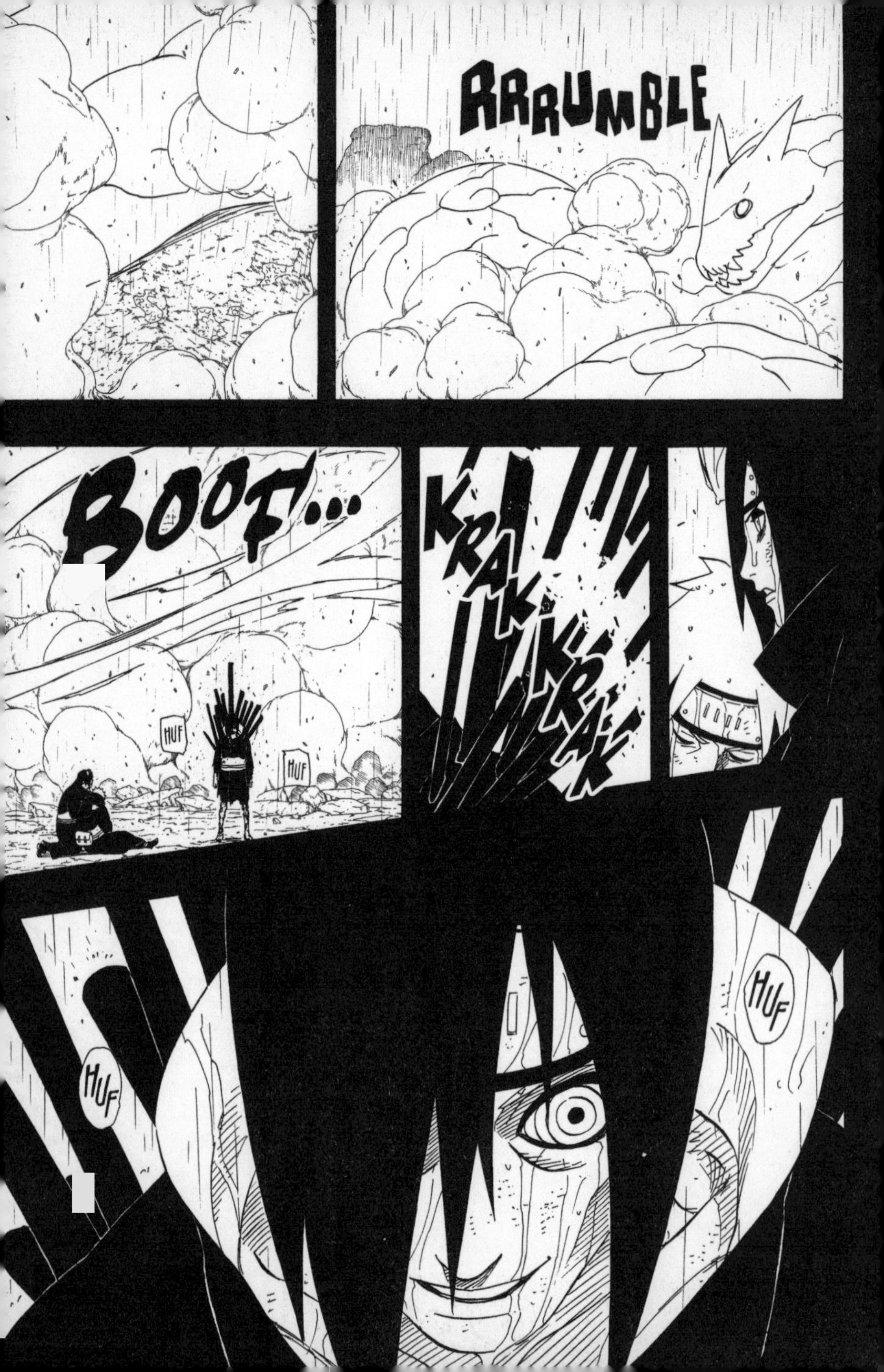
RRRUMBLE
KRAK
KRAK
KRAK
BOOF...
HUF
HUF
HUF
HUF

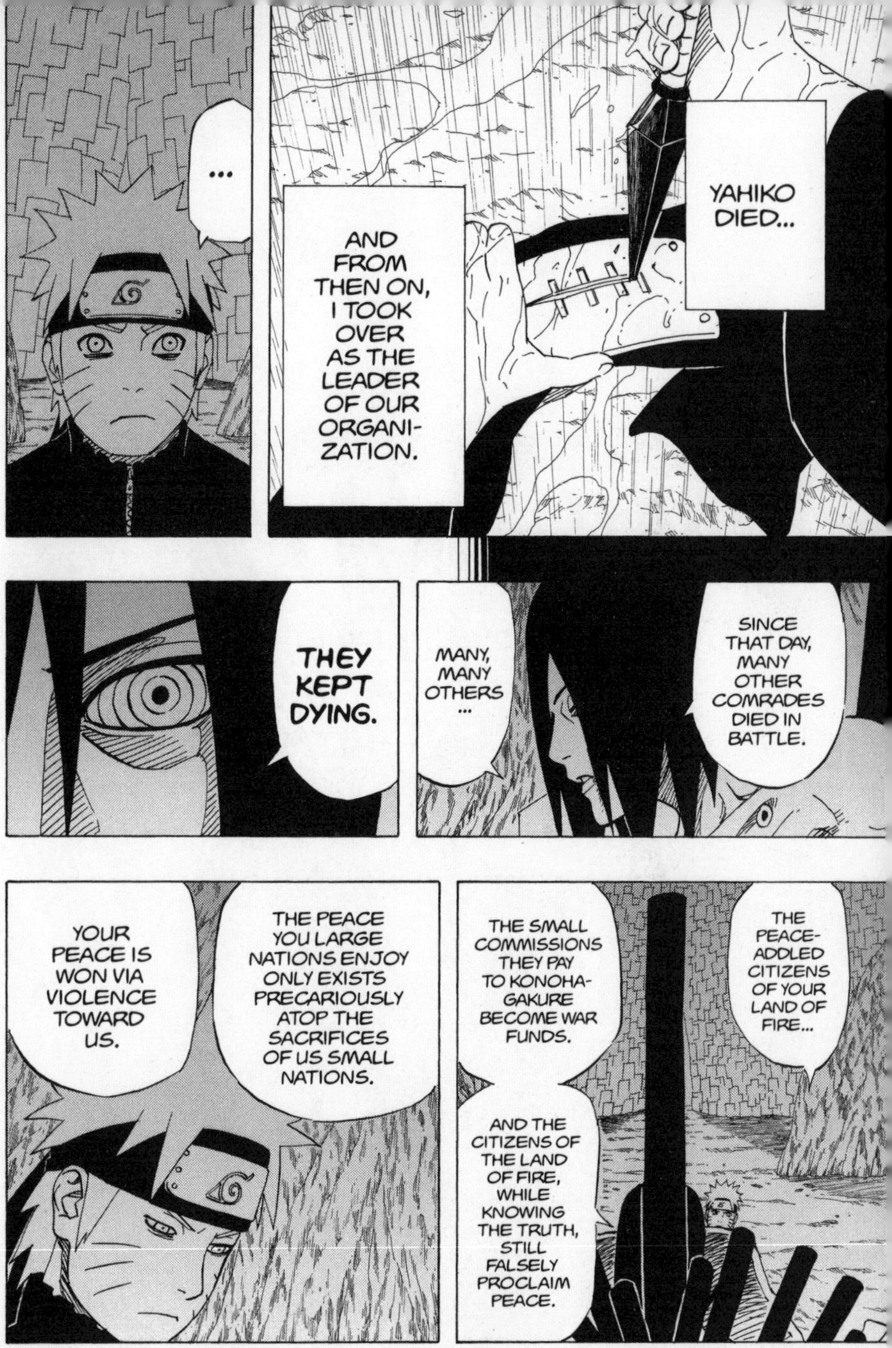
YAHIKO DIED...
AND FROM THEN ON, I TOOK OVER AS THE LEADER OF OUR ORGANIZATION.
...
SINCE THAT DAY, MANY OTHER COMRADES DIED IN BATTLE.
MANY, MANY OTHERS ...
THEY KEPT DYING.
THE PEACE-ADDLED CITIZENS OF YOUR LAND OF FIRE...
THE SMALL COMMISSIONS THEY PAY TO KONOHAGAKURE BECOME WAR FUNDS.
AND THE CITIZENS OF THE LAND OF FIRE, WHILE KNOWING THE TRUTH, STILL FALSELY PROCLAIM PEACE.
THE PEACE YOU LARGE NATIONS ENJOY ONLY EXISTS PRECARIOUSLY ATOP THE SACRIFICES OF US SMALL NATIONS.
YOUR PEACE IS WON VIA VIOLENCE TOWARD US.

READ THIS WAY

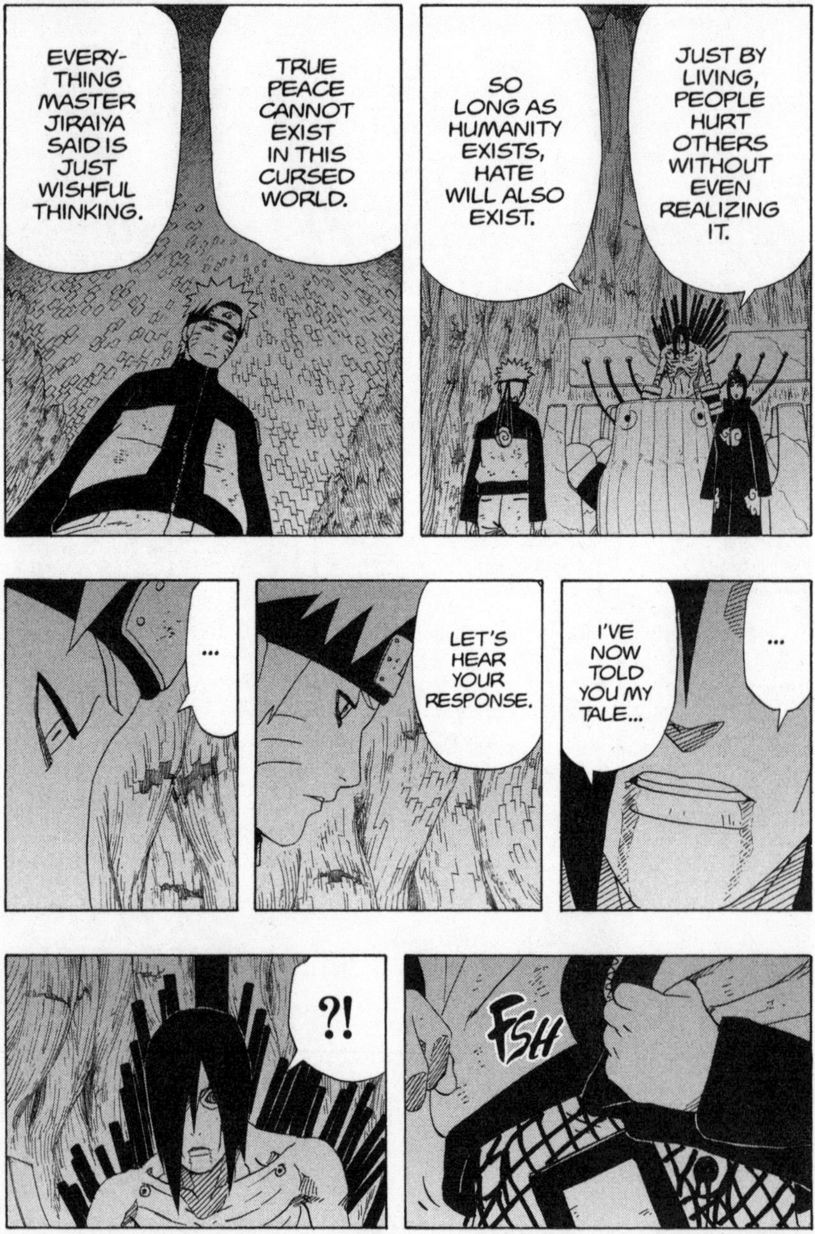
JUST BY LIVING, PEOPLE HURT OTHERS WITHOUT EVEN REALIZING IT.
SO LONG AS HUMANITY EXISTS, HATE WILL ALSO EXIST.
TRUE PEACE CANNOT EXIST IN THIS CURSED WORLD.
EVERYTHING MASTER JIRAIYA SAID IS JUST WISHFUL THINKING.
...
I'VE NOW TOLD YOU MY TALE...
LET'S HEAR YOUR RESPONSE.
...
FSH
?!

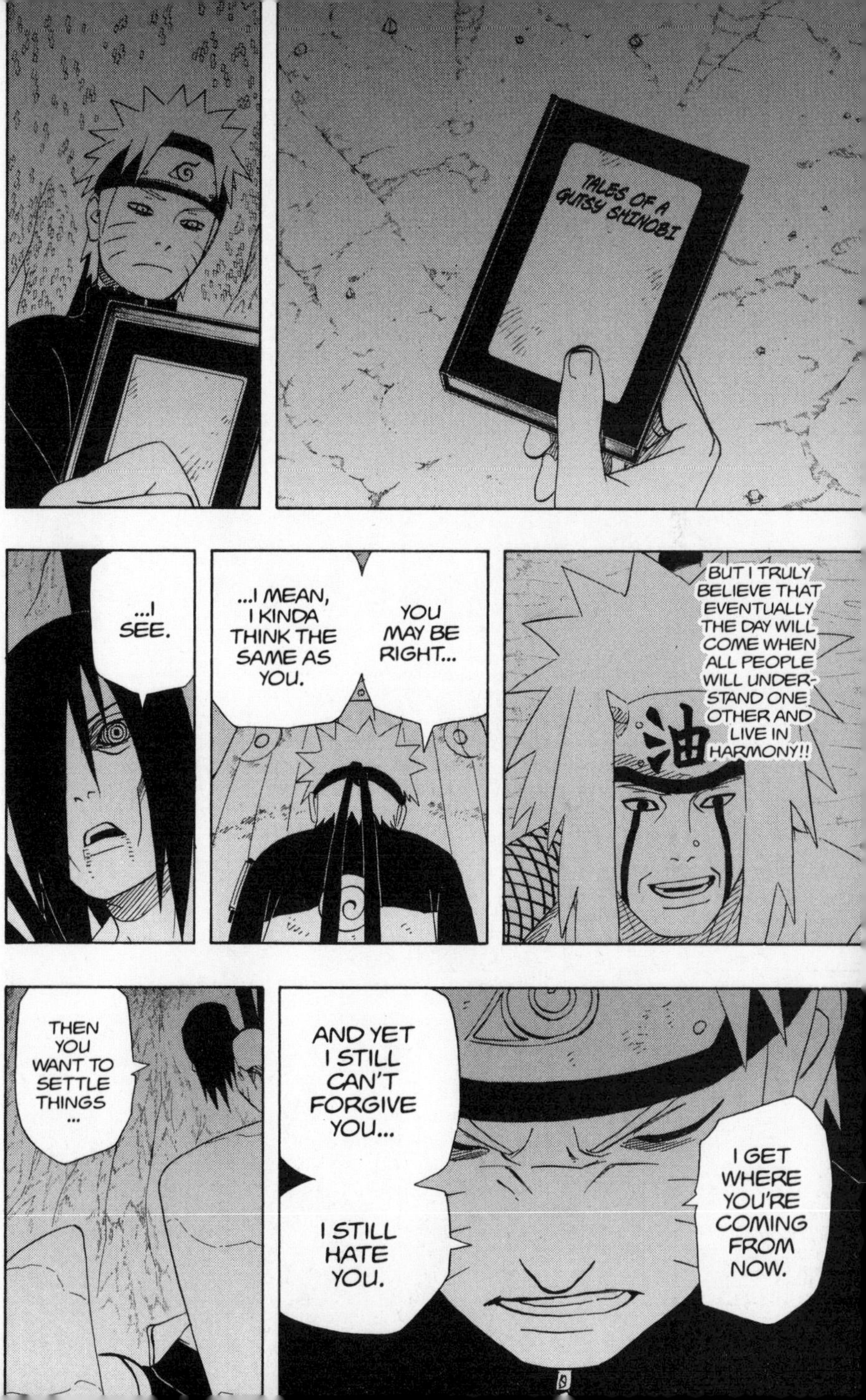
TALES OF A GUTSY SHINOBI
BUT I TRULY BELIEVE THAT EVENTUALLY THE DAY WILL COME WHEN ALL PEOPLE WILL UNDER-STAND ONE OTHER AND LIVE IN HARMONY!!
YOU MAY BE RIGHT...
...I MEAN, I KINDA THINK THE SAME AS YOU.
...I SEE.
I GET WHERE YOU'RE COMING FROM NOW.
AND YET I STILL CAN'T FORGIVE YOU...
I STILL HATE YOU.
THEN YOU WANT TO SETTLE THINGS ...

READ THIS WAY

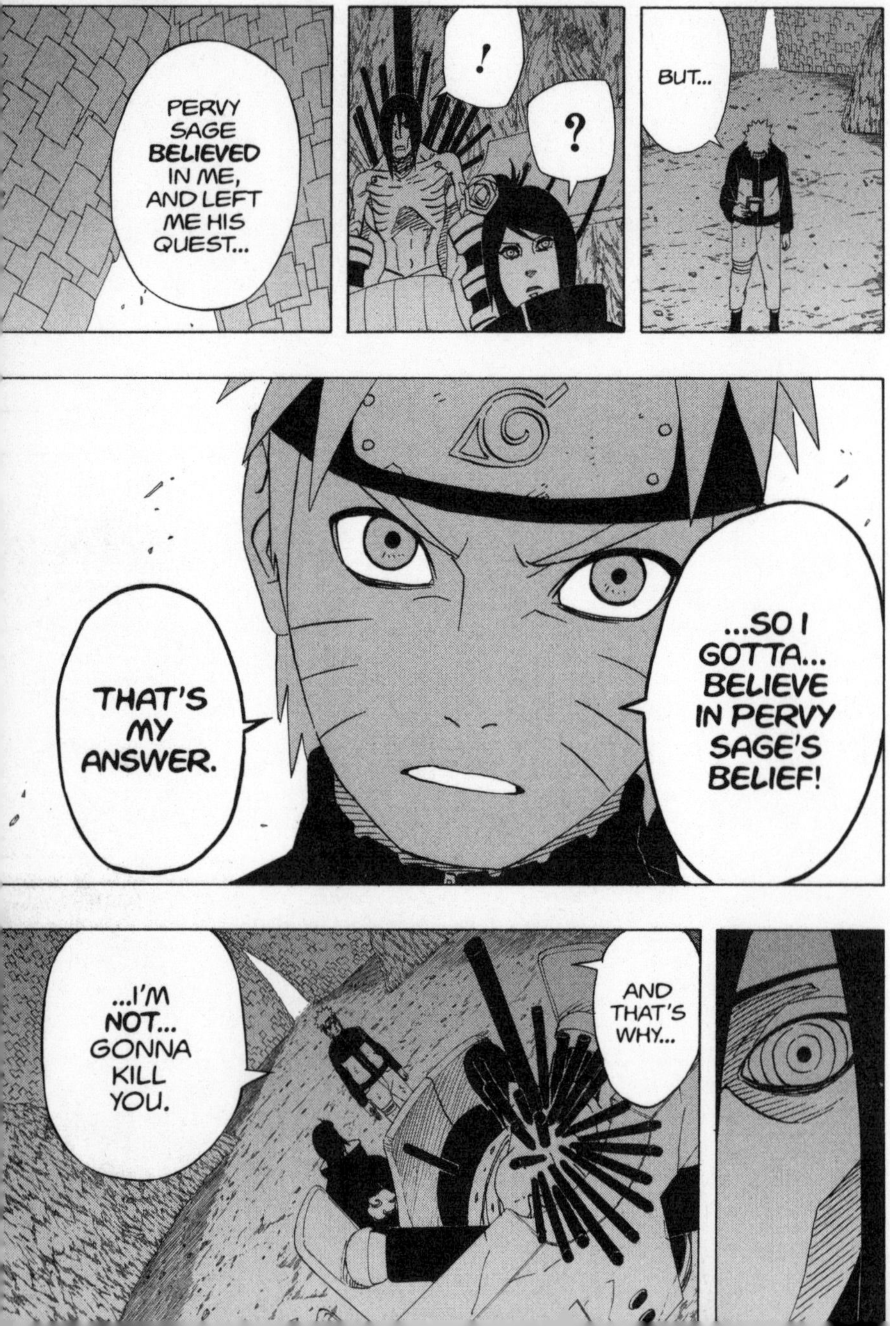
BUT...
!
?
PERVY SAGE BELIEVED IN ME, AND LEFT ME HIS QUEST...
...SO I GOTTA... BELIEVE IN PERVY SAGE'S BELIEF!
THAT'S MY ANSWER.
AND THAT'S WHY...
...I'M NOT... GONNA KILL YOU.

NARUTO

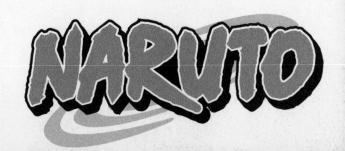

Number 448: Heirloom...!!

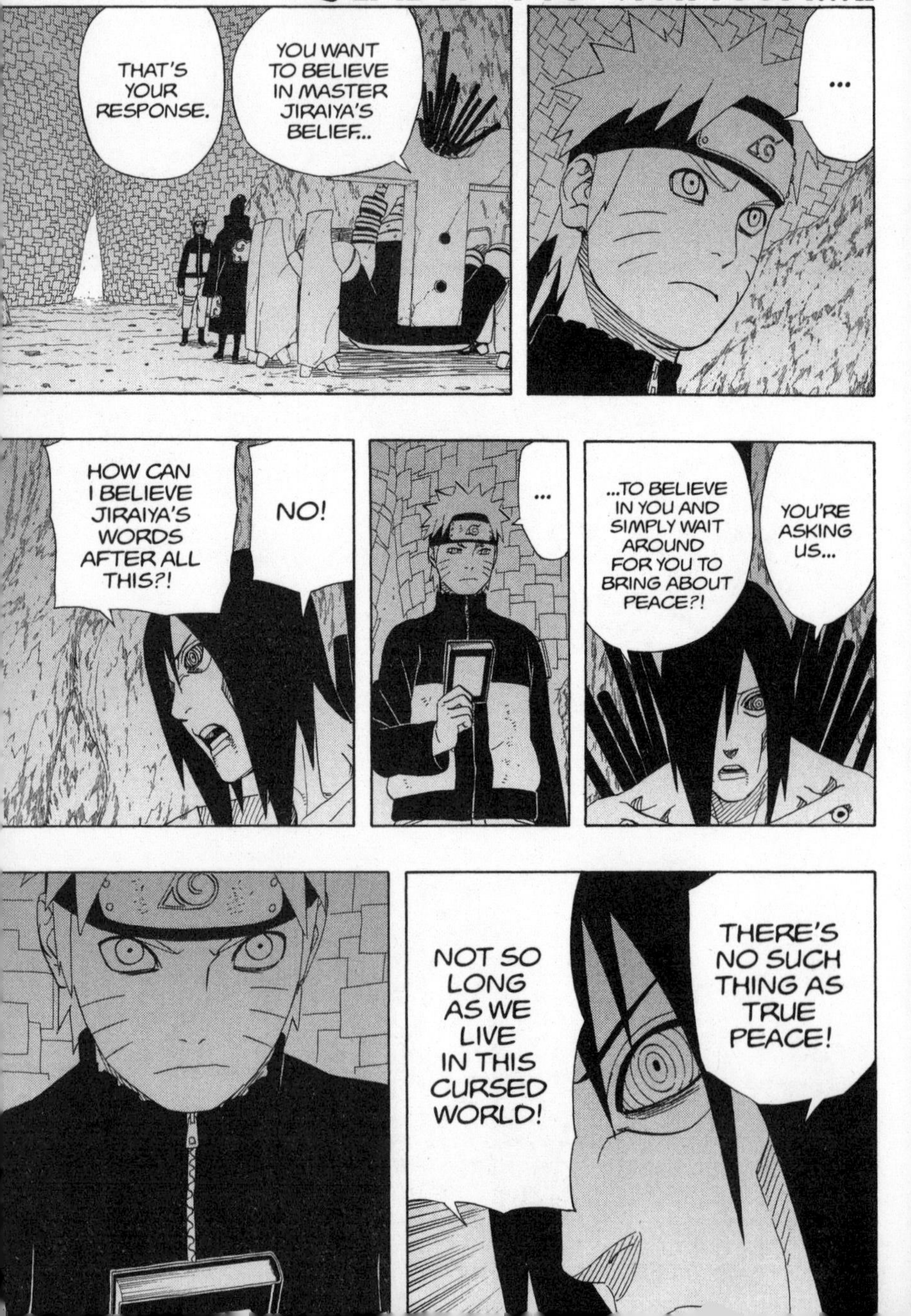
...
YOU WANT TO BELIEVE IN MASTER JIRAIYA'S BELIEF...
THAT'S YOUR RESPONSE.
YOU'RE ASKING US...
...TO BELIEVE IN YOU AND SIMPLY WAIT AROUND FOR YOU TO BRING ABOUT PEACE?!
...
NO!
HOW CAN I BELIEVE JIRAIYA'S WORDS AFTER ALL THIS?!
THERE'S NO SUCH THING AS TRUE PEACE!
NOT SO LONG AS WE LIVE IN THIS CURSED WORLD!

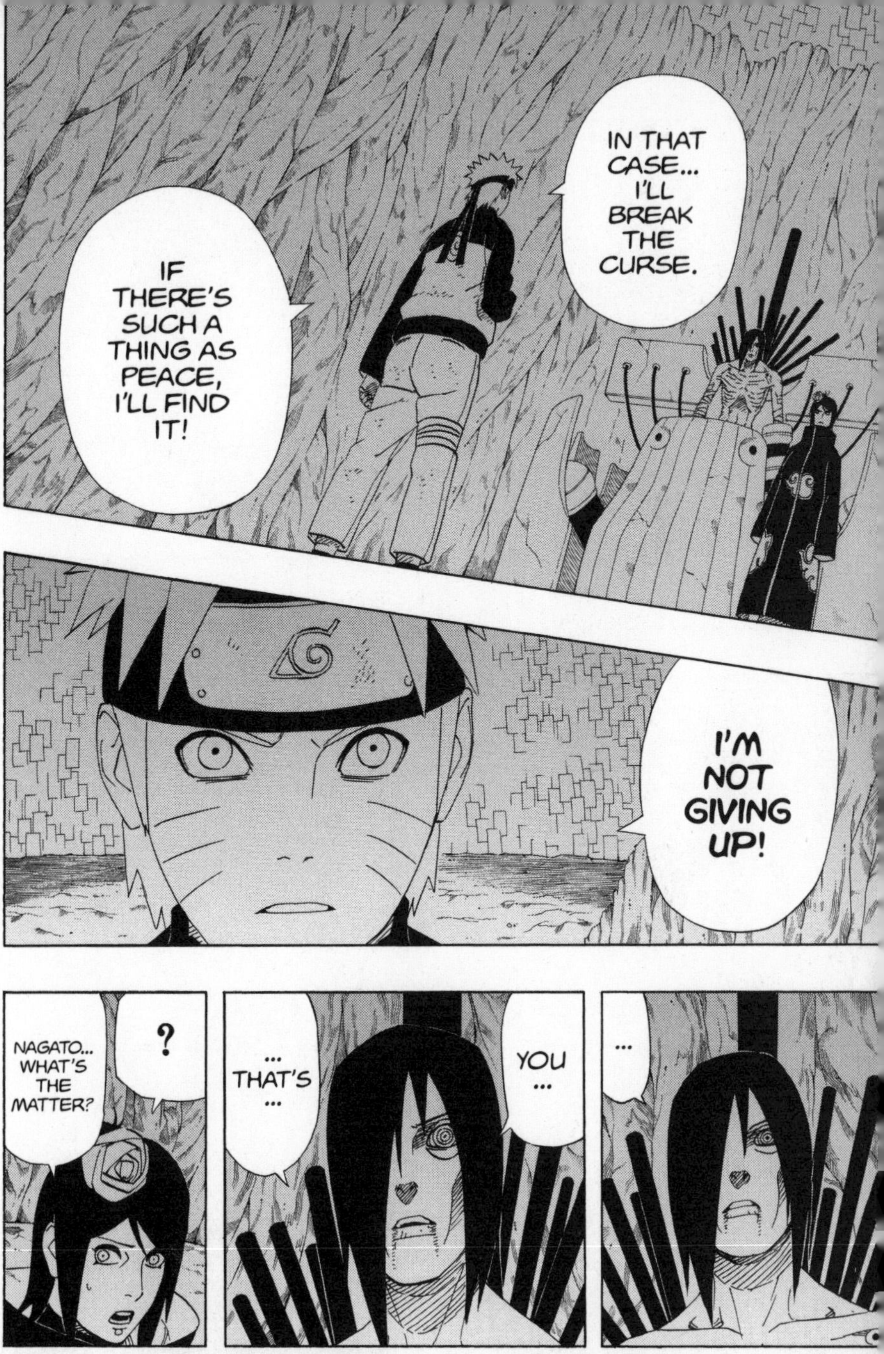
IN THAT CASE... I'LL BREAK THE CURSE.
IF THERE'S SUCH A THING AS PEACE, I'LL FIND IT!
I'M NOT GIVING UP!
...
YOU ...
... THAT'S ...
?
NAGATO... WHAT'S THE MATTER?

READ THIS WAY

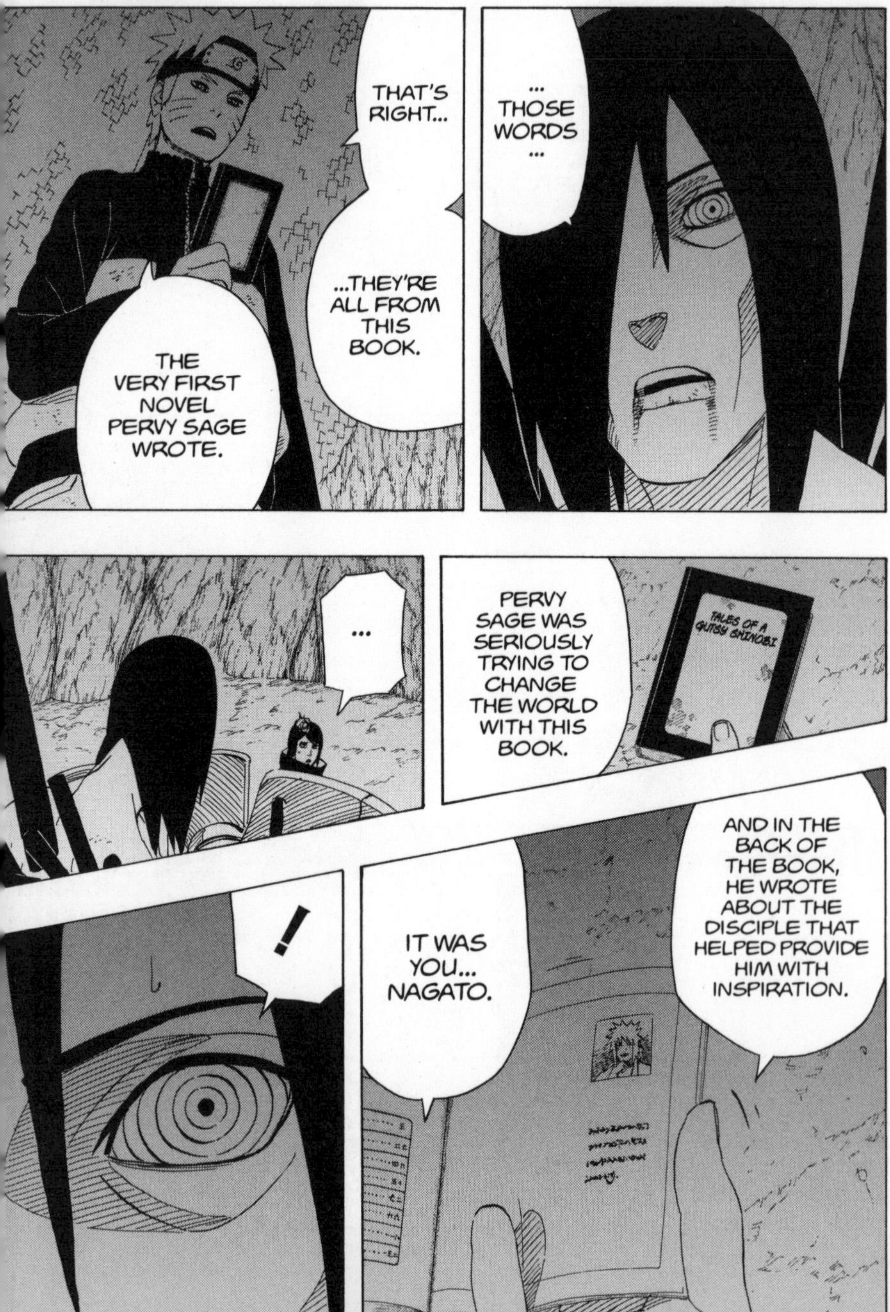
... THOSE WORDS ...
THAT'S RIGHT...
...THEY'RE ALL FROM THIS BOOK.
THE VERY FIRST NOVEL PERVY SAGE WROTE.
TALES OF A GUTSY SHINOBI
PERVY SAGE WAS SERIOUSLY TRYING TO CHANGE THE WORLD WITH THIS BOOK.
...
AND IN THE BACK OF THE BOOK, HE WROTE ABOUT THE DISCIPLE THAT HELPED PROVIDE HIM WITH INSPIRATION.
IT WAS YOU... NAGATO.
!

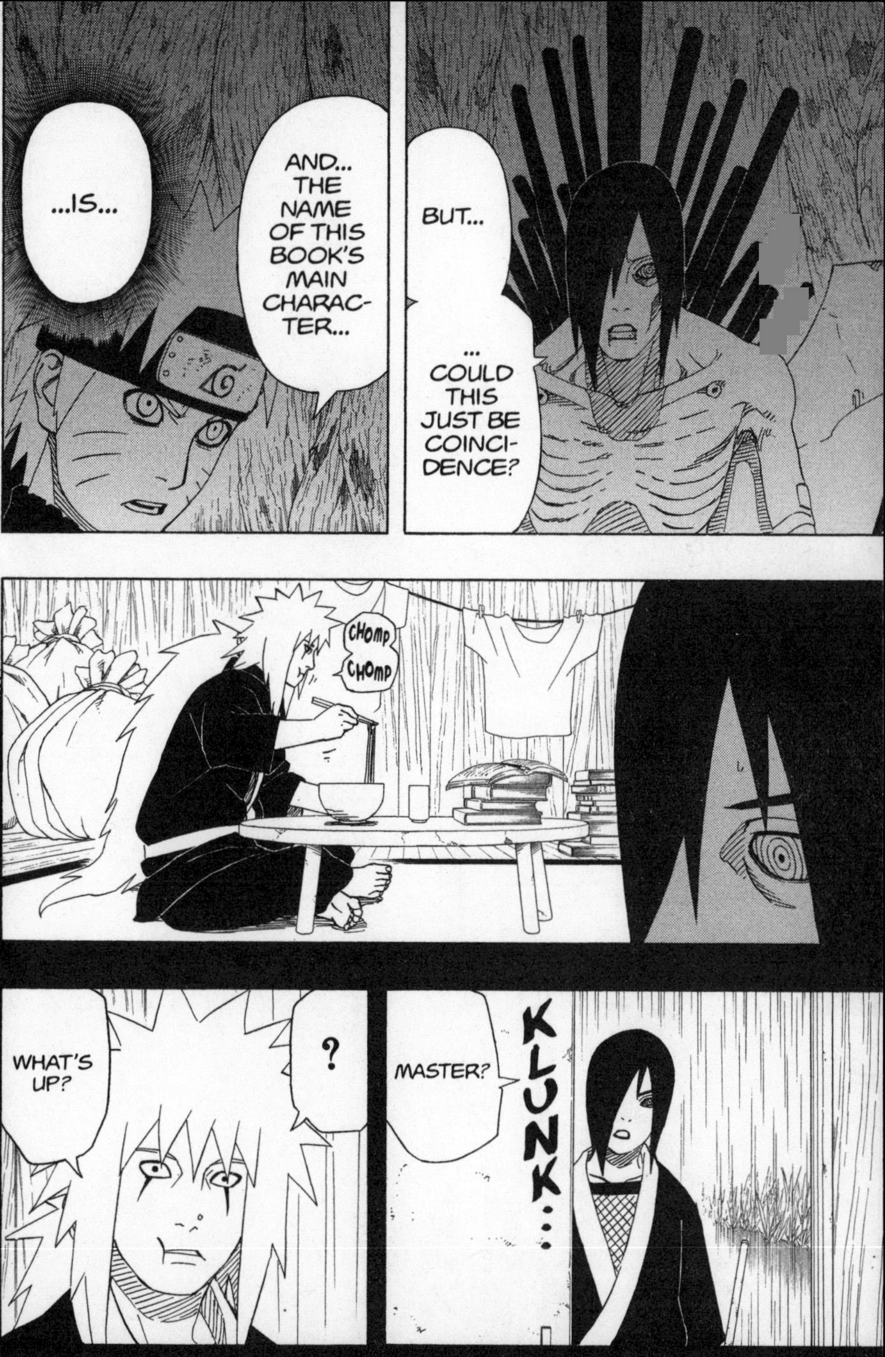
BUT...
... COULD THIS JUST BE COINCIDENCE?
AND... THE NAME OF THIS BOOK'S MAIN CHARACTER...
...IS...
CHOMP
CHOMP
KLUNK...
MASTER?
?
WHAT'S UP?

READ THIS WAY

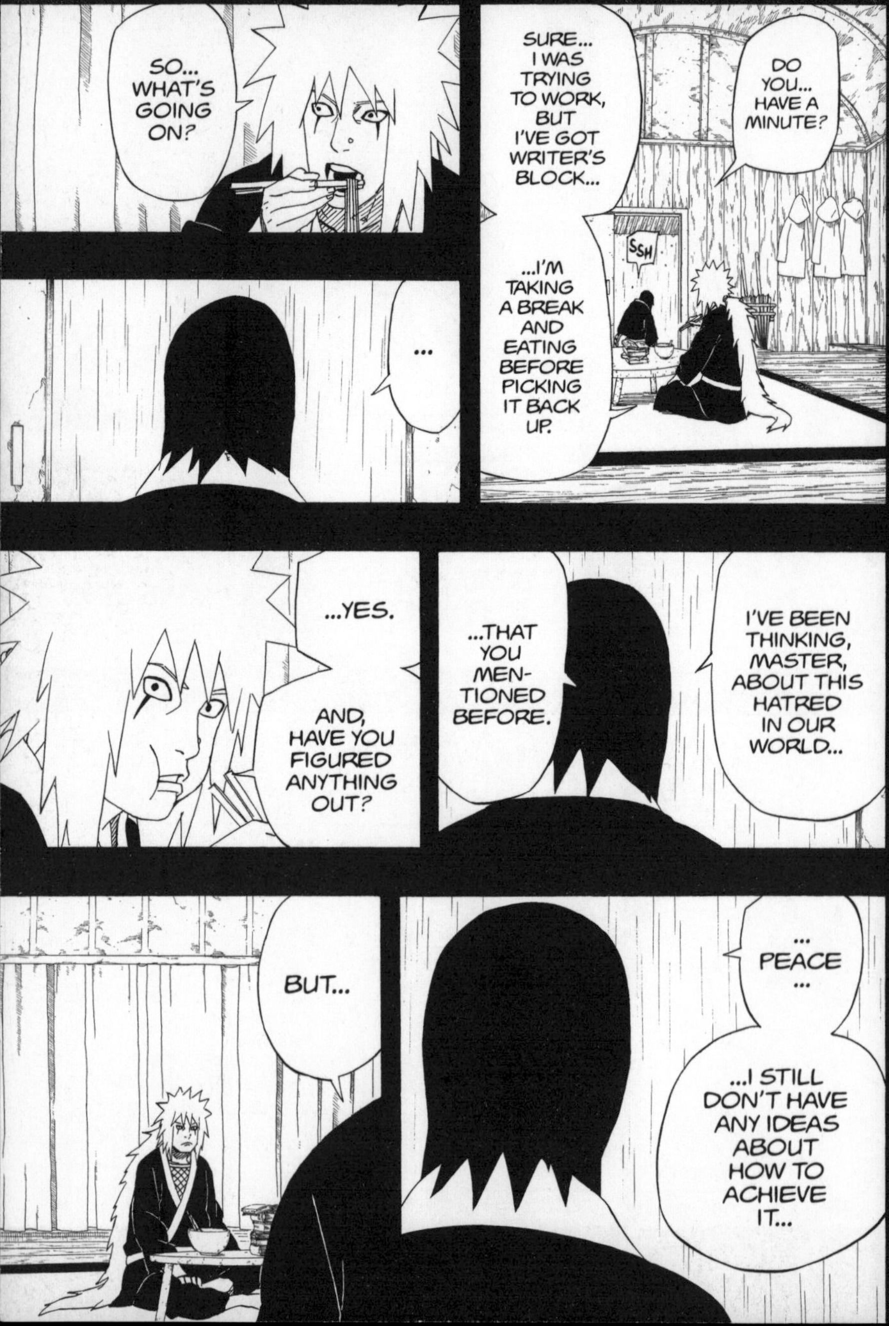
DO YOU... HAVE A MINUTE?
SURE... I WAS TRYING TO WORK, BUT I'VE GOT WRITER'S BLOCK...
SSH
...I'M TAKING A BREAK AND EATING BEFORE PICKING IT BACK UP.
SO... WHAT'S GOING ON?
...
I'VE BEEN THINKING, MASTER, ABOUT THIS HATRED IN OUR WORLD...
...THAT YOU MENTIONED BEFORE.
...YES.
AND, HAVE YOU FIGURED ANYTHING OUT?
... PEACE ...
...I STILL DON'T HAVE ANY IDEAS ABOUT HOW TO ACHIEVE IT...
BUT...

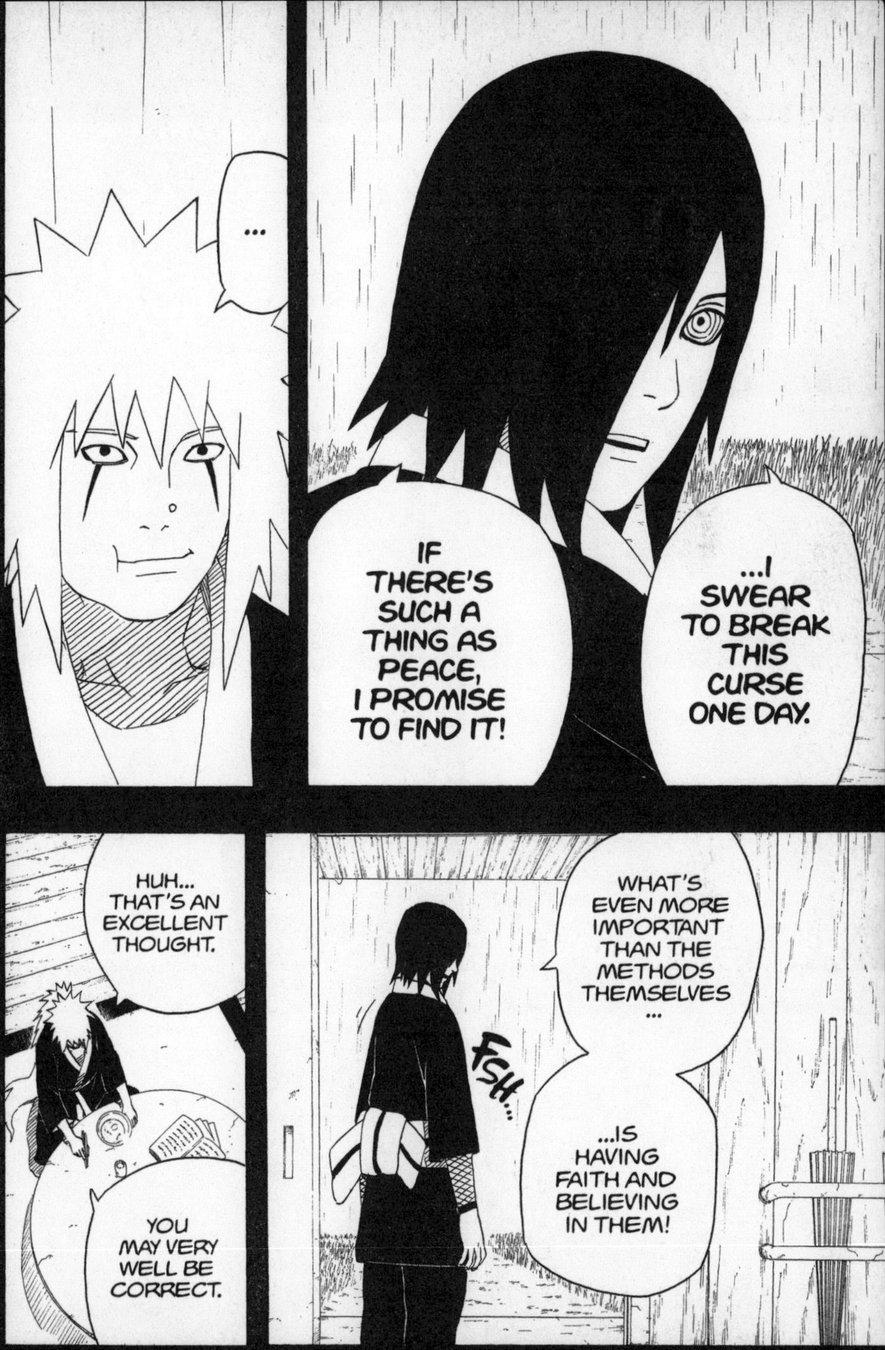
...I SWEAR TO BREAK THIS CURSE ONE DAY.
IF THERE'S SUCH A THING AS PEACE, I PROMISE TO FIND IT!
...
WHAT'S EVEN MORE IMPORTANT THAN THE METHODS THEMSELVES ...
FSH...
...IS HAVING FAITH AND BELIEVING IN THEM!
HUH... THAT'S AN EXCELLENT THOUGHT.
YOU MAY VERY WELL BE CORRECT.

READ THIS WAY

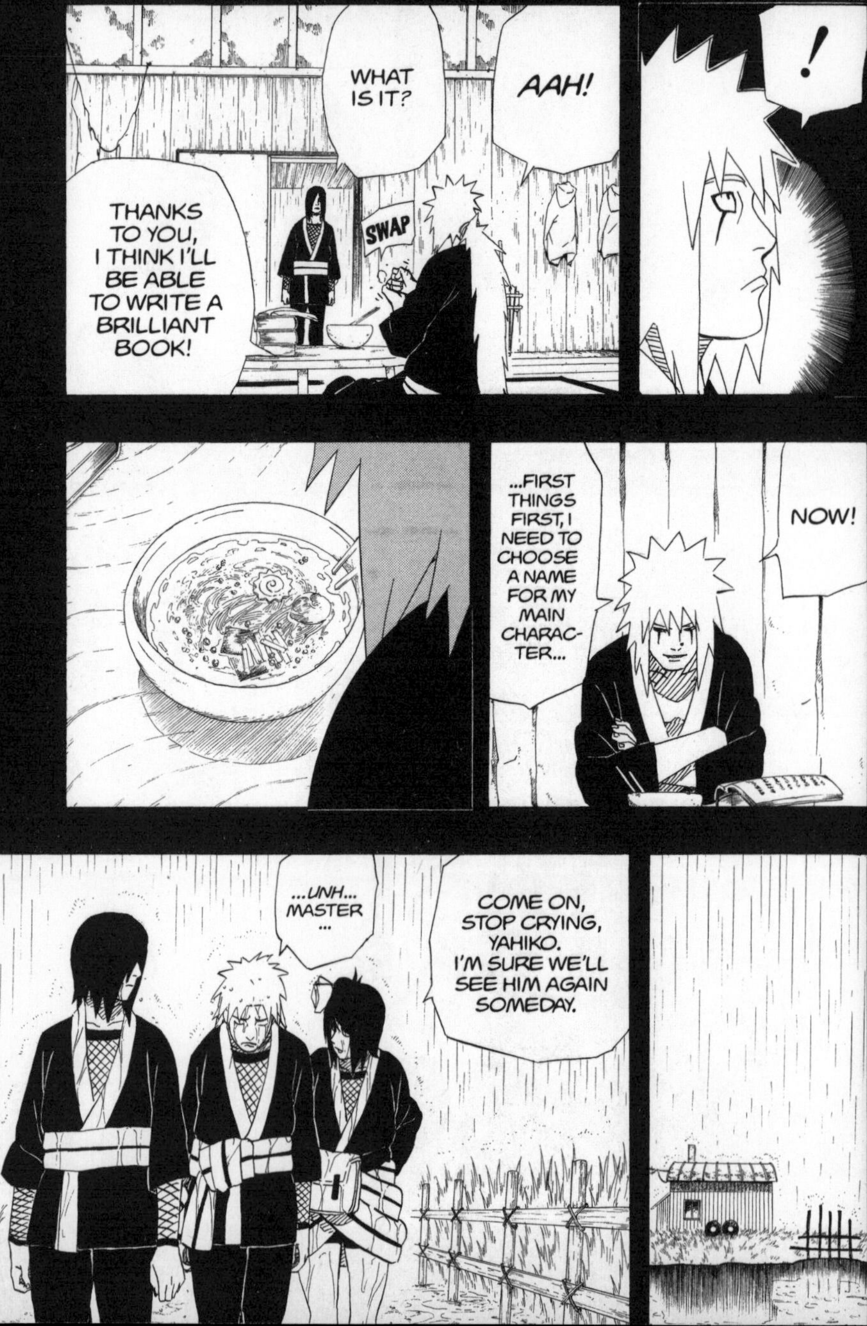
!
AAH!
WHAT IS IT?
SWAP
THANKS TO YOU, I THINK I'LL BE ABLE TO WRITE A BRILLIANT BOOK!
NOW!
...FIRST THINGS FIRST, I NEED TO CHOOSE A NAME FOR MY MAIN CHARACTER...
COME ON, STOP CRYING, YAHIKO. I'M SURE WE'LL SEE HIM AGAIN SOMEDAY.
...UNH... MASTER ...

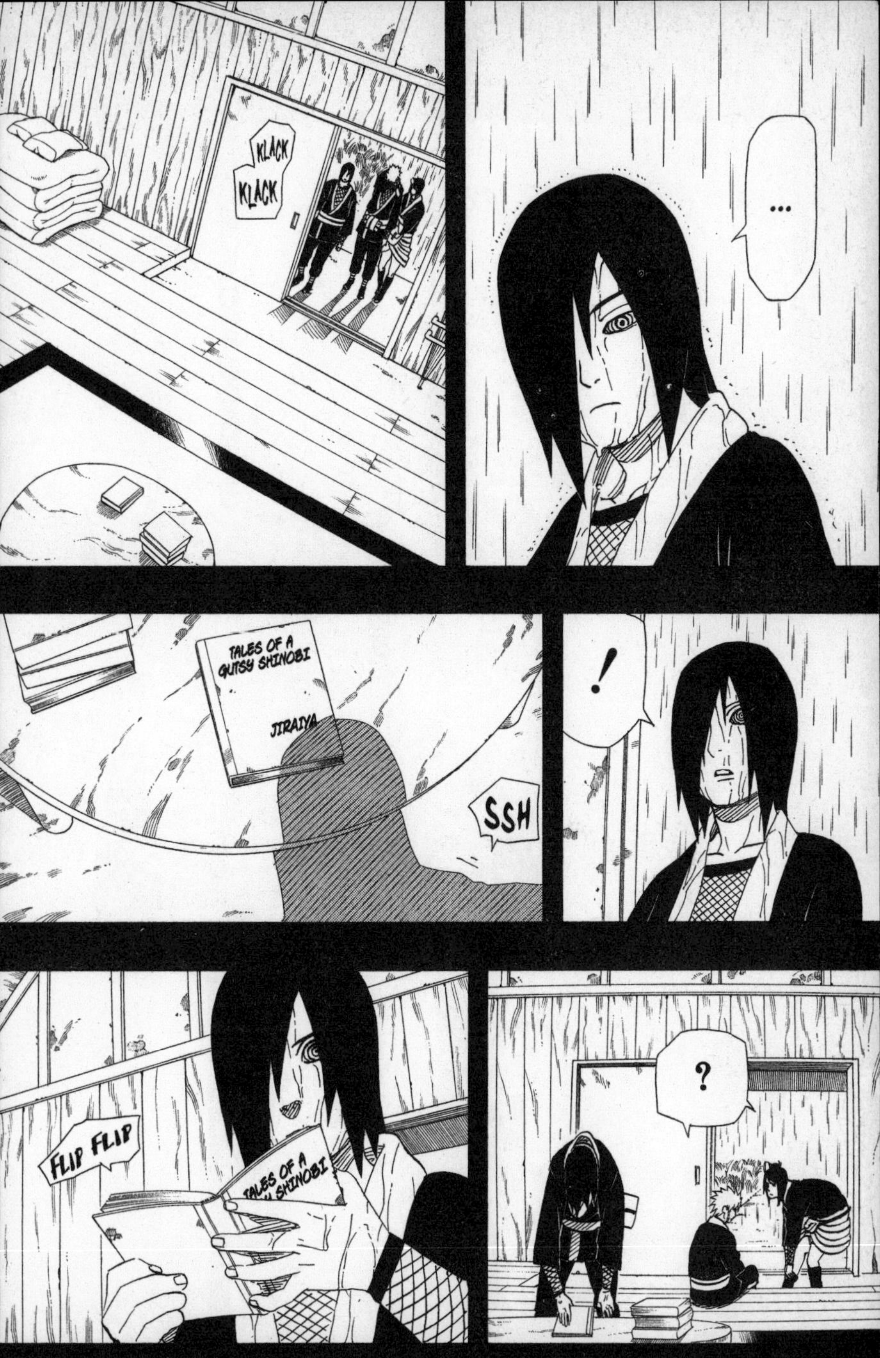
...
KLACK
KLACK
!
TALES OF A GUTSY SHINOBI
JIRAIYA
SSH
?
FLIP FLIP
TALES OF A
SHINOBI

READ THIS WAY

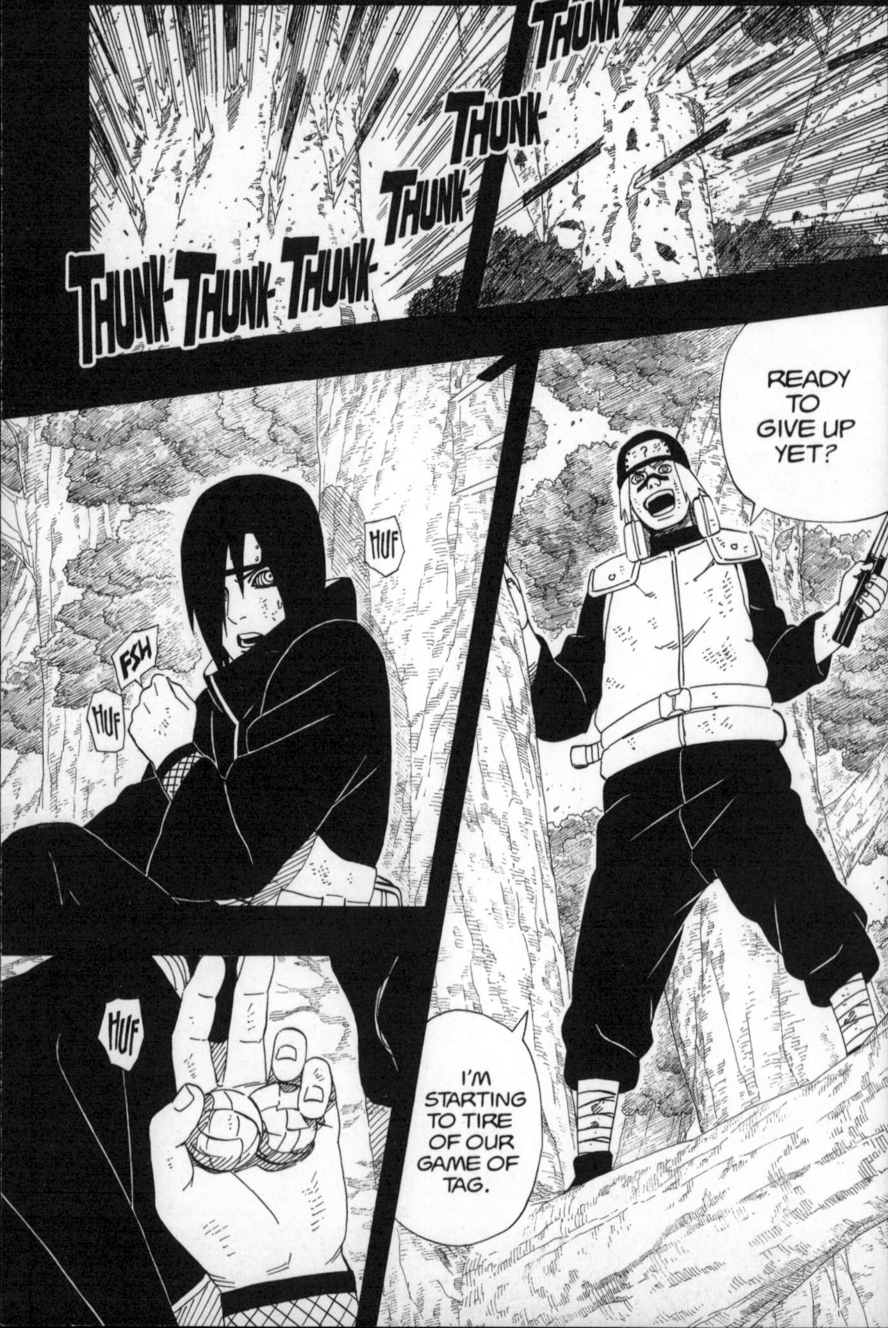
THUNK-THUNK-THUNK-THUNK-THUNK-THUNK
READY TO GIVE UP YET?
HUF
FSH
HUF
HUF
I'M STARTING TO TIRE OF OUR GAME OF TAG.

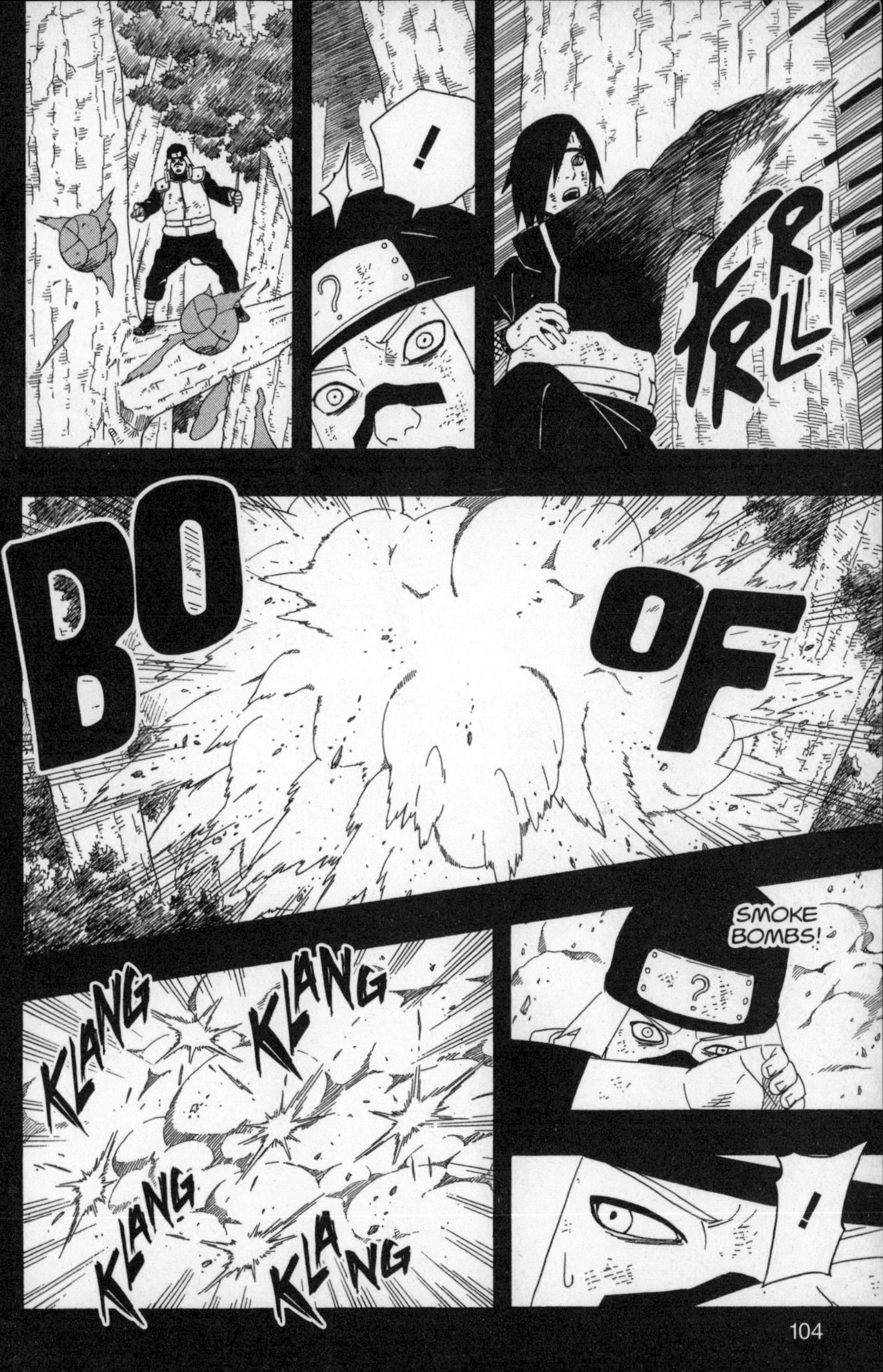
FRRLL
!
BOOF
SMOKE BOMBS!
!
KLANG
KLANG
KLANG
KLANG

READ THIS WAY

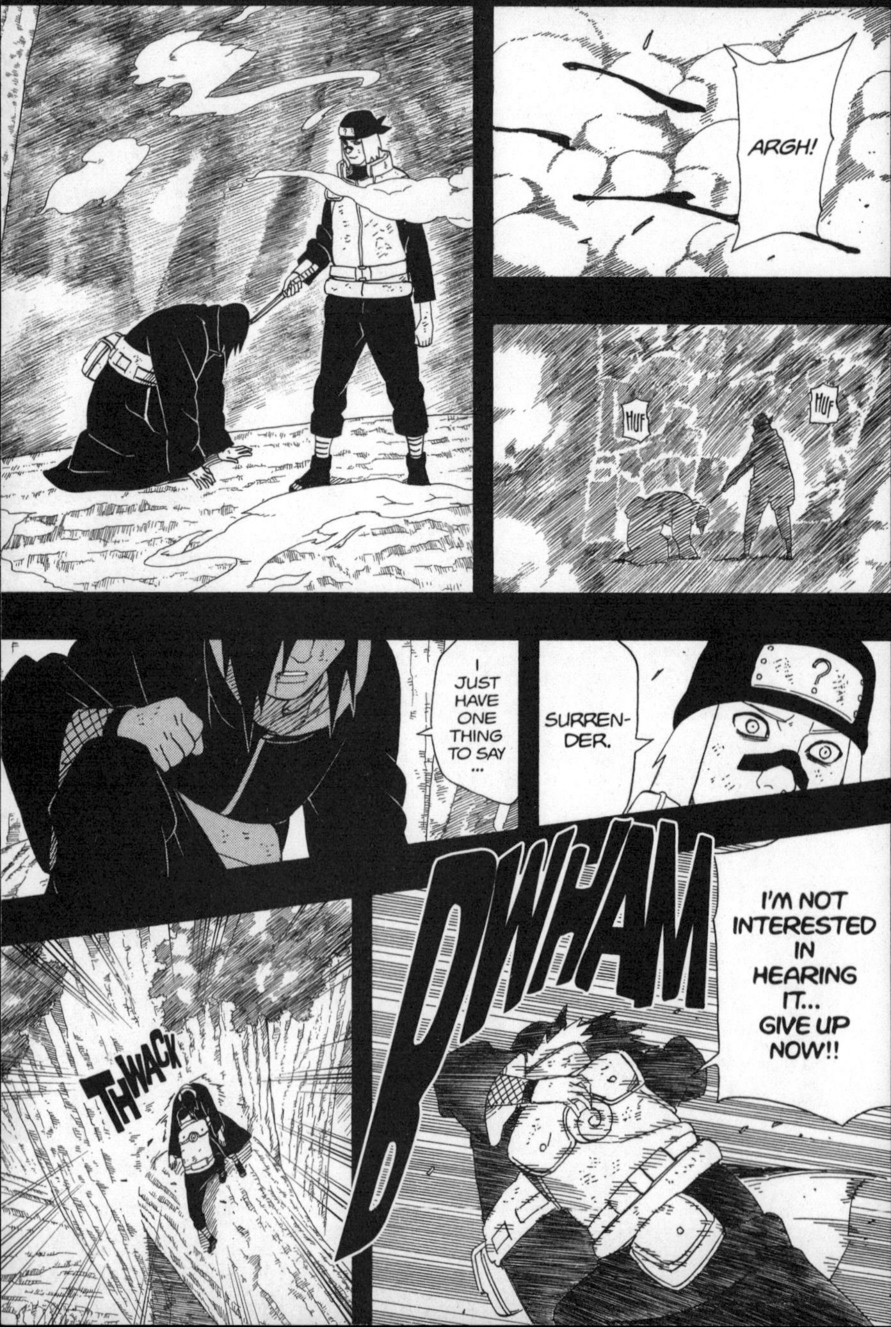

ARGH!
HUF
HUF
SURRENDER.
I JUST HAVE ONE THING TO SAY...
DWHAM
I'M NOT INTERESTED IN HEARING IT... GIVE UP NOW!!
THWACK

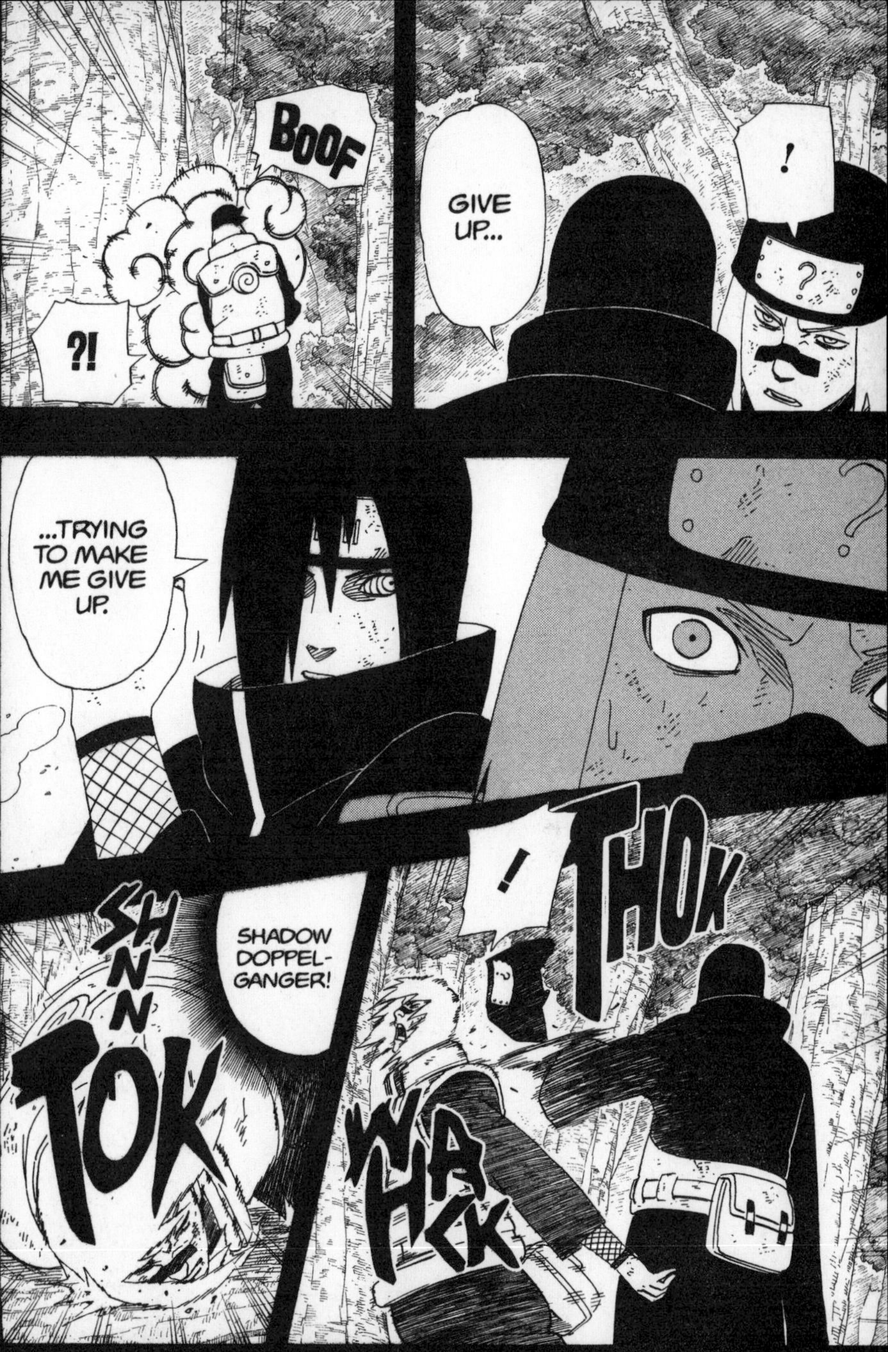
!
GIVE UP...
BOOF
?!
...TRYING TO MAKE ME GIVE UP.
THOK
!
WHACK
SHADOW DOPPEL-GANGER!
SHNN
TOK

READ THIS WAY

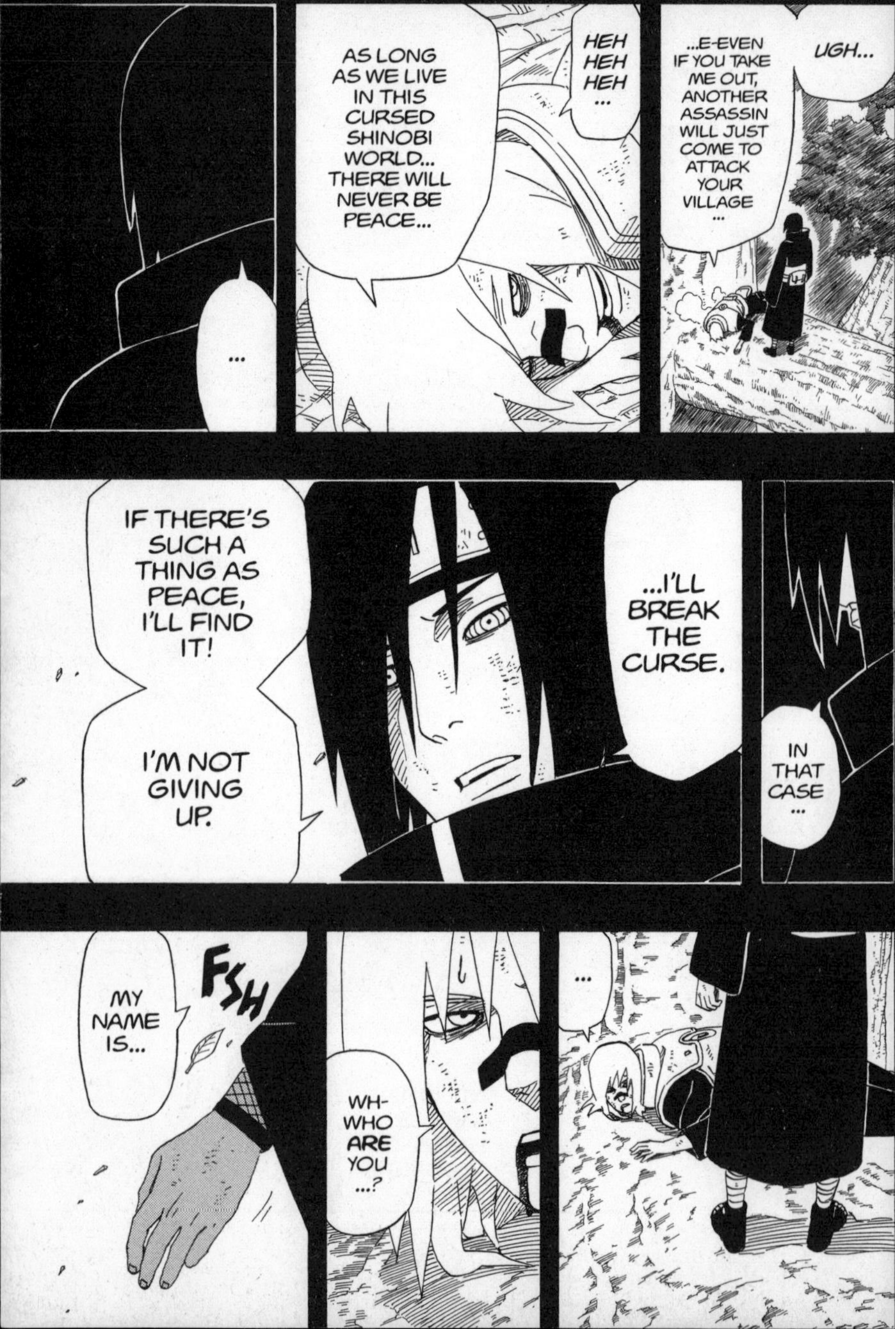
UGH...
...E-EVEN IF YOU TAKE ME OUT, ANOTHER ASSASSIN WILL JUST COME TO ATTACK YOUR VILLAGE...
HEH HEH HEH...
AS LONG AS WE LIVE IN THIS CURSED SHINOBI WORLD... THERE WILL NEVER BE PEACE...
...
IN THAT CASE...
...I'LL BREAK THE CURSE.
IF THERE'S SUCH A THING AS PEACE, I'LL FIND IT!
I'M NOT GIVING UP.
...
WH-WHO ARE YOU...?
FSH
MY NAME IS...

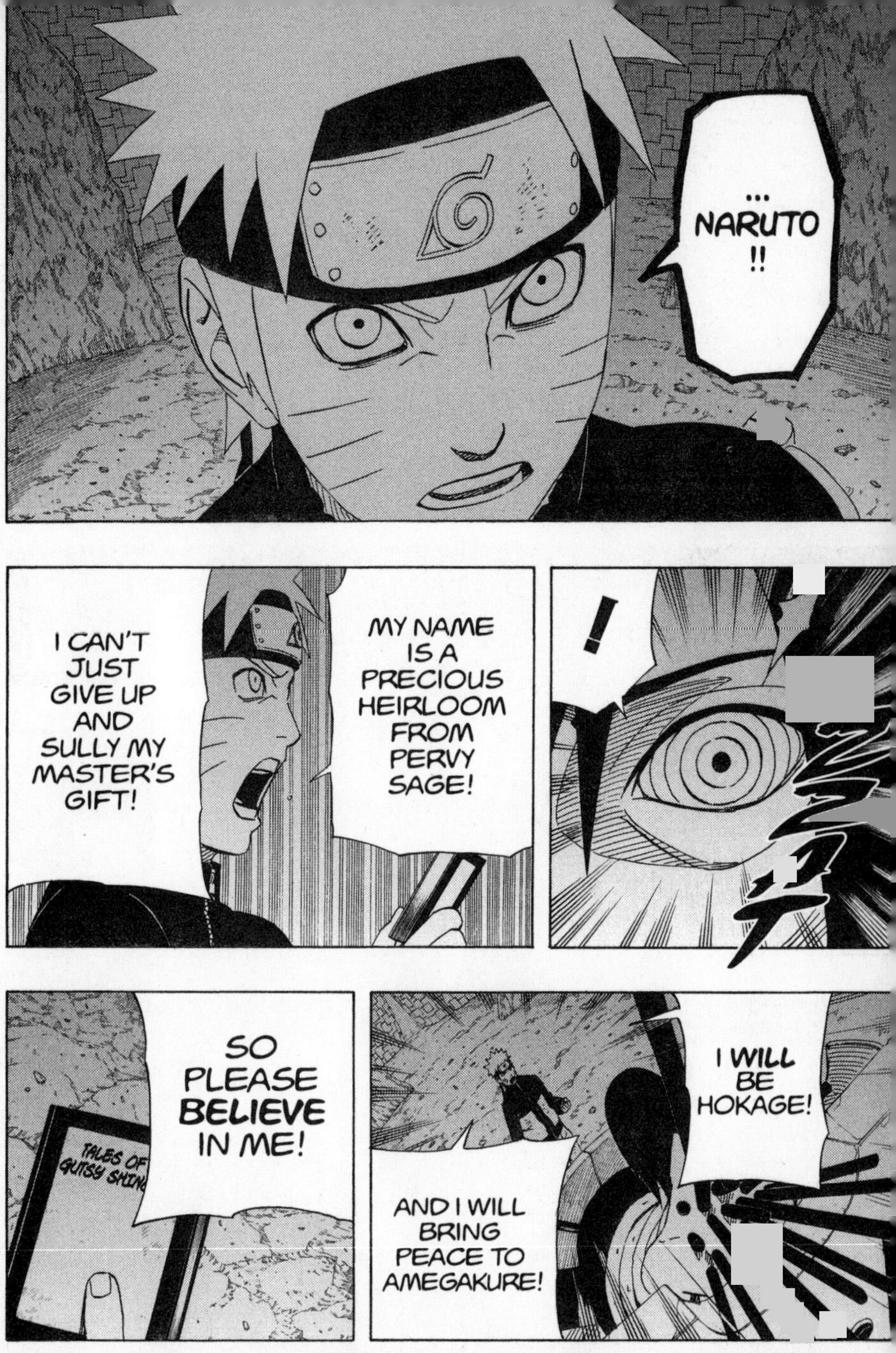
... NARUTO !!
!
MY NAME IS A PRECIOUS HEIRLOOM FROM PERVY SAGE!
I CAN'T JUST GIVE UP AND SULLY MY MASTER'S GIFT!
I WILL BE HOKAGE!
AND I WILL BRING PEACE TO AMEGAKURE!
SO PLEASE **BELIEVE** IN ME!

READ THIS WAY

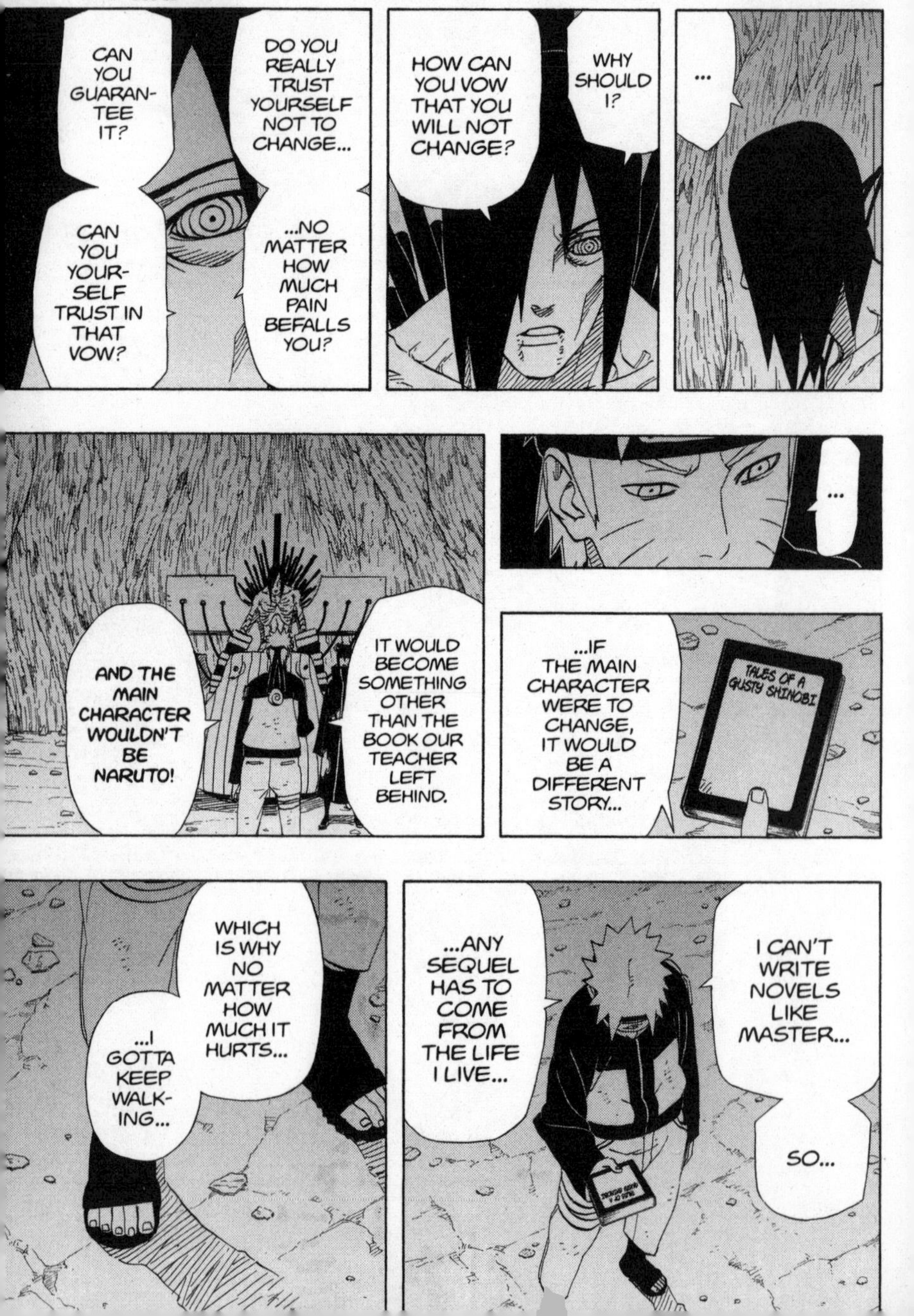
...
WHY SHOULD I?
HOW CAN YOU VOW THAT YOU WILL NOT CHANGE?
DO YOU REALLY TRUST YOURSELF NOT TO CHANGE...
...NO MATTER HOW MUCH PAIN BEFALLS YOU?
CAN YOU GUARANTEE IT?
CAN YOU YOURSELF TRUST IN THAT VOW?
...
TALES OF A GUSTY SHINOBI
...IF THE MAIN CHARACTER WERE TO CHANGE, IT WOULD BE A DIFFERENT STORY...
IT WOULD BECOME SOMETHING OTHER THAN THE BOOK OUR TEACHER LEFT BEHIND.
AND THE MAIN CHARACTER WOULDN'T BE NARUTO!
I CAN'T WRITE NOVELS LIKE MASTER...
SO...
...ANY SEQUEL HAS TO COME FROM THE LIFE I LIVE...
WHICH IS WHY NO MATTER HOW MUCH IT HURTS...
...I GOTTA KEEP WALKING...

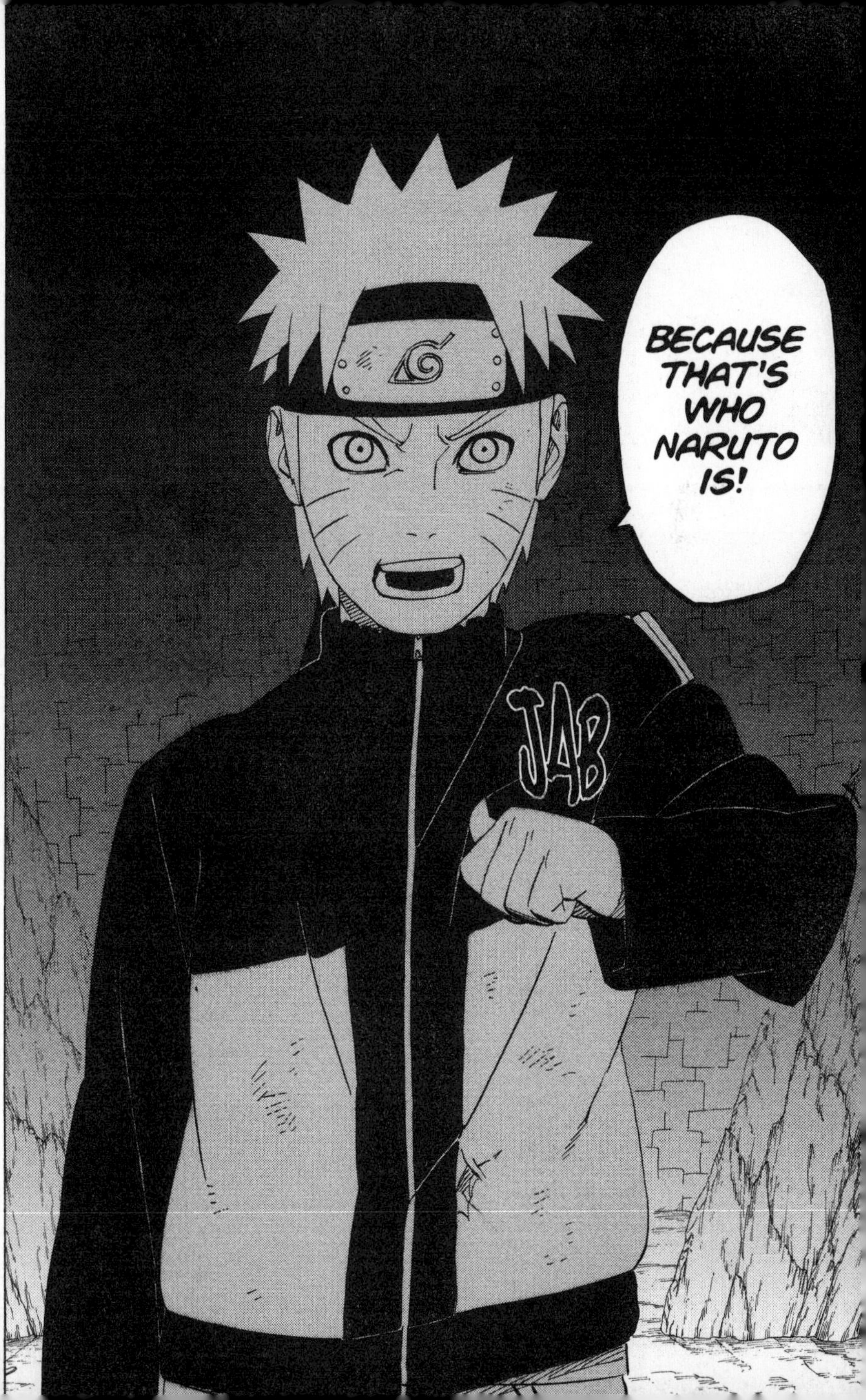
BECAUSE THAT'S WHO NARUTO IS!
JAB

READ THIS WAY

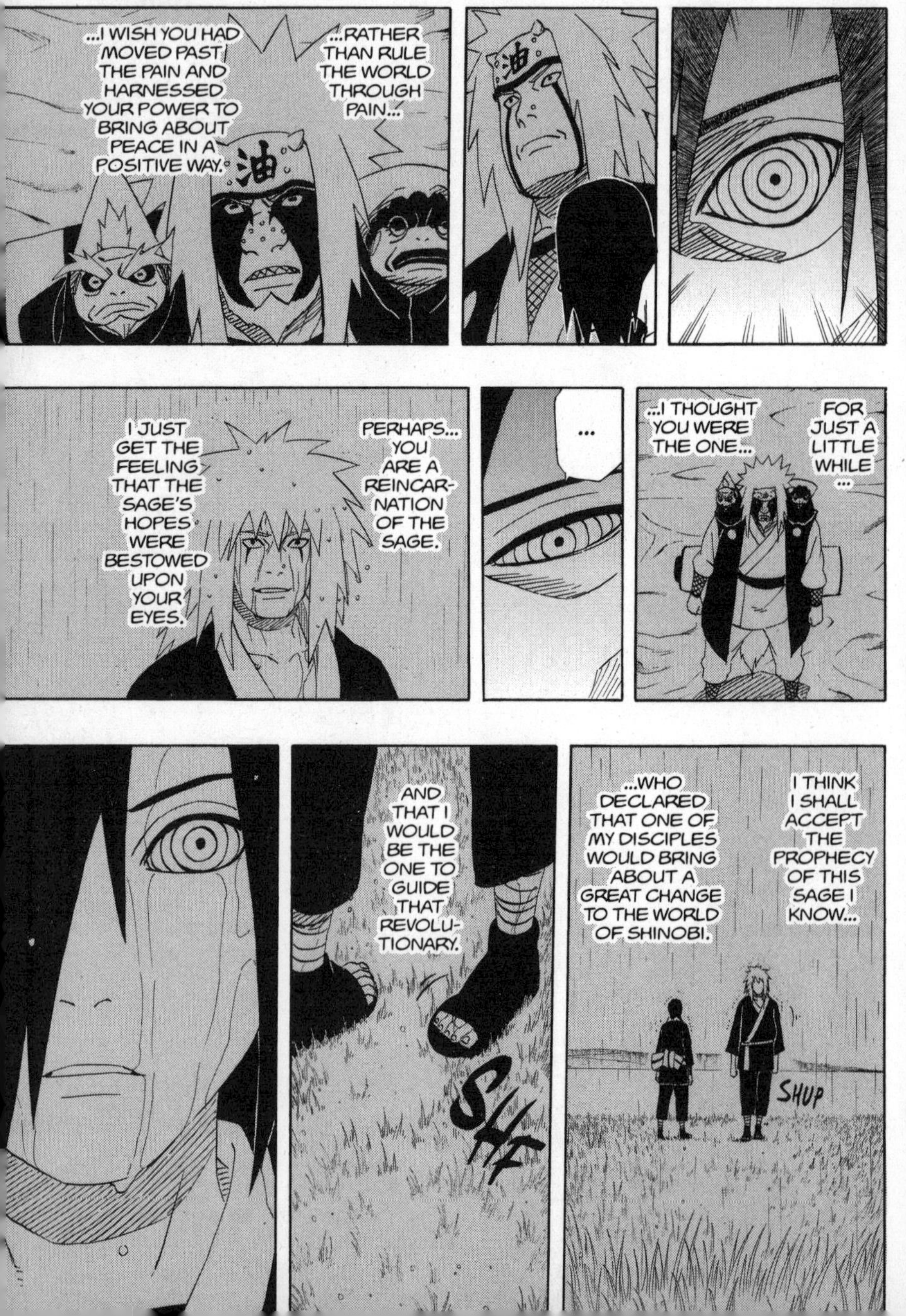
...RATHER THAN RULE THE WORLD THROUGH PAIN...
...I WISH YOU HAD MOVED PAST THE PAIN AND HARNESSED YOUR POWER TO BRING ABOUT PEACE IN A POSITIVE WAY.
FOR JUST A LITTLE WHILE...
...I THOUGHT YOU WERE THE ONE...
...
PERHAPS... YOU ARE A REINCARNATION OF THE SAGE.
I JUST GET THE FEELING THAT THE SAGE'S HOPES WERE BESTOWED UPON YOUR EYES.
I THINK I SHALL ACCEPT THE PROPHECY OF THIS SAGE I KNOW...
...WHO DECLARED THAT ONE OF MY DISCIPLES WOULD BRING ABOUT A GREAT CHANGE TO THE WORLD OF SHINOBI.
SHUP
AND THAT I WOULD BE THE ONE TO GUIDE THAT REVOLUTIONARY.
SHF

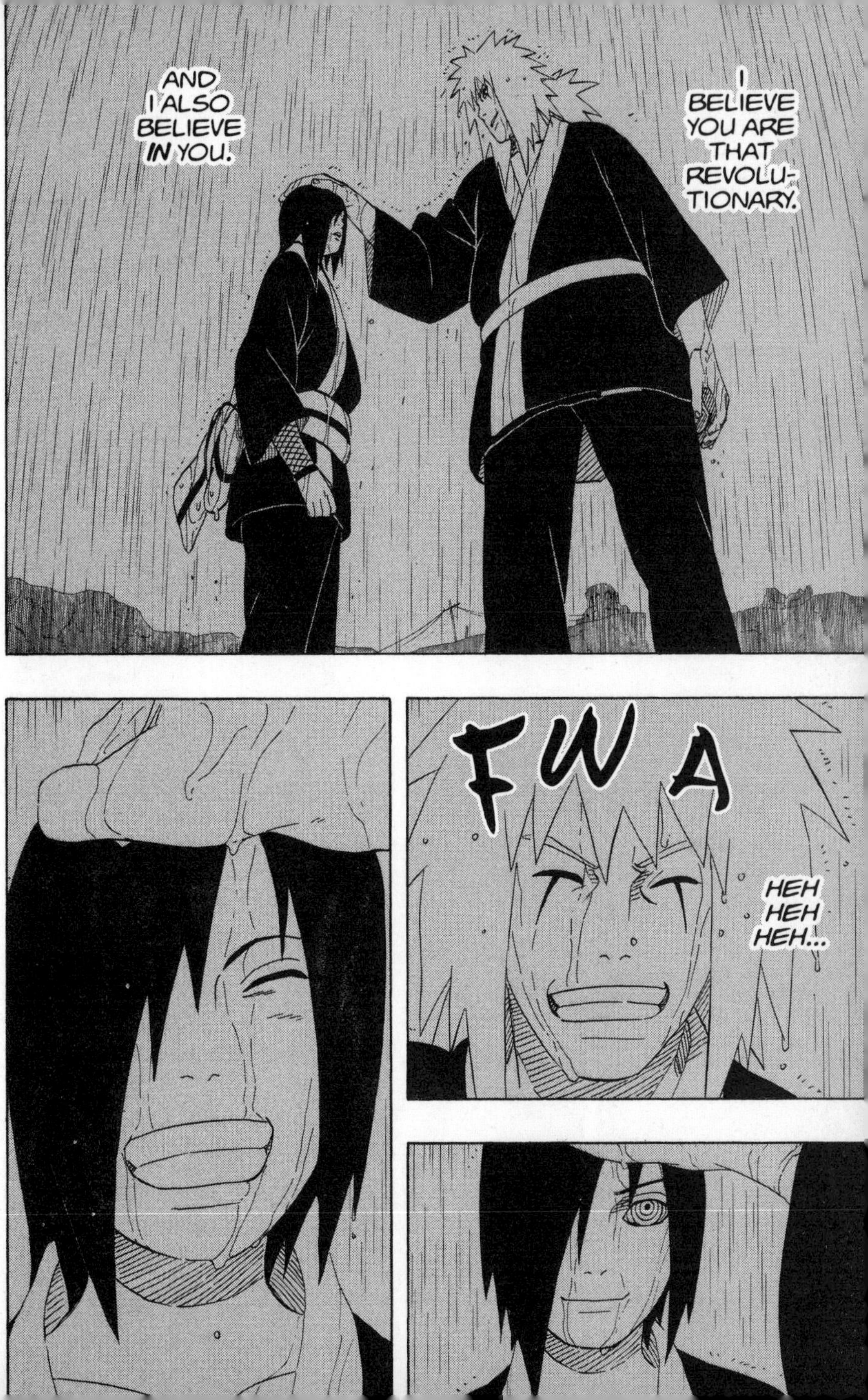
I BELIEVE YOU ARE THAT REVOLUTIONARY.
AND I ALSO BELIEVE **IN** YOU.
FWA
HEH HEH HEH...

READ THIS WAY

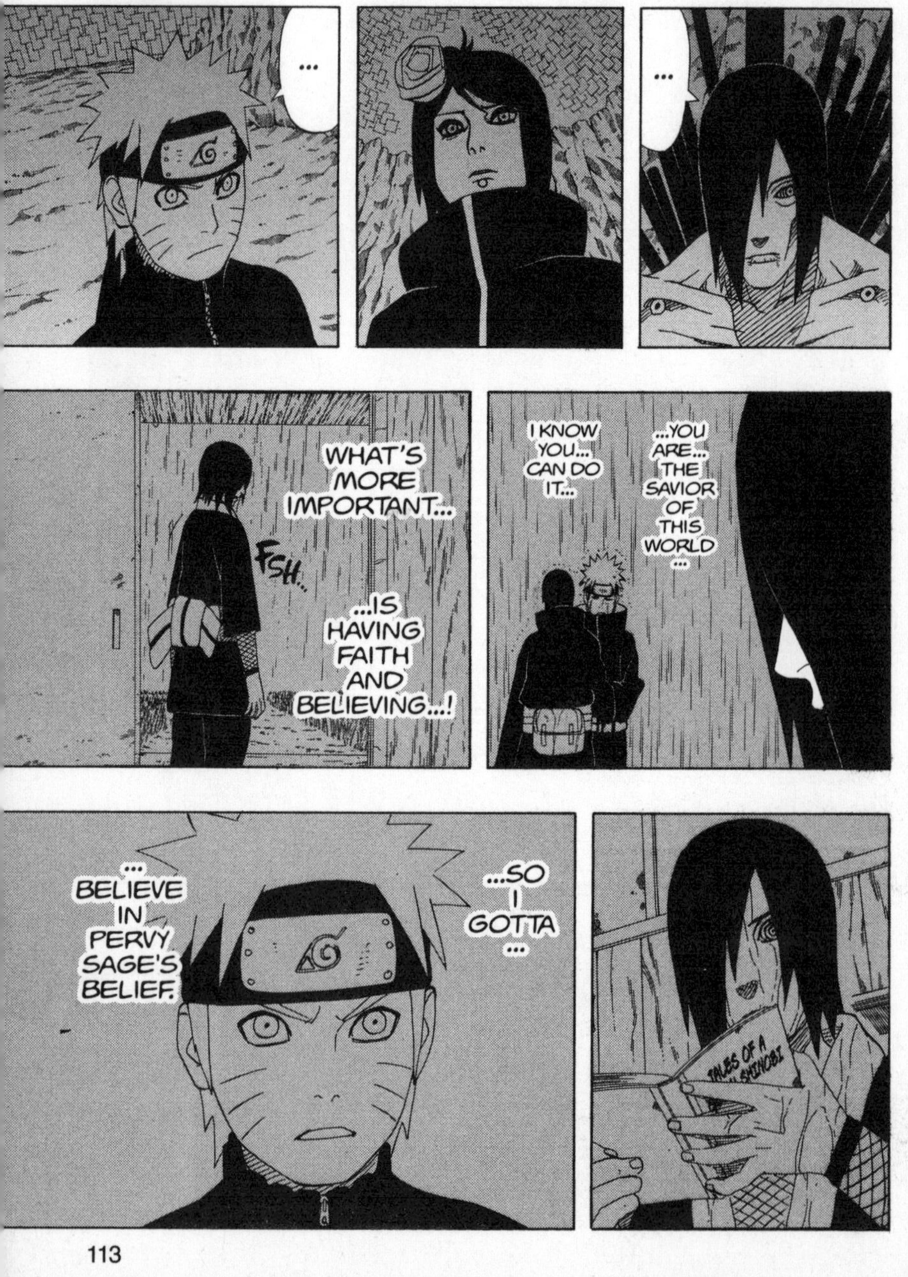
...
...
...YOU ARE... THE SAVIOR OF THIS WORLD...
I KNOW YOU... CAN DO IT...
WHAT'S MORE IMPORTANT...
FSH...
...IS HAVING FAITH AND BELIEVING...!
TALES OF A
SHINOBI
...SO I GOTTA...
...BELIEVE IN PERVY SAGE'S BELIEF.

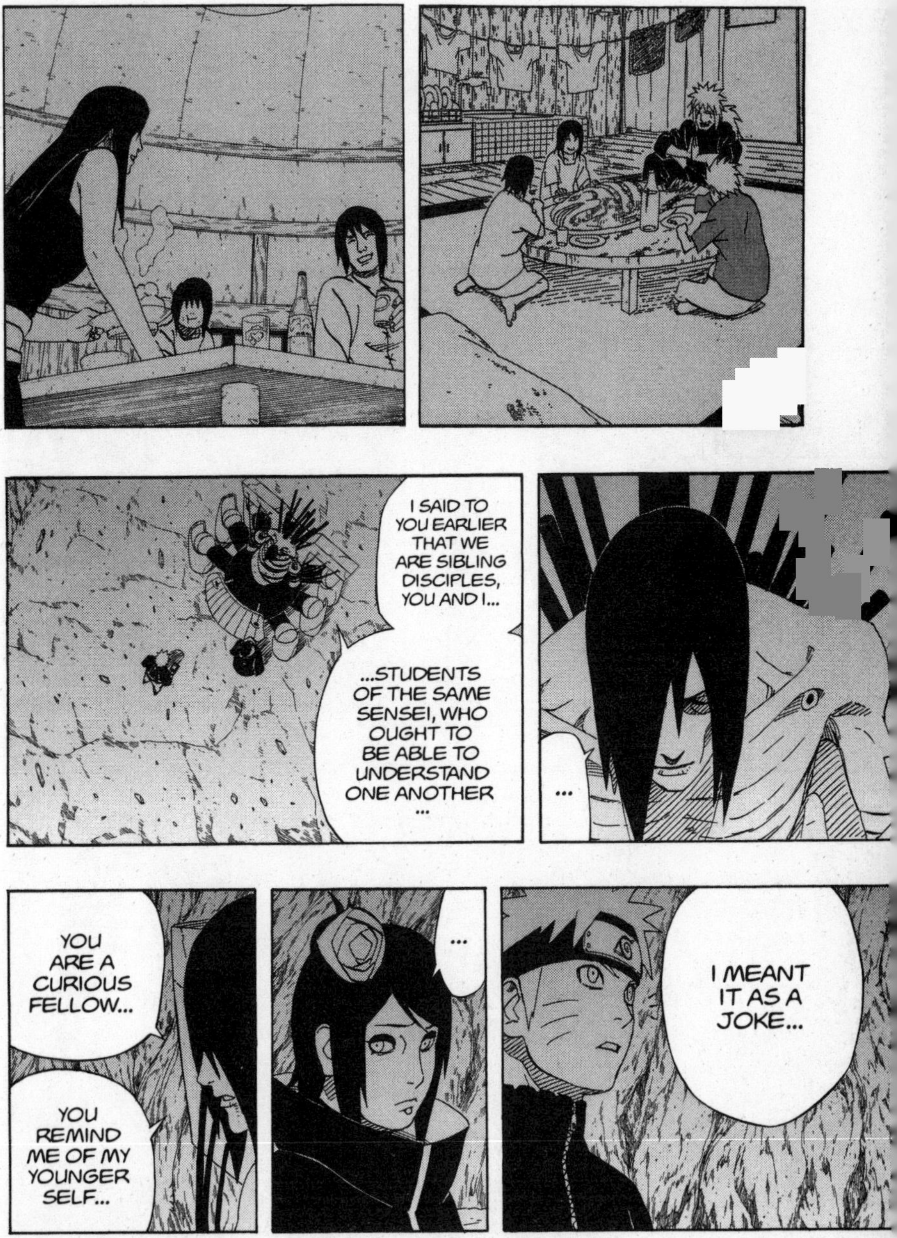
...
I SAID TO YOU EARLIER THAT WE ARE SIBLING DISCIPLES, YOU AND I...
...STUDENTS OF THE SAME SENSEI, WHO OUGHT TO BE ABLE TO UNDERSTAND ONE ANOTHER ...
I MEANT IT AS A JOKE...
...
YOU ARE A CURIOUS FELLOW...
YOU REMIND ME OF MY YOUNGER SELF...

READ THIS WAY

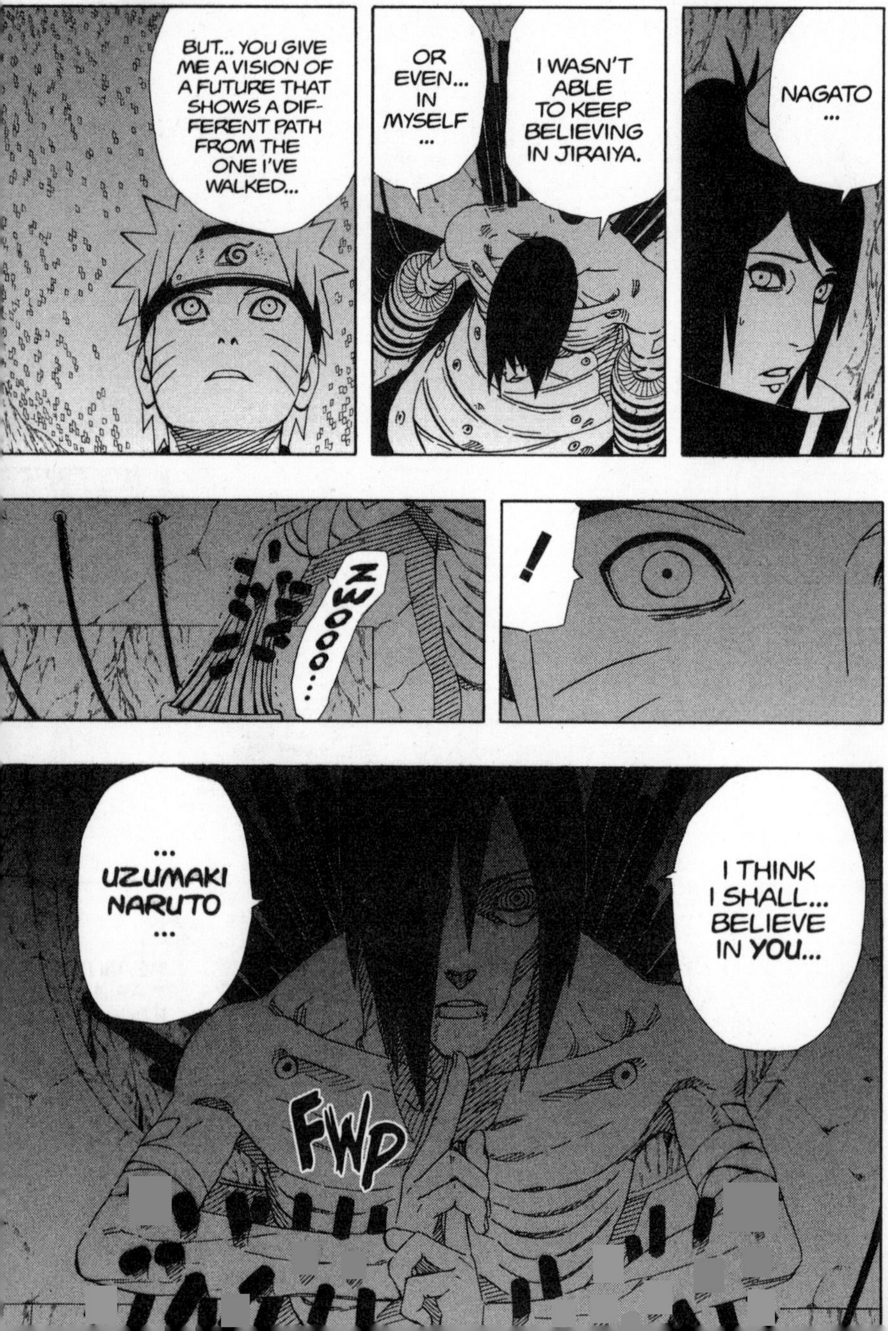
NAGATO ...
I WASN'T ABLE TO KEEP BELIEVING IN JIRAIYA.
OR EVEN... IN MYSELF ...
BUT... YOU GIVE ME A VISION OF A FUTURE THAT SHOWS A DIF-FERENT PATH FROM THE ONE I'VE WALKED...
!
ZWOOOO...
I THINK I SHALL... BELIEVE IN YOU...
... UZUMAKI NARUTO ...
FWD

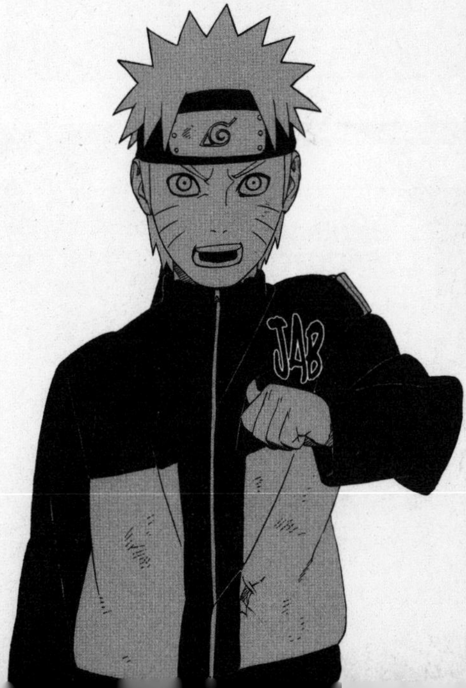
JAB

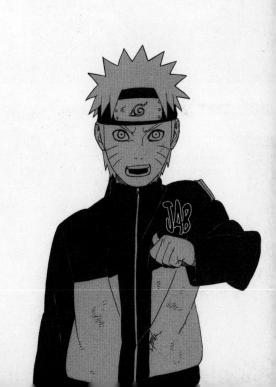

Number 449: The Blossom of Hope

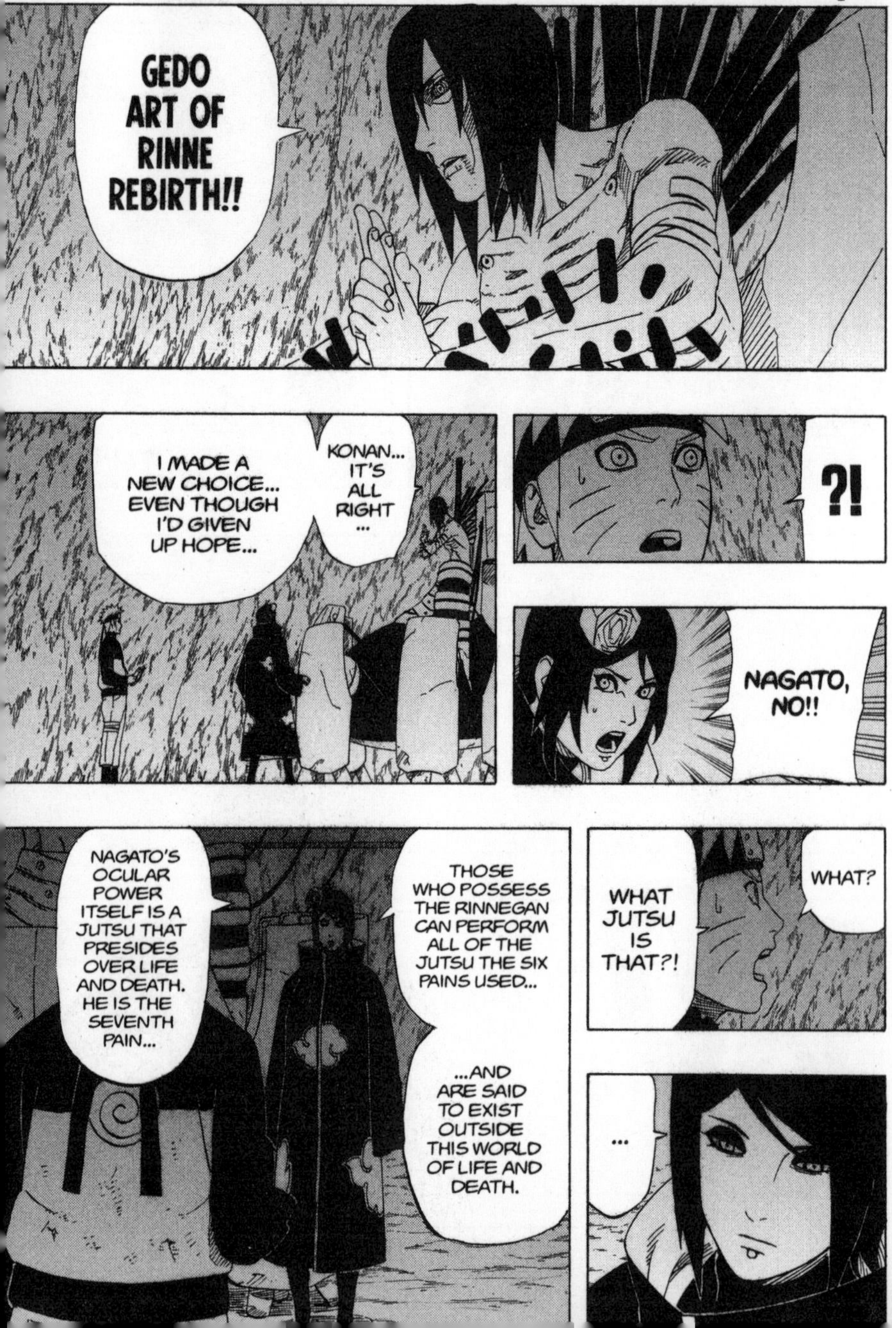

GEDO ART OF RINNE REBIRTH!!
?!
NAGATO, NO!!
KONAN... IT'S ALL RIGHT...
I MADE A NEW CHOICE... EVEN THOUGH I'D GIVEN UP HOPE...
WHAT?
WHAT JUTSU IS THAT?!
...
THOSE WHO POSSESS THE RINNEGAN CAN PERFORM ALL OF THE JUTSU THE SIX PAINS USED...
...AND ARE SAID TO EXIST OUTSIDE THIS WORLD OF LIFE AND DEATH.
NAGATO'S OCULAR POWER ITSELF IS A JUTSU THAT PRESIDES OVER LIFE AND DEATH. HE IS THE SEVENTH PAIN...

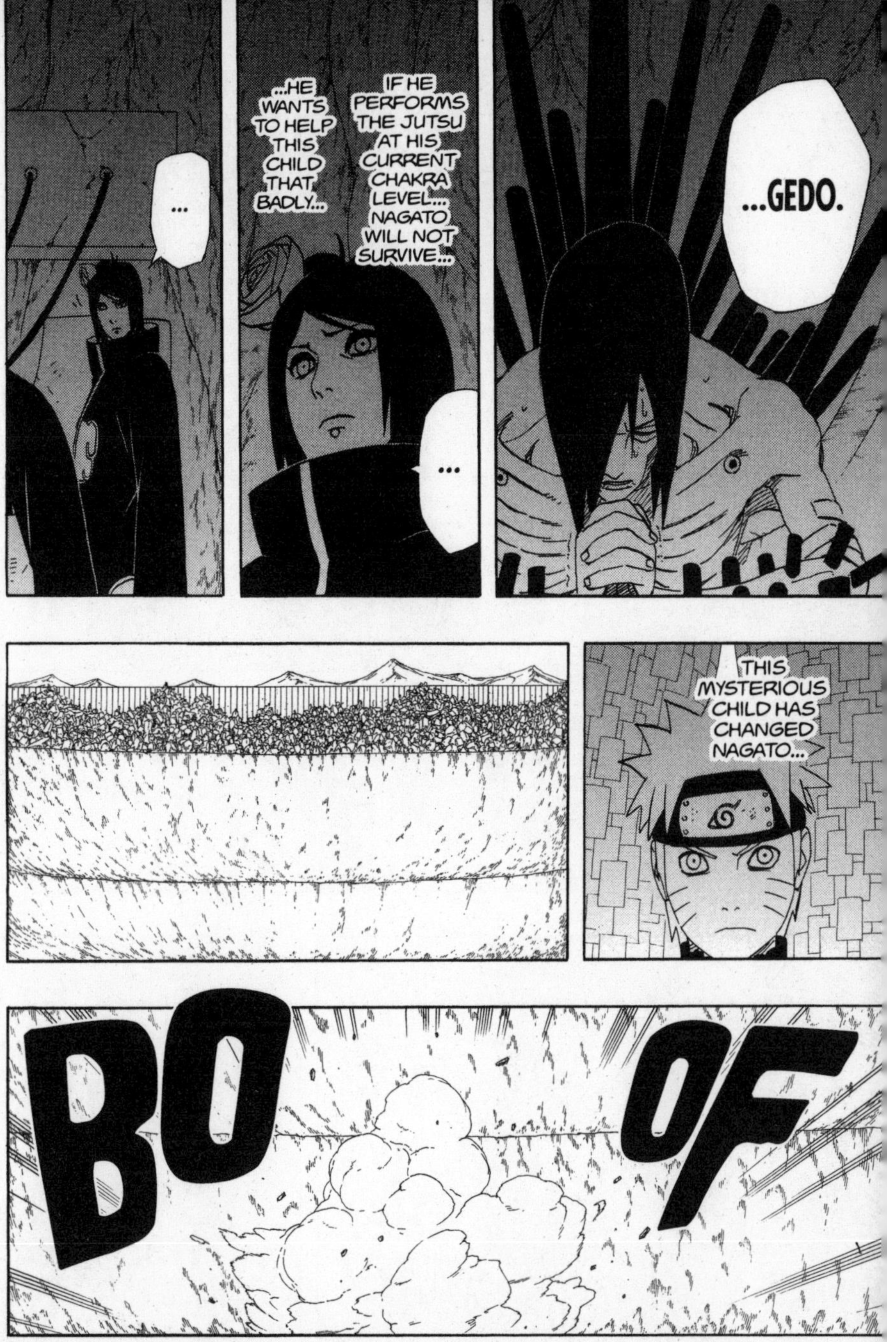
...GEDO.
IF HE PERFORMS THE JUTSU AT HIS CURRENT CHAKRA LEVEL... NAGATO WILL NOT SURVIVE...
...HE WANTS TO HELP THIS CHILD THAT BADLY...
...
...
THIS MYSTERIOUS CHILD HAS CHANGED NAGATO...
BOOF

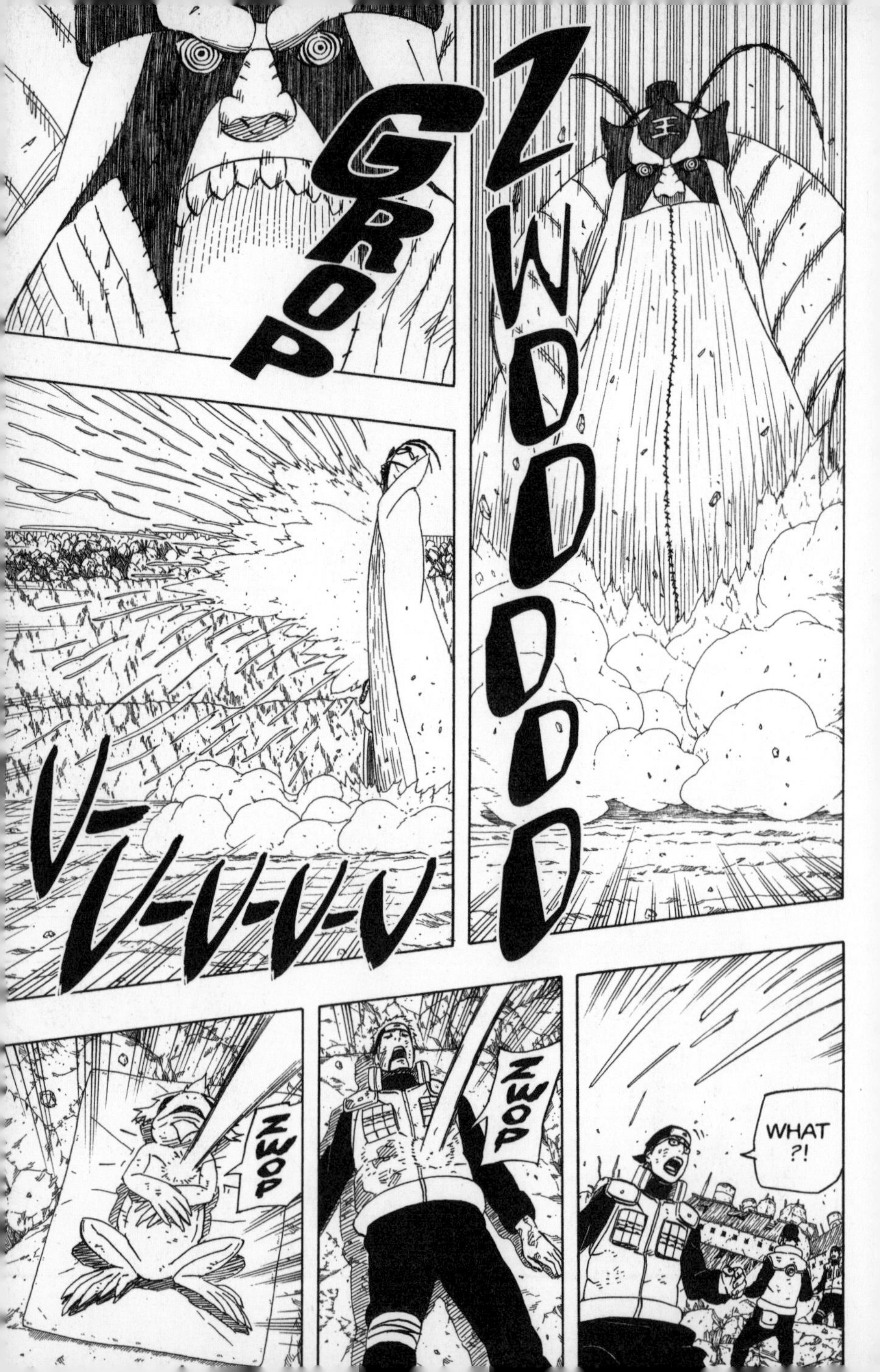
ZWOOOOO
GROP
V-V-V-V-V-V
WHAT ?!
ZWOP
ZWOP

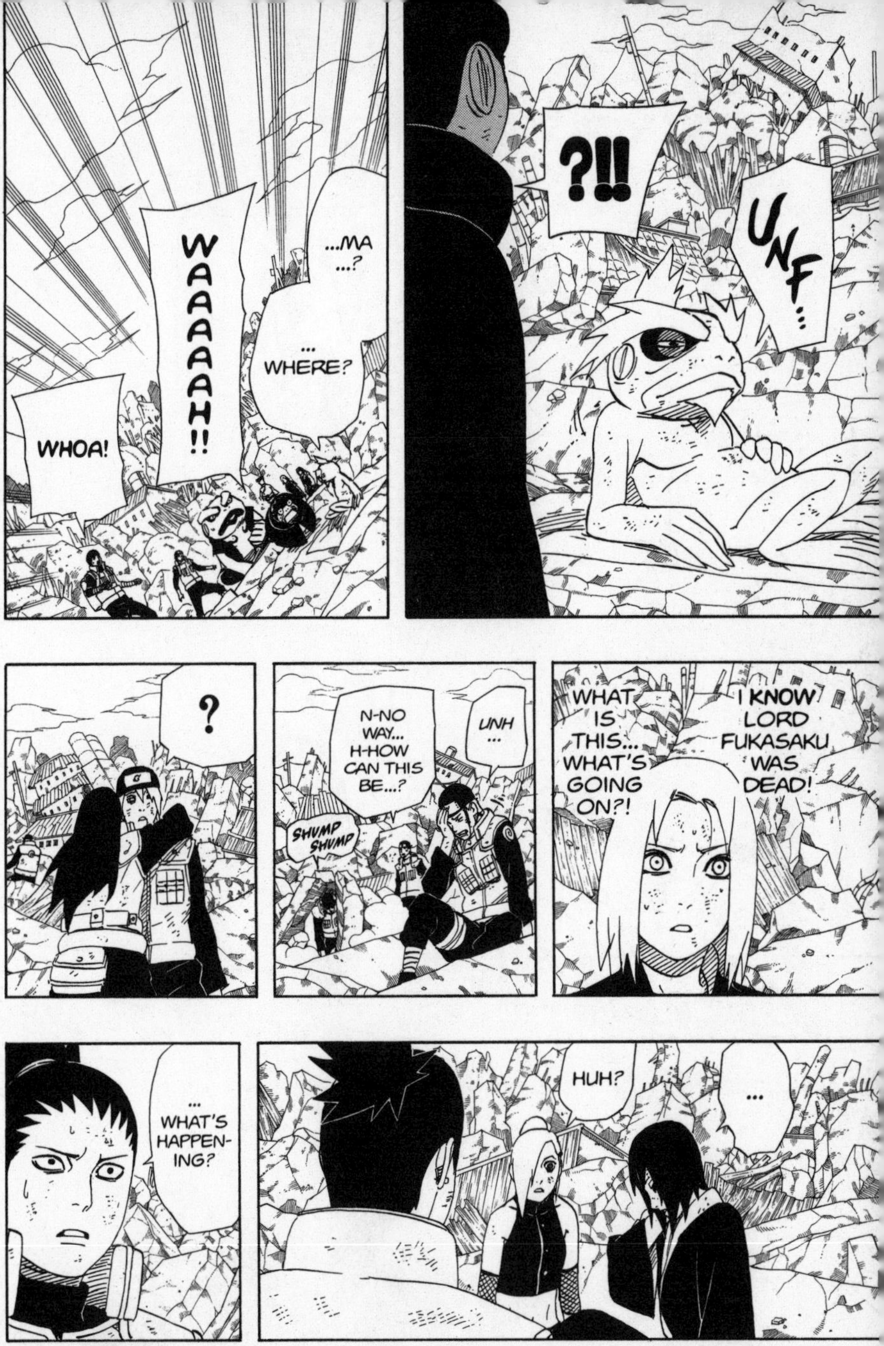
?!!
UNF...
...MA ...?
... WHERE?
WAAAAAAH!!
WHOA!
I KNOW LORD FUKASAKU WAS DEAD!
WHAT IS THIS... WHAT'S GOING ON?!
UNH ...
N-NO WAY... H-HOW CAN THIS BE...?
SHUMP SHUMP
?
...
HUH?
... WHAT'S HAPPEN-ING?

READ THIS WAY

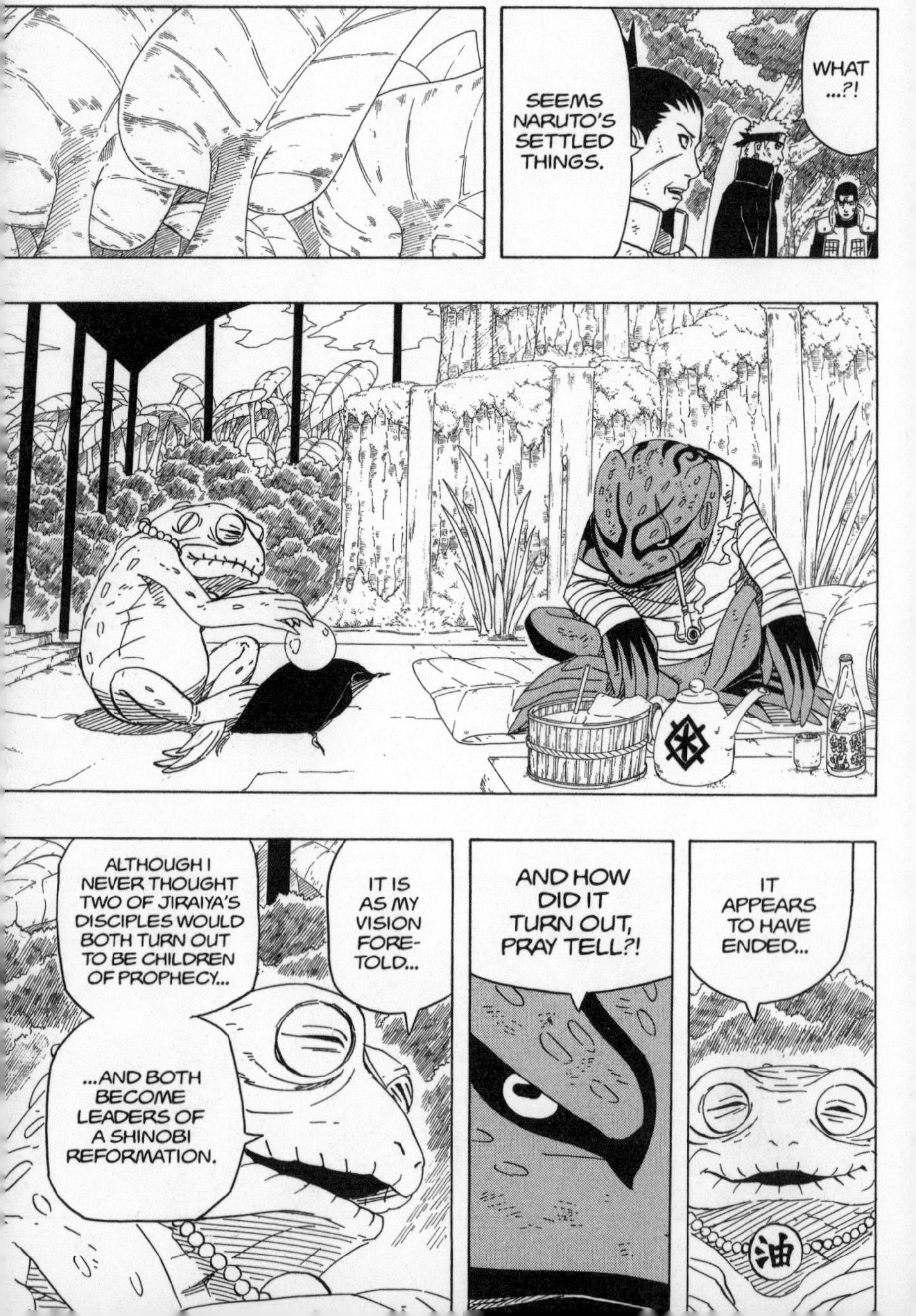
WHAT ...?!
SEEMS NARUTO'S SETTLED THINGS.
IT APPEARS TO HAVE ENDED...
AND HOW DID IT TURN OUT, PRAY TELL?!
IT IS AS MY VISION FORE-TOLD...
ALTHOUGH I NEVER THOUGHT TWO OF JIRAIYA'S DISCIPLES WOULD BOTH TURN OUT TO BE CHILDREN OF PROPHECY...
...AND BOTH BECOME LEADERS OF A SHINOBI REFORMATION.

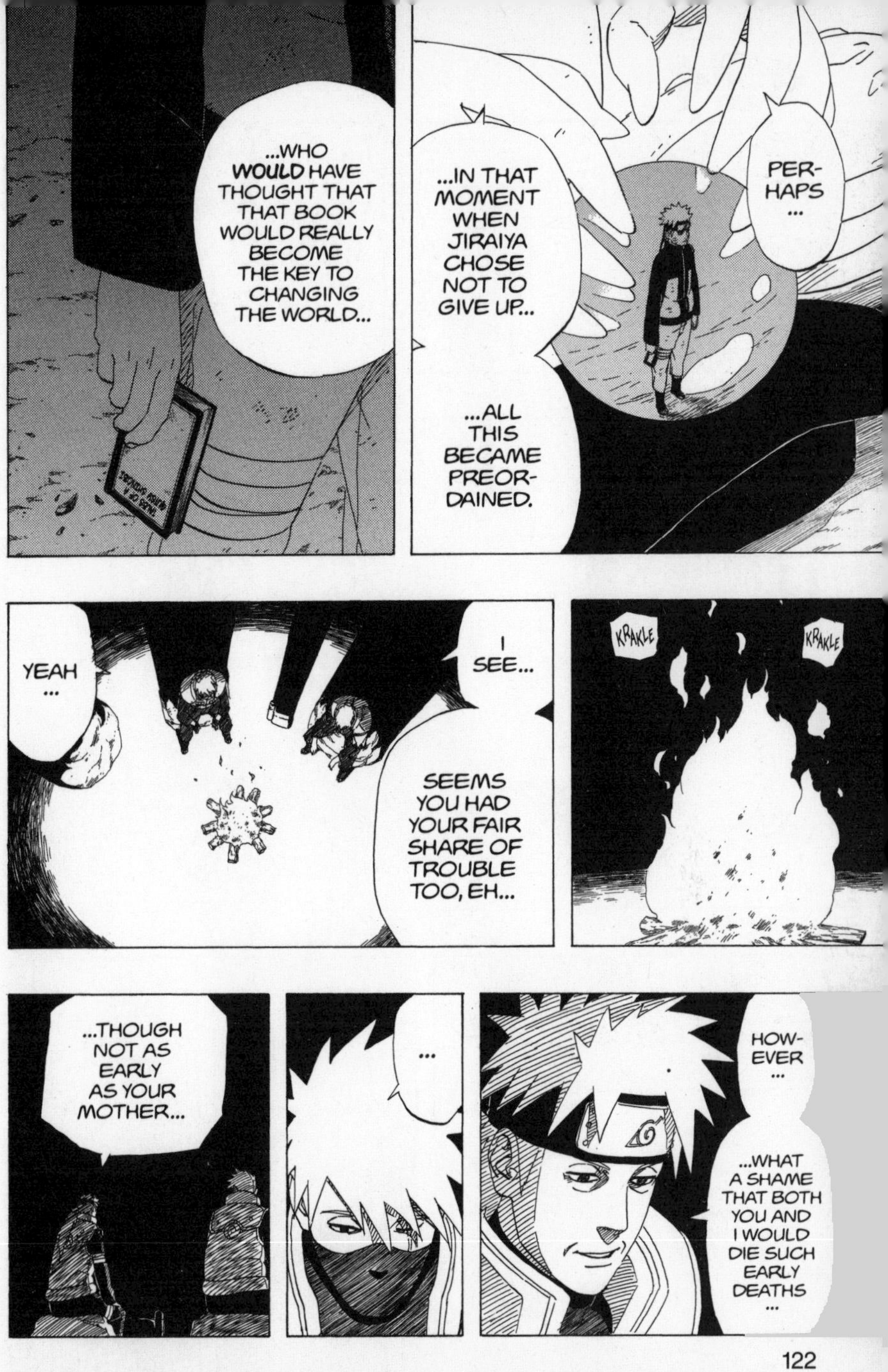
PER-HAPS ...
...IN THAT MOMENT WHEN JIRAIYA CHOSE NOT TO GIVE UP...
...ALL THIS BECAME PREOR-DAINED.
...WHO **WOULD** HAVE THOUGHT THAT THAT BOOK WOULD REALLY BECOME THE KEY TO CHANGING THE WORLD...
KRAKLE
KRAKLE
I SEE...
SEEMS YOU HAD YOUR FAIR SHARE OF TROUBLE TOO, EH...
YEAH ...
HOW-EVER ...
...WHAT A SHAME THAT BOTH YOU AND I WOULD DIE SUCH EARLY DEATHS ...
...
...THOUGH NOT AS EARLY AS YOUR MOTHER...

READ THIS WAY

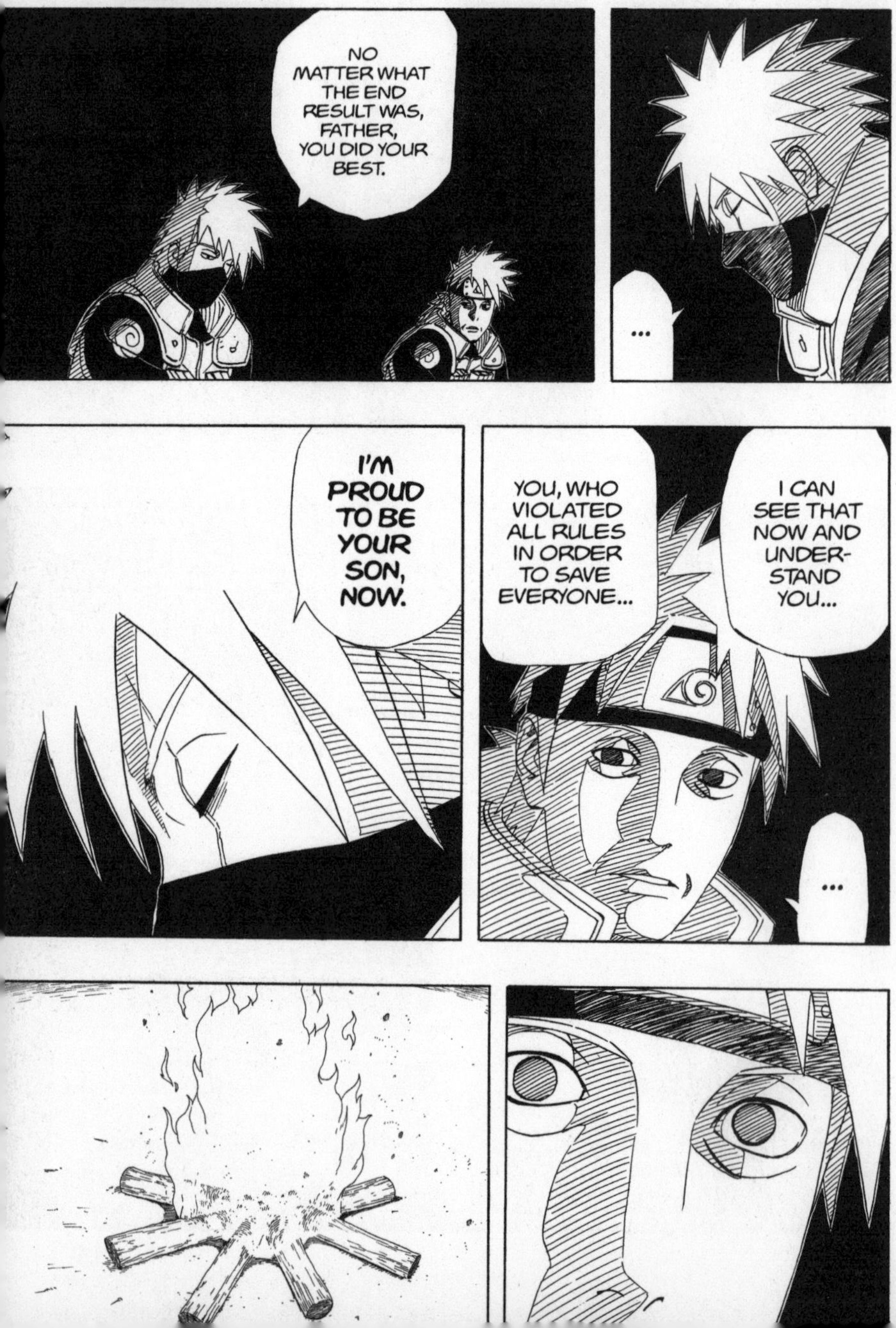
...
NO MATTER WHAT THE END RESULT WAS, FATHER, YOU DID YOUR BEST.
I CAN SEE THAT NOW AND UNDER-STAND YOU...
YOU, WHO VIOLATED ALL RULES IN ORDER TO SAVE EVERYONE...
...
I'M PROUD TO BE YOUR SON, NOW.

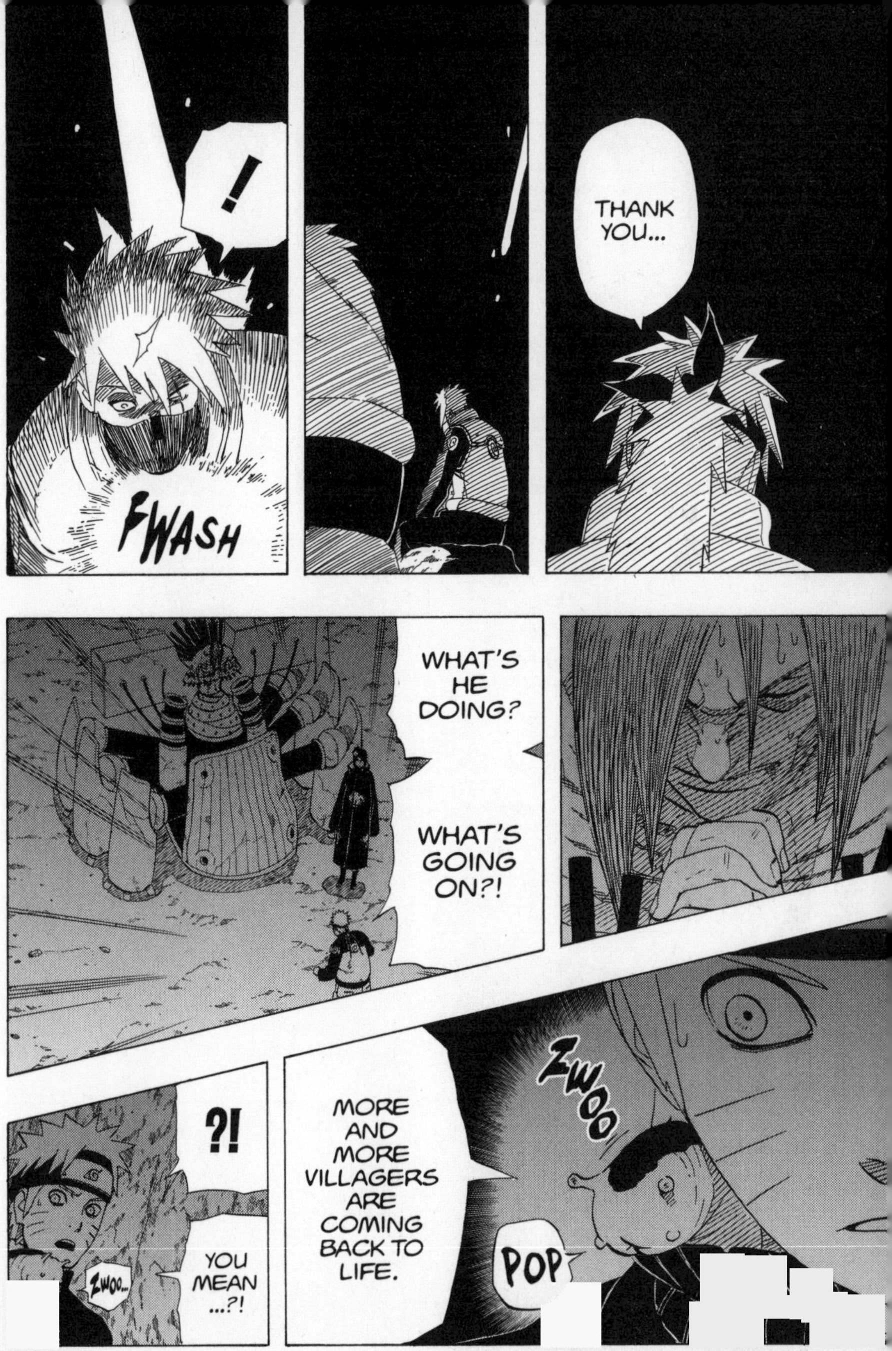
THANK YOU...
!
FWASH
WHAT'S HE DOING?
WHAT'S GOING ON?!
ZWOO
POP
MORE AND MORE VILLAGERS ARE COMING BACK TO LIFE.
?!
YOU MEAN ...?!
ZWOO...

READ THIS WAY

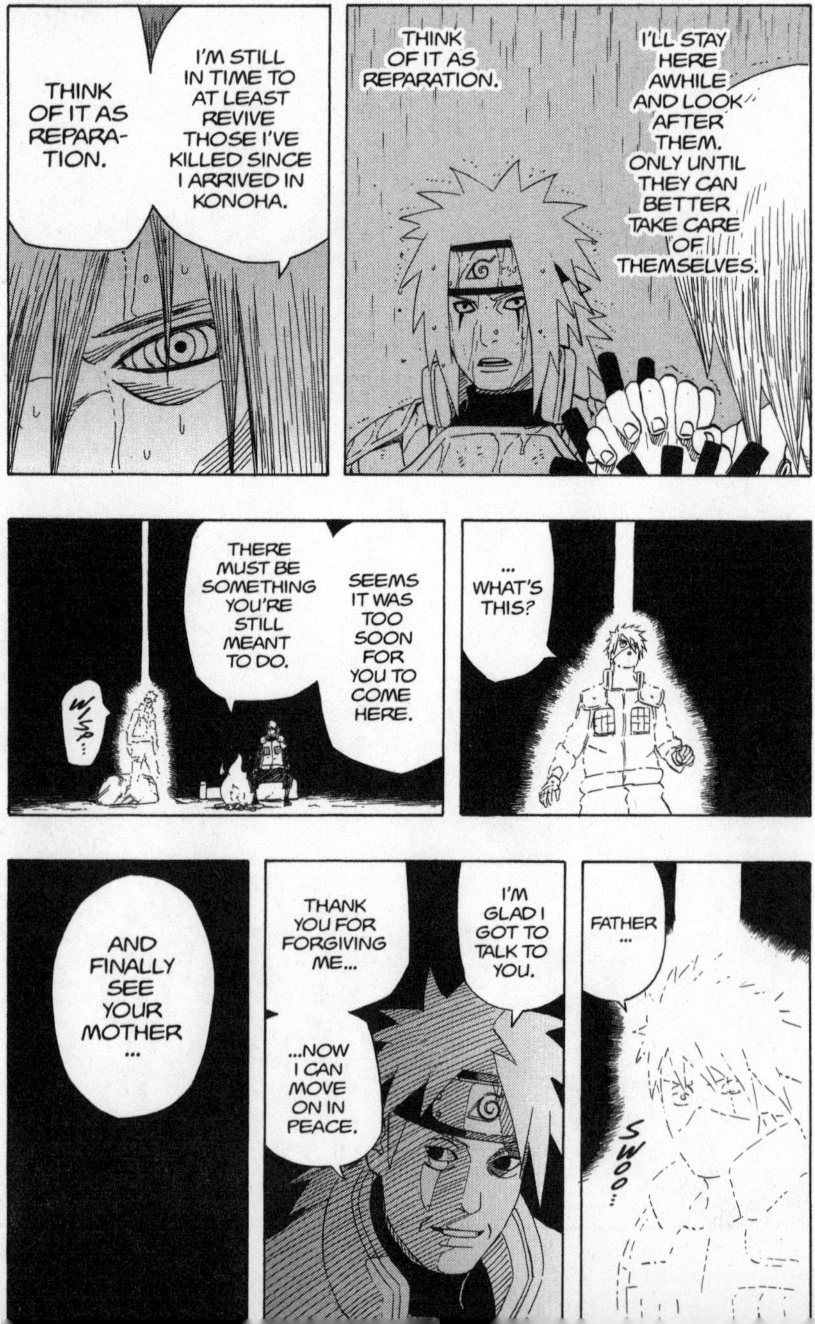
I'LL STAY HERE AWHILE AND LOOK AFTER THEM. ONLY UNTIL THEY CAN BETTER TAKE CARE OF THEMSELVES.
THINK OF IT AS REPARATION.
I'M STILL IN TIME TO AT LEAST REVIVE THOSE I'VE KILLED SINCE I ARRIVED IN KONOHA.
THINK OF IT AS REPARA-TION.
... WHAT'S THIS?
SEEMS IT WAS TOO SOON FOR YOU TO COME HERE.
THERE MUST BE SOMETHING YOU'RE STILL MEANT TO DO.
FATHER...
SWOO...
I'M GLAD I GOT TO TALK TO YOU.
THANK YOU FOR FORGIVING ME...
...NOW I CAN MOVE ON IN PEACE.
AND FINALLY SEE YOUR MOTHER...

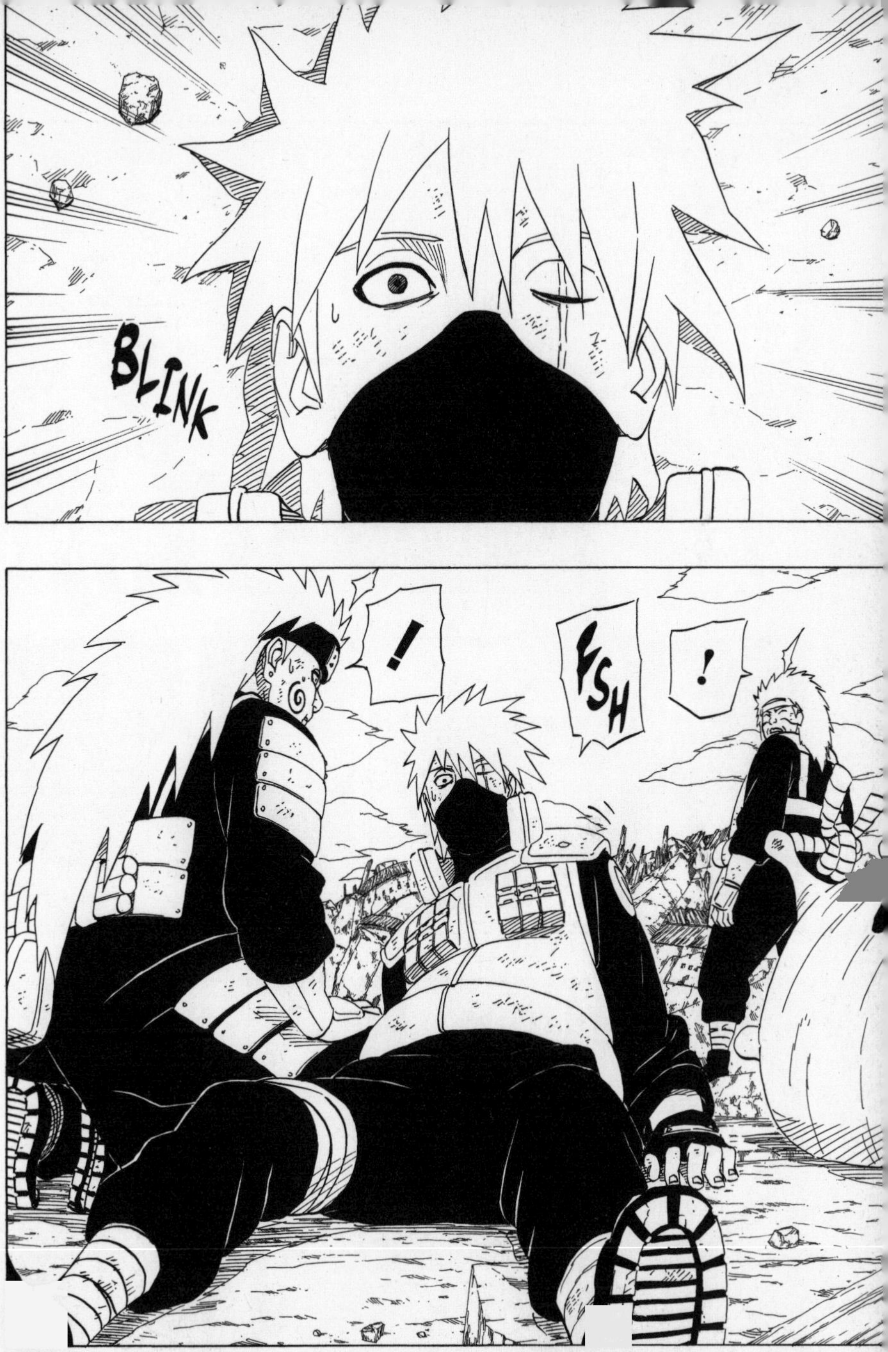
BLINK
!
FSH
!

READ THIS WAY

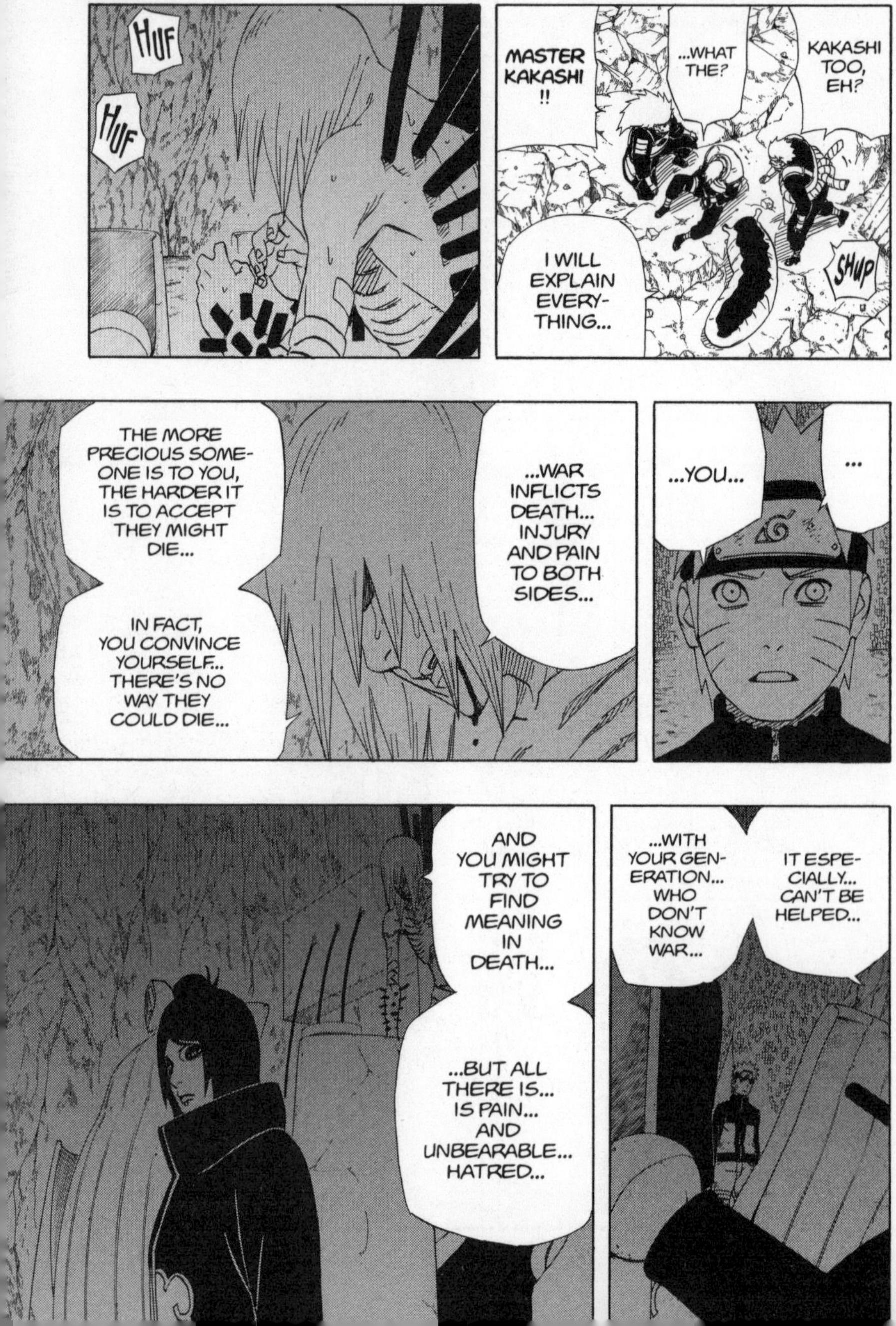
KAKASHI TOO, EH?
...WHAT THE?
MASTER KAKASHI !!
SHUP
I WILL EXPLAIN EVERY-THING...
HUF
HUF
...
...YOU...
...WAR INFLICTS DEATH... INJURY AND PAIN TO BOTH SIDES...
THE MORE PRECIOUS SOME-ONE IS TO YOU, THE HARDER IT IS TO ACCEPT THEY MIGHT DIE...
IN FACT, YOU CONVINCE YOURSELF... THERE'S NO WAY THEY COULD DIE...
IT ESPE-CIALLY... CAN'T BE HELPED...
...WITH YOUR GEN-ERATION... WHO DON'T KNOW WAR...
AND YOU MIGHT TRY TO FIND MEANING IN DEATH...
...BUT ALL THERE IS... IS PAIN... AND UNBEARABLE... HATRED...

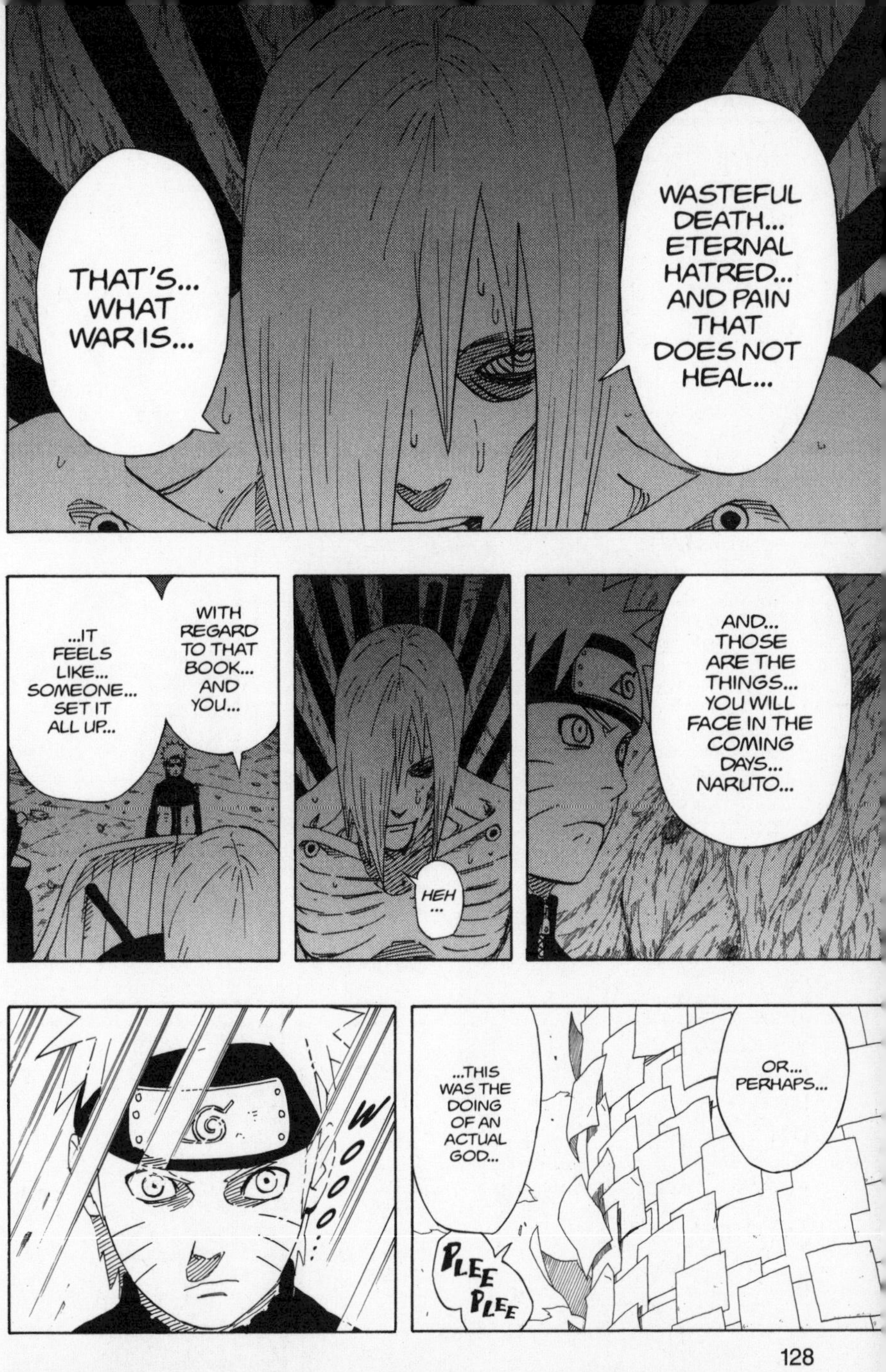
WASTEFUL DEATH... ETERNAL HATRED... AND PAIN THAT DOES NOT HEAL...
THAT'S... WHAT WAR IS...
AND... THOSE ARE THE THINGS... YOU WILL FACE IN THE COMING DAYS... NARUTO...
HEH...
WITH REGARD TO THAT BOOK... AND YOU...
...IT FEELS LIKE... SOMEONE... SET IT ALL UP...
OR... PERHAPS...
...THIS WAS THE DOING OF AN ACTUAL GOD...
PLEE PLEE
WOOOOO

READ THIS WAY

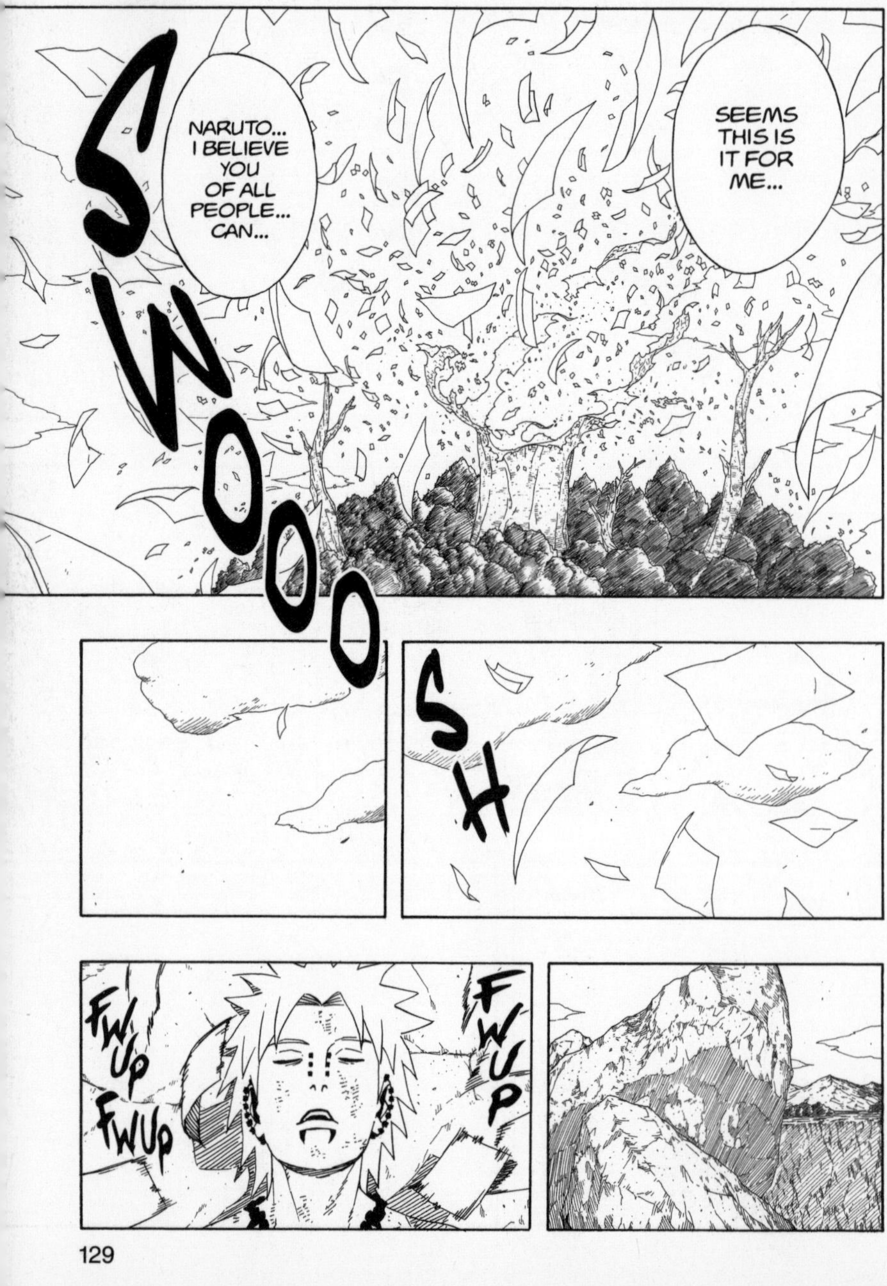
SEEMS THIS IS IT FOR ME...
NARUTO... I BELIEVE YOU OF ALL PEOPLE... CAN...
SWOOOOSH
FWUP
FWUP
FWUP

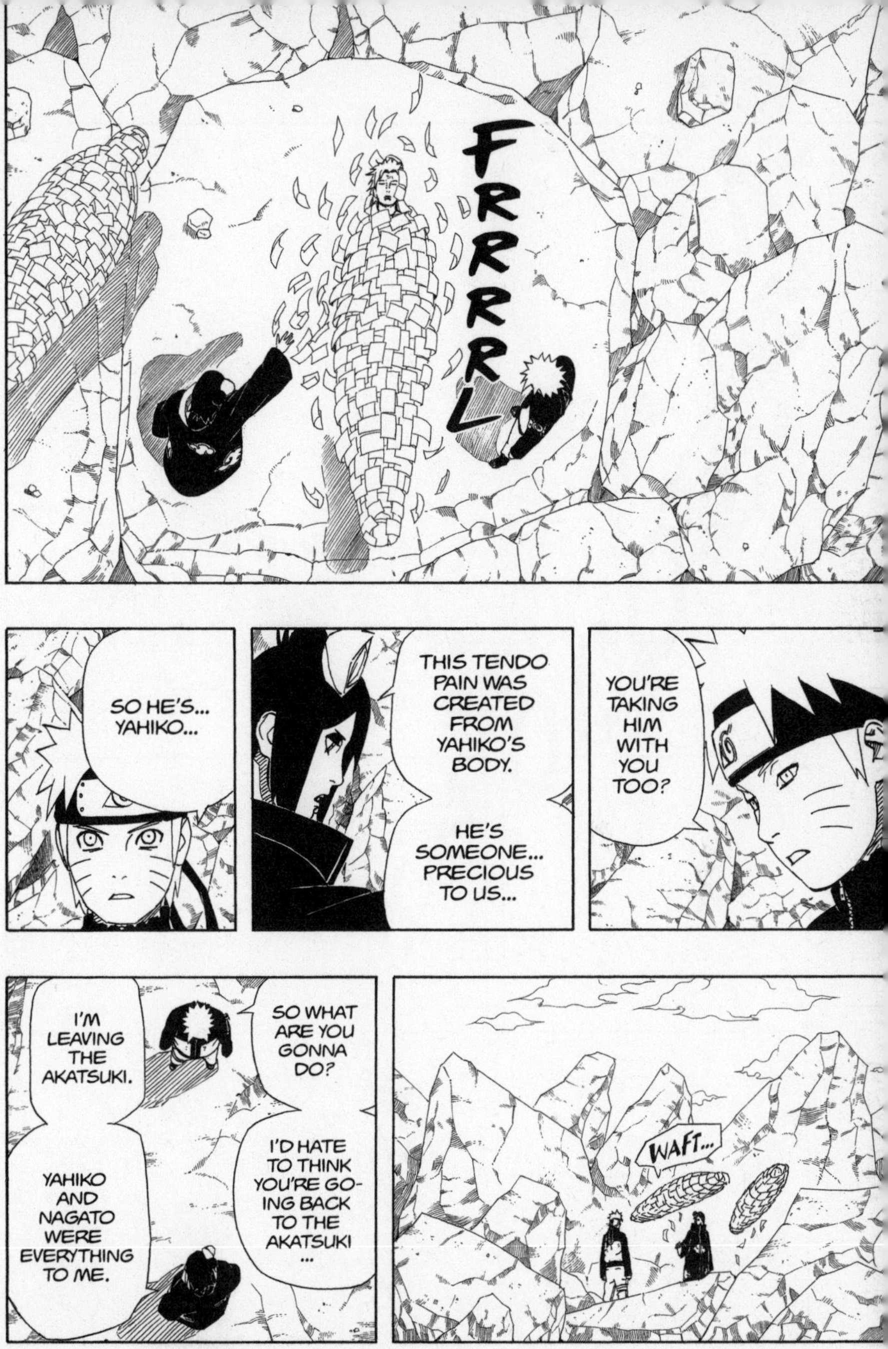
FRRRRL
YOU'RE TAKING HIM WITH YOU TOO?
THIS TENDO PAIN WAS CREATED FROM YAHIKO'S BODY.
HE'S SOMEONE... PRECIOUS TO US...
SO HE'S... YAHIKO...
WAFT...
SO WHAT ARE YOU GONNA DO?
I'D HATE TO THINK YOU'RE GO-ING BACK TO THE AKATSUKI...
I'M LEAVING THE AKATSUKI.
YAHIKO AND NAGATO WERE EVERYTHING TO ME.

READ THIS WAY

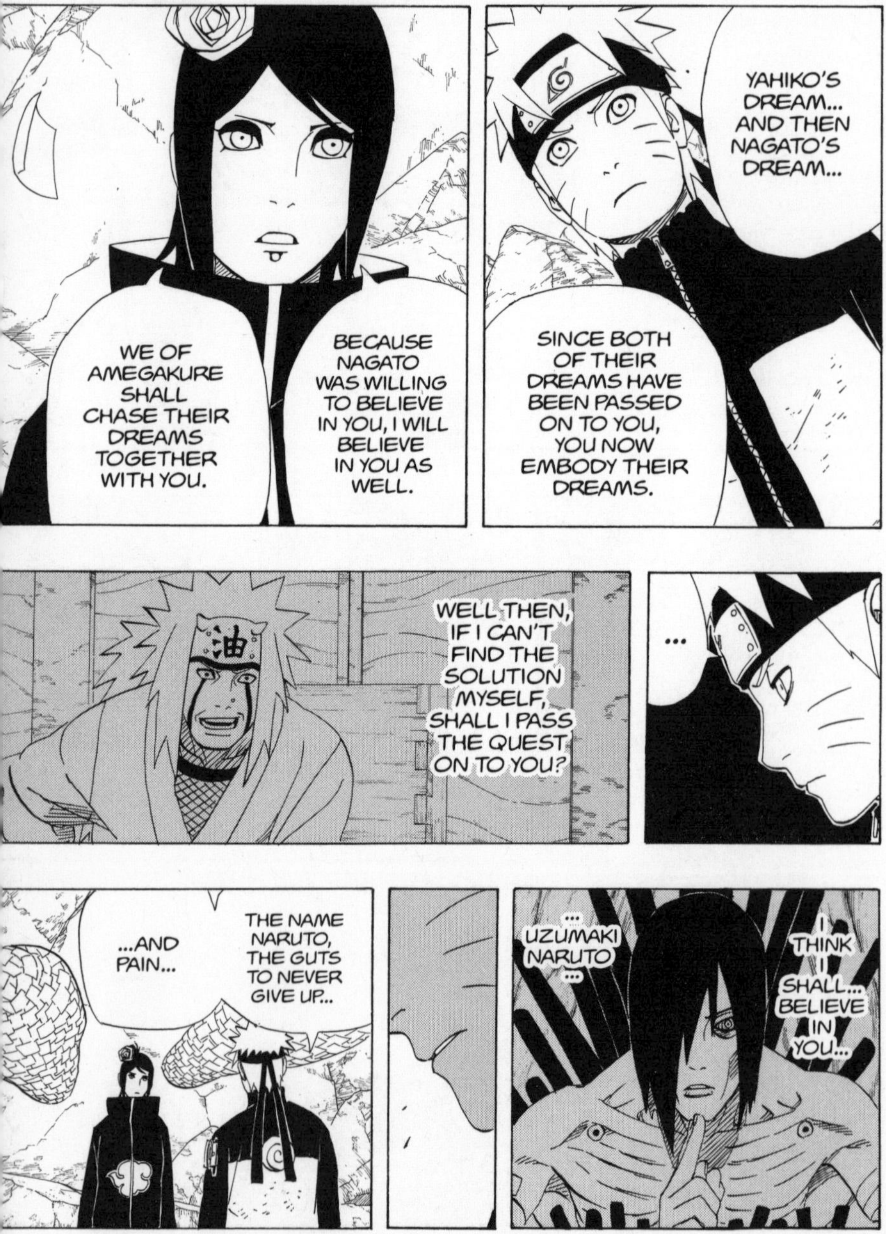
YAHIKO'S DREAM... AND THEN NAGATO'S DREAM...
SINCE BOTH OF THEIR DREAMS HAVE BEEN PASSED ON TO YOU, YOU NOW EMBODY THEIR DREAMS.
BECAUSE NAGATO WAS WILLING TO BELIEVE IN YOU, I WILL BELIEVE IN YOU AS WELL.
WE OF AMEGAKURE SHALL CHASE THEIR DREAMS TOGETHER WITH YOU.
...
WELL THEN, IF I CAN'T FIND THE SOLUTION MYSELF, SHALL I PASS THE QUEST ON TO YOU?
I THINK I SHALL... BELIEVE IN YOU...
...UZUMAKI NARUTO...
THE NAME NARUTO, THE GUTS TO NEVER GIVE UP...
...AND PAIN...

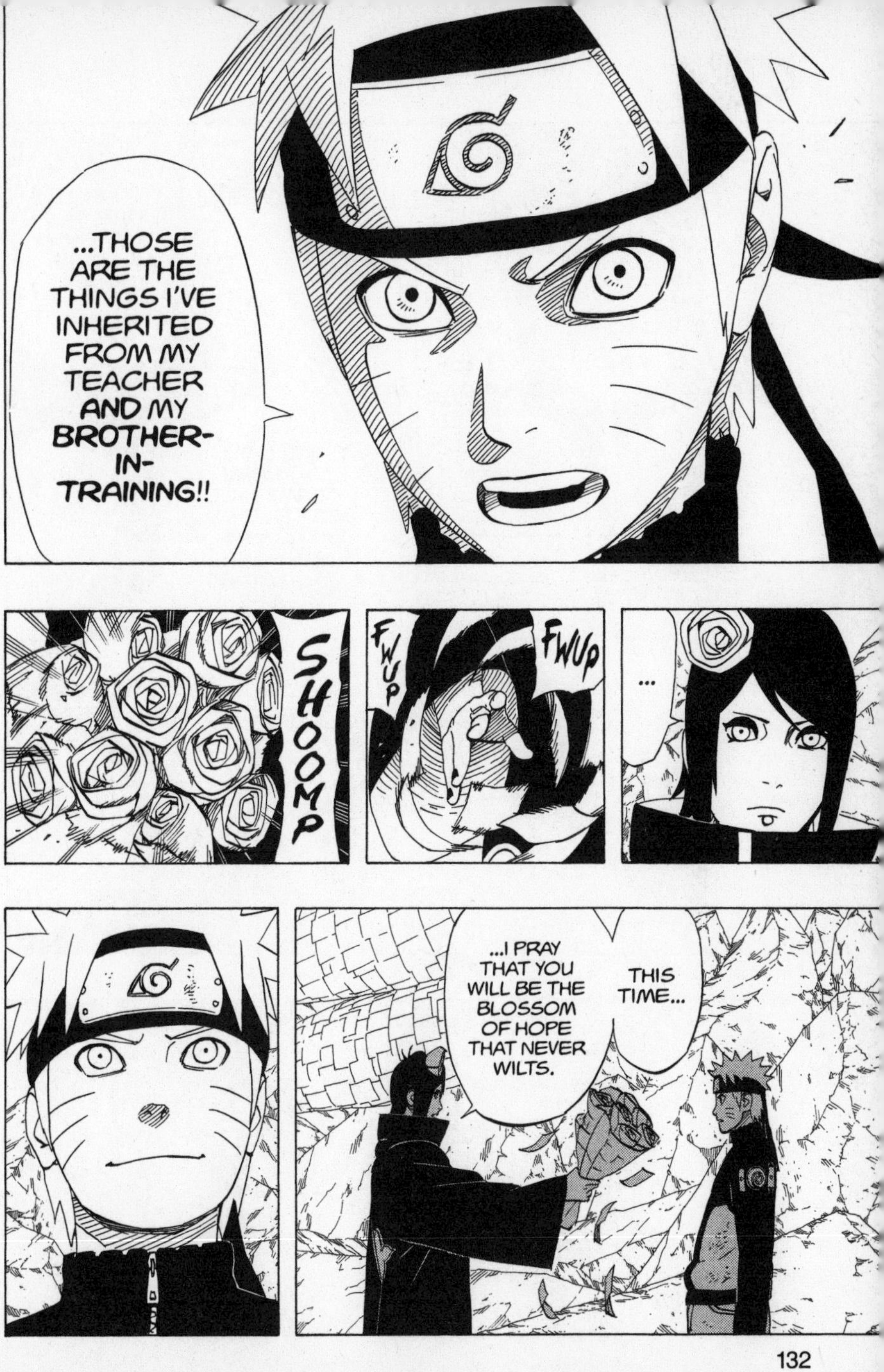
...THOSE ARE THE THINGS I'VE INHERITED FROM MY TEACHER AND MY BROTHER-IN-TRAINING!!
...
FWUP
FWUP
SHOOMP
THIS TIME...
...I PRAY THAT YOU WILL BE THE BLOSSOM OF HOPE THAT NEVER WILTS.

READ THIS WAY

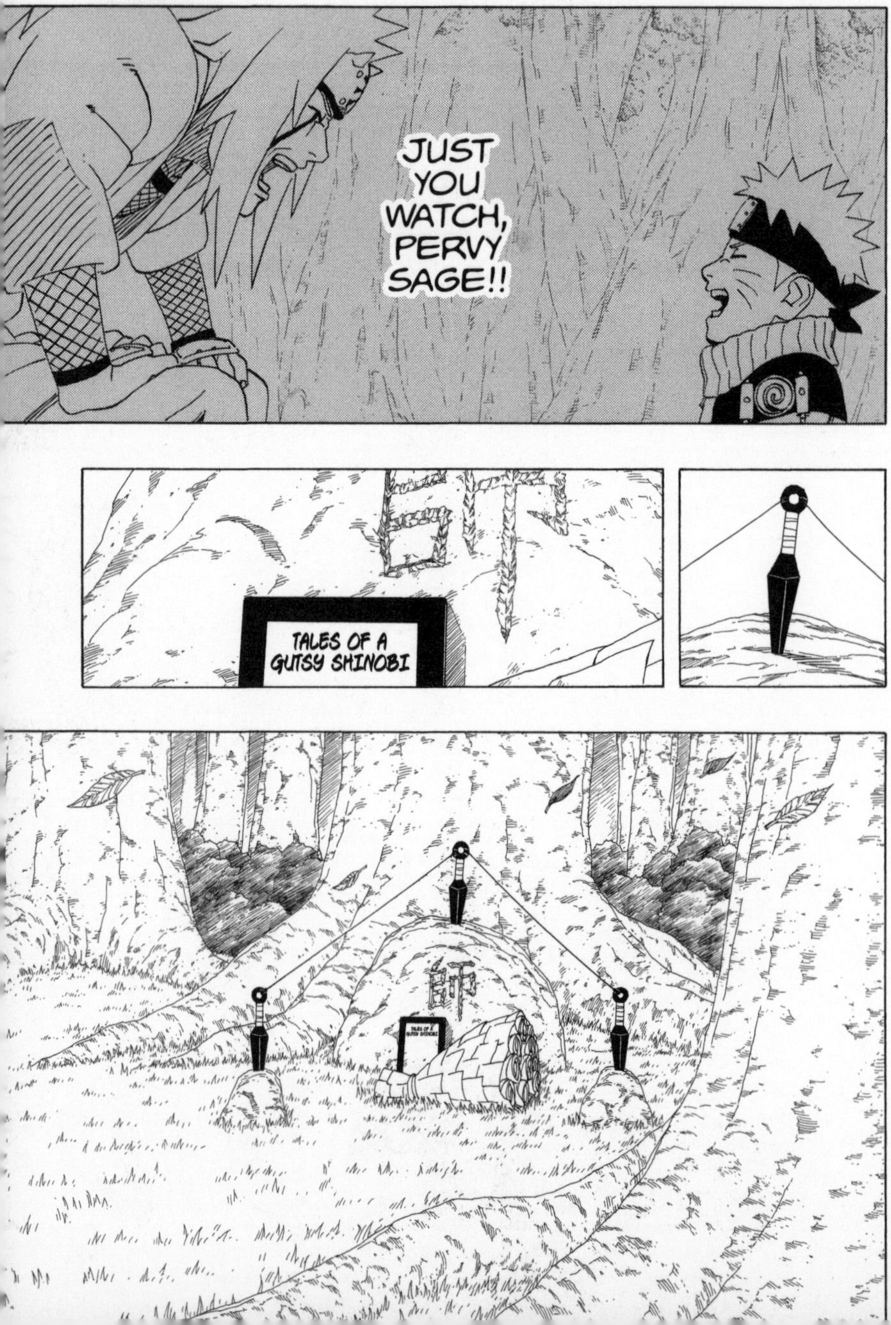
JUST YOU WATCH, PERVY SAGE!!
TALES OF A GUTSY SHINOBI

NARUTO

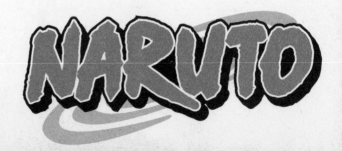

Number 450: The Cheering Village!!

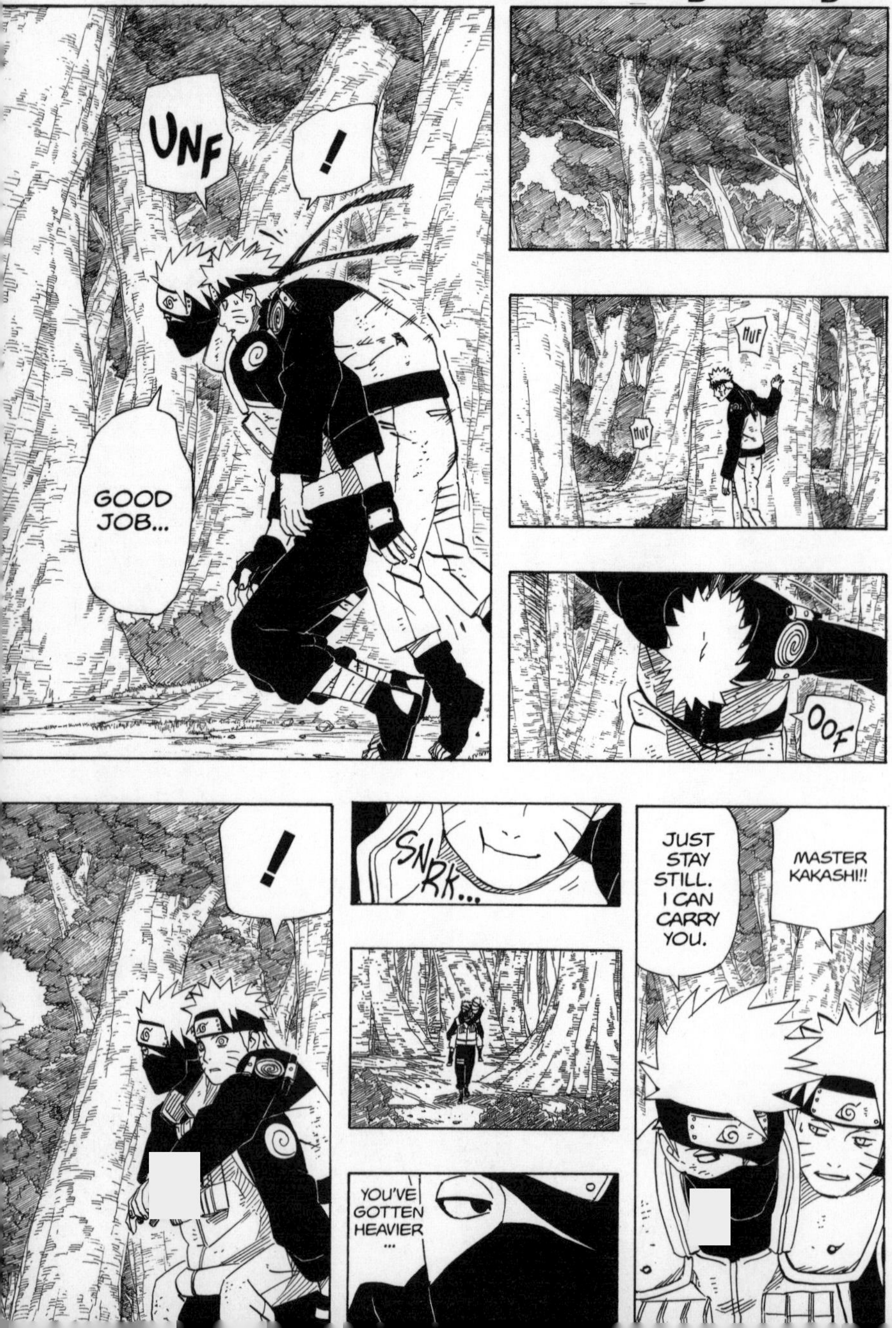
MUF
MUF
OOF
!
UNF
GOOD JOB...
MASTER KAKASHI!!
JUST STAY STILL. I CAN CARRY YOU.
SNRK...
YOU'VE GOTTEN HEAVIER ...
!

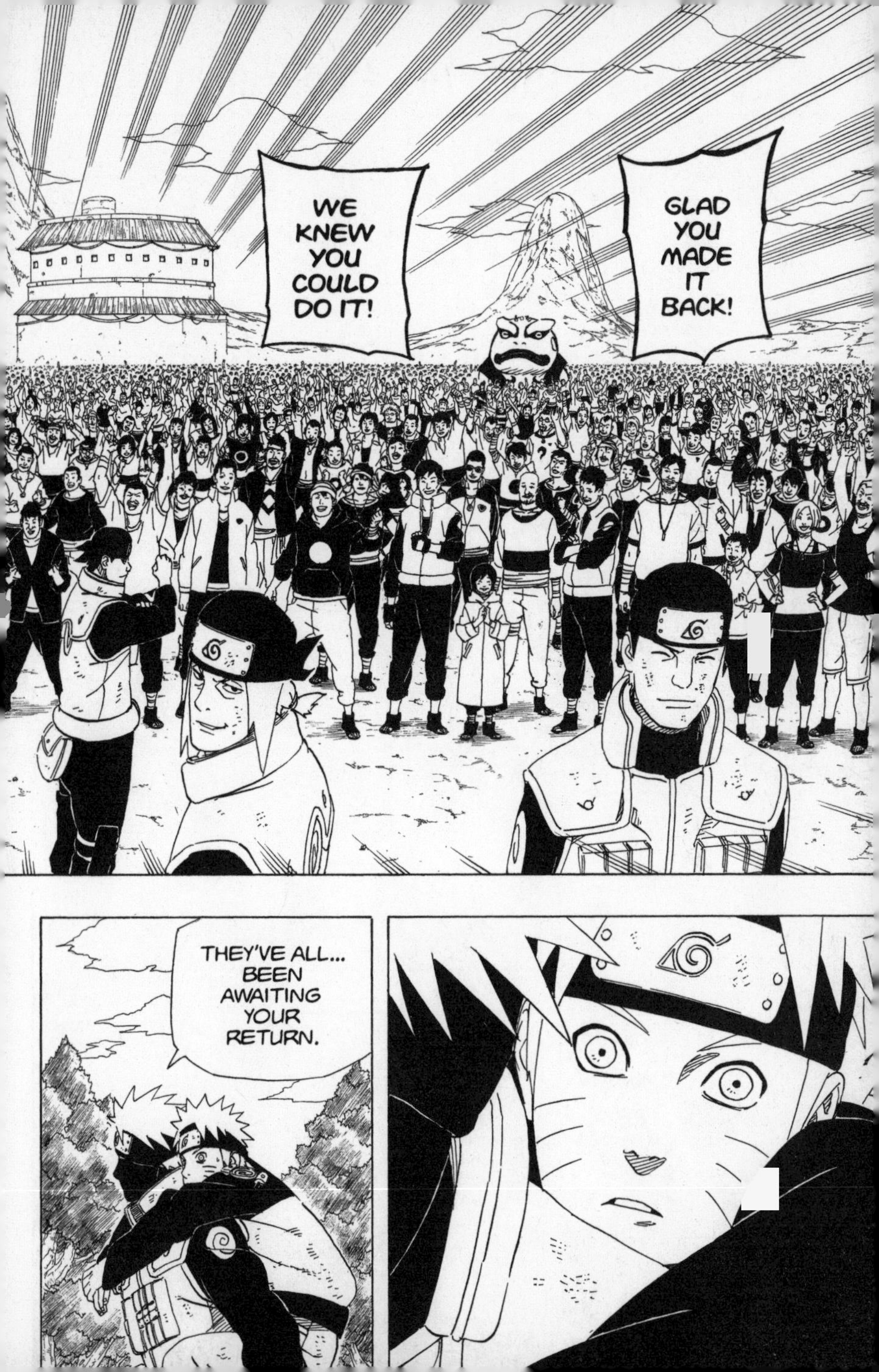
GLAD YOU MADE IT BACK!
WE KNEW YOU COULD DO IT!
THEY'VE ALL... BEEN AWAITING YOUR RETURN.

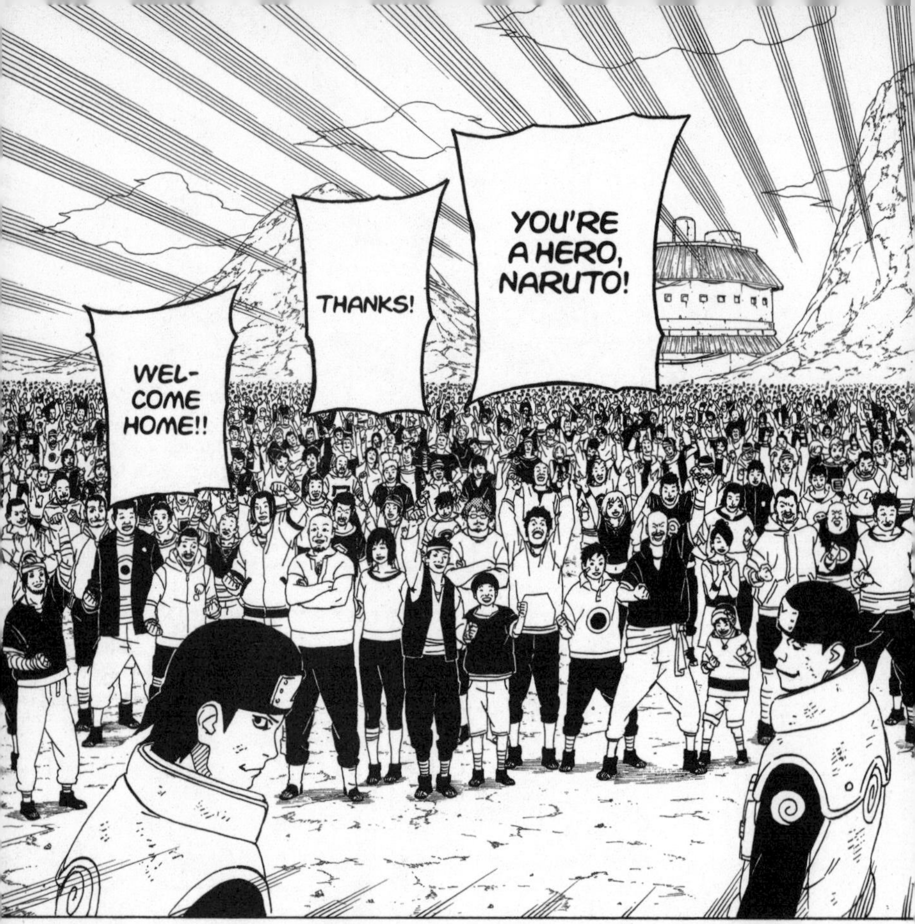
YOU'RE A HERO, NARUTO!
THANKS!
WEL-COME HOME!!

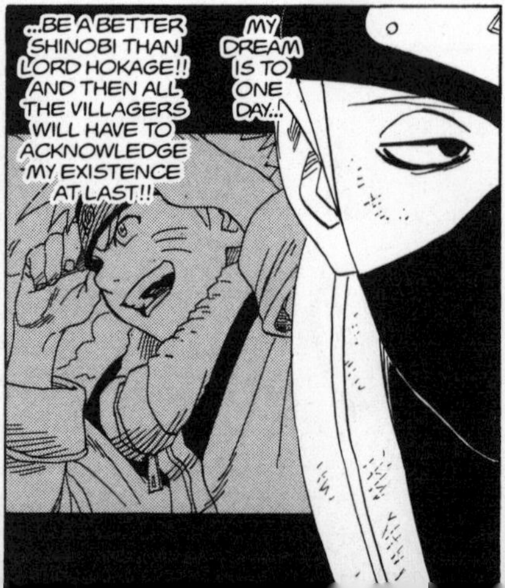
MY DREAM IS TO ONE DAY...
...BE A BETTER SHINOBI THAN LORD HOKAGE!! AND THEN ALL THE VILLAGERS WILL HAVE TO ACKNOWLEDGE MY EXISTENCE AT LAST!!

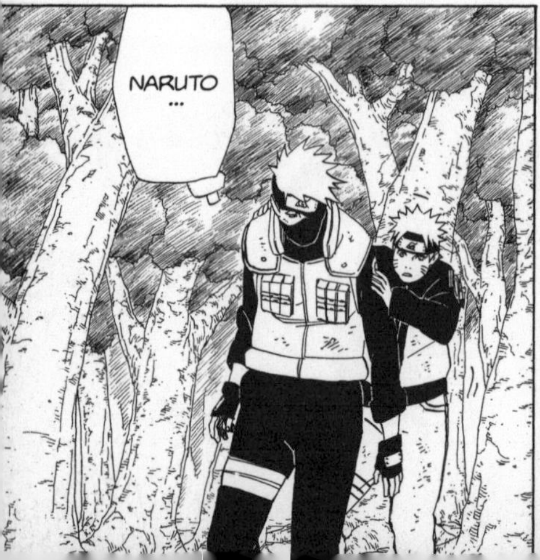
NARUTO ...

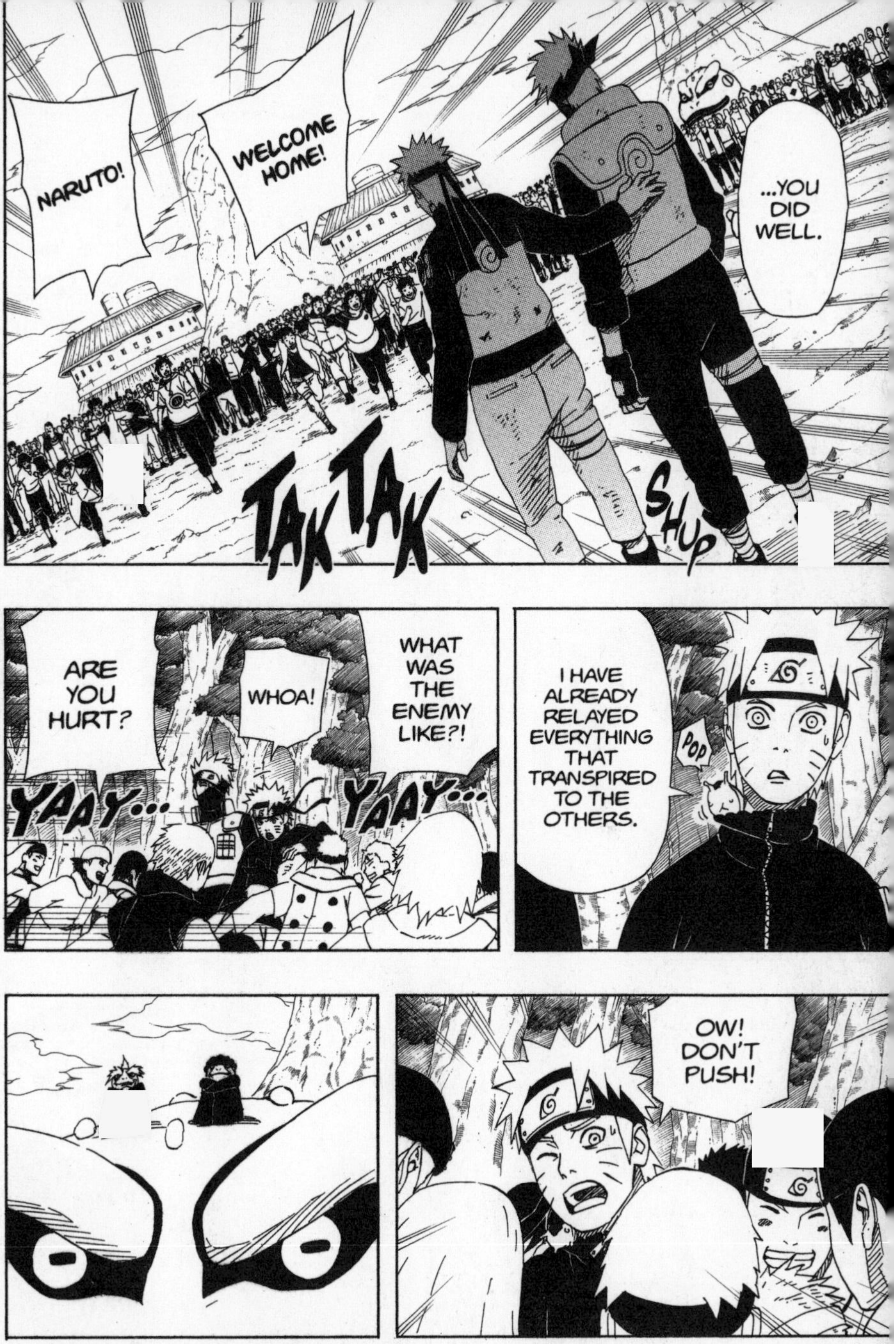
...YOU DID WELL.
WELCOME HOME!
NARUTO!
SHUP
TAK TAK
I HAVE ALREADY RELAYED EVERYTHING THAT TRANSPIRED TO THE OTHERS.
POP
WHAT WAS THE ENEMY LIKE?!
WHOA!
ARE YOU HURT?
YAAY...
YAAY...
OW! DON'T PUSH!

READ THIS WAY

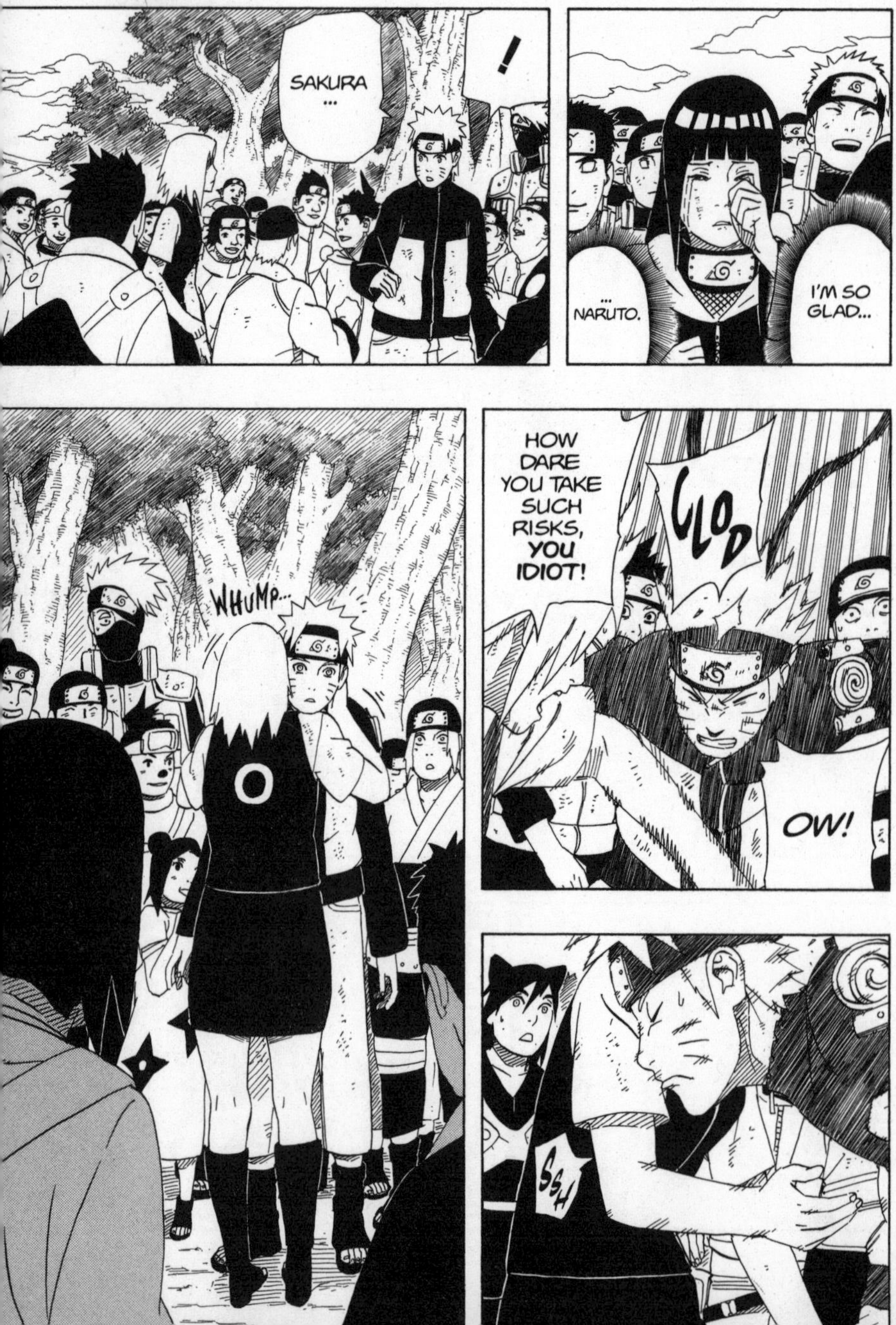
I'M SO GLAD...
... NARUTO.
!
SAKURA ...
CLOD
HOW DARE YOU TAKE SUCH RISKS, YOU IDIOT!
OW!
SSH
WHUMP...

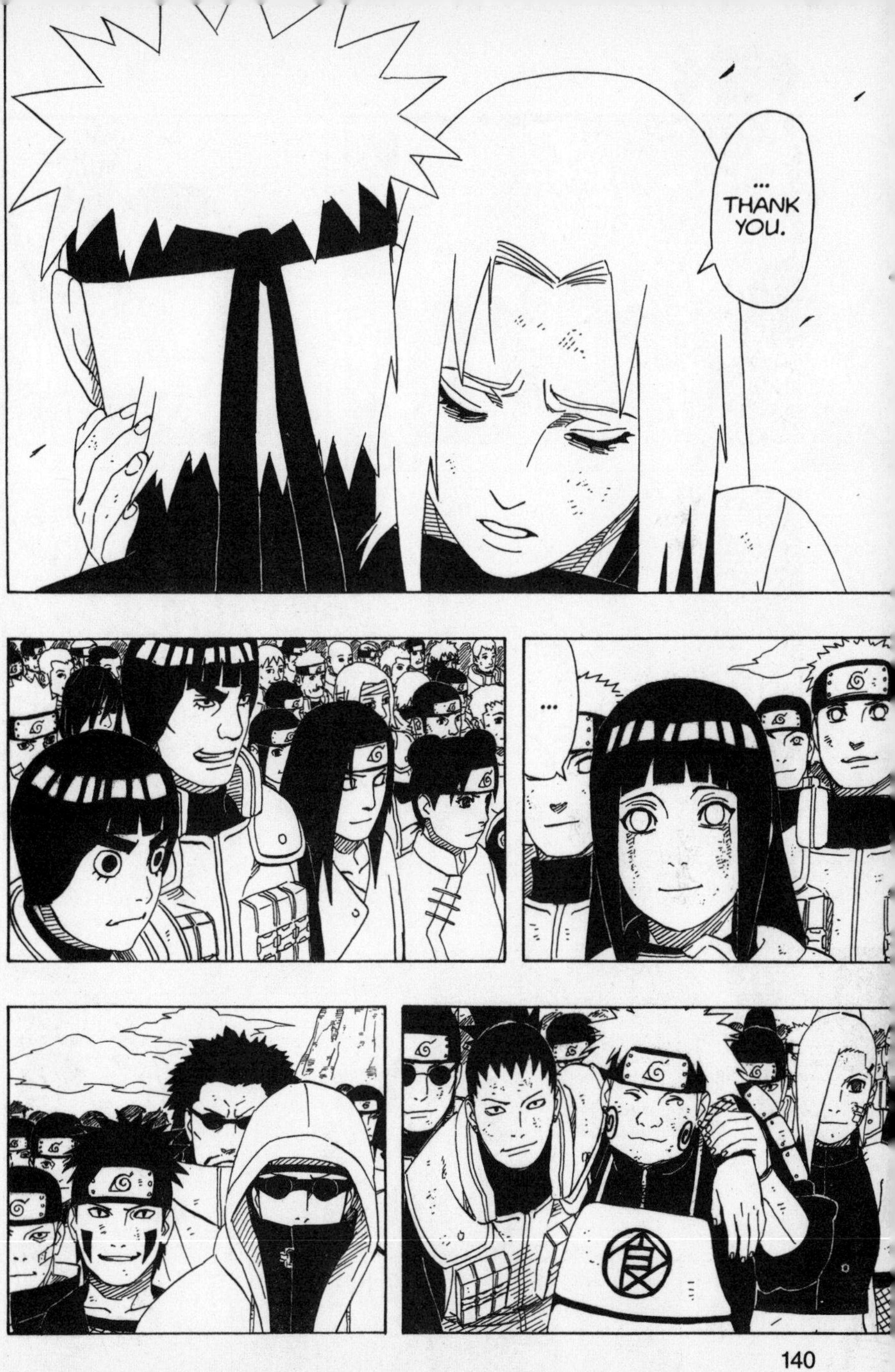
...THANK YOU.
...

READ THIS WAY

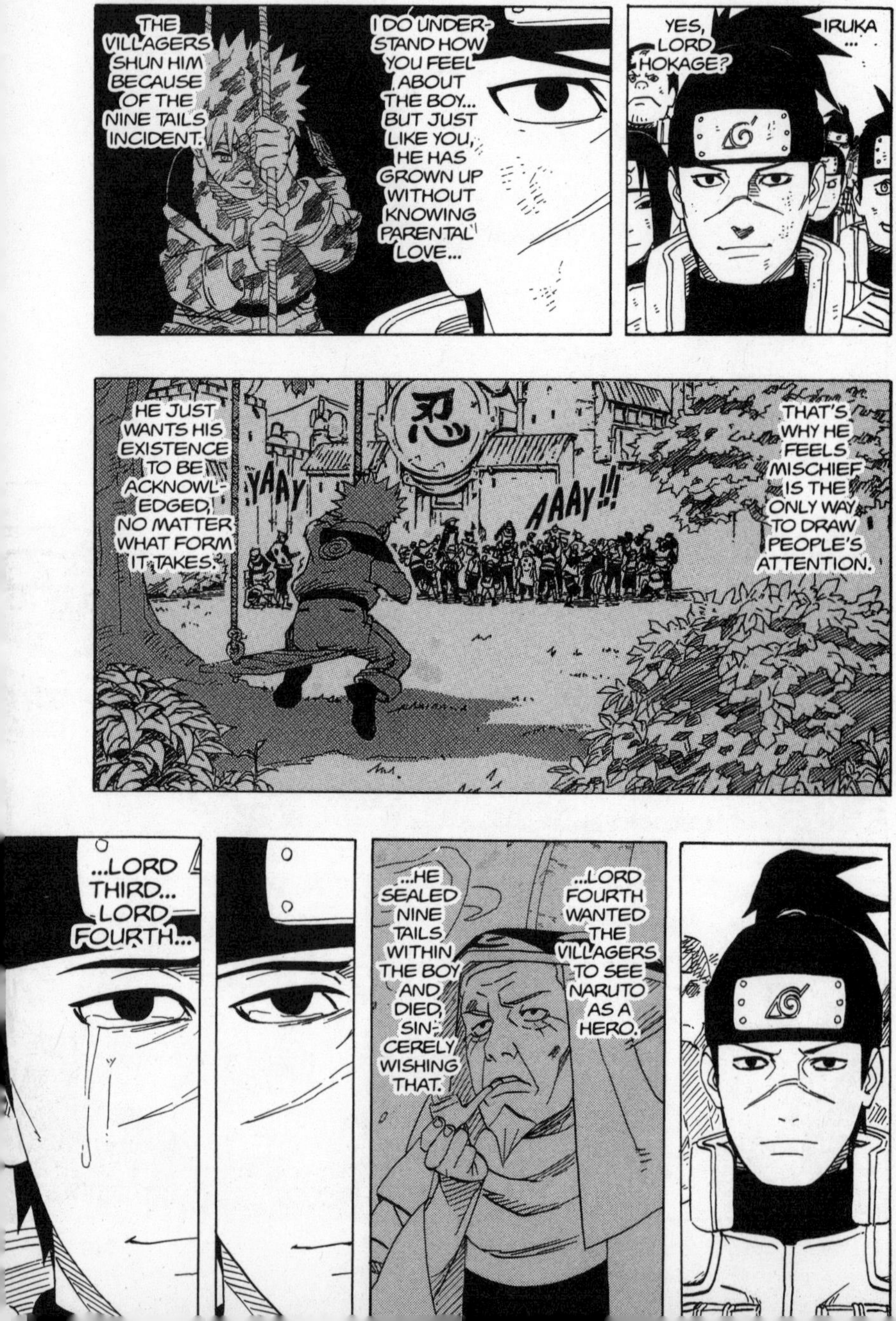
IRUKA ...
YES, LORD HOKAGE?
I DO UNDERSTAND HOW YOU FEEL ABOUT THE BOY... BUT JUST LIKE YOU, HE HAS GROWN UP WITHOUT KNOWING PARENTAL LOVE...
THE VILLAGERS SHUN HIM BECAUSE OF THE NINE TAILS INCIDENT.
THAT'S WHY HE FEELS MISCHIEF IS THE ONLY WAY TO DRAW PEOPLE'S ATTENTION.
AAAY!!!
YAAY
HE JUST WANTS HIS EXISTENCE TO BE ACKNOWLEDGED, NO MATTER WHAT FORM IT TAKES.
...LORD FOURTH WANTED THE VILLAGERS TO SEE NARUTO AS A HERO.
...HE SEALED NINE TAILS WITHIN THE BOY AND DIED, SINCERELY WISHING THAT.
...LORD THIRD... LORD FOURTH...

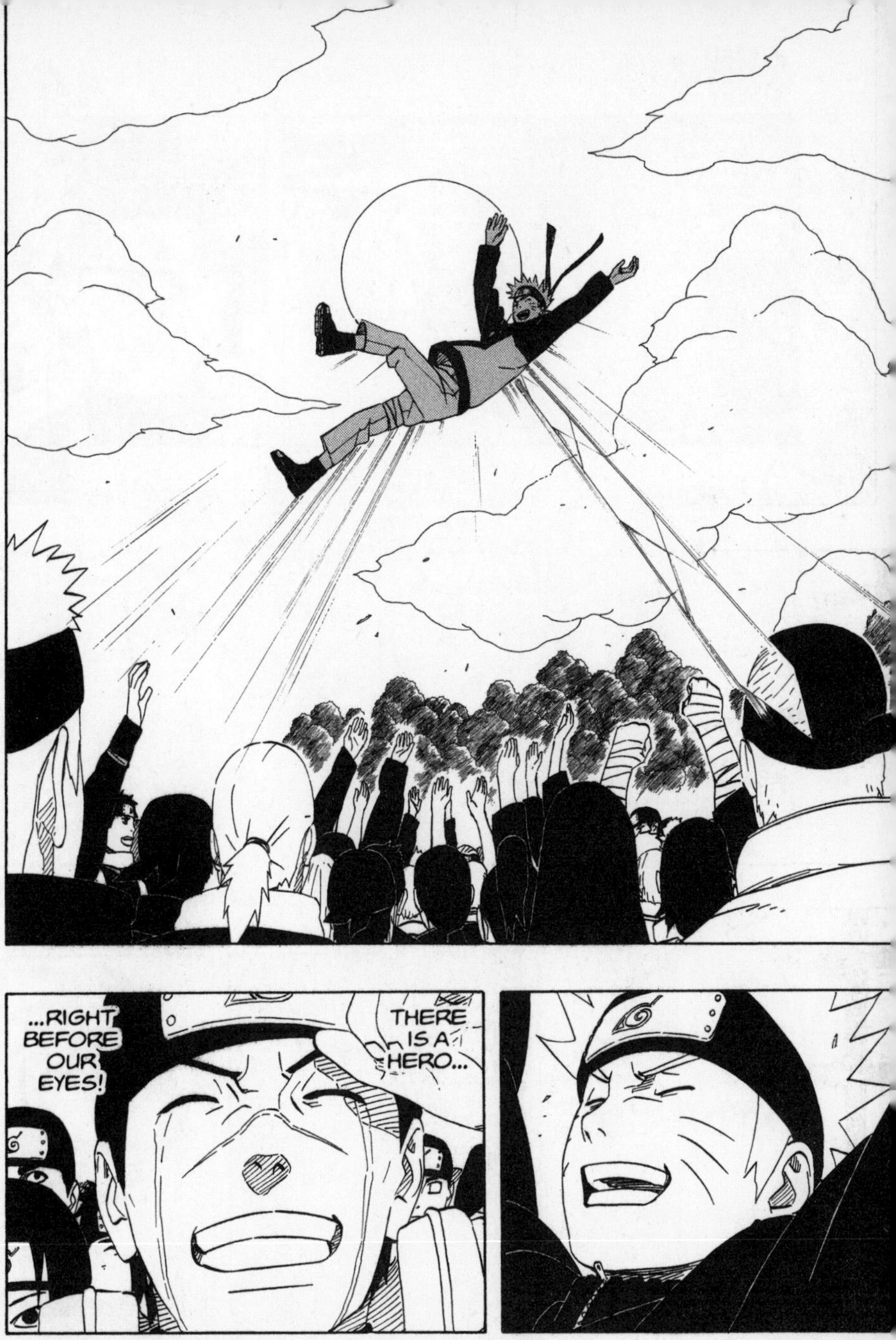
THERE IS A HERO...
...RIGHT BEFORE OUR EYES!

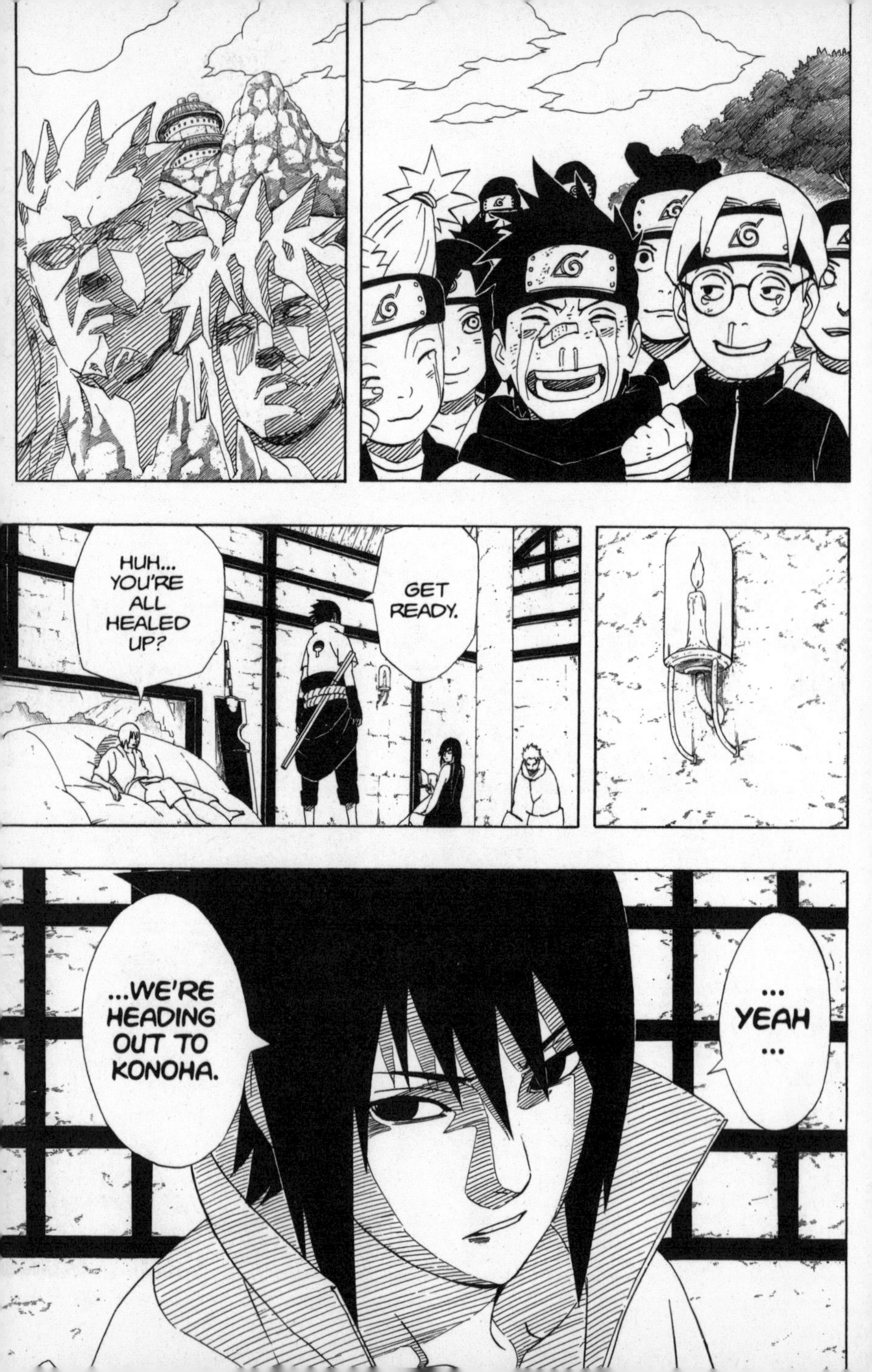
GET READY.
HUH... YOU'RE ALL HEALED UP?
... YEAH ...
...WE'RE HEADING OUT TO KONOHA.

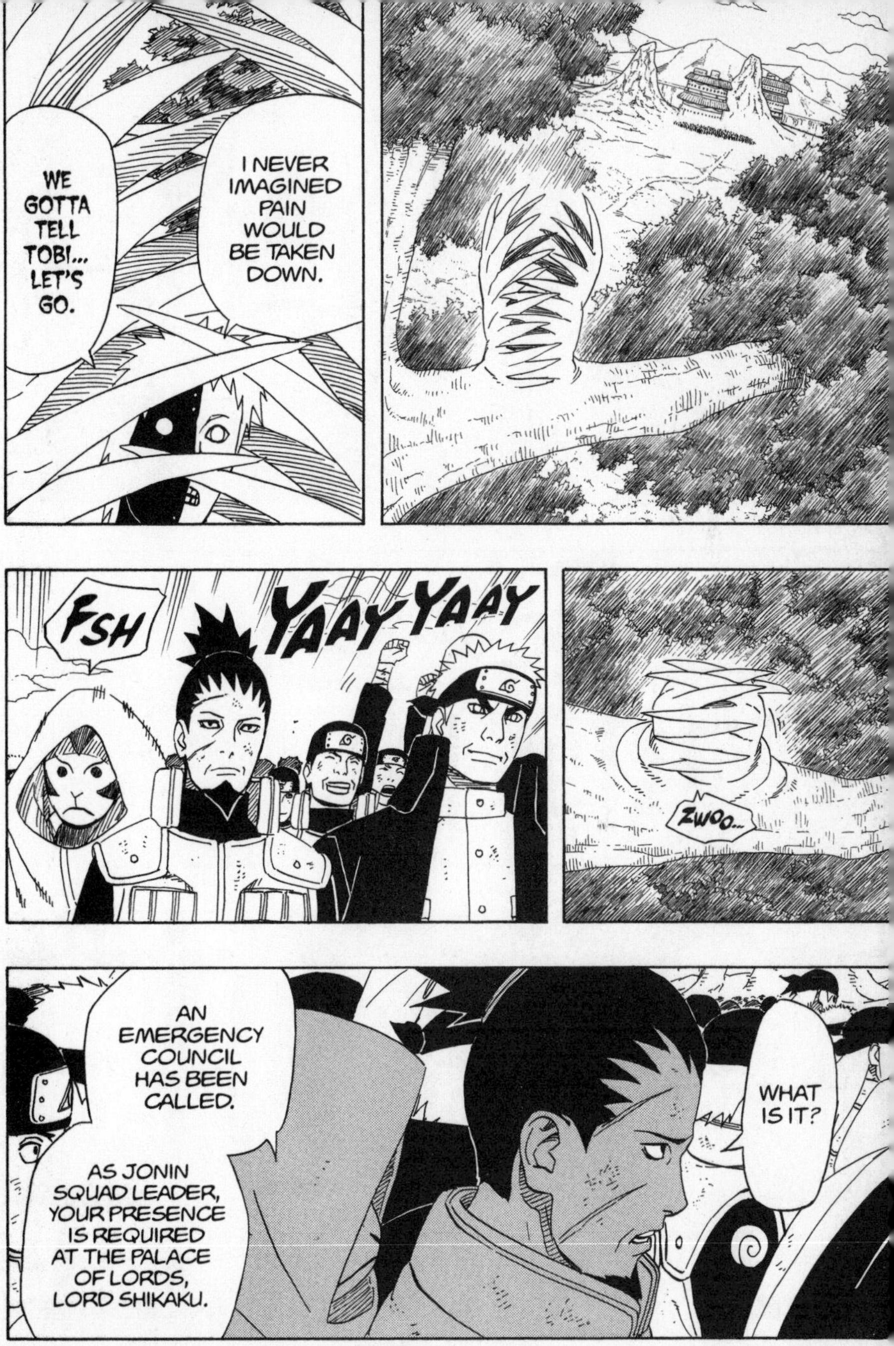
I NEVER IMAGINED PAIN WOULD BE TAKEN DOWN.
WE GOTTA TELL TOBI... LET'S GO.
ZWOO...
YAAY YAAY
FSH
WHAT IS IT?
AN EMERGENCY COUNCIL HAS BEEN CALLED.
AS JONIN SQUAD LEADER, YOUR PRESENCE IS REQUIRED AT THE PALACE OF LORDS, LORD SHIKAKU.

READ THIS WAY

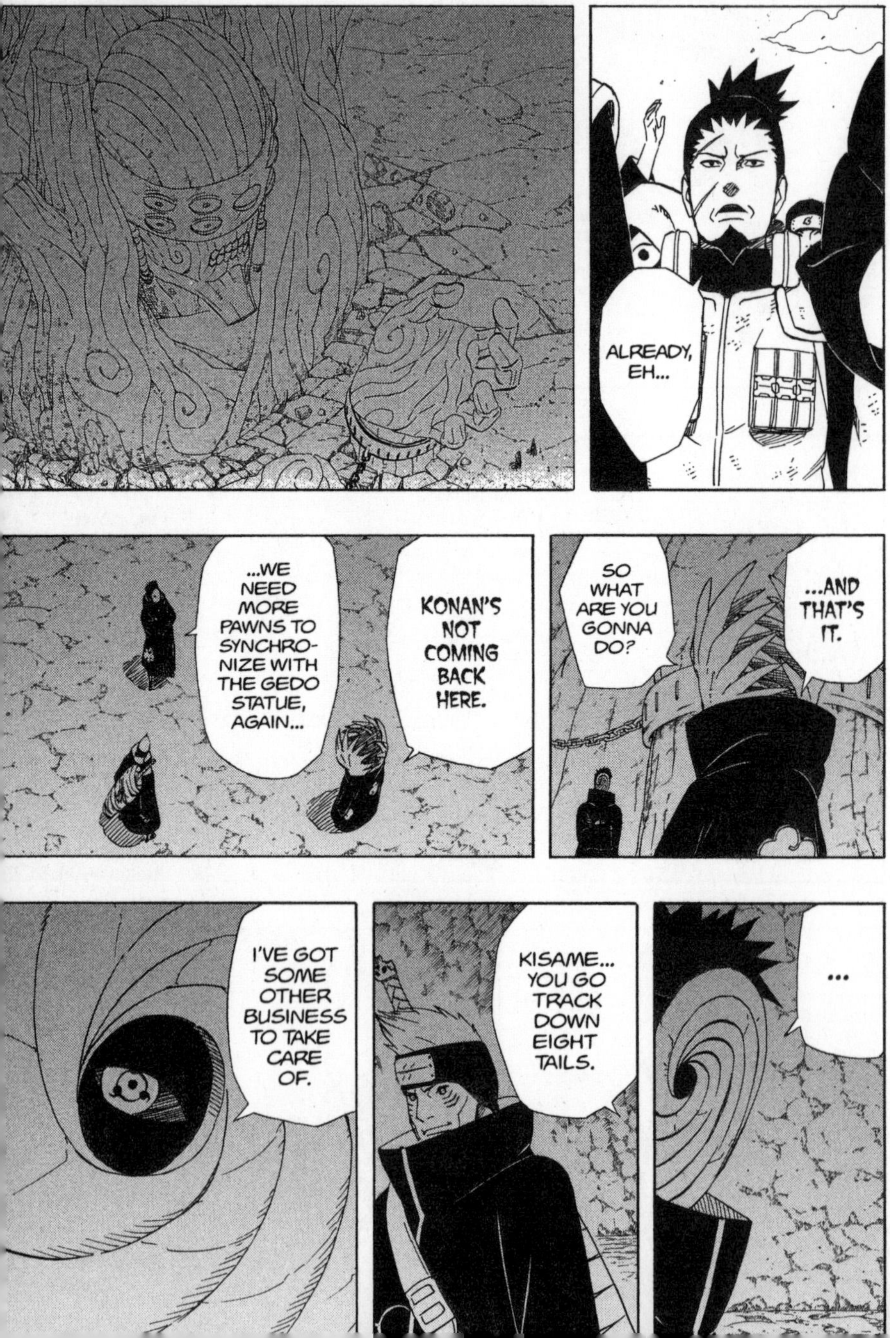
ALREADY, EH...
...AND THAT'S IT.
SO WHAT ARE YOU GONNA DO?
KONAN'S NOT COMING BACK HERE.
...WE NEED MORE PAWNS TO SYNCHRONIZE WITH THE GEDO STATUE, AGAIN...
...
KISAME... YOU GO TRACK DOWN EIGHT TAILS.
I'VE GOT SOME OTHER BUSINESS TO TAKE CARE OF.

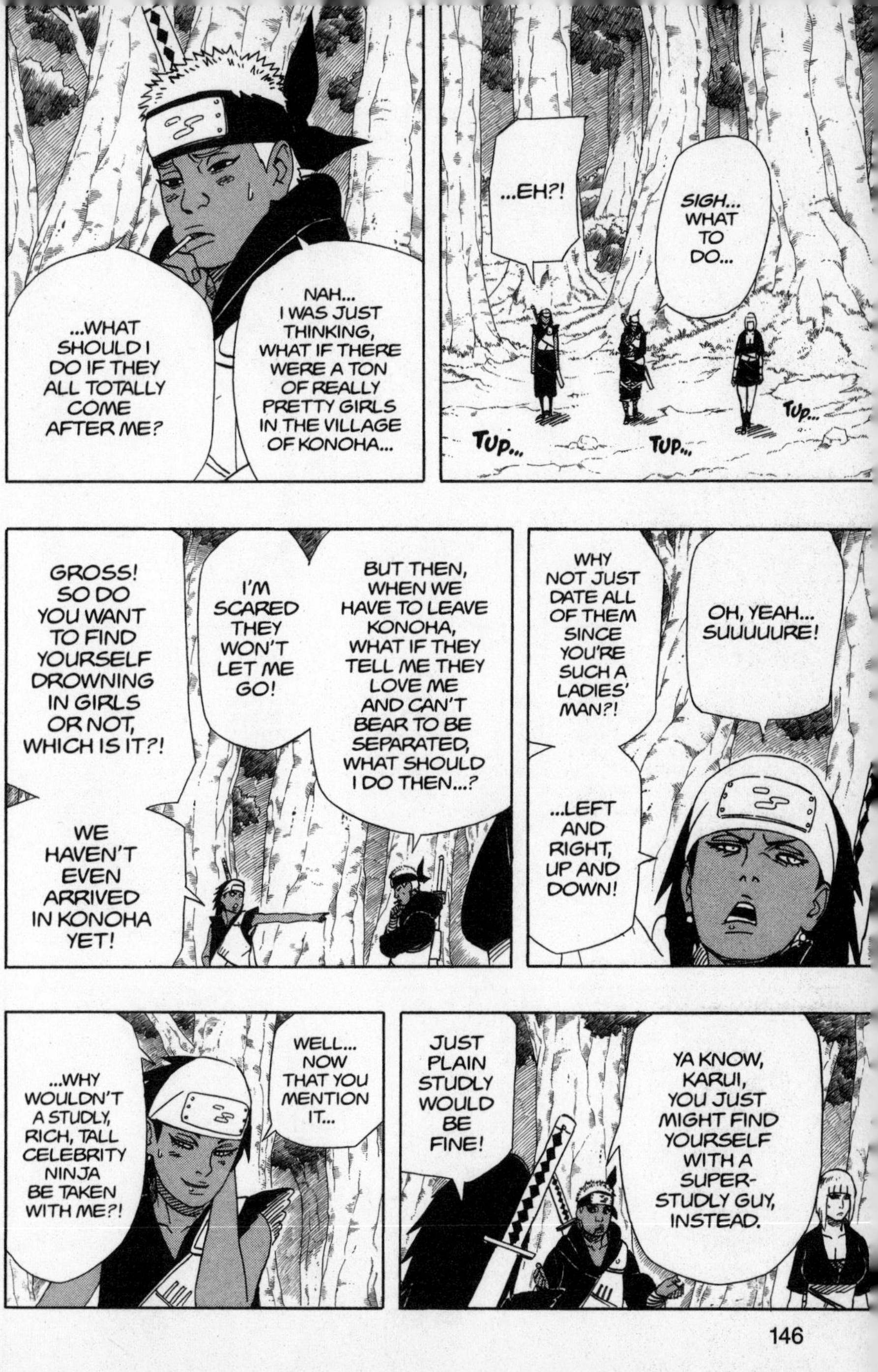
SIGH... WHAT TO DO...
...EH?!
TUP...
TUP...
TUP...
NAH... I WAS JUST THINKING, WHAT IF THERE WERE A TON OF REALLY PRETTY GIRLS IN THE VILLAGE OF KONOHA...
...WHAT SHOULD I DO IF THEY ALL TOTALLY COME AFTER ME?
OH, YEAH... SUUUUURE!
WHY NOT JUST DATE ALL OF THEM SINCE YOU'RE SUCH A LADIES' MAN?!
...LEFT AND RIGHT, UP AND DOWN!
BUT THEN, WHEN WE HAVE TO LEAVE KONOHA, WHAT IF THEY TELL ME THEY LOVE ME AND CAN'T BEAR TO BE SEPARATED, WHAT SHOULD I DO THEN...?
I'M SCARED THEY WON'T LET ME GO!
GROSS! SO DO YOU WANT TO FIND YOURSELF DROWNING IN GIRLS OR NOT, WHICH IS IT?!
WE HAVEN'T EVEN ARRIVED IN KONOHA YET!
YA KNOW, KARUI, YOU JUST MIGHT FIND YOURSELF WITH A SUPER-STUDLY GUY, INSTEAD.
JUST PLAIN STUDLY WOULD BE FINE!
WELL... NOW THAT YOU MENTION IT...
...WHY WOULDN'T A STUDLY, RICH, TALL CELEBRITY NINJA BE TAKEN WITH ME?!

READ THIS WAY

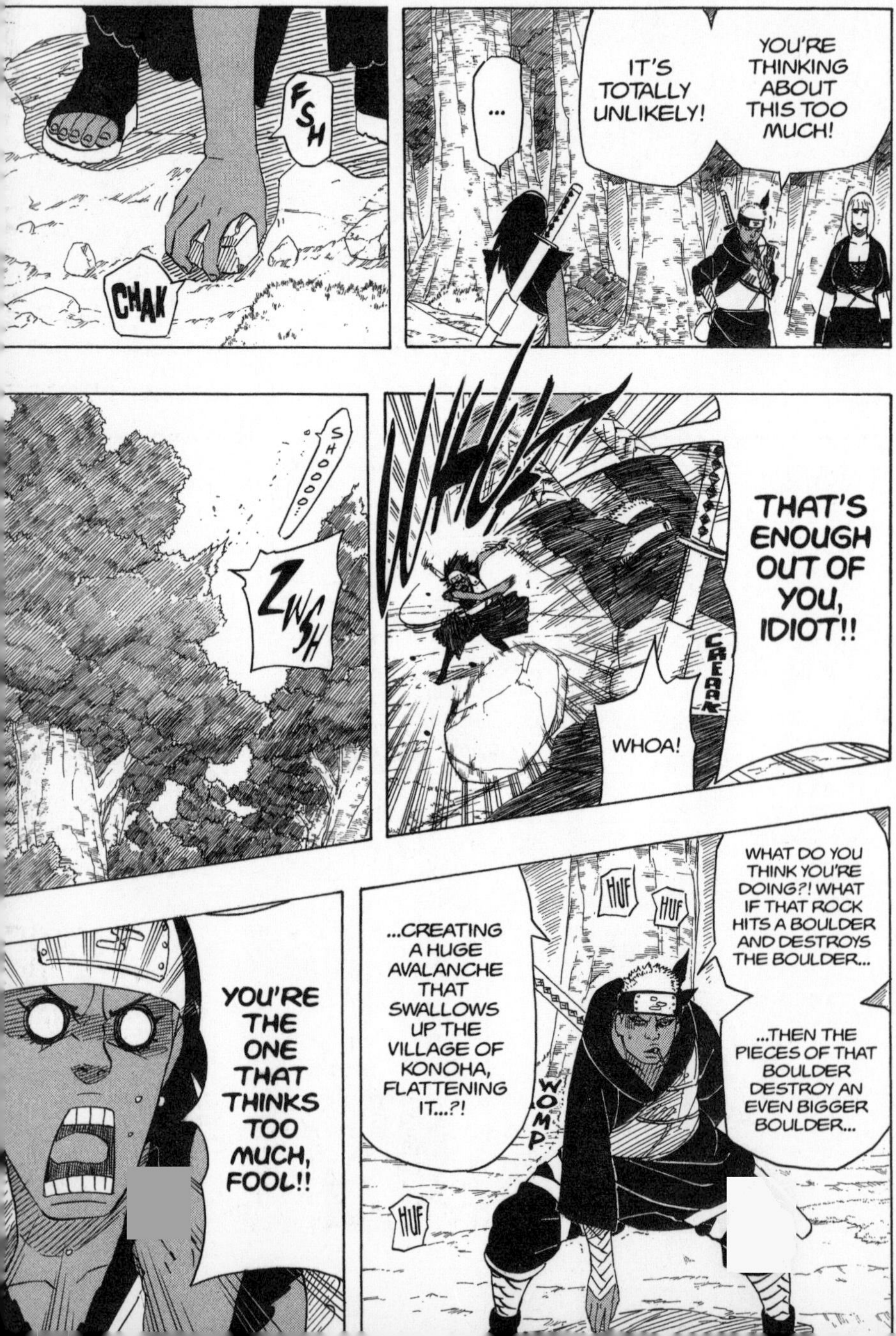
YOU'RE THINKING ABOUT THIS TOO MUCH!
IT'S TOTALLY UNLIKELY!
...
FSH
CHAK
THAT'S ENOUGH OUT OF YOU, IDIOT!!
CREAAK
WHOA!
SHOOOO...
ZWSH
WHAT DO YOU THINK YOU'RE DOING?! WHAT IF THAT ROCK HITS A BOULDER AND DESTROYS THE BOULDER...
...THEN THE PIECES OF THAT BOULDER DESTROY AN EVEN BIGGER BOULDER...
HUF
HUF
...CREATING A HUGE AVALANCHE THAT SWALLOWS UP THE VILLAGE OF KONOHA, FLATTENING IT...?!
WOMP
HUF
YOU'RE THE ONE THAT THINKS TOO MUCH, FOOL!!

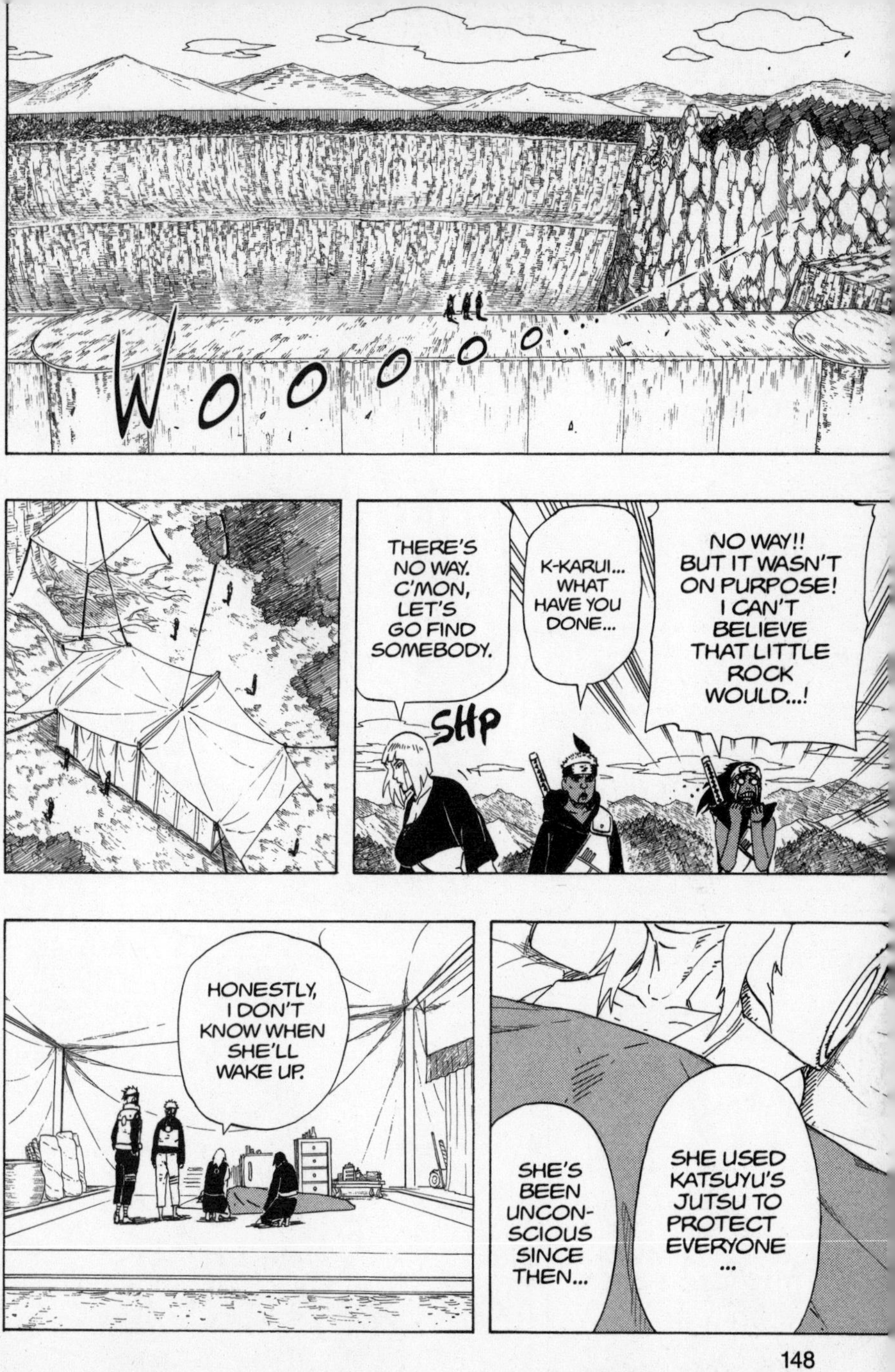
WOOOOO...
NO WAY!! BUT IT WASN'T ON PURPOSE! I CAN'T BELIEVE THAT LITTLE ROCK WOULD...!
K-KARUI... WHAT HAVE YOU DONE...
THERE'S NO WAY. C'MON, LET'S GO FIND SOMEBODY.
SHP
SHE USED KATSUYU'S JUTSU TO PROTECT EVERYONE...
SHE'S BEEN UNCON-SCIOUS SINCE THEN...
HONESTLY, I DON'T KNOW WHEN SHE'LL WAKE UP.

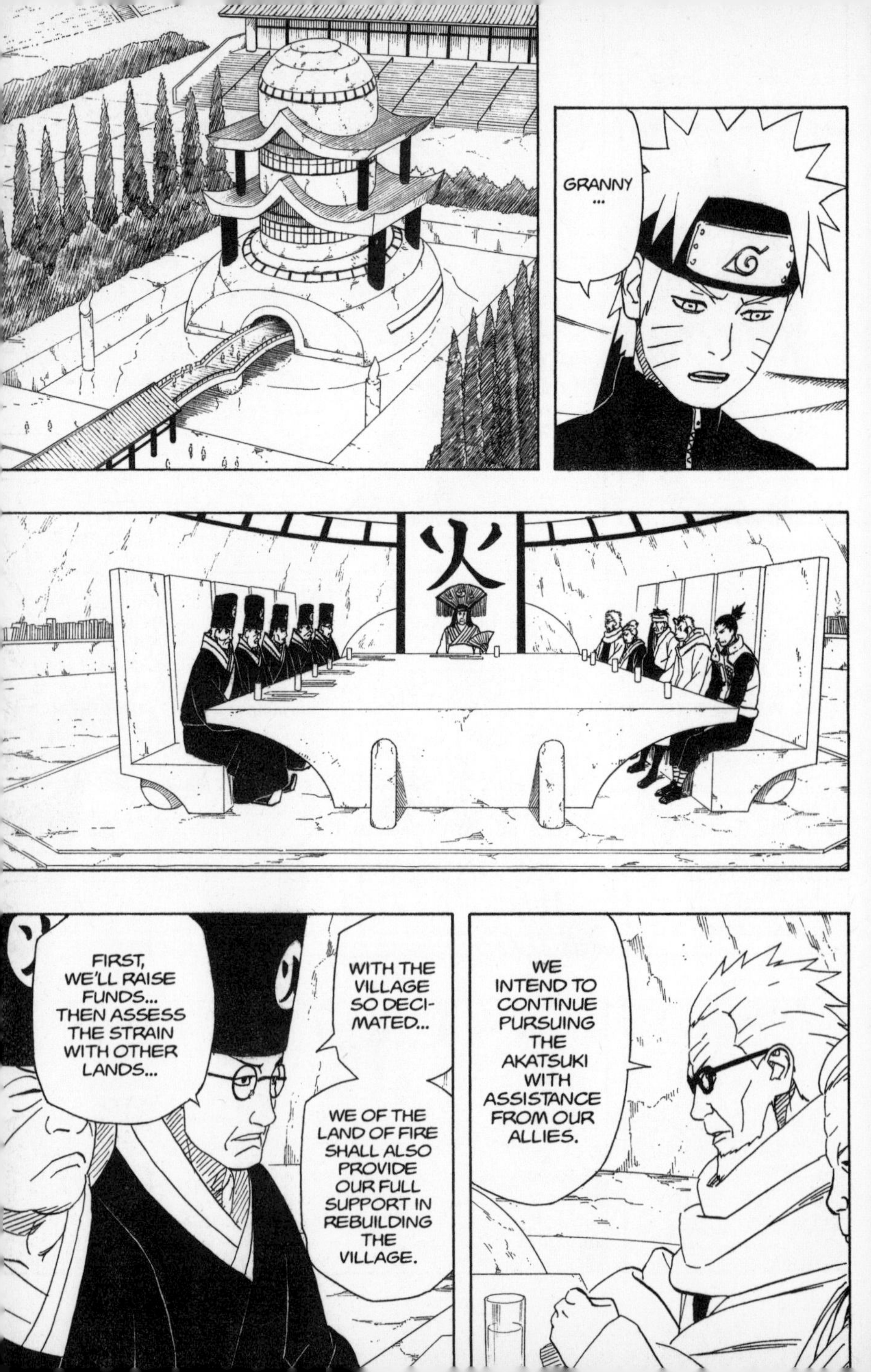
GRANNY ...
火
WE INTEND TO CONTINUE PURSUING THE AKATSUKI WITH ASSISTANCE FROM OUR ALLIES.
WITH THE VILLAGE SO DECIMATED...
WE OF THE LAND OF FIRE SHALL ALSO PROVIDE OUR FULL SUPPORT IN REBUILDING THE VILLAGE.
FIRST, WE'LL RAISE FUNDS... THEN ASSESS THE STRAIN WITH OTHER LANDS...

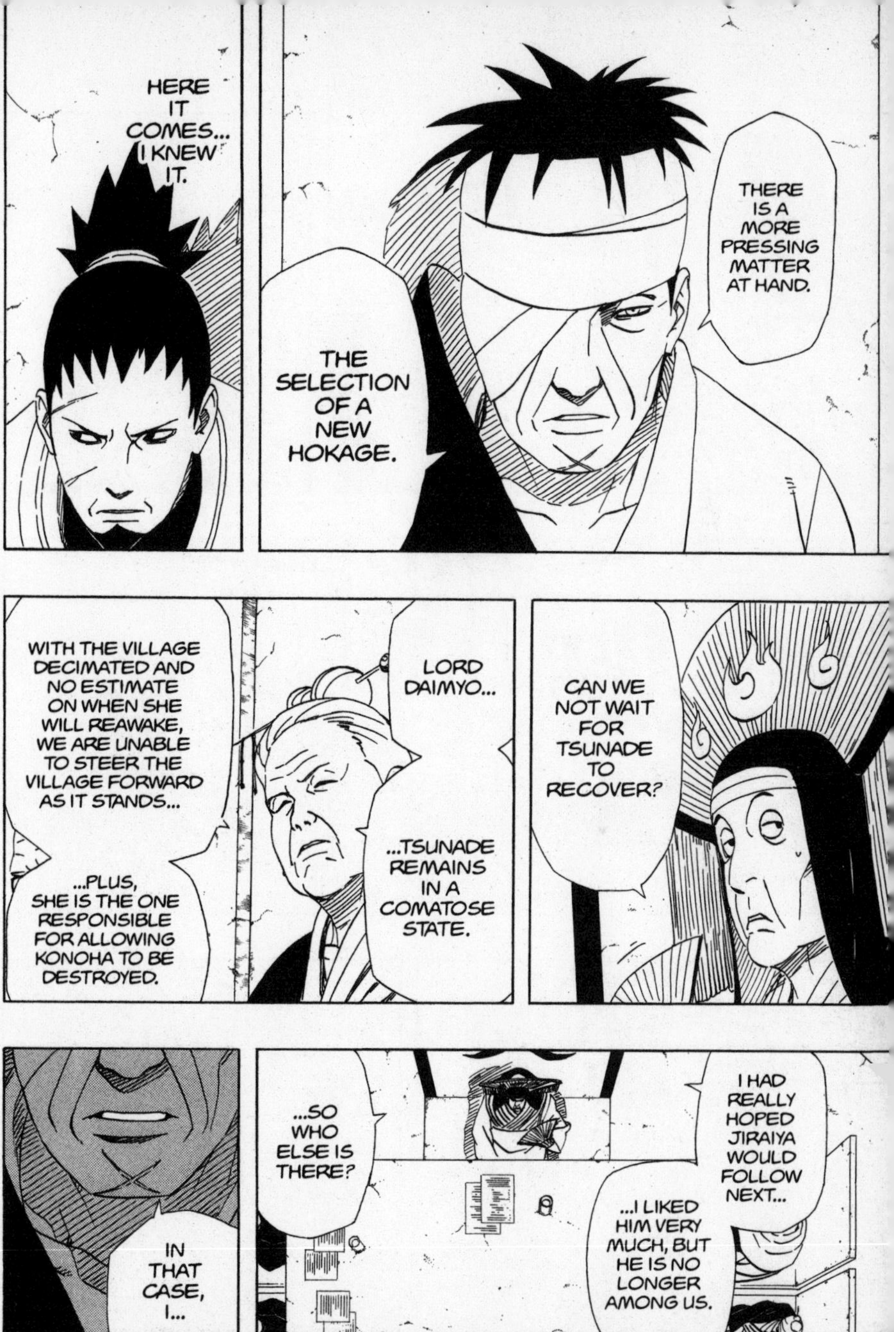
THERE IS A MORE PRESSING MATTER AT HAND.
THE SELECTION OF A NEW HOKAGE.
HERE IT COMES... I KNEW IT.
CAN WE NOT WAIT FOR TSUNADE TO RECOVER?
LORD DAIMYO...
...TSUNADE REMAINS IN A COMATOSE STATE.
WITH THE VILLAGE DECIMATED AND NO ESTIMATE ON WHEN SHE WILL REAWAKE, WE ARE UNABLE TO STEER THE VILLAGE FORWARD AS IT STANDS...
...PLUS, SHE IS THE ONE RESPONSIBLE FOR ALLOWING KONOHA TO BE DESTROYED.
I HAD REALLY HOPED JIRAIYA WOULD FOLLOW NEXT...
...I LIKED HIM VERY MUCH, BUT HE IS NO LONGER AMONG US.
...SO WHO ELSE IS THERE?
IN THAT CASE, I...

READ THIS WAY

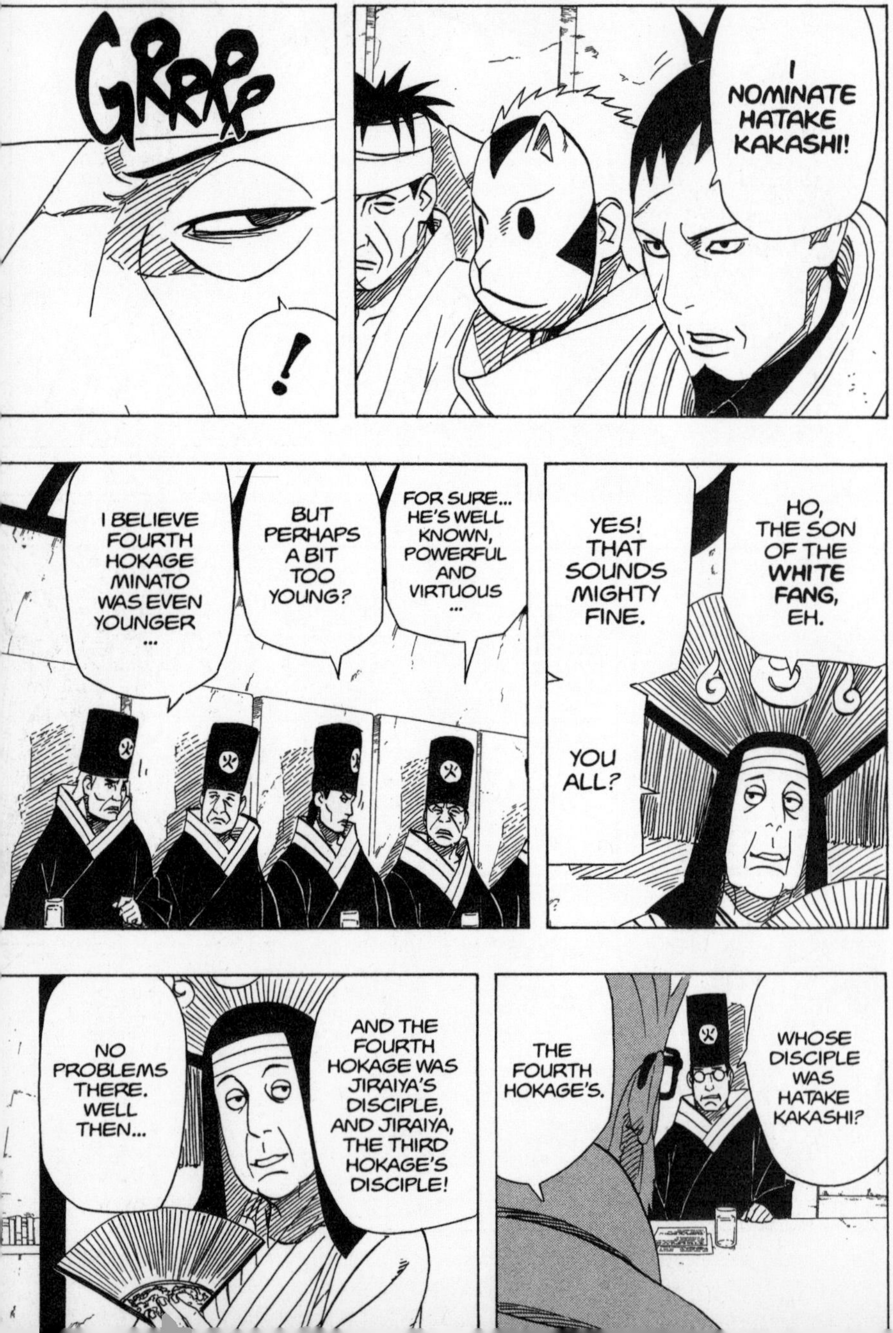
I NOMINATE HATAKE KAKASHI!
GRRRR
!
HO, THE SON OF THE WHITE FANG, EH.
YES! THAT SOUNDS MIGHTY FINE.
YOU ALL?
FOR SURE... HE'S WELL KNOWN, POWERFUL AND VIRTUOUS ...
BUT PERHAPS A BIT TOO YOUNG?
I BELIEVE FOURTH HOKAGE MINATO WAS EVEN YOUNGER ...
WHOSE DISCIPLE WAS HATAKE KAKASHI?
THE FOURTH HOKAGE'S.
AND THE FOURTH HOKAGE WAS JIRAIYA'S DISCIPLE, AND JIRAIYA, THE THIRD HOKAGE'S DISCIPLE!
NO PROBLEMS THERE. WELL THEN...

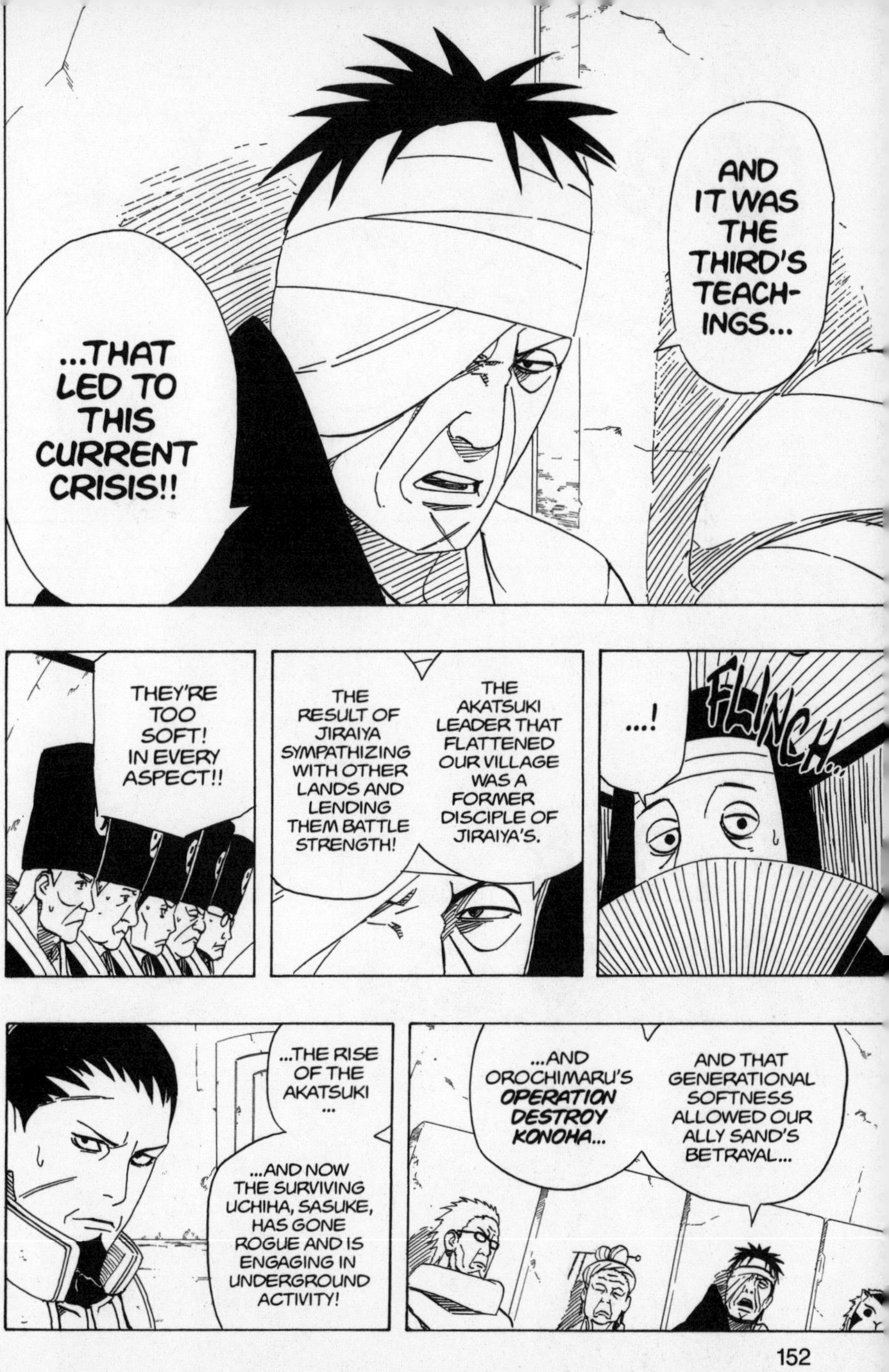
AND IT WAS THE THIRD'S TEACH- INGS...
...THAT LED TO THIS CURRENT CRISIS!!
FLINCH...
...!
THE AKATSUKI LEADER THAT FLATTENED OUR VILLAGE WAS A FORMER DISCIPLE OF JIRAIYA'S.
THE RESULT OF JIRAIYA SYMPATHIZING WITH OTHER LANDS AND LENDING THEM BATTLE STRENGTH!
THEY'RE TOO SOFT! IN EVERY ASPECT!!
AND THAT GENERATIONAL SOFTNESS ALLOWED OUR ALLY SAND'S BETRAYAL...
...AND OROCHIMARU'S *OPERATION DESTROY KONOHA*...
...THE RISE OF THE AKATSUKI ...
...AND NOW THE SURVIVING UCHIHA, SASUKE, HAS GONE ROGUE AND IS ENGAGING IN UNDERGROUND ACTIVITY!

READ THIS WAY

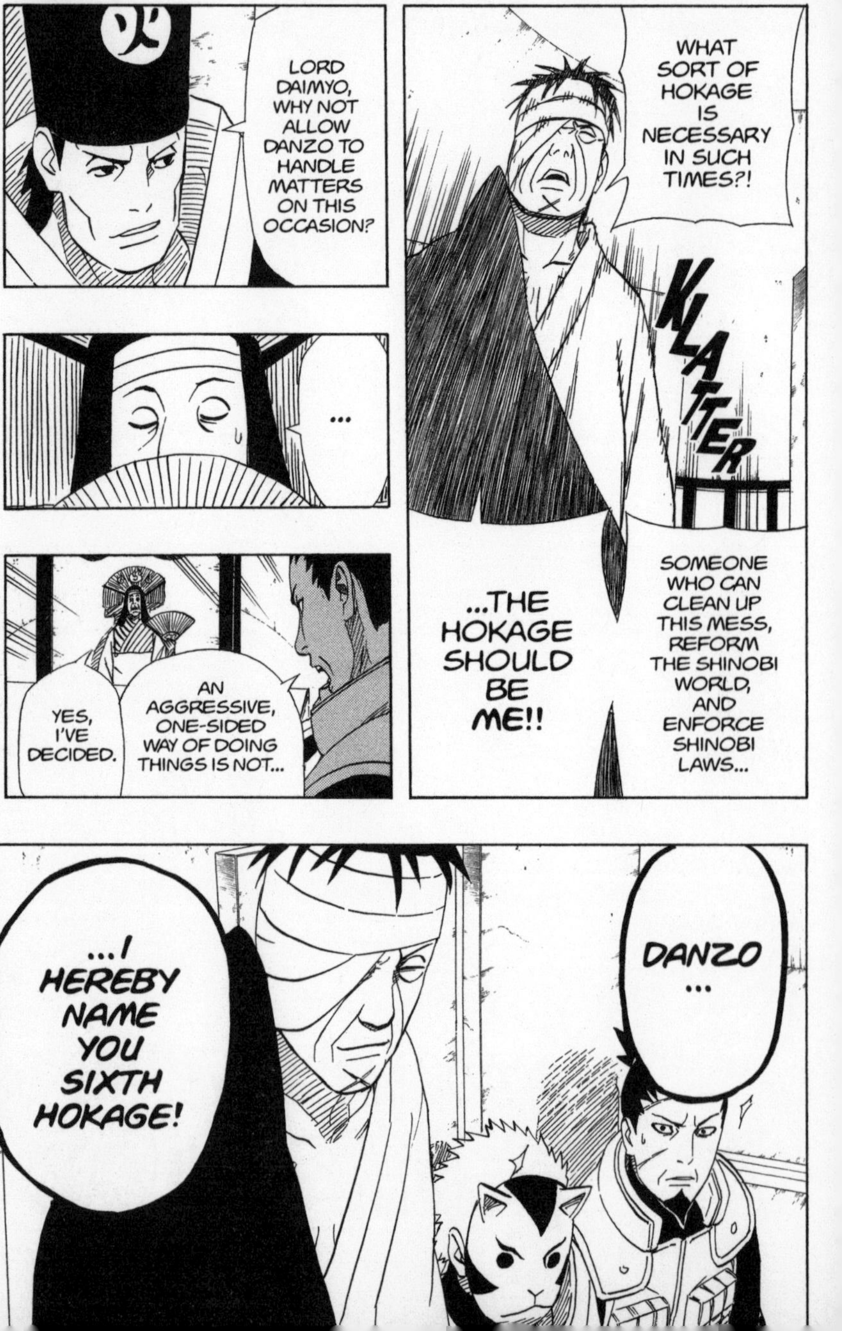
WHAT SORT OF HOKAGE IS NECESSARY IN SUCH TIMES?!
KLATTER
SOMEONE WHO CAN CLEAN UP THIS MESS, REFORM THE SHINOBI WORLD, AND ENFORCE SHINOBI LAWS...
...THE HOKAGE SHOULD BE ME!!
LORD DAIMYO, WHY NOT ALLOW DANZO TO HANDLE MATTERS ON THIS OCCASION?
...
AN AGGRESSIVE, ONE-SIDED WAY OF DOING THINGS IS NOT...
YES, I'VE DECIDED.
DANZO...
...I HEREBY NAME YOU SIXTH HOKAGE!

NARUTO

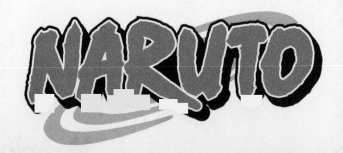

Number 451: Sasuke's Disposal!!

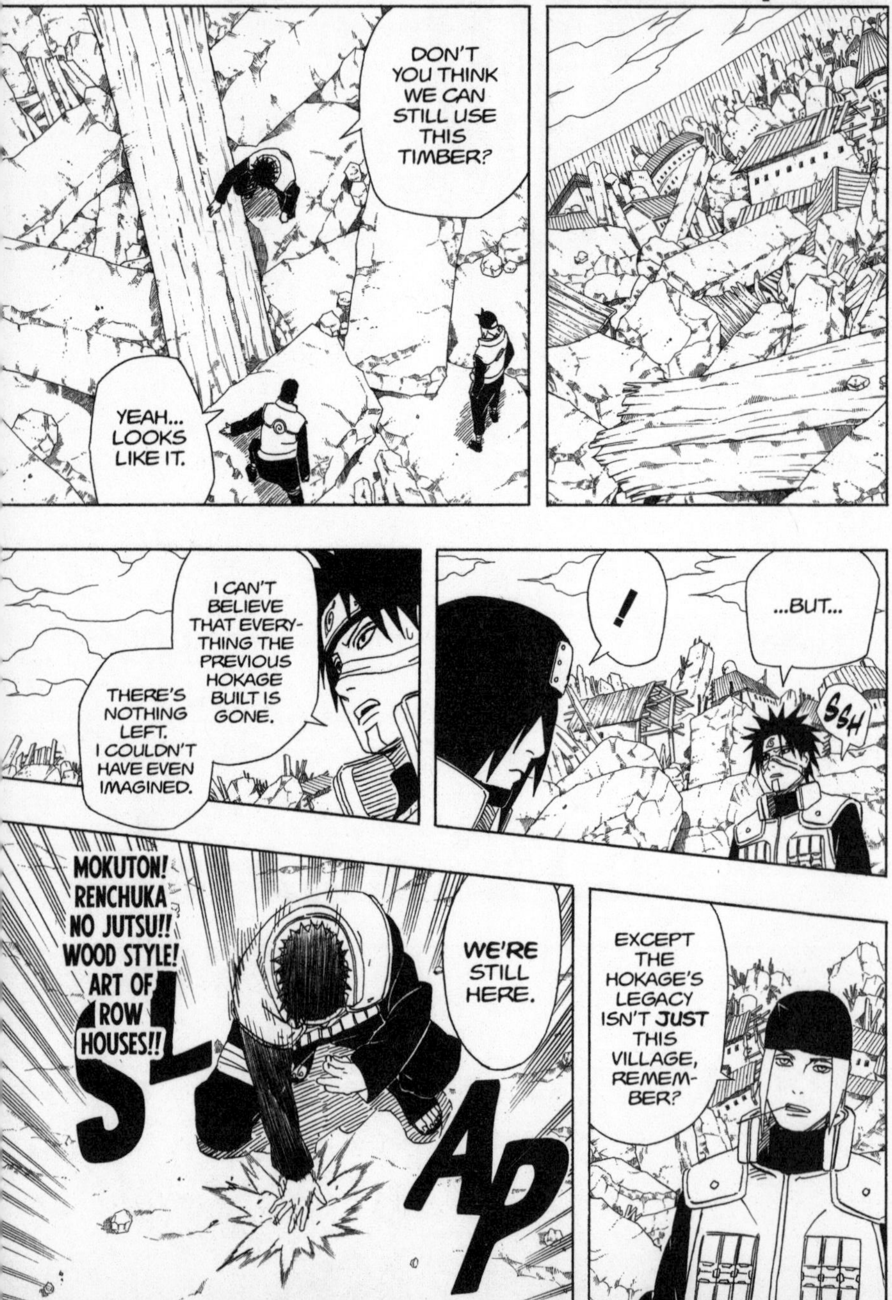

DON'T YOU THINK WE CAN STILL USE THIS TIMBER?
YEAH... LOOKS LIKE IT.
!
...BUT...
SSH
I CAN'T BELIEVE THAT EVERY-THING THE PREVIOUS HOKAGE BUILT IS GONE.
THERE'S NOTHING LEFT. I COULDN'T HAVE EVEN IMAGINED.
EXCEPT THE HOKAGE'S LEGACY ISN'T JUST THIS VILLAGE, REMEM-BER?
WE'RE STILL HERE.
MOKUTON! RENCHUKA NO JUTSU!! WOOD STYLE! ART OF ROW HOUSES!!
SLAP

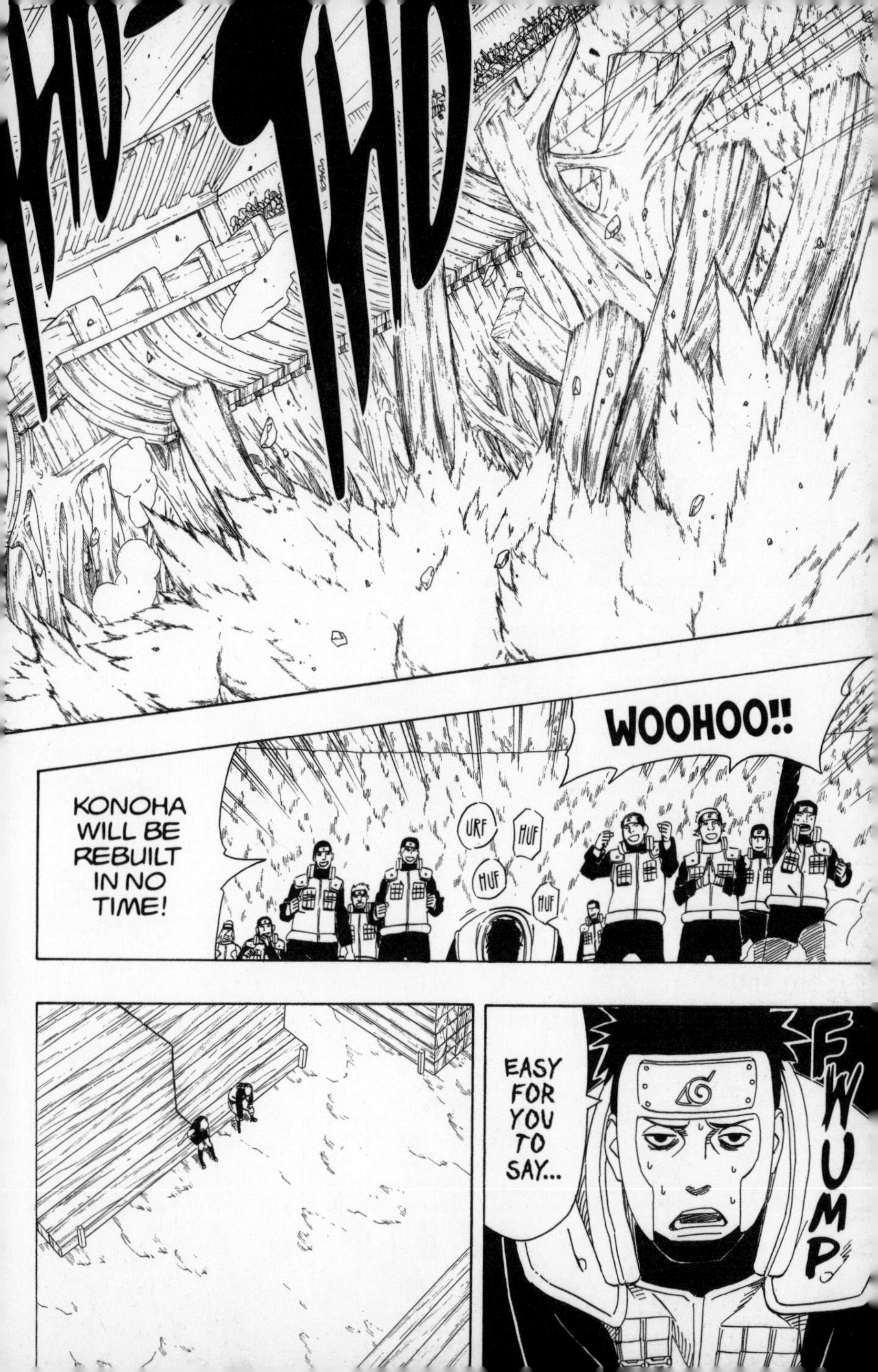
WOOHOO!!
HUF
URF
HUF
HUF
KONOHA WILL BE REBUILT IN NO TIME!
FWUMP
EASY FOR YOU TO SAY...

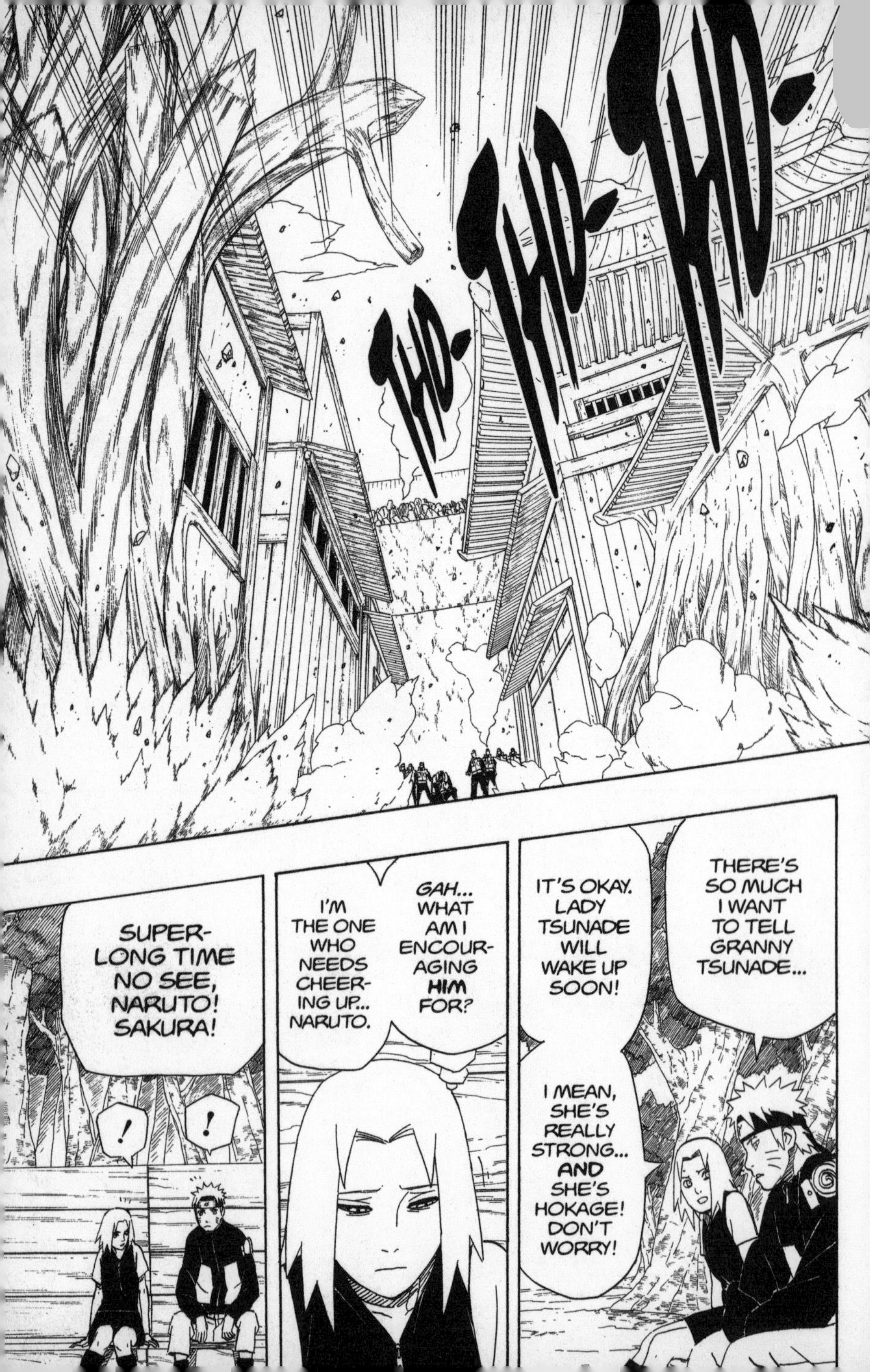
THD- THD- THD-
THERE'S SO MUCH I WANT TO TELL GRANNY TSUNADE...
IT'S OKAY. LADY TSUNADE WILL WAKE UP SOON!
I MEAN, SHE'S REALLY STRONG... AND SHE'S HOKAGE! DON'T WORRY!
GAH... WHAT AM I ENCOURAGING HIM FOR?
I'M THE ONE WHO NEEDS CHEERING UP... NARUTO.
SUPER-LONG TIME NO SEE, NARUTO! SAKURA!
!
!

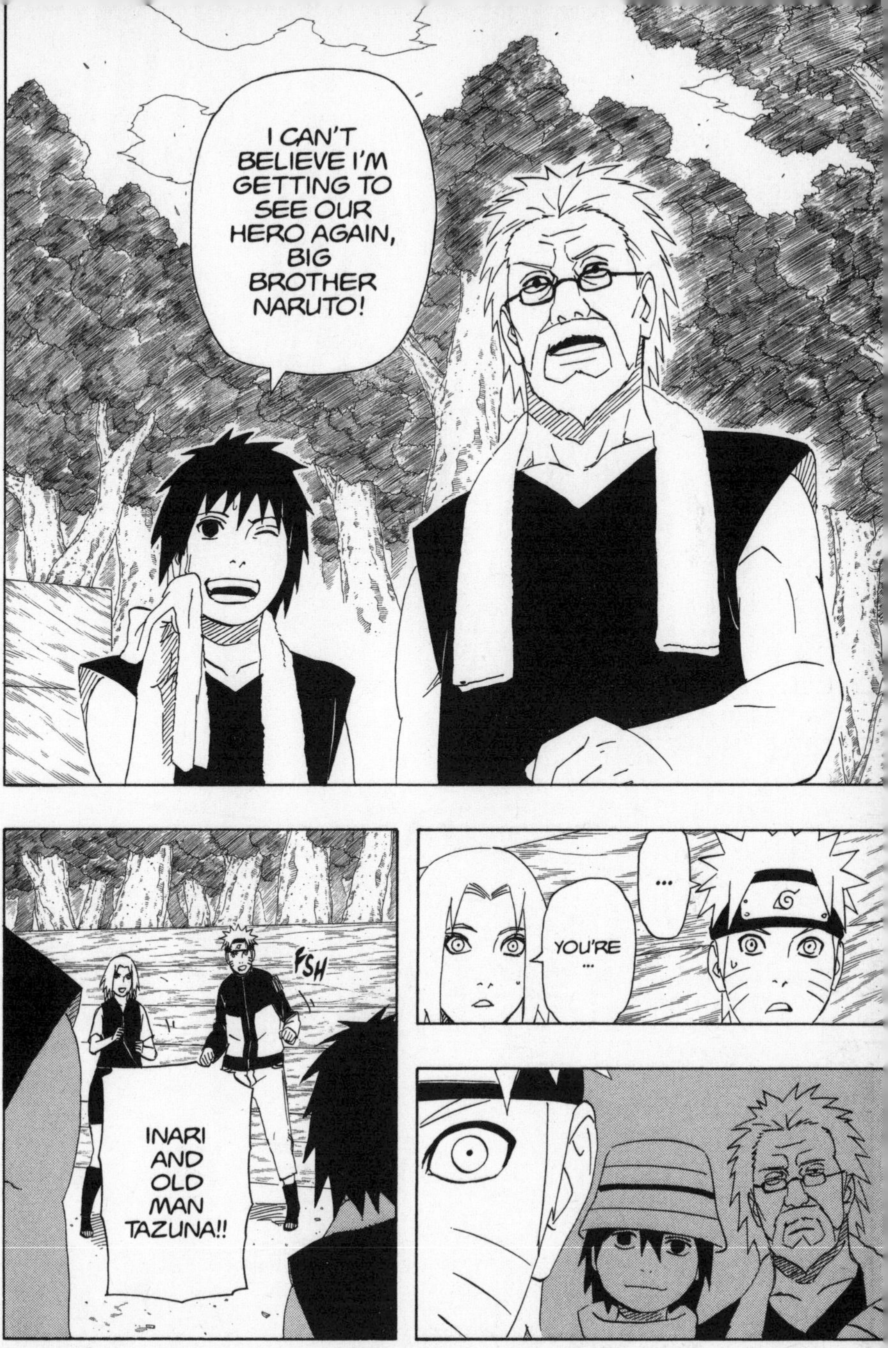
I CAN'T BELIEVE I'M GETTING TO SEE OUR HERO AGAIN, BIG BROTHER NARUTO!
...
YOU'RE ...
FSH
INARI AND OLD MAN TAZUNA!!

READ THIS WAY

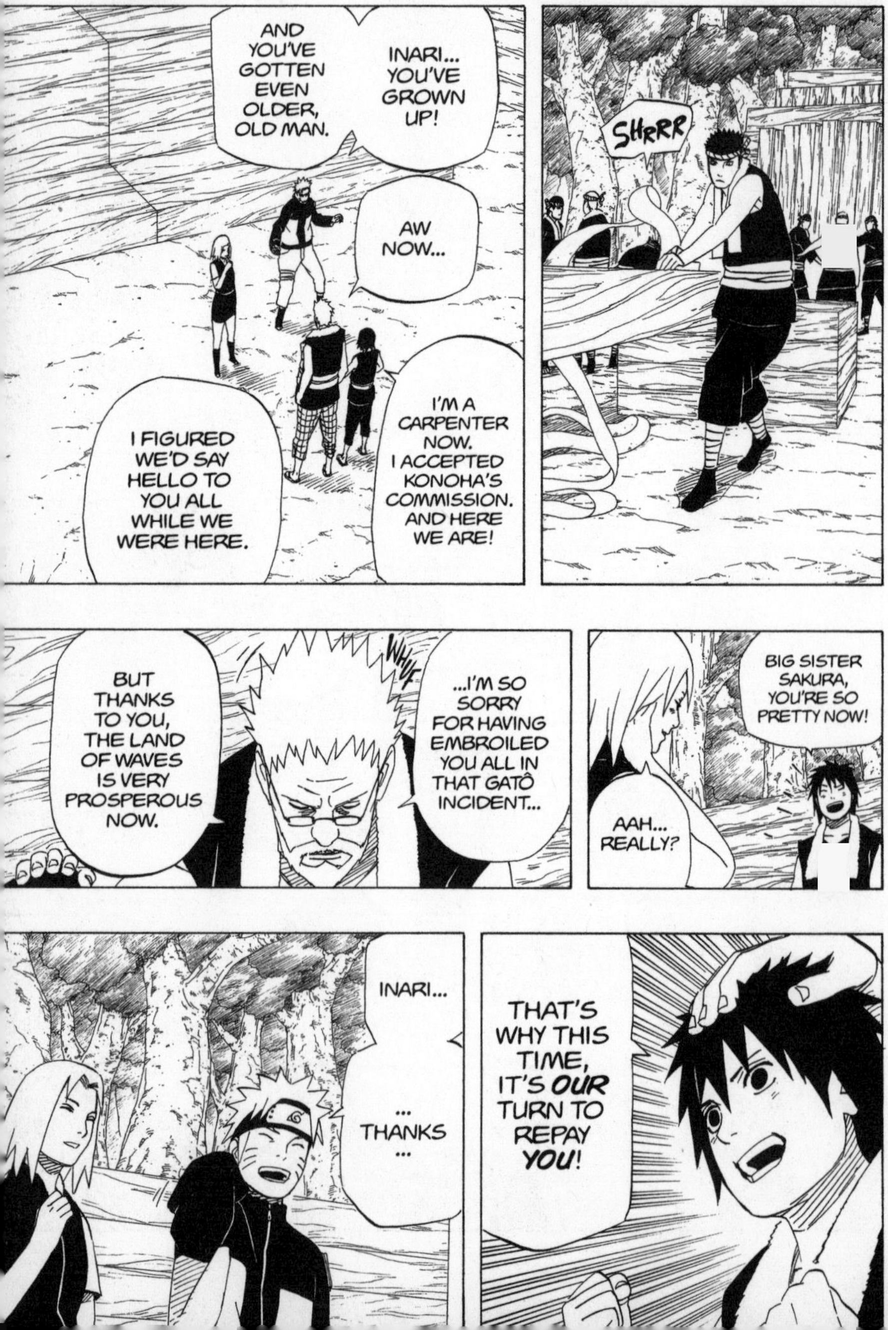
SHRRR
INARI... YOU'VE GROWN UP!
AND YOU'VE GOTTEN EVEN OLDER, OLD MAN.
AW NOW...
I'M A CARPENTER NOW. I ACCEPTED KONOHA'S COMMISSION. AND HERE WE ARE!
I FIGURED WE'D SAY HELLO TO YOU ALL WHILE WE WERE HERE.
BIG SISTER SAKURA, YOU'RE SO PRETTY NOW!
AAH... REALLY?
WHUF
...I'M SO SORRY FOR HAVING EMBROILED YOU ALL IN THAT GATÔ INCIDENT...
BUT THANKS TO YOU, THE LAND OF WAVES IS VERY PROSPEROUS NOW.
THAT'S WHY THIS TIME, IT'S OUR TURN TO REPAY YOU!
INARI...
... THANKS ...

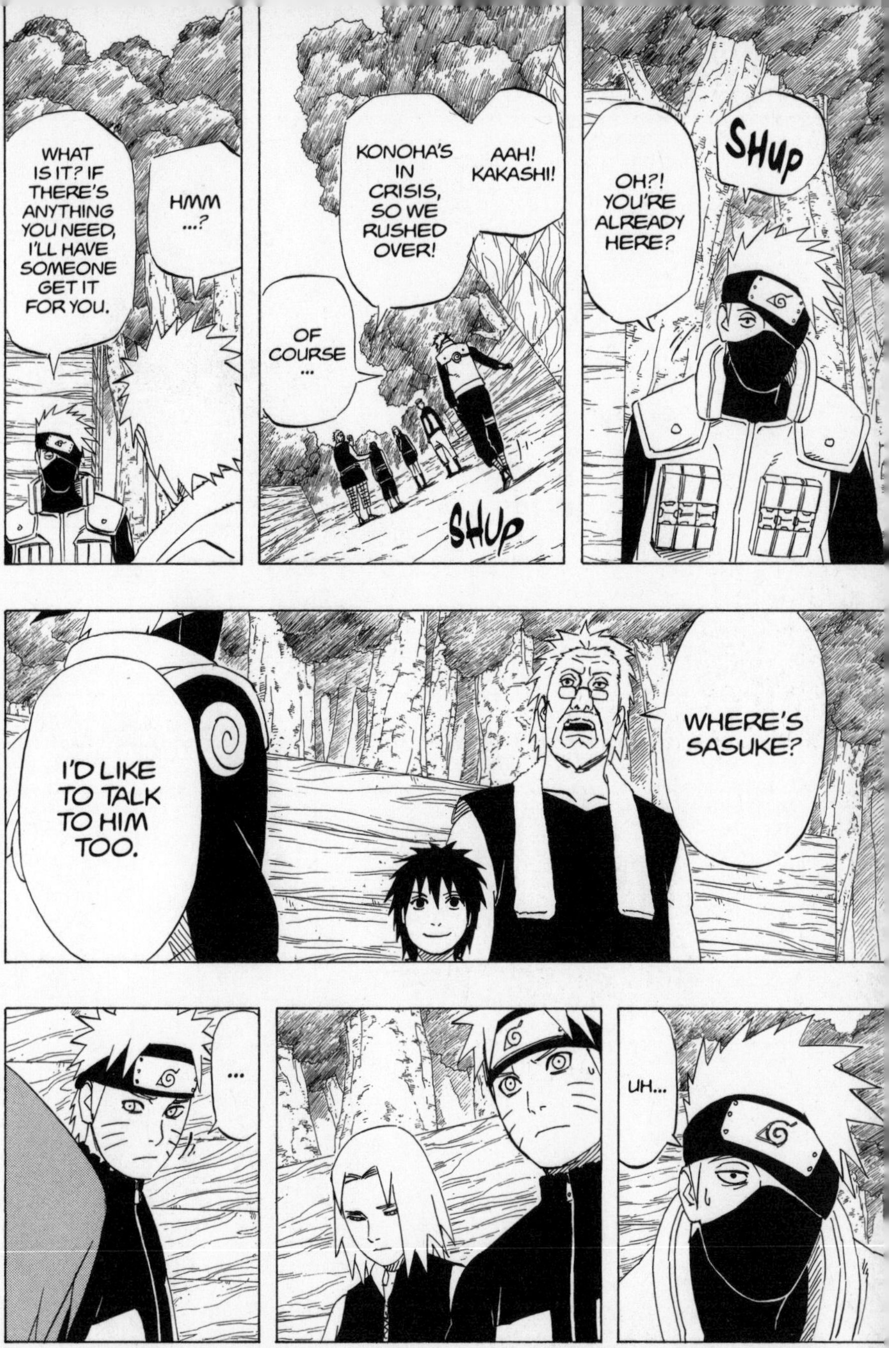
SHUP
OH?! YOU'RE ALREADY HERE?
AAH! KAKASHI!
KONOHA'S IN CRISIS, SO WE RUSHED OVER!
OF COURSE ...
SHUP
HMM ...?
WHAT IS IT? IF THERE'S ANYTHING YOU NEED, I'LL HAVE SOMEONE GET IT FOR YOU.
WHERE'S SASUKE?
I'D LIKE TO TALK TO HIM TOO.
UH...
...

READ THIS WAY

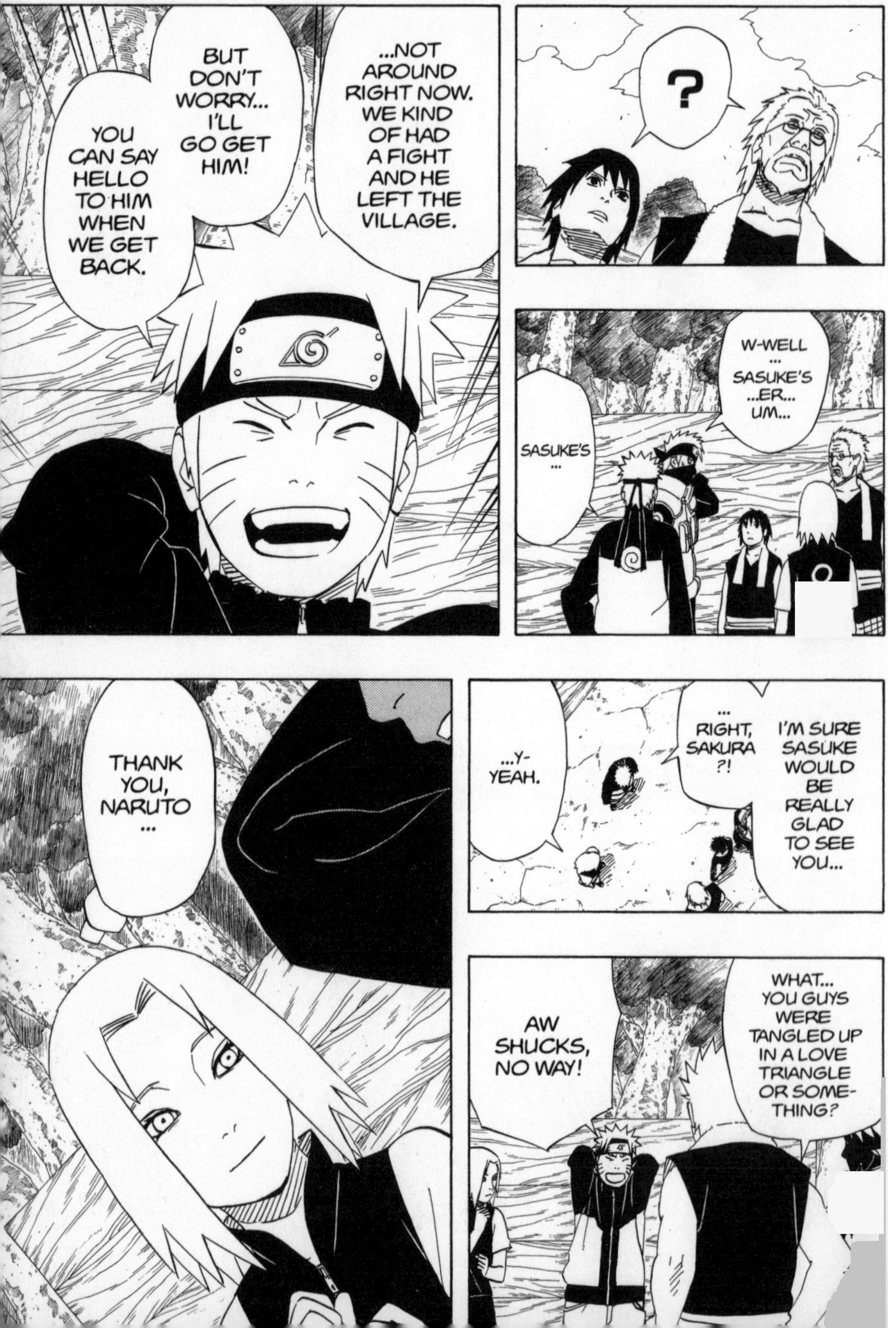
?
W-WELL ... SASUKE'S ...ER... UM...
SASUKE'S ...
...NOT AROUND RIGHT NOW. WE KIND OF HAD A FIGHT AND HE LEFT THE VILLAGE.
BUT DON'T WORRY... I'LL GO GET HIM!
YOU CAN SAY HELLO TO HIM WHEN WE GET BACK.
I'M SURE SASUKE WOULD BE REALLY GLAD TO SEE YOU...
... RIGHT, SAKURA ?!
...Y-YEAH.
WHAT... YOU GUYS WERE TANGLED UP IN A LOVE TRIANGLE OR SOME-THING?
AW SHUCKS, NO WAY!
THANK YOU, NARUTO ...

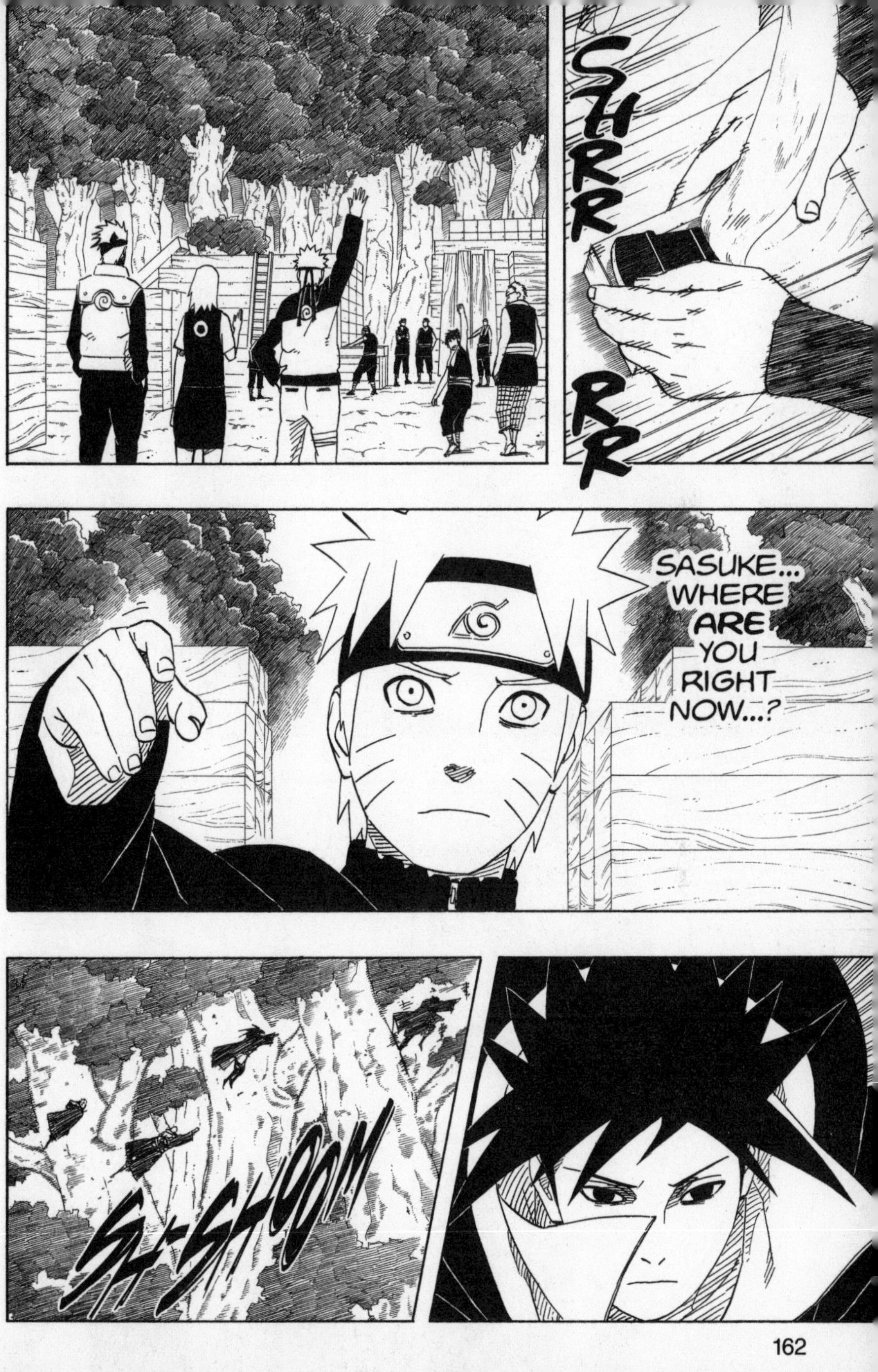
SHRR
RR
SASUKE... WHERE ARE YOU RIGHT NOW...?
SH-SHOOM

READ THIS WAY

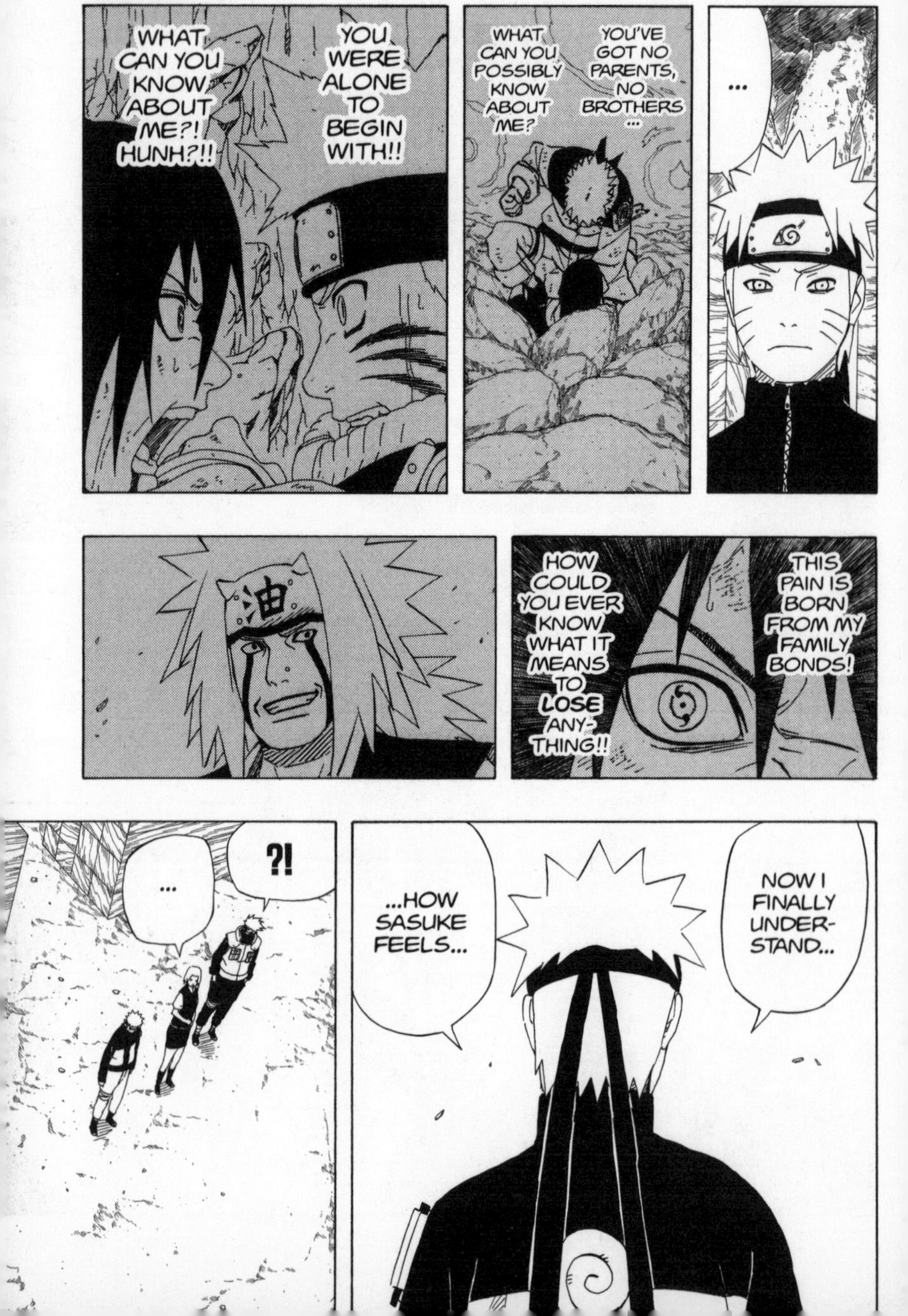

...
YOU'VE GOT NO PARENTS, NO BROTHERS ...
WHAT CAN YOU POSSIBLY KNOW ABOUT ME?
YOU WERE ALONE TO BEGIN WITH!!
WHAT CAN YOU KNOW ABOUT ME?! HUNH?!!
THIS PAIN IS BORN FROM MY FAMILY BONDS!
HOW COULD YOU EVER KNOW WHAT IT MEANS TO LOSE ANYTHING!!
NOW I FINALLY UNDERSTAND...
...HOW SASUKE FEELS...
?!
...

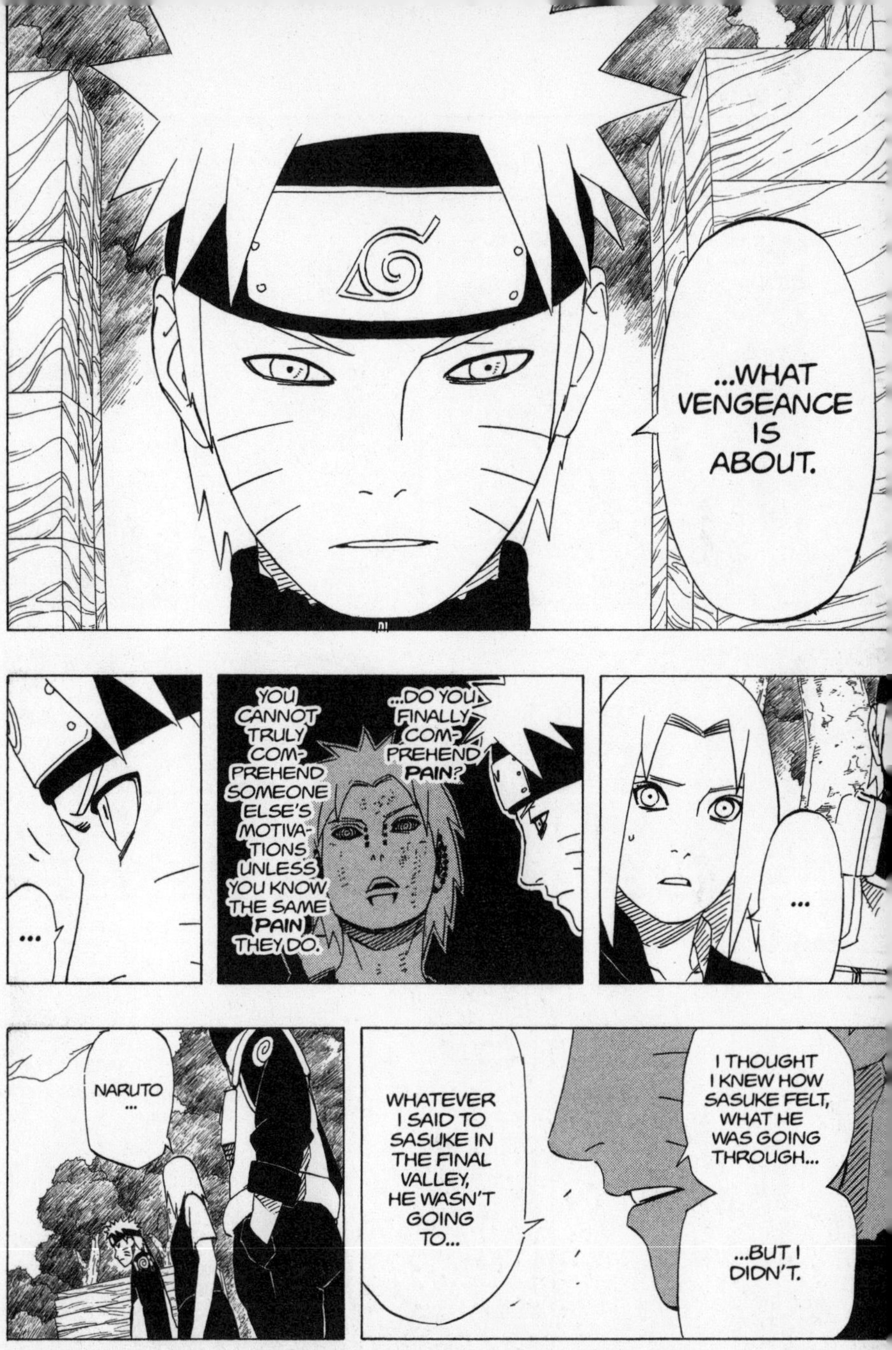
...WHAT VENGEANCE IS ABOUT.
...
...DO YOU FINALLY COM- PREHEND PAIN?
YOU CANNOT TRULY COM- PREHEND SOMEONE ELSE'S MOTIVA- TIONS UNLESS YOU KNOW THE SAME PAIN THEY DO.
...
I THOUGHT I KNEW HOW SASUKE FELT, WHAT HE WAS GOING THROUGH...
...BUT I DIDN'T.
WHATEVER I SAID TO SASUKE IN THE FINAL VALLEY, HE WASN'T GOING TO...
NARUTO ...

READ THIS WAY

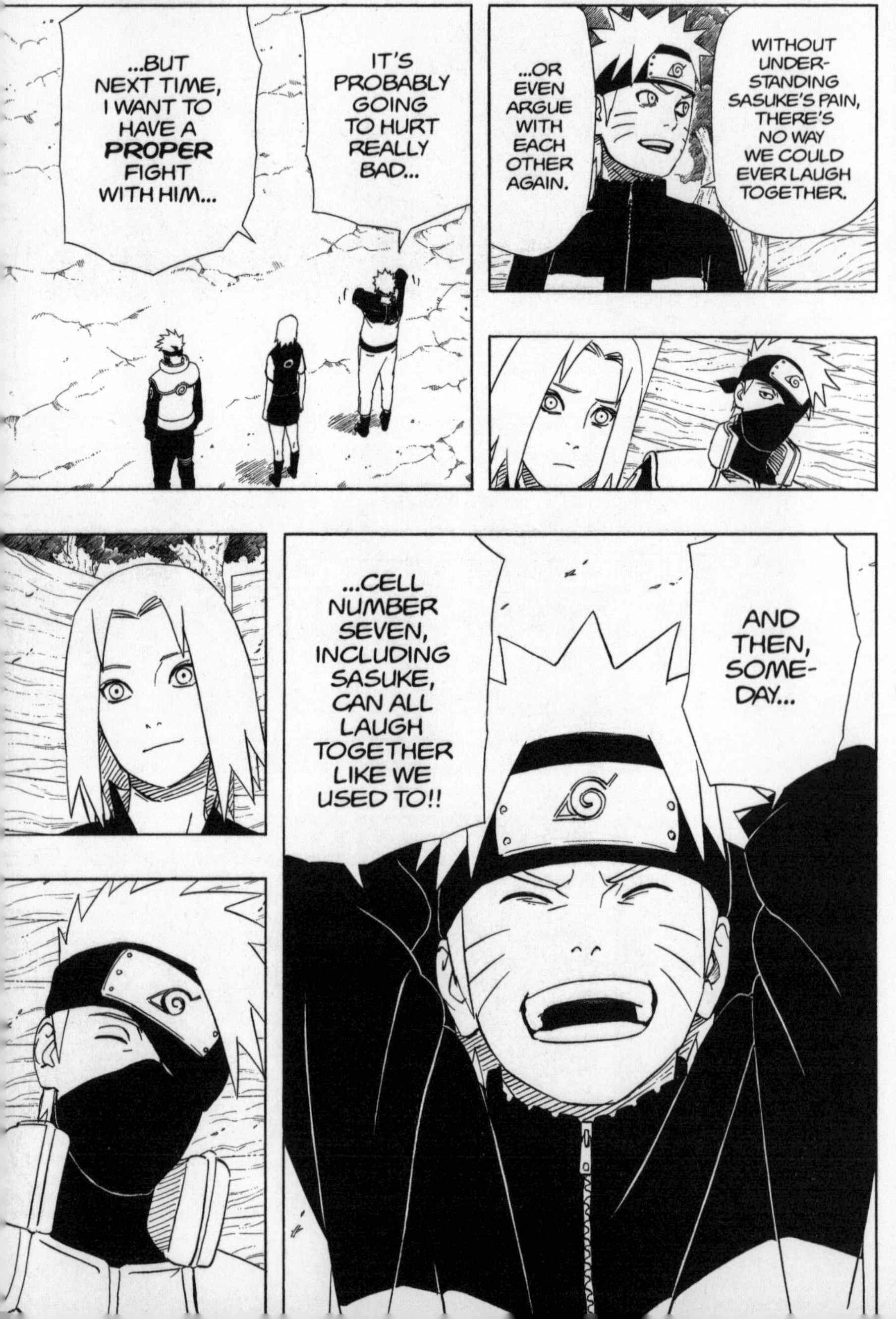
WITHOUT UNDER-STANDING SASUKE'S PAIN, THERE'S NO WAY WE COULD EVER LAUGH TOGETHER.
...OR EVEN ARGUE WITH EACH OTHER AGAIN.
IT'S PROBABLY GOING TO HURT REALLY BAD...
...BUT NEXT TIME, I WANT TO HAVE A **PROPER** FIGHT WITH HIM...
AND THEN, SOME-DAY...
...CELL NUMBER SEVEN, INCLUDING SASUKE, CAN ALL LAUGH TOGETHER LIKE WE USED TO!!

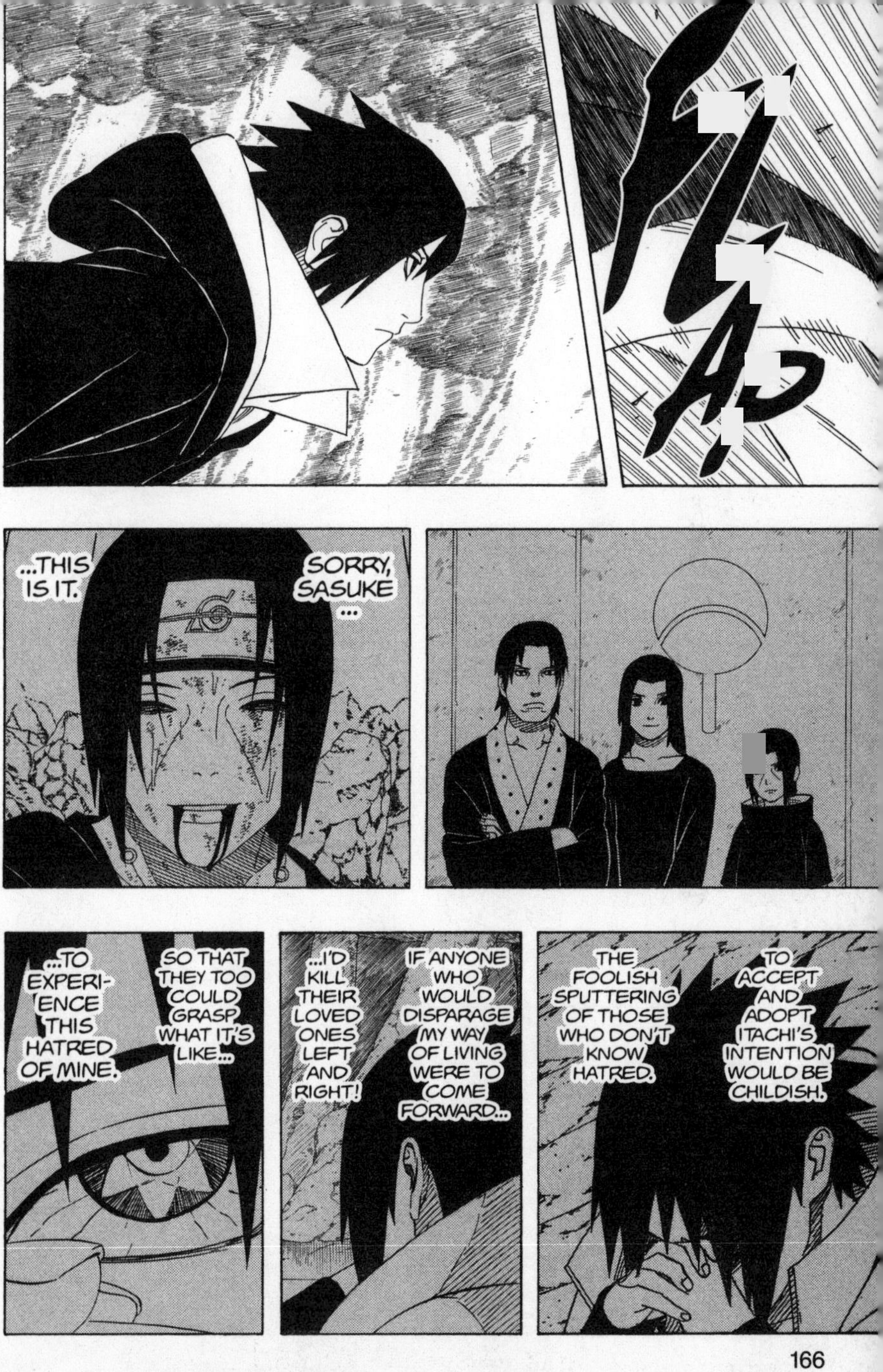

SORRY, SASUKE ...
...THIS IS IT.
TO ACCEPT AND ADOPT ITACHI'S INTENTION WOULD BE CHILDISH.
THE FOOLISH SPUTTERING OF THOSE WHO DON'T KNOW HATRED.
IF ANYONE WHO WOULD DISPARAGE MY WAY OF LIVING WERE TO COME FORWARD...
...I'D KILL THEIR LOVED ONES LEFT AND RIGHT!
SO THAT THEY TOO COULD GRASP WHAT IT'S LIKE...
...TO EXPERIENCE THIS HATRED OF MINE.

READ THIS WAY

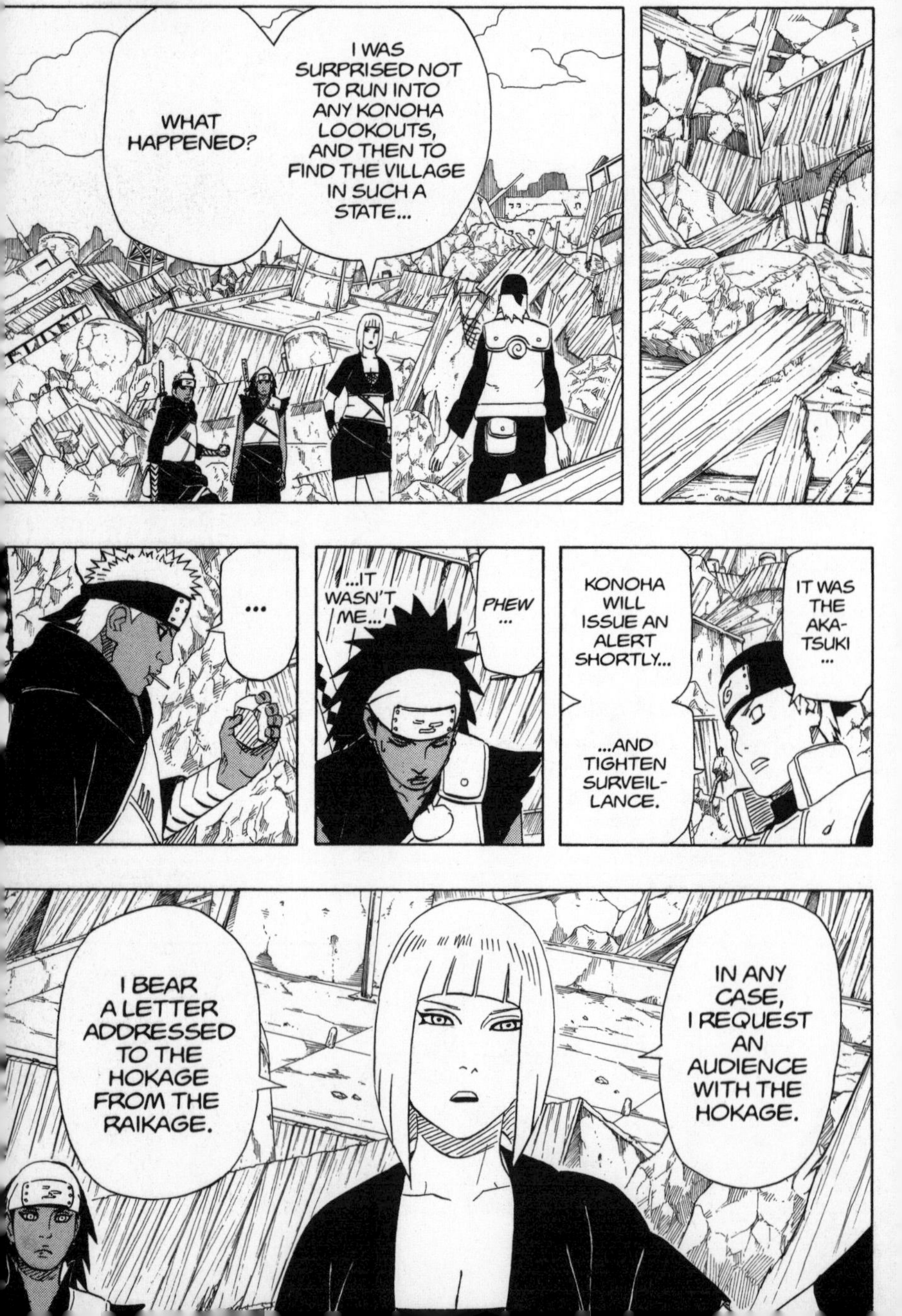
I WAS SURPRISED NOT TO RUN INTO ANY KONOHA LOOKOUTS, AND THEN TO FIND THE VILLAGE IN SUCH A STATE...
WHAT HAPPENED?
IT WAS THE AKA-TSUKI...
KONOHA WILL ISSUE AN ALERT SHORTLY...
...AND TIGHTEN SURVEIL-LANCE.
PHEW...
...IT WASN'T ME...!
...
IN ANY CASE, I REQUEST AN AUDIENCE WITH THE HOKAGE.
I BEAR A LETTER ADDRESSED TO THE HOKAGE FROM THE RAIKAGE.

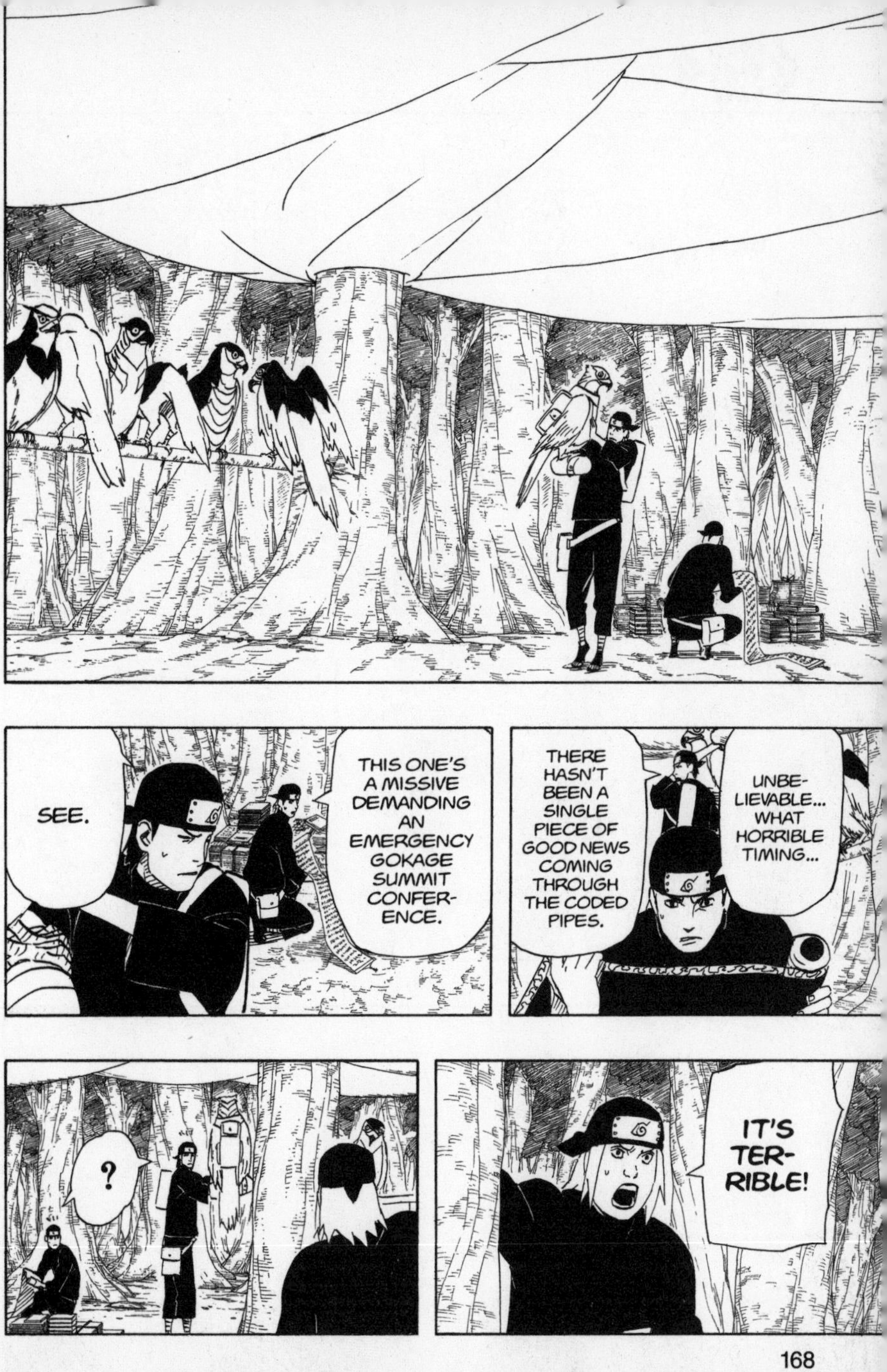
UNBE-LIEVABLE... WHAT HORRIBLE TIMING...
THERE HASN'T BEEN A SINGLE PIECE OF GOOD NEWS COMING THROUGH THE CODED PIPES.
THIS ONE'S A MISSIVE DEMANDING AN EMERGENCY GOKAGE SUMMIT CONFER-ENCE.
SEE.
IT'S TER-RIBLE!
?

READ THIS WAY

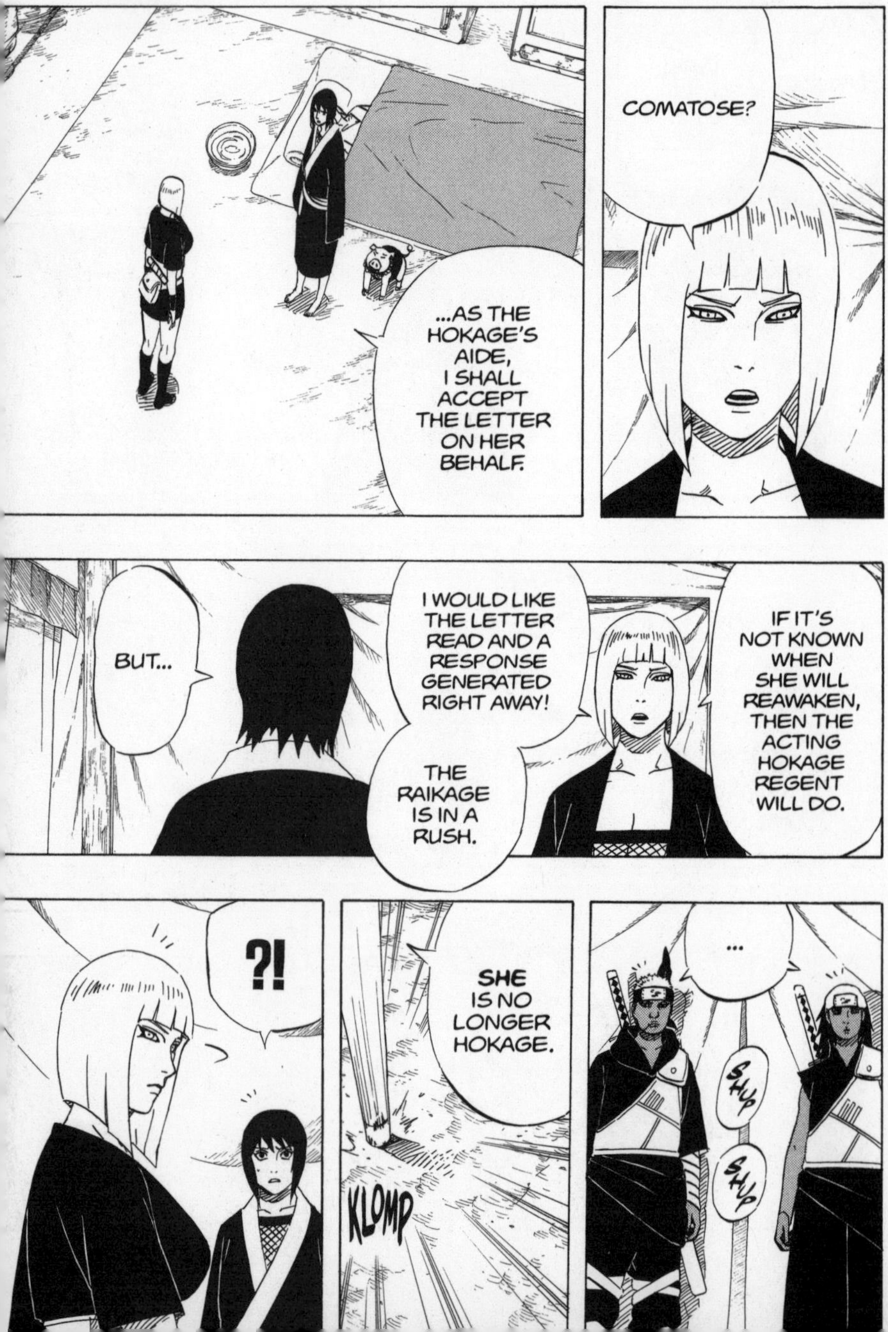
COMATOSE?
...AS THE HOKAGE'S AIDE, I SHALL ACCEPT THE LETTER ON HER BEHALF.
IF IT'S NOT KNOWN WHEN SHE WILL REAWAKEN, THEN THE ACTING HOKAGE REGENT WILL DO.
I WOULD LIKE THE LETTER READ AND A RESPONSE GENERATED RIGHT AWAY!
THE RAIKAGE IS IN A RUSH.
BUT...
...
SHUP
SHUP
SHE IS NO LONGER HOKAGE.
KLOMP
?!

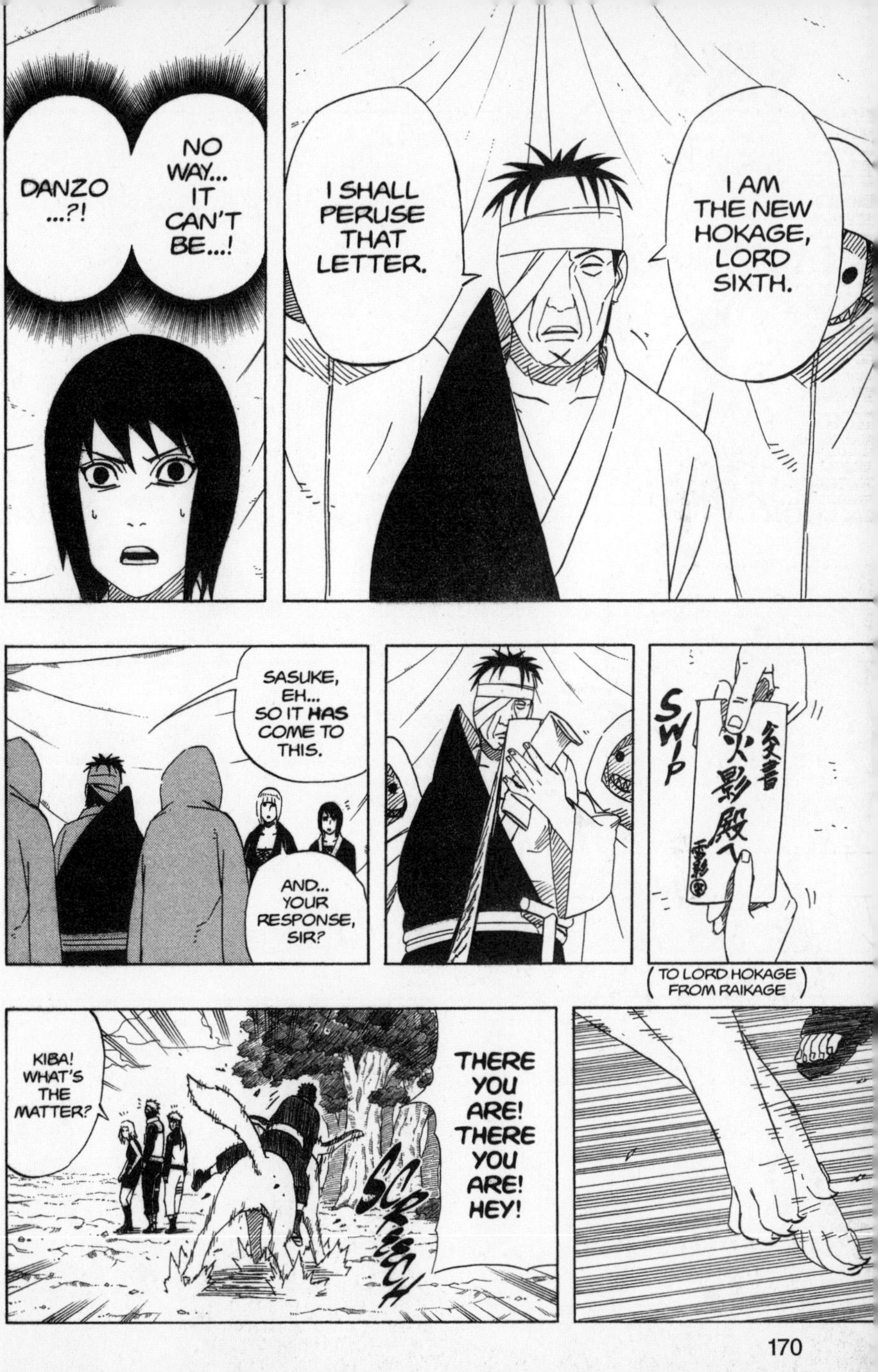
I AM THE NEW HOKAGE, LORD SIXTH.
I SHALL PERUSE THAT LETTER.
NO WAY... IT CAN'T BE...!
DANZO ...?!
SWIP
火影殿へ
雷影
(TO LORD HOKAGE FROM RAIKAGE)
SASUKE, EH... SO IT HAS COME TO THIS.
AND... YOUR RESPONSE, SIR?
THERE YOU ARE! THERE YOU ARE! HEY!
SCREECH
KIBA! WHAT'S THE MATTER?

READ THIS WAY

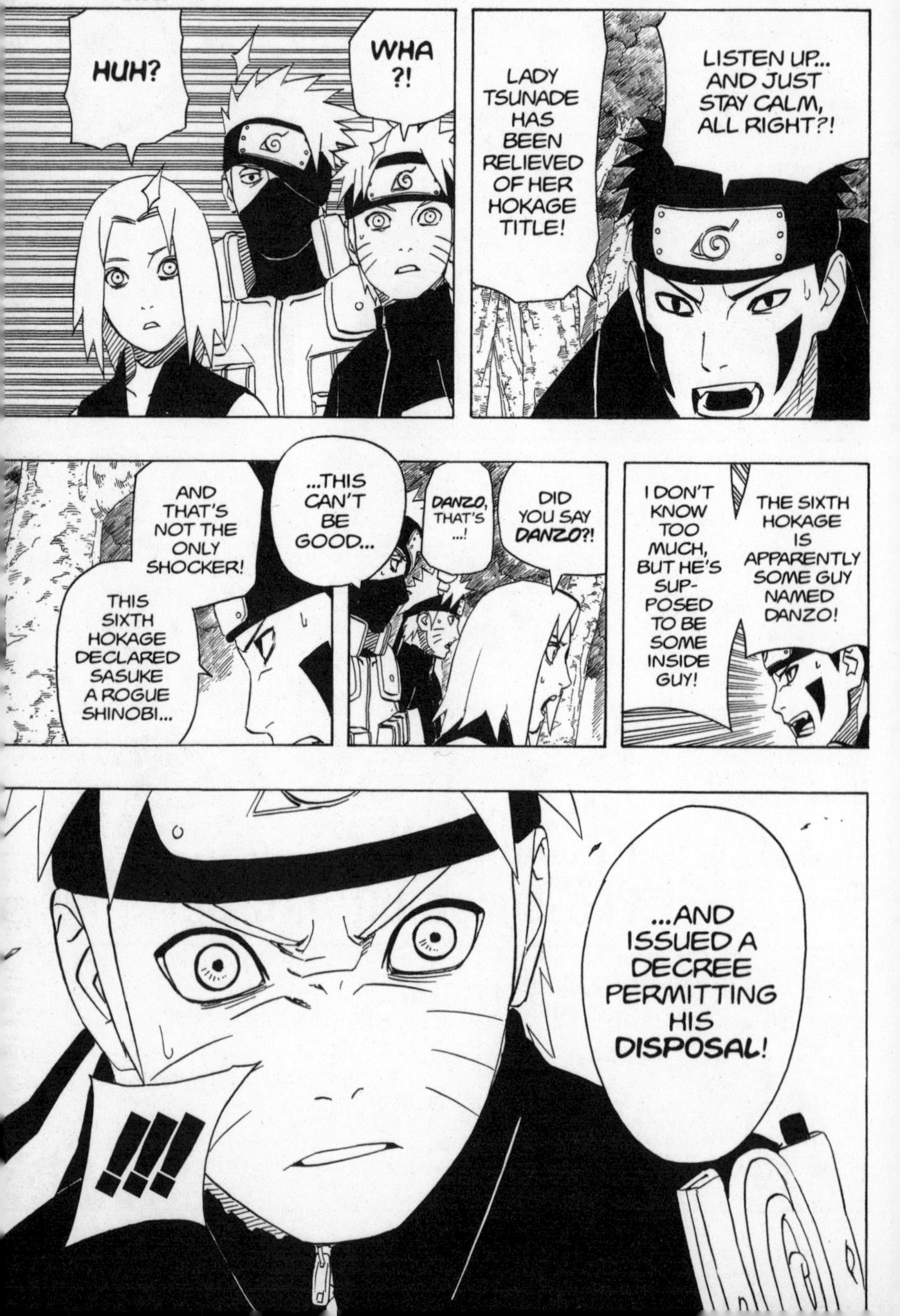
LISTEN UP... AND JUST STAY CALM, ALL RIGHT?!
LADY TSUNADE HAS BEEN RELIEVED OF HER HOKAGE TITLE!
WHA ?!
HUH?
THE SIXTH HOKAGE IS APPARENTLY SOME GUY NAMED DANZO!
I DON'T KNOW TOO MUCH, BUT HE'S SUP-POSED TO BE SOME INSIDE GUY!
DID YOU SAY DANZO?!
DANZO, THAT'S ...!
...THIS CAN'T BE GOOD...
AND THAT'S NOT THE ONLY SHOCKER!
THIS SIXTH HOKAGE DECLARED SASUKE A ROGUE SHINOBI...
...AND ISSUED A DECREE PERMITTING HIS DISPOSAL!
!!!

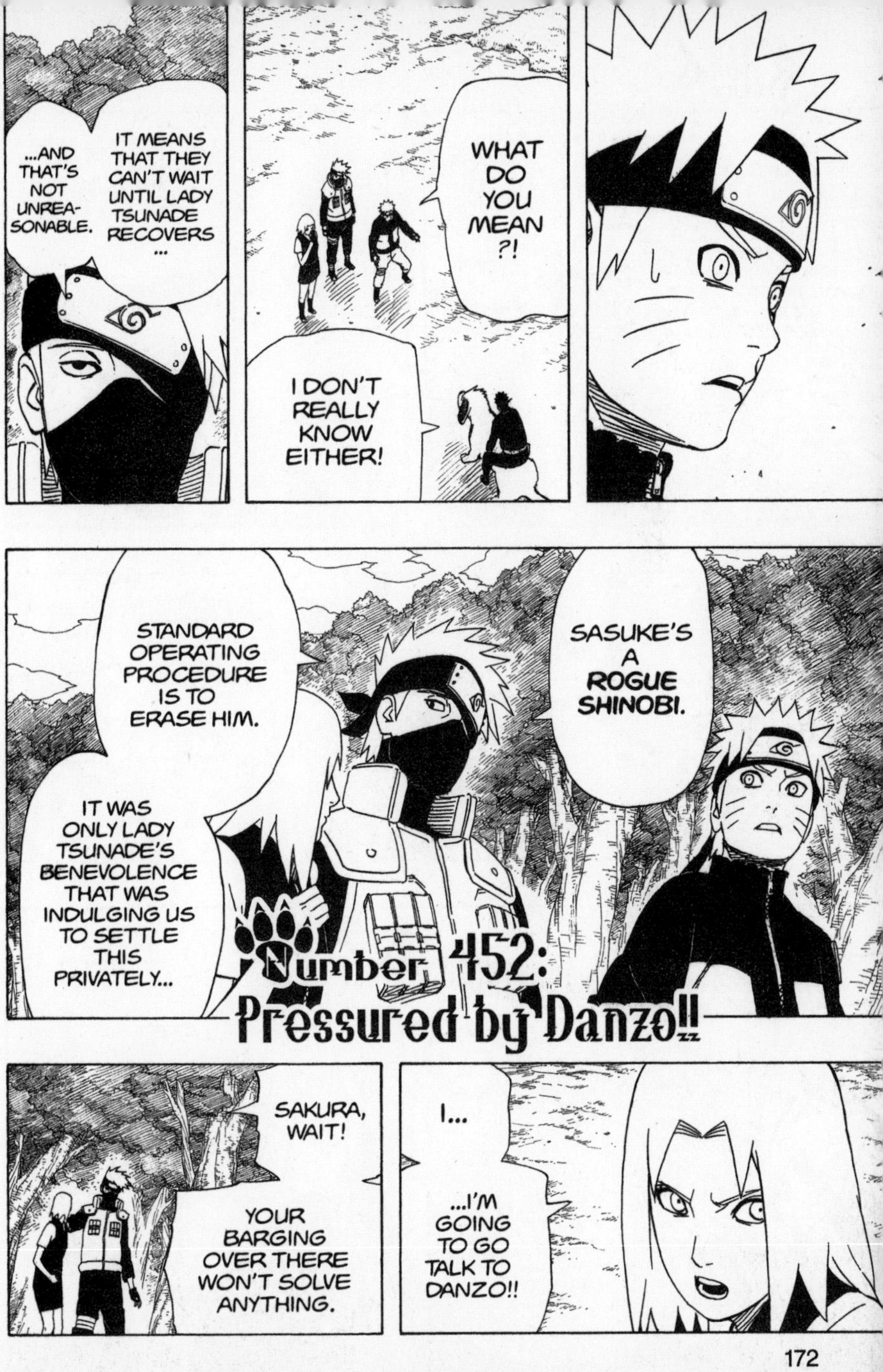
WHAT DO YOU MEAN?!
I DON'T REALLY KNOW EITHER!
IT MEANS THAT THEY CAN'T WAIT UNTIL LADY TSUNADE RECOVERS...
...AND THAT'S NOT UNREASONABLE.
SASUKE'S A ROGUE SHINOBI.
STANDARD OPERATING PROCEDURE IS TO ERASE HIM.
IT WAS ONLY LADY TSUNADE'S BENEVOLENCE THAT WAS INDULGING US TO SETTLE THIS PRIVATELY...
Number 452: Pressured by Danzo!!
I...
...I'M GOING TO GO TALK TO DANZO!!
SAKURA, WAIT!
YOUR BARGING OVER THERE WON'T SOLVE ANYTHING.

READ THIS WAY

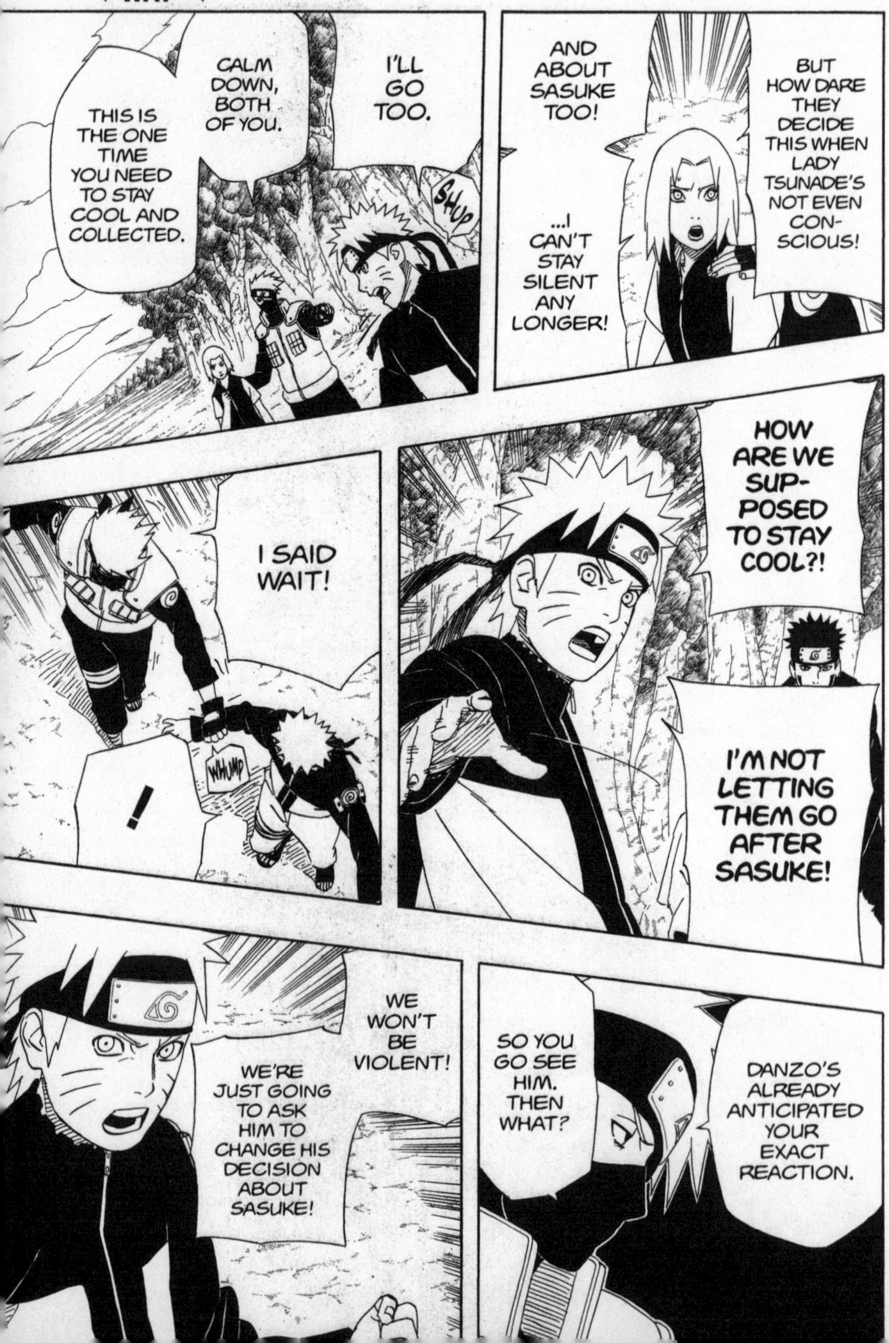
BUT HOW DARE THEY DECIDE THIS WHEN LADY TSUNADE'S NOT EVEN CONSCIOUS!
AND ABOUT SASUKE TOO!
...I CAN'T STAY SILENT ANY LONGER!
I'LL GO TOO.
SHUP
CALM DOWN, BOTH OF YOU.
THIS IS THE ONE TIME YOU NEED TO STAY COOL AND COLLECTED.
HOW ARE WE SUPPOSED TO STAY COOL?!
I'M NOT LETTING THEM GO AFTER SASUKE!
I SAID WAIT!
WHUMP
!
DANZO'S ALREADY ANTICIPATED YOUR EXACT REACTION.
SO YOU GO SEE HIM. THEN WHAT?
WE WON'T BE VIOLENT!
WE'RE JUST GOING TO ASK HIM TO CHANGE HIS DECISION ABOUT SASUKE!

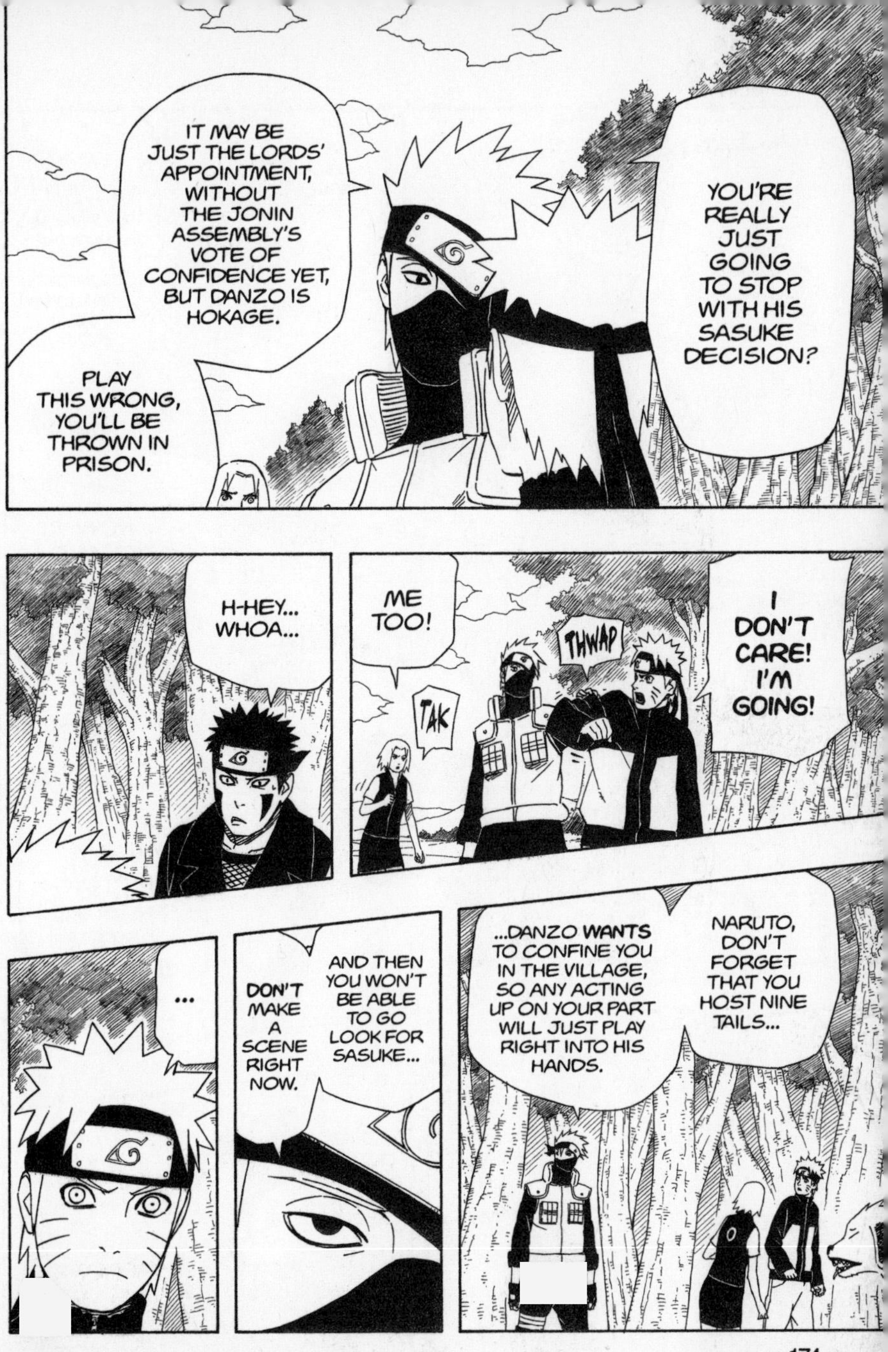
YOU'RE REALLY JUST GOING TO STOP WITH HIS SASUKE DECISION?
IT MAY BE JUST THE LORDS' APPOINTMENT, WITHOUT THE JONIN ASSEMBLY'S VOTE OF CONFIDENCE YET, BUT DANZO IS HOKAGE.
PLAY THIS WRONG, YOU'LL BE THROWN IN PRISON.
I DON'T CARE! I'M GOING!
THWAP
TAK
ME TOO!
H-HEY... WHOA...
NARUTO, DON'T FORGET THAT YOU HOST NINE TAILS...
...DANZO **WANTS** TO CONFINE YOU IN THE VILLAGE, SO ANY ACTING UP ON YOUR PART WILL JUST PLAY RIGHT INTO HIS HANDS.
AND THEN YOU WON'T BE ABLE TO GO LOOK FOR SASUKE...
DON'T MAKE A SCENE RIGHT NOW.
...

READ THIS WAY

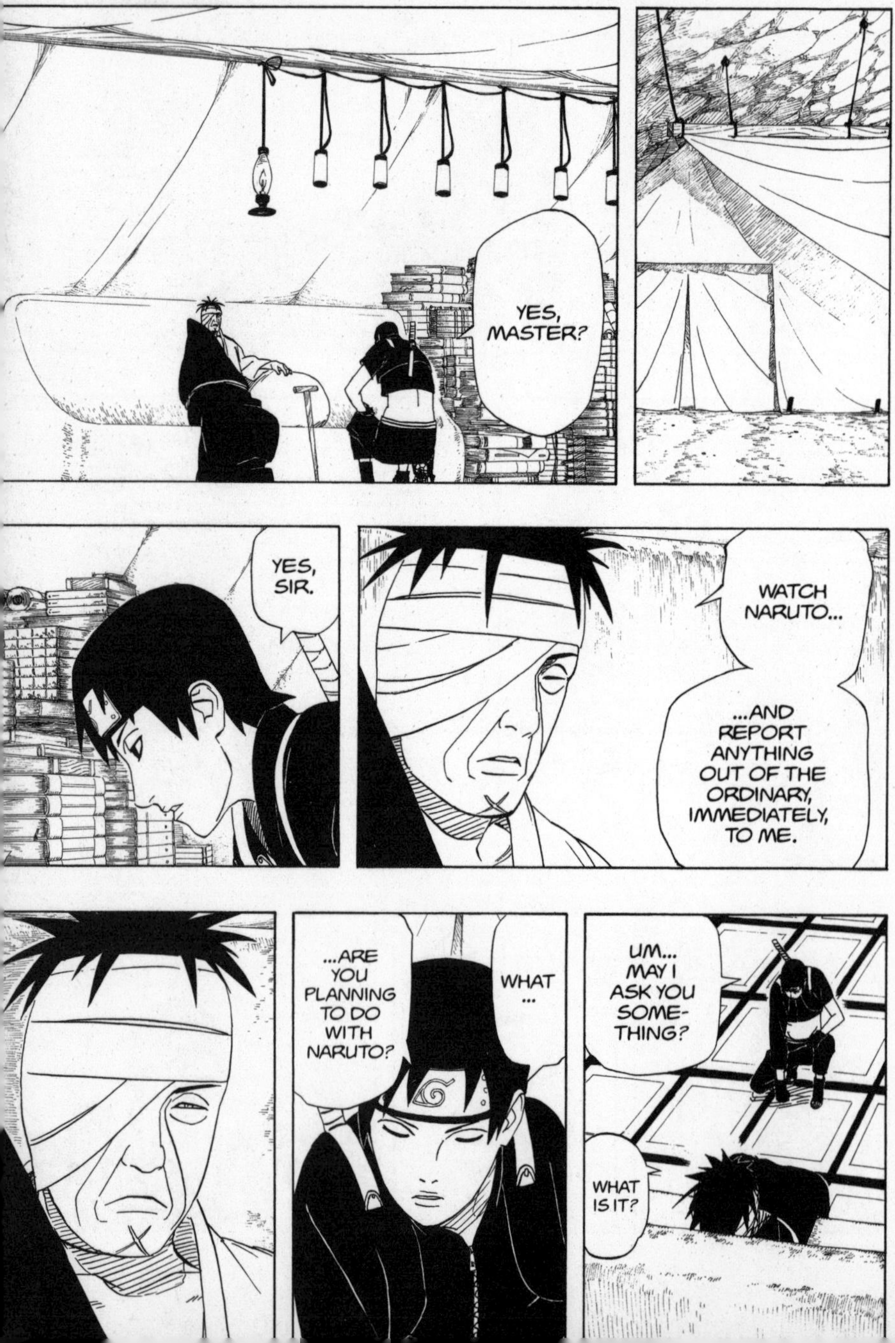
YES, MASTER?
WATCH NARUTO...
...AND REPORT ANYTHING OUT OF THE ORDINARY, IMMEDIATELY, TO ME.
YES, SIR.
UM... MAY I ASK YOU SOMETHING?
WHAT IS IT?
WHAT ...
...ARE YOU PLANNING TO DO WITH NARUTO?

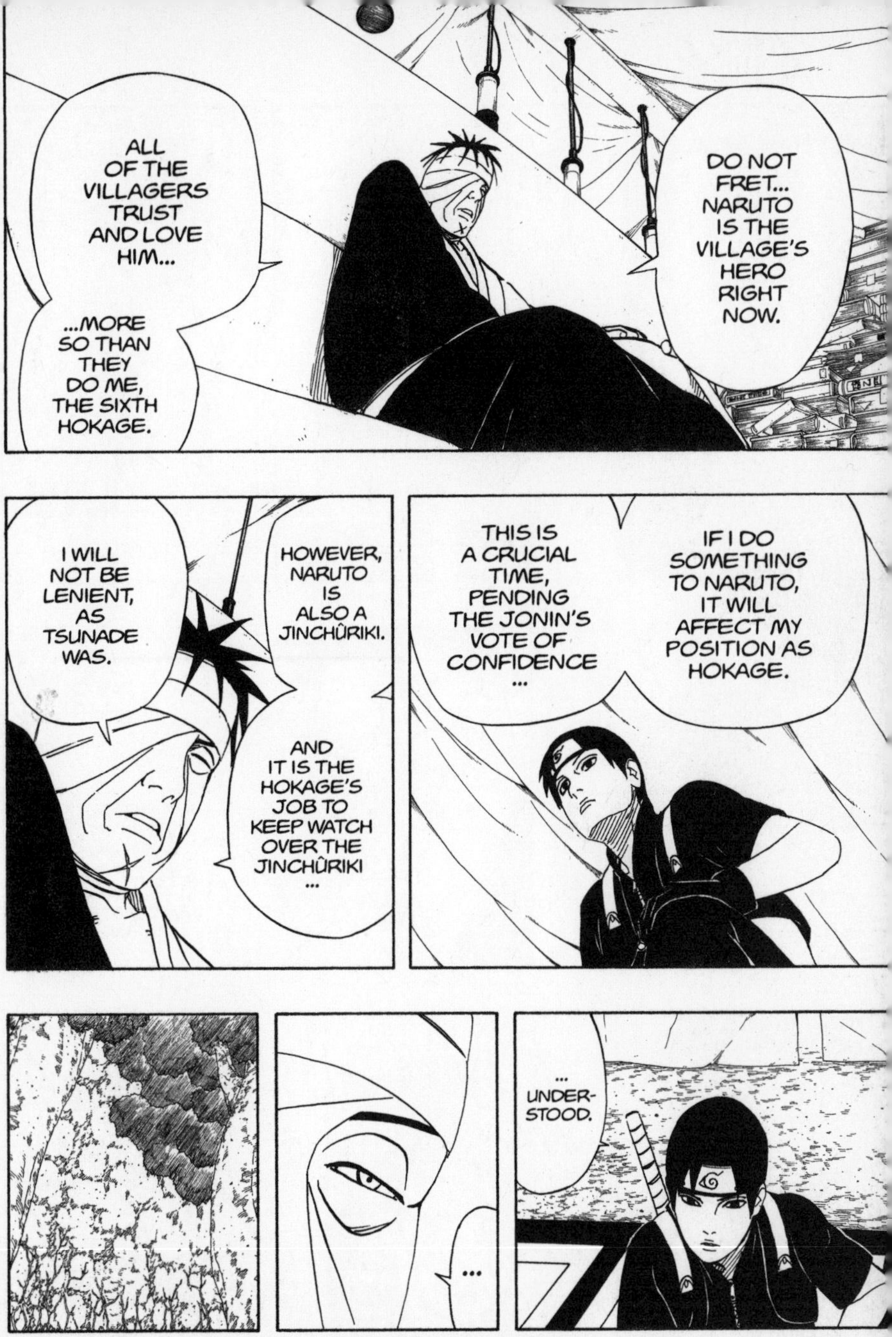
DO NOT FRET... NARUTO IS THE VILLAGE'S HERO RIGHT NOW.
ALL OF THE VILLAGERS TRUST AND LOVE HIM...
...MORE SO THAN THEY DO ME, THE SIXTH HOKAGE.
IF I DO SOMETHING TO NARUTO, IT WILL AFFECT MY POSITION AS HOKAGE.
THIS IS A CRUCIAL TIME, PENDING THE JONIN'S VOTE OF CONFIDENCE ...
HOWEVER, NARUTO IS ALSO A JINCHÛRIKI.
AND IT IS THE HOKAGE'S JOB TO KEEP WATCH OVER THE JINCHÛRIKI ...
I WILL NOT BE LENIENT, AS TSUNADE WAS.
... UNDER-STOOD.
...

READ THIS WAY

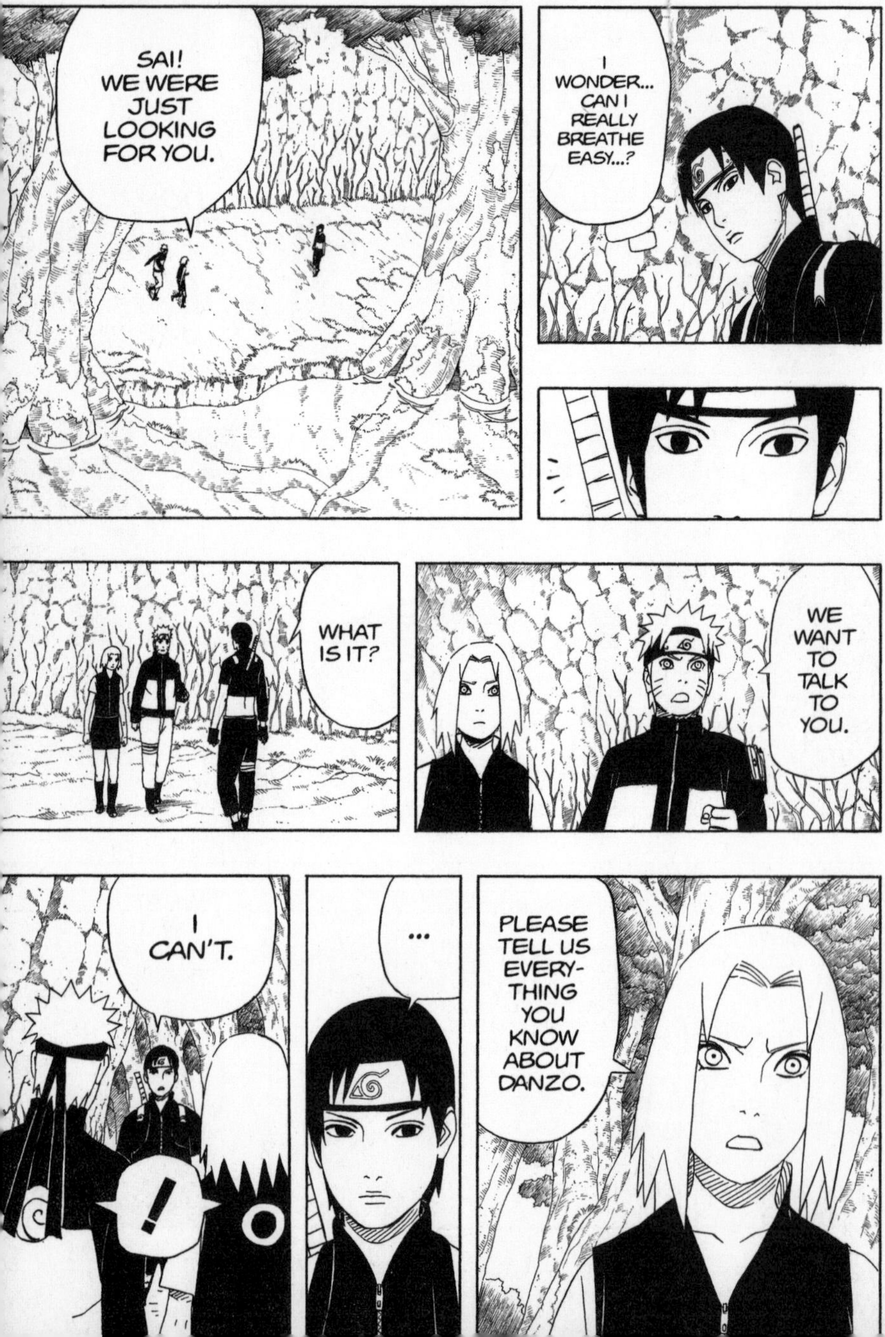
I WONDER... CAN I REALLY BREATHE EASY...?
SAI! WE WERE JUST LOOKING FOR YOU.
WE WANT TO TALK TO YOU.
WHAT IS IT?
PLEASE TELL US EVERY-THING YOU KNOW ABOUT DANZO.
...
I CAN'T.
!

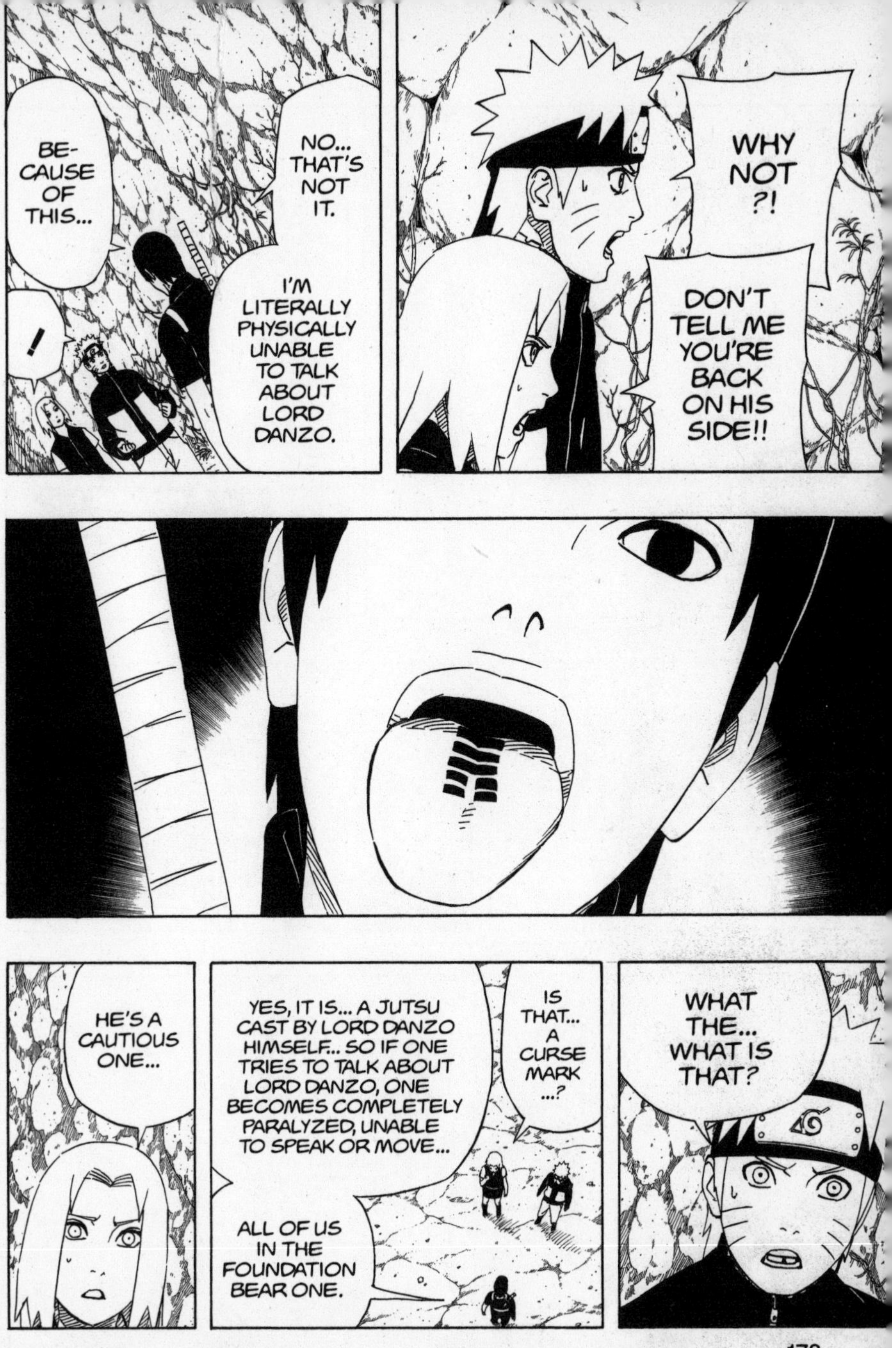
WHY NOT ?!
DON'T TELL ME YOU'RE BACK ON HIS SIDE!!
NO... THAT'S NOT IT.
I'M LITERALLY PHYSICALLY UNABLE TO TALK ABOUT LORD DANZO.
BE-CAUSE OF THIS...
!
WHAT THE... WHAT IS THAT?
IS THAT... A CURSE MARK ...?
YES, IT IS... A JUTSU CAST BY LORD DANZO HIMSELF... SO IF ONE TRIES TO TALK ABOUT LORD DANZO, ONE BECOMES COMPLETELY PARALYZED, UNABLE TO SPEAK OR MOVE...
ALL OF US IN THE FOUNDATION BEAR ONE.
HE'S A CAUTIOUS ONE...

READ THIS WAY

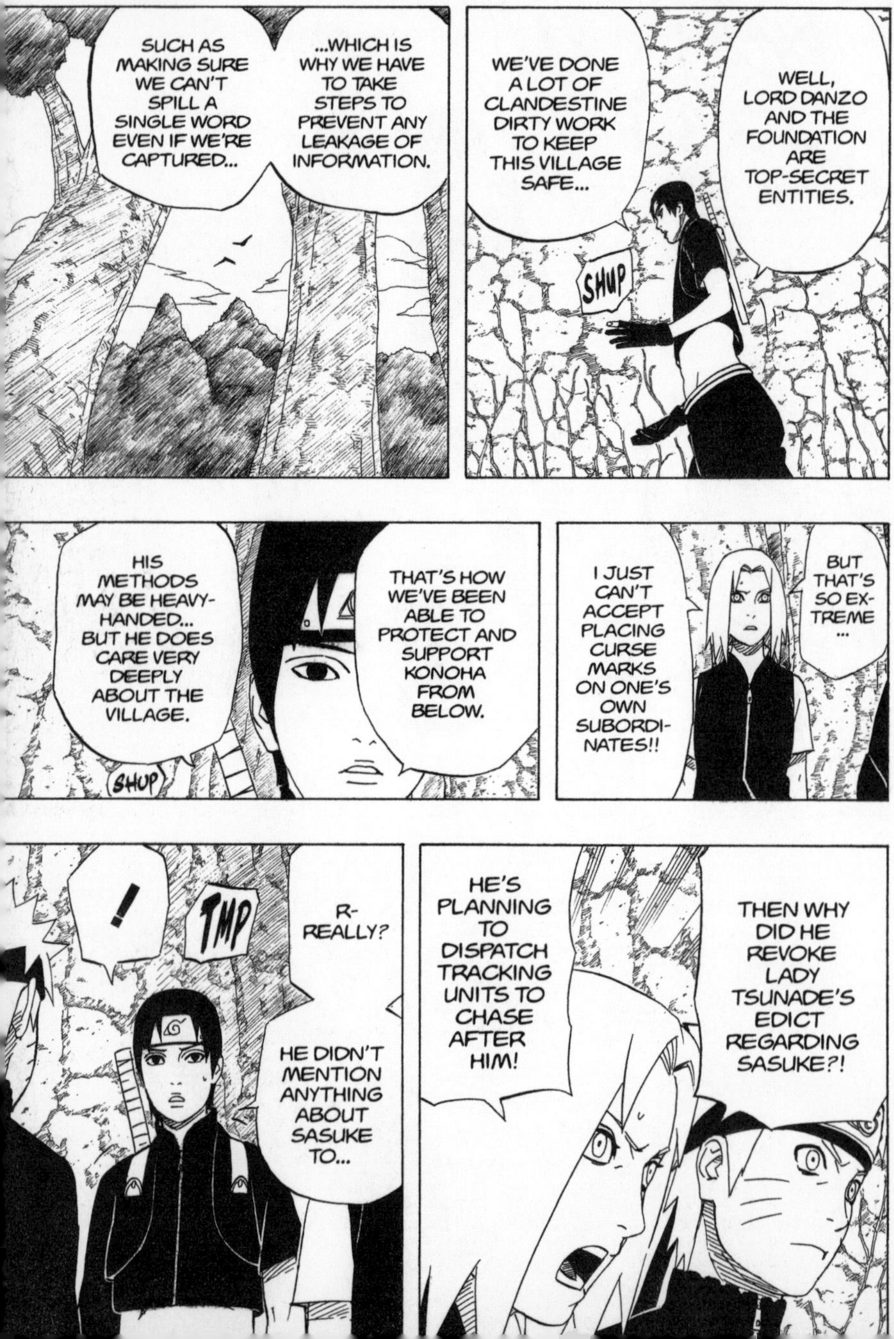
WELL, LORD DANZO AND THE FOUNDATION ARE TOP-SECRET ENTITIES.
WE'VE DONE A LOT OF CLANDESTINE DIRTY WORK TO KEEP THIS VILLAGE SAFE...
SHUP
...WHICH IS WHY WE HAVE TO TAKE STEPS TO PREVENT ANY LEAKAGE OF INFORMATION.
SUCH AS MAKING SURE WE CAN'T SPILL A SINGLE WORD EVEN IF WE'RE CAPTURED...
BUT THAT'S SO EXTREME ...
I JUST CAN'T ACCEPT PLACING CURSE MARKS ON ONE'S OWN SUBORDINATES!!
THAT'S HOW WE'VE BEEN ABLE TO PROTECT AND SUPPORT KONOHA FROM BELOW.
HIS METHODS MAY BE HEAVY-HANDED... BUT HE DOES CARE VERY DEEPLY ABOUT THE VILLAGE.
SHUP
THEN WHY DID HE REVOKE LADY TSUNADE'S EDICT REGARDING SASUKE?!
HE'S PLANNING TO DISPATCH TRACKING UNITS TO CHASE AFTER HIM!
R-REALLY?
TMP
!
HE DIDN'T MENTION ANYTHING ABOUT SASUKE TO...

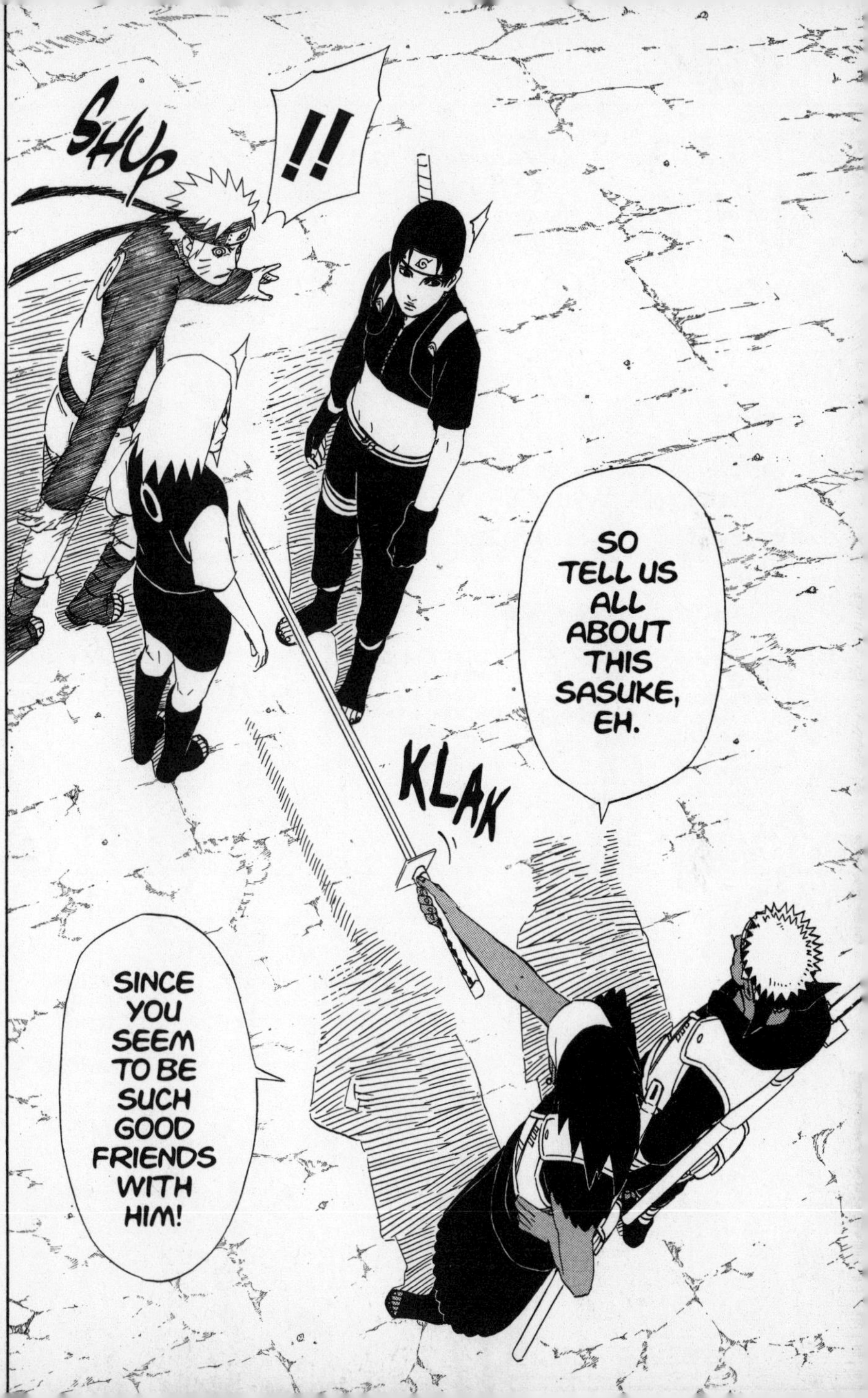
SHUP
!!
SO TELL US ALL ABOUT THIS SASUKE, EH.
KLAK
SINCE YOU SEEM TO BE SUCH GOOD FRIENDS WITH HIM!

READ THIS WAY

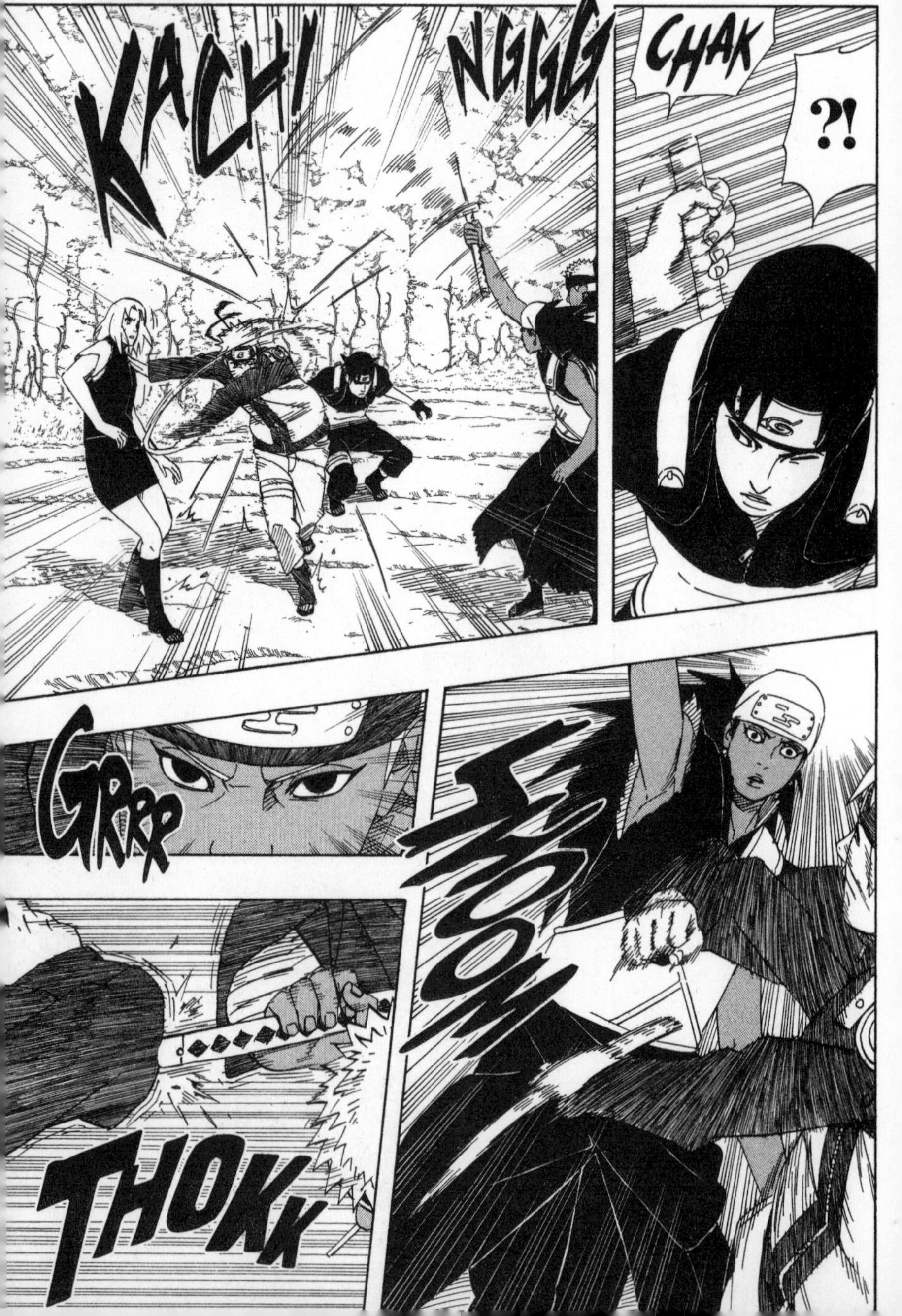
CHAK
?!
KACHI
NGGG
WHOOM
GRRR
THOKK

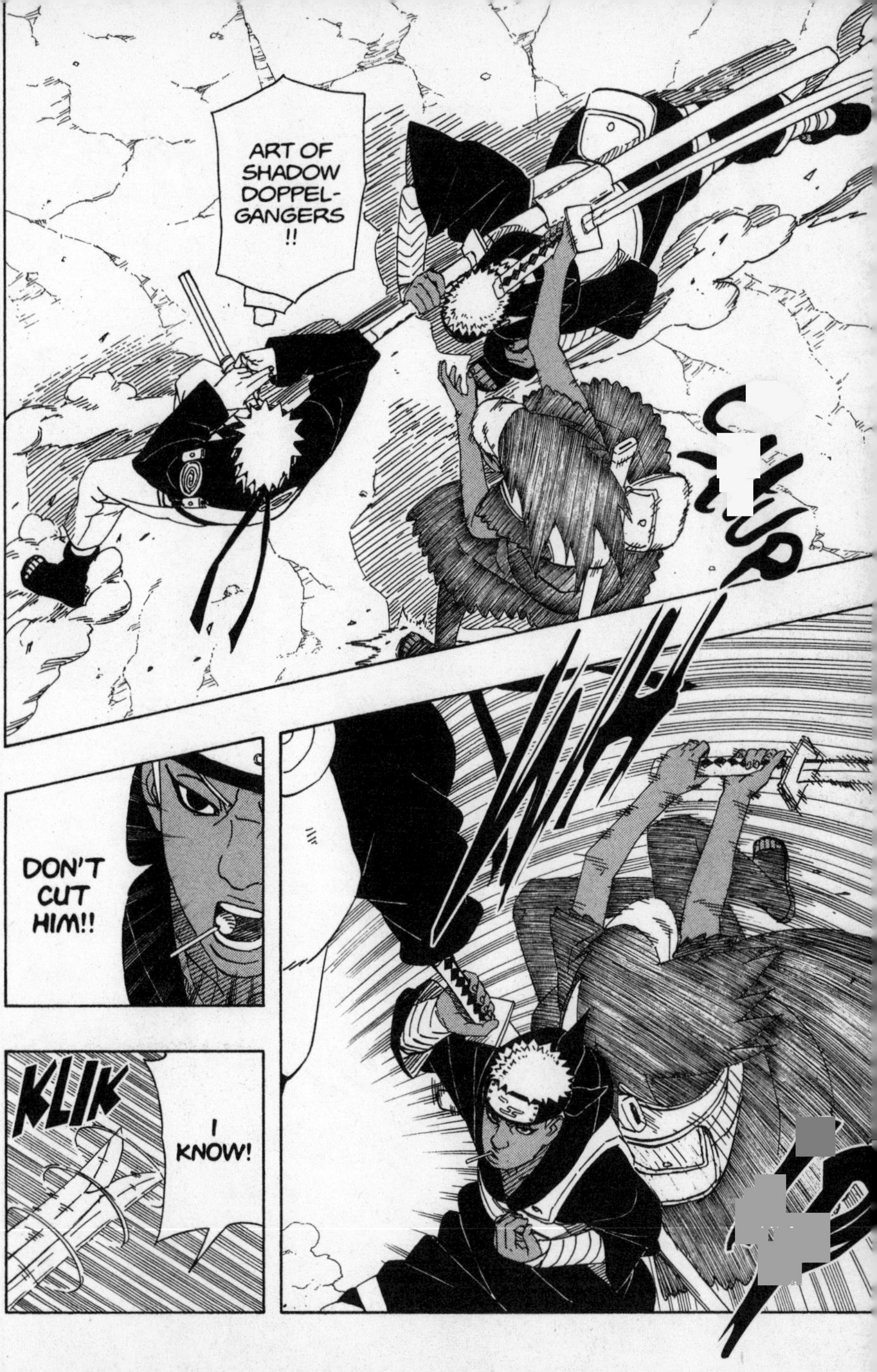

ART OF SHADOW DOPPEL-GANGERS!!
DON'T CUT HIM!!
KLIK
I KNOW!

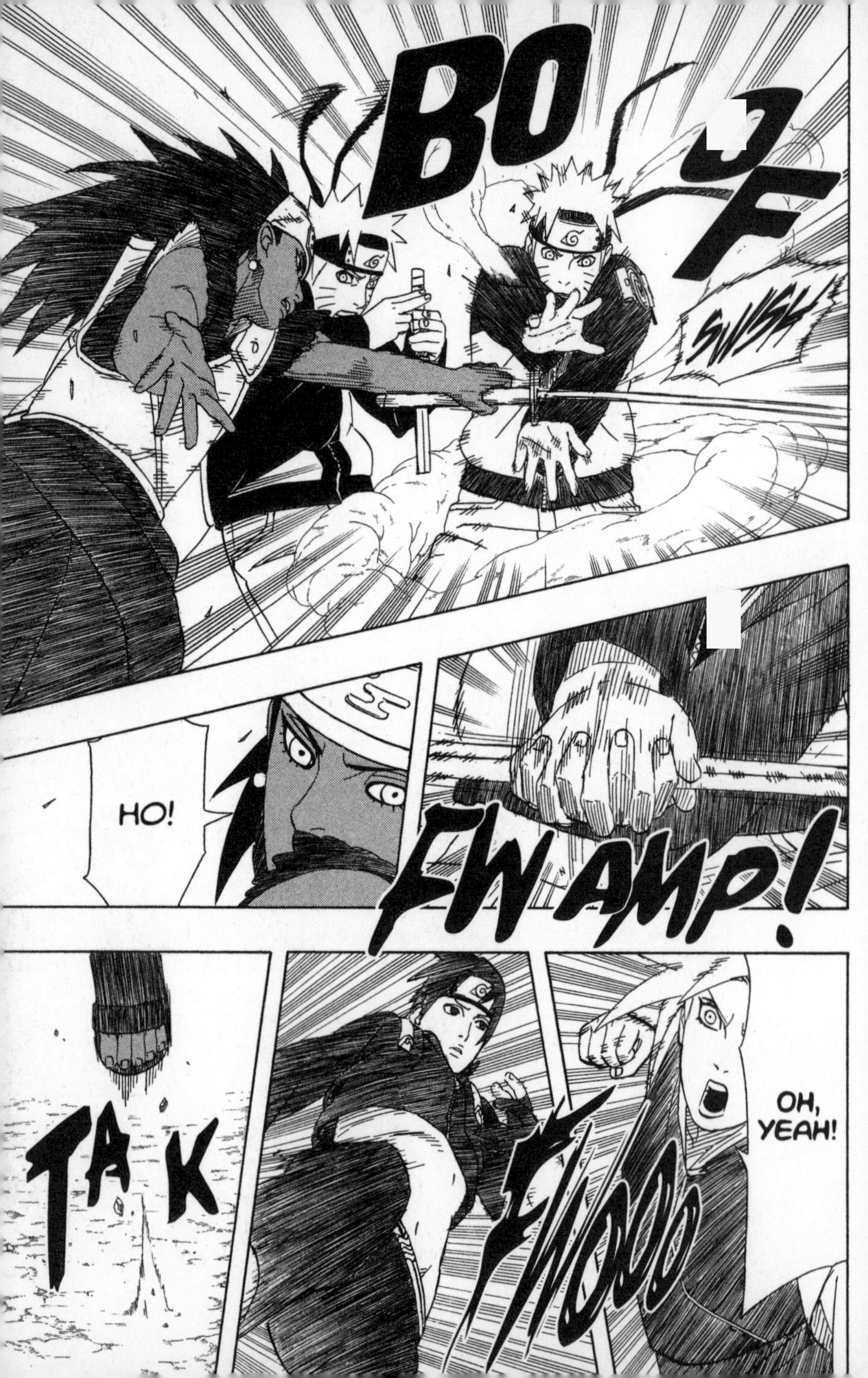
BOOF
SWISH
FWAMP!
HO!
OH, YEAH!
TAK

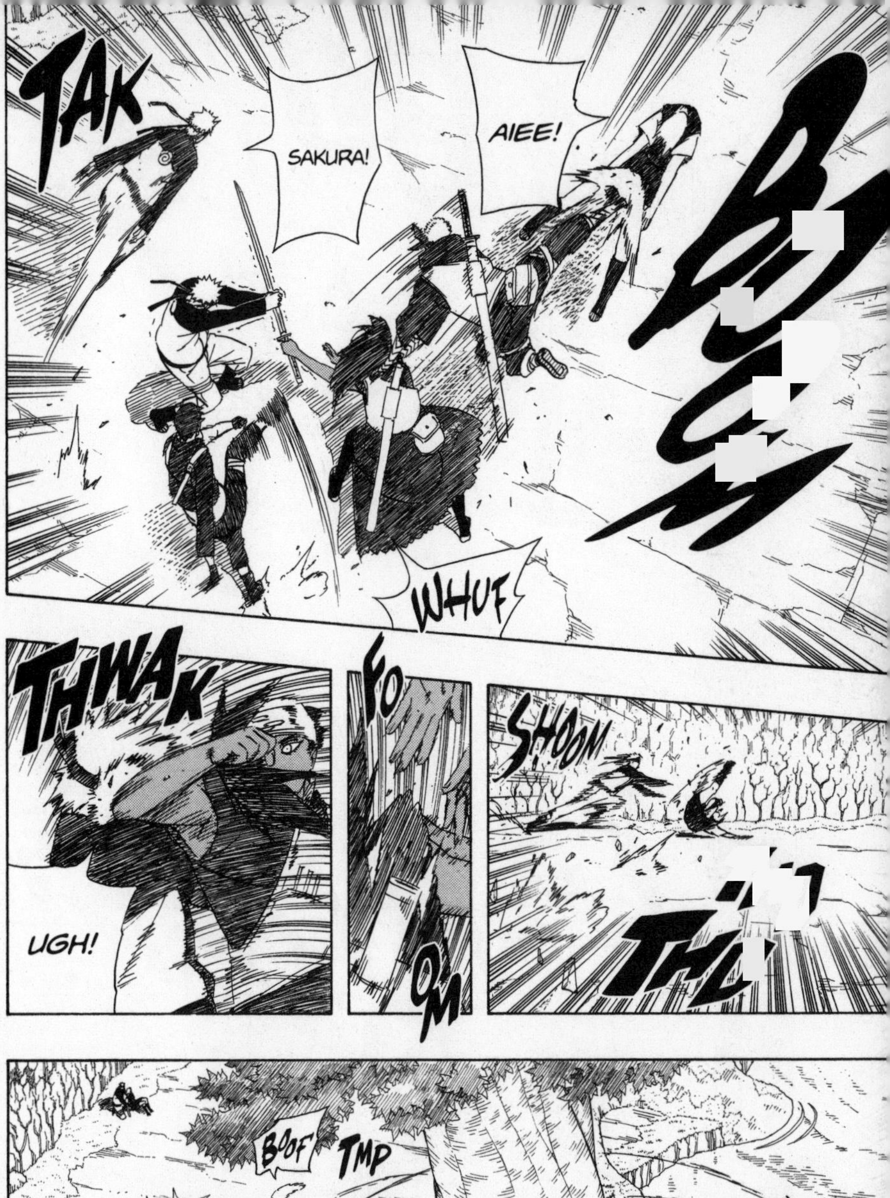
AIEE!
SAKURA!
TAK
WHUF
SHOOM
THWAK
UGH!
SPLASH SPLASH
TAK
TMP
BOOF

READ THIS WAY

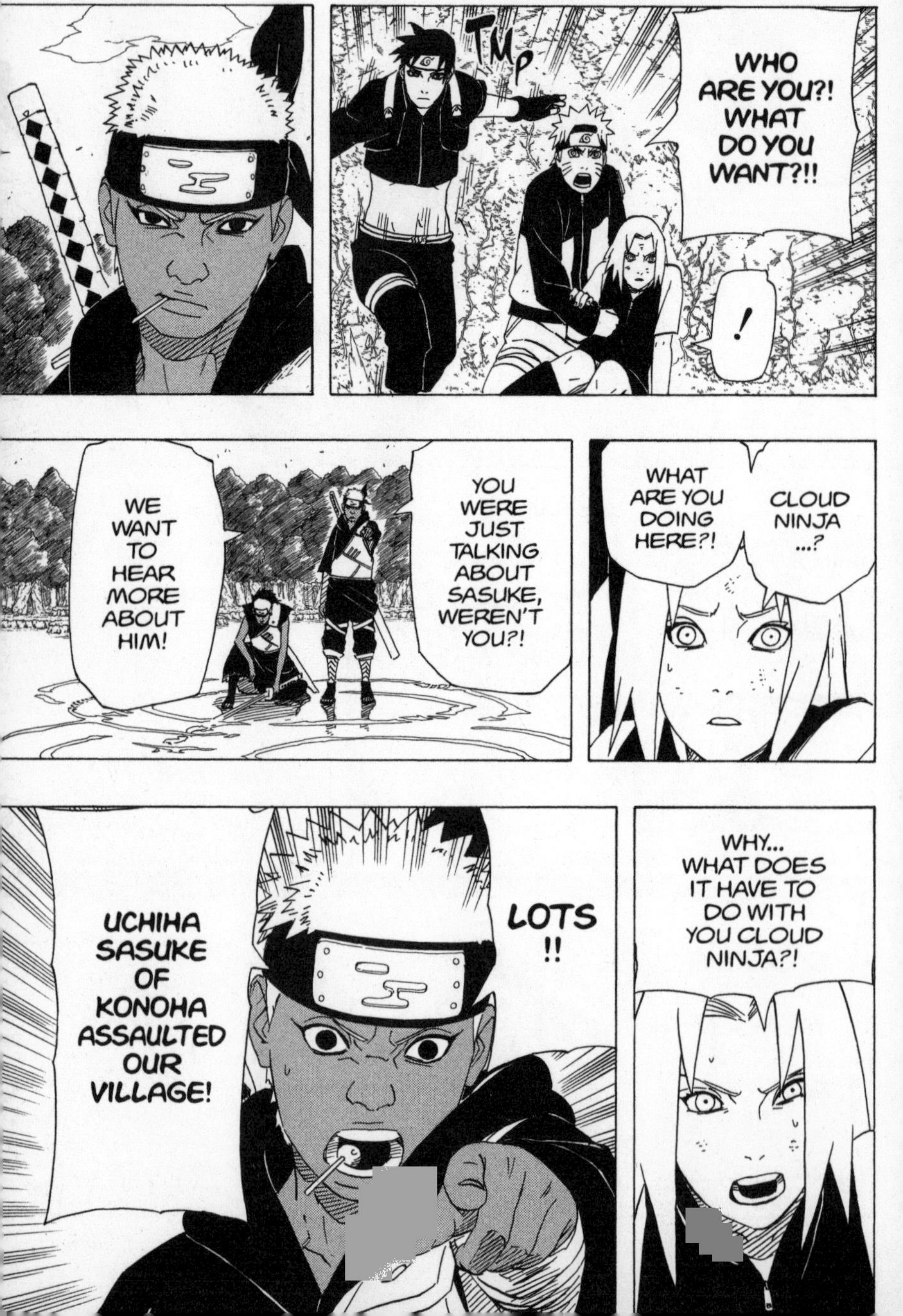
WHO ARE YOU?! WHAT DO YOU WANT?!!
TMP
!
CLOUD NINJA ...?
WHAT ARE YOU DOING HERE?!
YOU WERE JUST TALKING ABOUT SASUKE, WEREN'T YOU?!
WE WANT TO HEAR MORE ABOUT HIM!
WHY... WHAT DOES IT HAVE TO DO WITH YOU CLOUD NINJA?!
LOTS !!
UCHIHA SASUKE OF KONOHA ASSAULTED OUR VILLAGE!

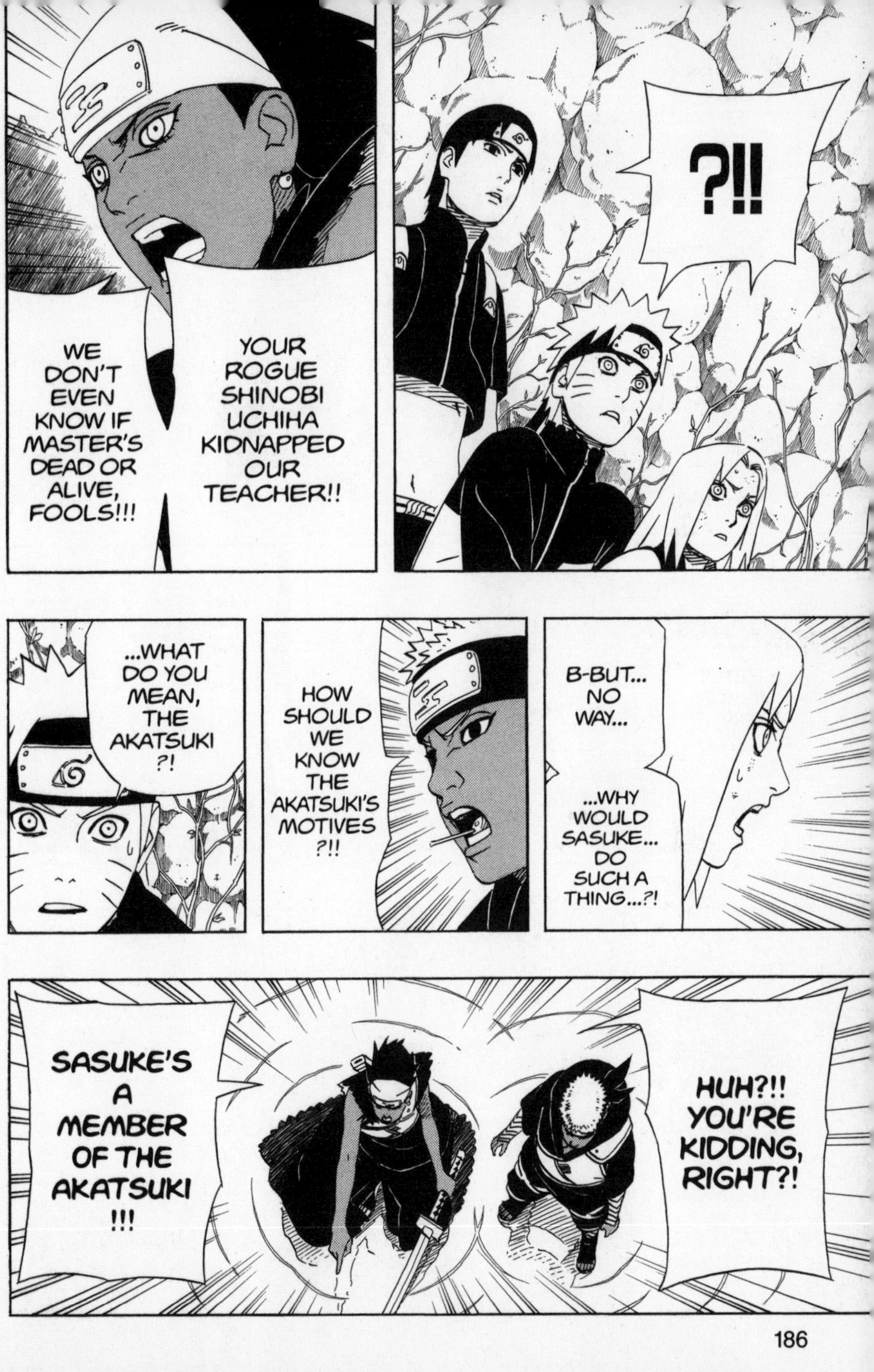
?!!
YOUR ROGUE SHINOBI UCHIHA KIDNAPPED OUR TEACHER!!
WE DON'T EVEN KNOW IF MASTER'S DEAD OR ALIVE, FOOLS!!!
B-BUT... NO WAY...
...WHY WOULD SASUKE... DO SUCH A THING...?!
HOW SHOULD WE KNOW THE AKATSUKI'S MOTIVES?!!
...WHAT DO YOU MEAN, THE AKATSUKI?!
SASUKE'S A MEMBER OF THE AKATSUKI!!!
HUH?!! YOU'RE KIDDING, RIGHT?!

READ THIS WAY

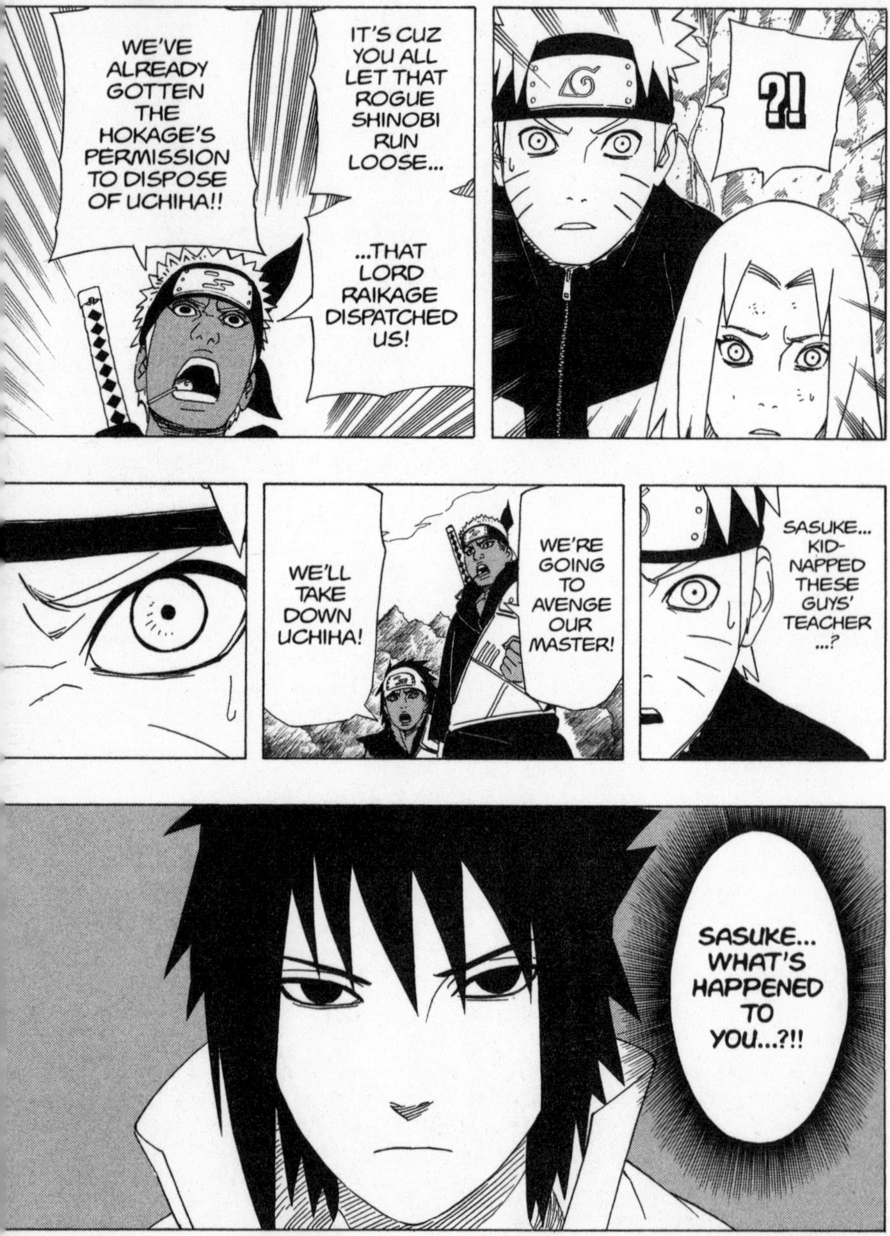
?!
IT'S CUZ YOU ALL LET THAT ROGUE SHINOBI RUN LOOSE...
...THAT LORD RAIKAGE DISPATCHED US!
WE'VE ALREADY GOTTEN THE HOKAGE'S PERMISSION TO DISPOSE OF UCHIHA!!
SASUKE... KID-NAPPED THESE GUYS' TEACHER ...?
WE'RE GOING TO AVENGE OUR MASTER!
WE'LL TAKE DOWN UCHIHA!
SASUKE... WHAT'S HAPPENED TO YOU...?!!

NARUTO

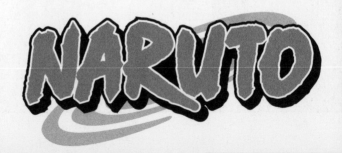

Number 453: Gokage Summit's Eve!!

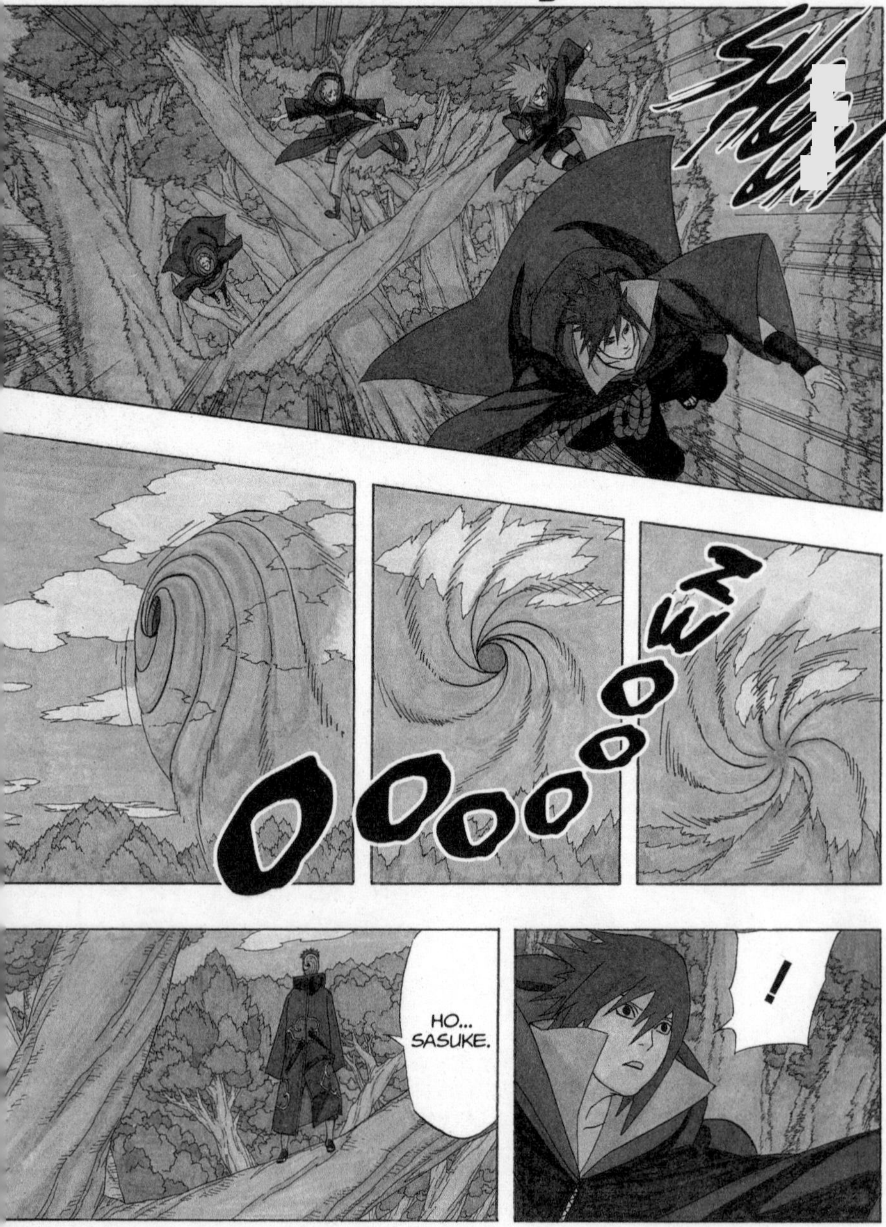
ZWOOOOOOO
!
HO... SASUKE.

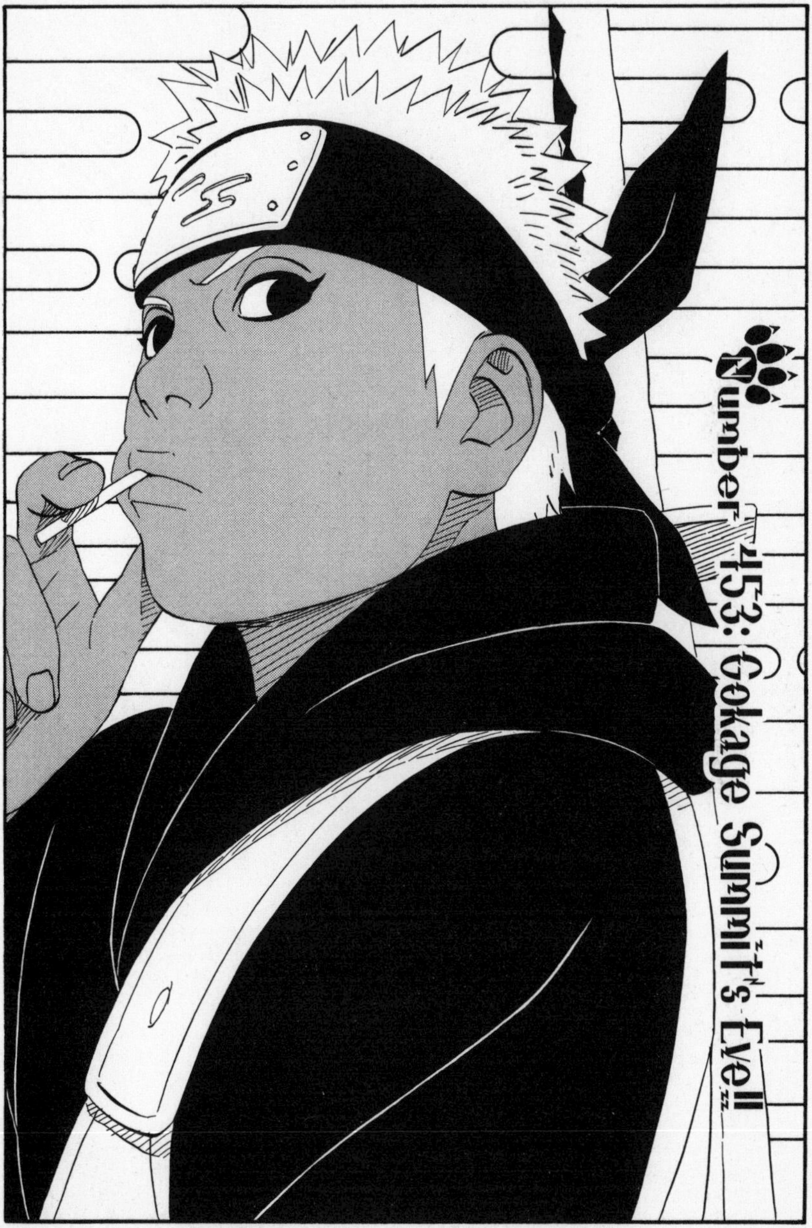
Number 453: Gokage Summit's Eve!!

READ THIS WAY

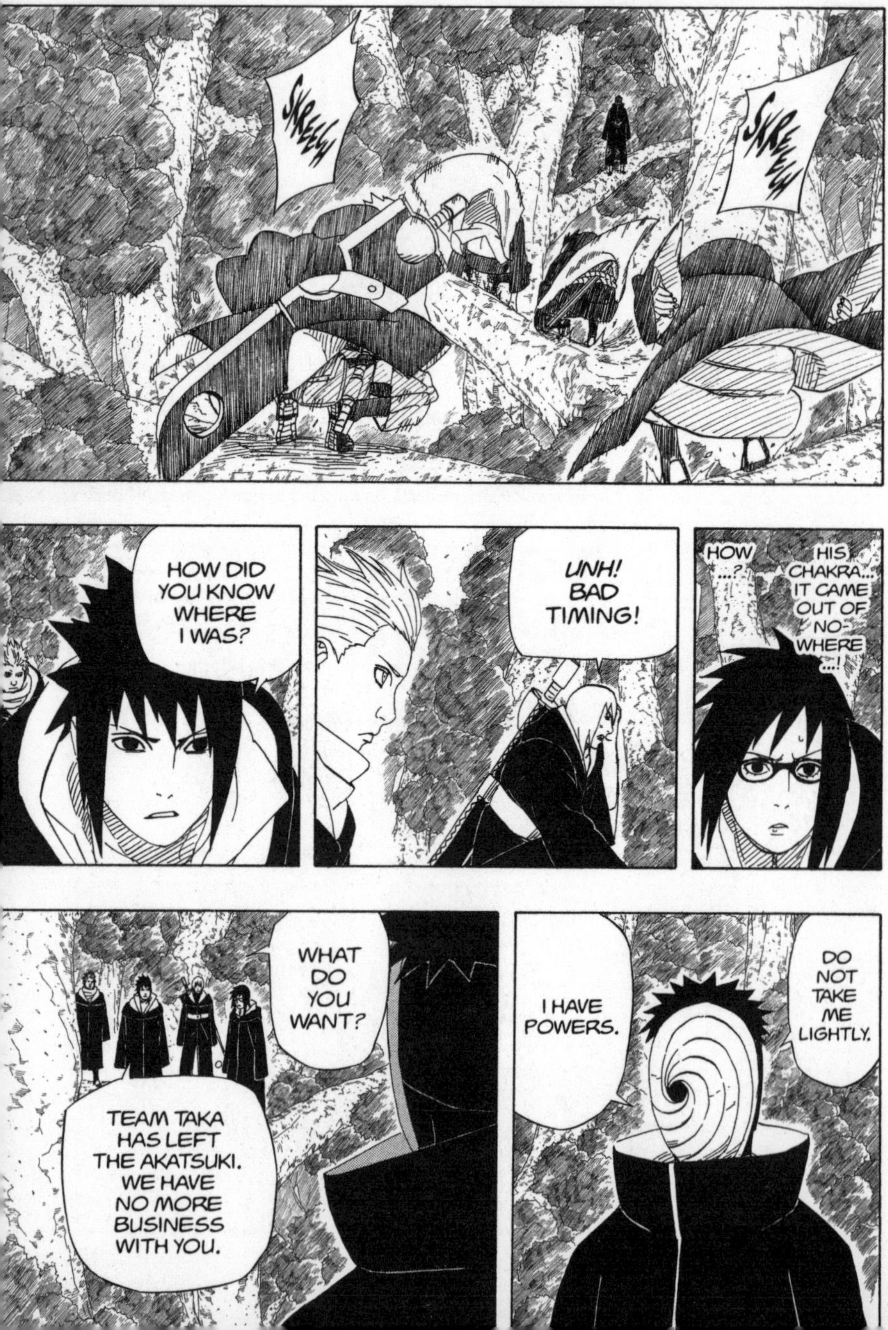
SKREEEH
SKREECH
HIS CHAKRA... IT CAME OUT OF NO-WHERE ...!
HOW ...?
UNH! BAD TIMING!
HOW DID YOU KNOW WHERE I WAS?
DO NOT TAKE ME LIGHTLY.
I HAVE POWERS.
WHAT DO YOU WANT?
TEAM TAKA HAS LEFT THE AKATSUKI. WE HAVE NO MORE BUSINESS WITH YOU.

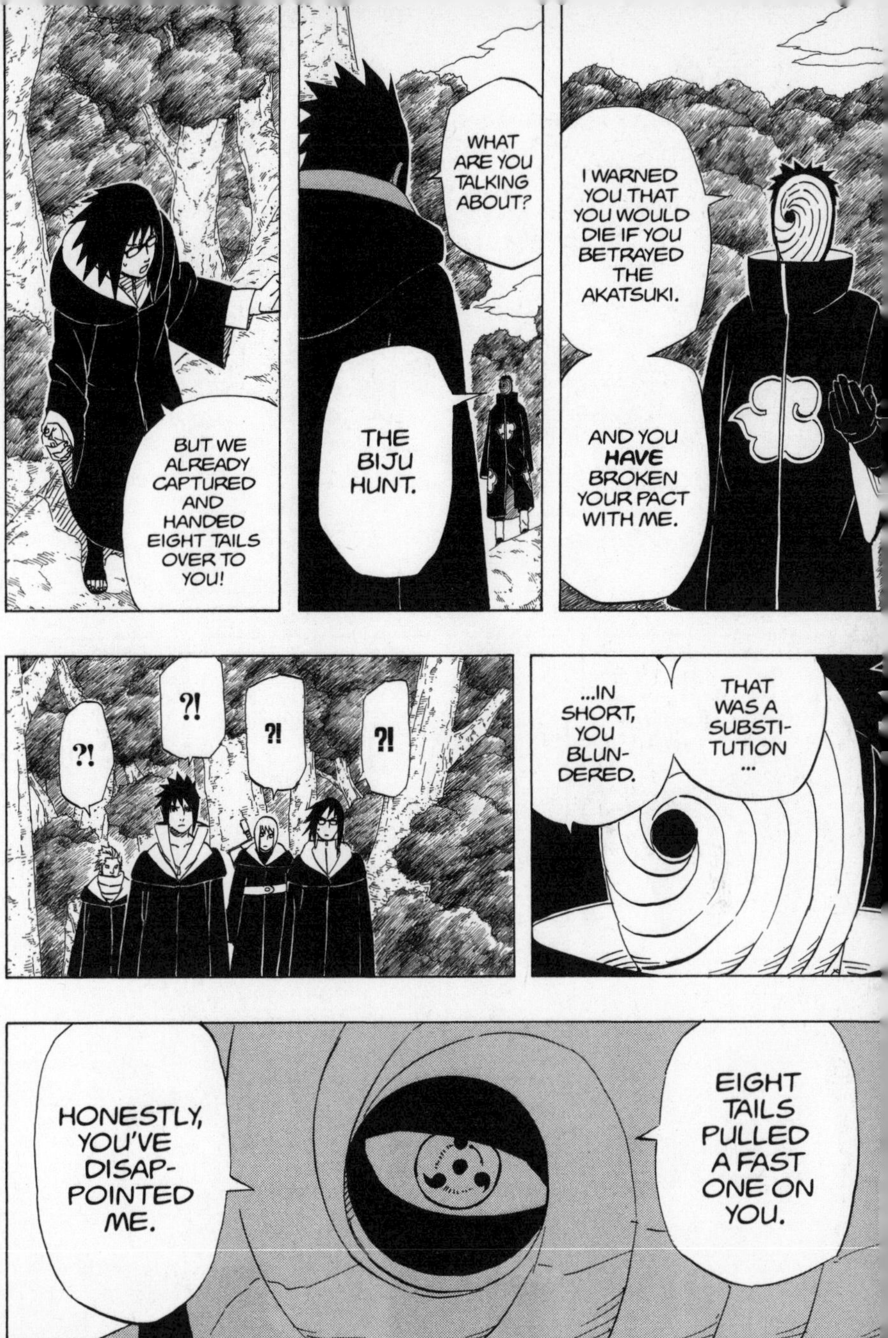
I WARNED YOU THAT YOU WOULD DIE IF YOU BETRAYED THE AKATSUKI.
AND YOU **HAVE** BROKEN YOUR PACT WITH ME.
WHAT ARE YOU TALKING ABOUT?
THE BIJU HUNT.
BUT WE ALREADY CAPTURED AND HANDED EIGHT TAILS OVER TO YOU!
THAT WAS A SUBSTI-TUTION ...
...IN SHORT, YOU BLUN-DERED.
?!
?!
?!
?!
EIGHT TAILS PULLED A FAST ONE ON YOU.
HONESTLY, YOU'VE DISAP-POINTED ME.

READ THIS WAY

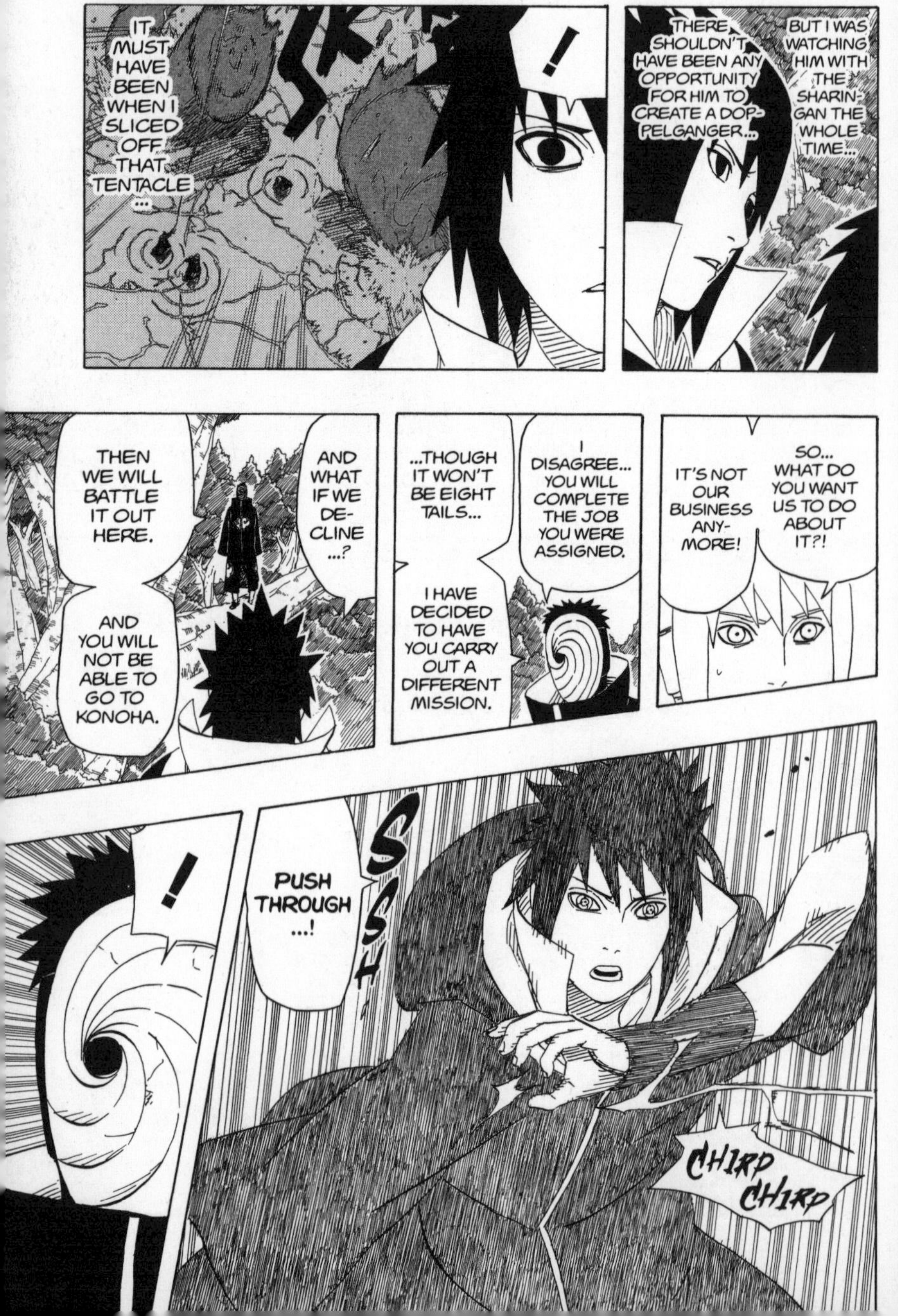

BUT I WAS WATCHING HIM WITH THE SHARINGAN THE WHOLE TIME...
THERE SHOULDN'T HAVE BEEN ANY OPPORTUNITY FOR HIM TO CREATE A DOPPELGANGER...
!
IT MUST HAVE BEEN WHEN I SLICED OFF THAT TENTACLE...
SO... WHAT DO YOU WANT US TO DO ABOUT IT?!
IT'S NOT OUR BUSINESS ANYMORE!
I DISAGREE... YOU WILL COMPLETE THE JOB YOU WERE ASSIGNED.
...THOUGH IT WON'T BE EIGHT TAILS...
I HAVE DECIDED TO HAVE YOU CARRY OUT A DIFFERENT MISSION.
AND WHAT IF WE DECLINE...?
THEN WE WILL BATTLE IT OUT HERE.
AND YOU WILL NOT BE ABLE TO GO TO KONOHA.
SSH
PUSH THROUGH...!
!
CHIRP CHIRP

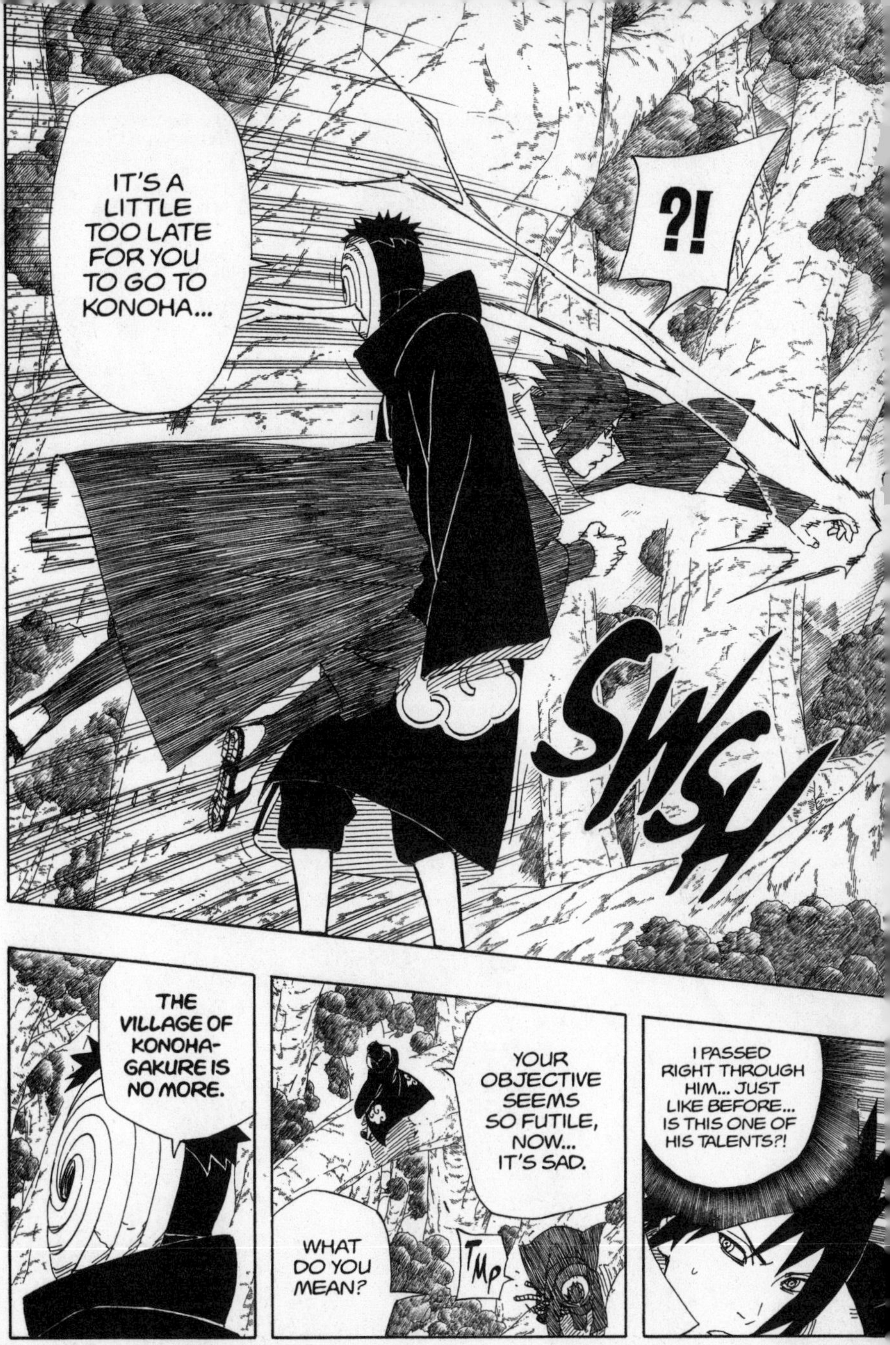
?!
IT'S A LITTLE TOO LATE FOR YOU TO GO TO KONOHA...
SWSH
I PASSED RIGHT THROUGH HIM... JUST LIKE BEFORE... IS THIS ONE OF HIS TALENTS?!
YOUR OBJECTIVE SEEMS SO FUTILE, NOW... IT'S SAD.
TMP
WHAT DO YOU MEAN?
THE VILLAGE OF KONOHA-GAKURE IS NO MORE.

READ THIS WAY

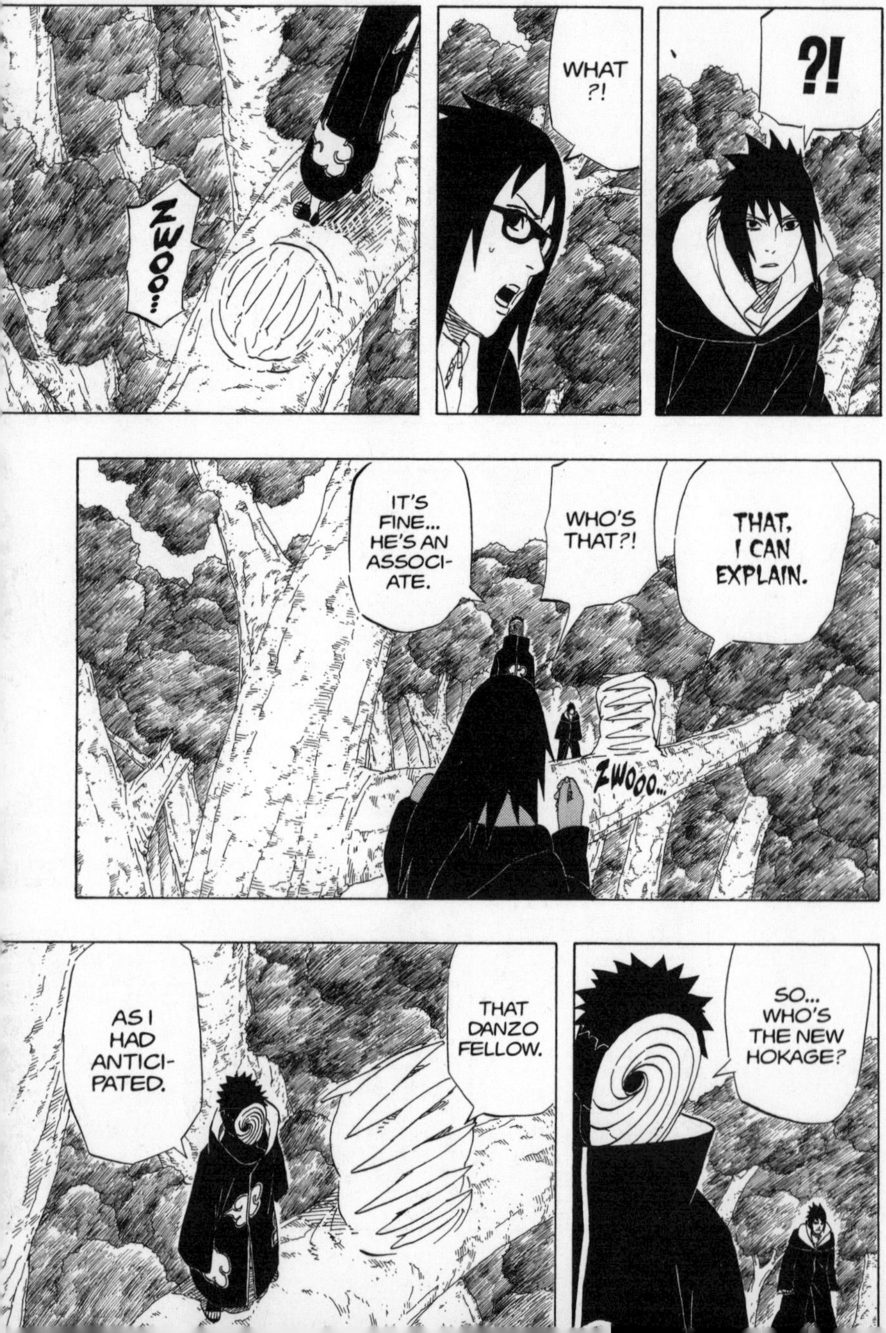
?!
WHAT ?!
ZWOO...
THAT, I CAN EXPLAIN.
WHO'S THAT?!
IT'S FINE... HE'S AN ASSOCI-ATE.
ZWOOO...
SO... WHO'S THE NEW HOKAGE?
THAT DANZO FELLOW.
AS I HAD ANTICI-PATED.

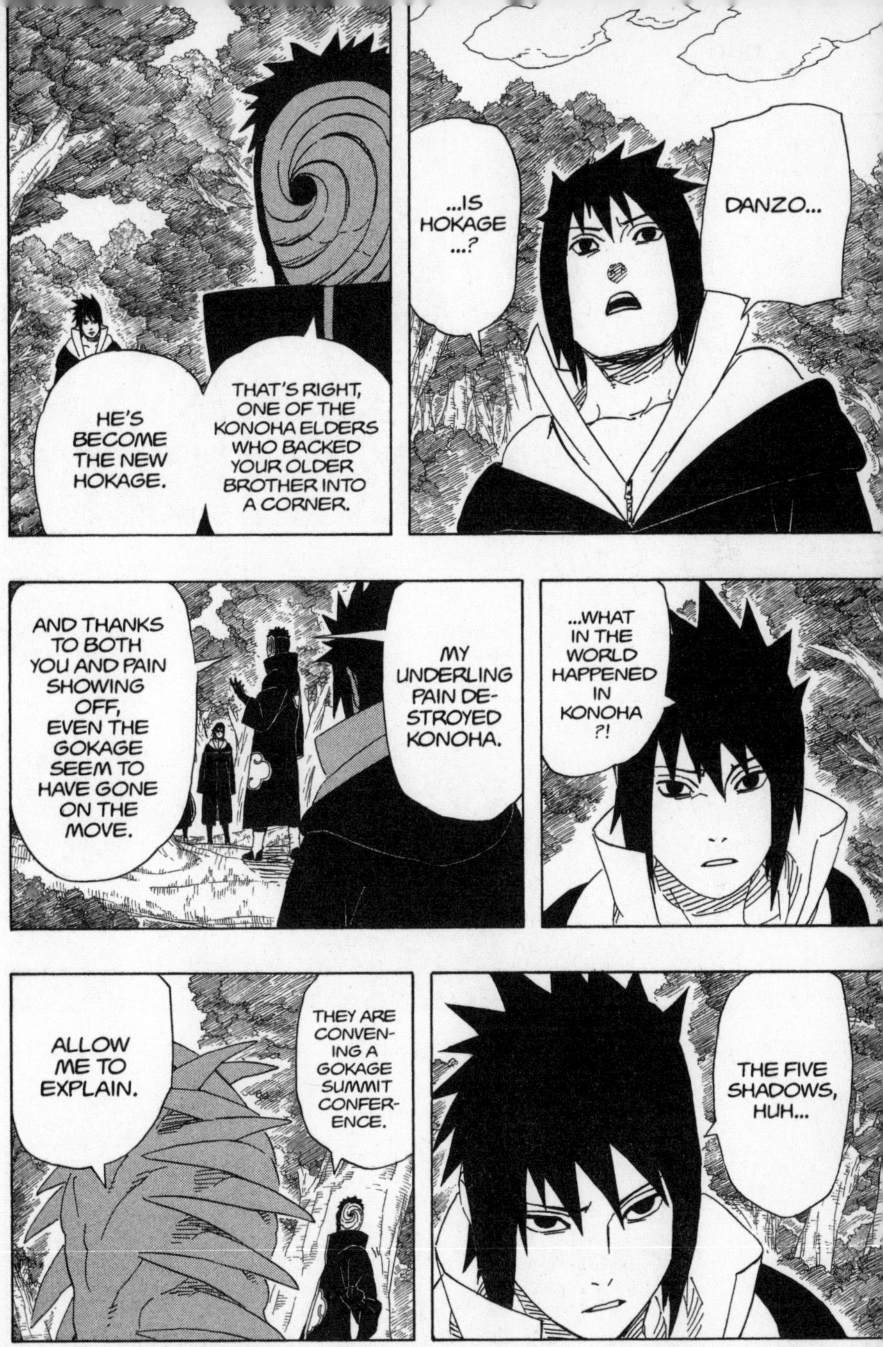
DANZO...
...IS HOKAGE ...?
THAT'S RIGHT, ONE OF THE KONOHA ELDERS WHO BACKED YOUR OLDER BROTHER INTO A CORNER.
HE'S BECOME THE NEW HOKAGE.
...WHAT IN THE WORLD HAPPENED IN KONOHA ?!
MY UNDERLING PAIN DE-STROYED KONOHA.
AND THANKS TO BOTH YOU AND PAIN SHOWING OFF, EVEN THE GOKAGE SEEM TO HAVE GONE ON THE MOVE.
THE FIVE SHADOWS, HUH...
THEY ARE CONVEN-ING A GOKAGE SUMMIT CONFER-ENCE.
ALLOW ME TO EXPLAIN.

READ THIS WAY

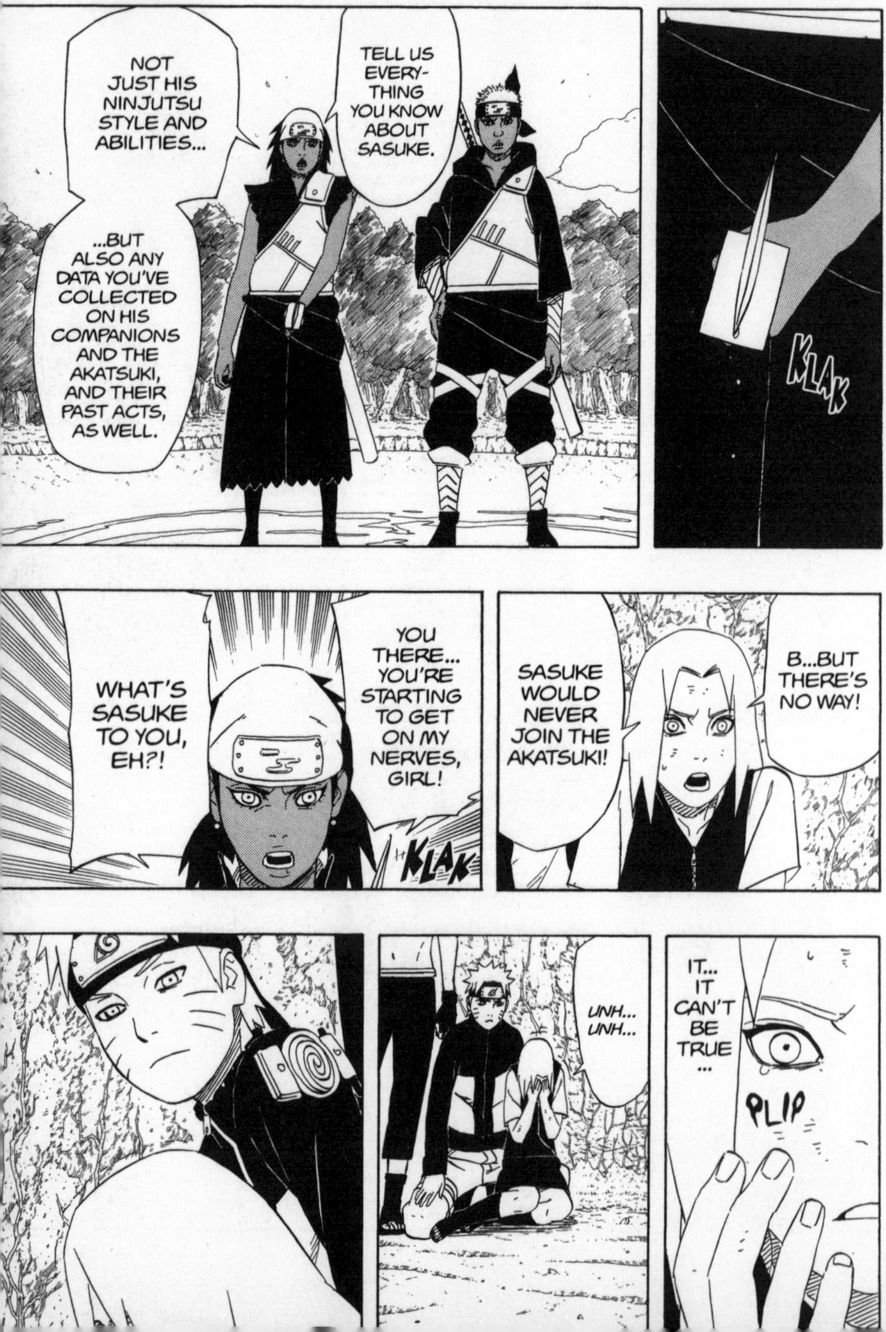
KLAK
TELL US EVERY-THING YOU KNOW ABOUT SASUKE.
NOT JUST HIS NINJUTSU STYLE AND ABILITIES...
...BUT ALSO ANY DATA YOU'VE COLLECTED ON HIS COMPANIONS AND THE AKATSUKI, AND THEIR PAST ACTS, AS WELL.
B...BUT THERE'S NO WAY!
SASUKE WOULD NEVER JOIN THE AKATSUKI!
YOU THERE... YOU'RE STARTING TO GET ON MY NERVES, GIRL!
WHAT'S SASUKE TO YOU, EH?!
KLAK
IT... IT CAN'T BE TRUE...
PLIP
UNH... UNH...

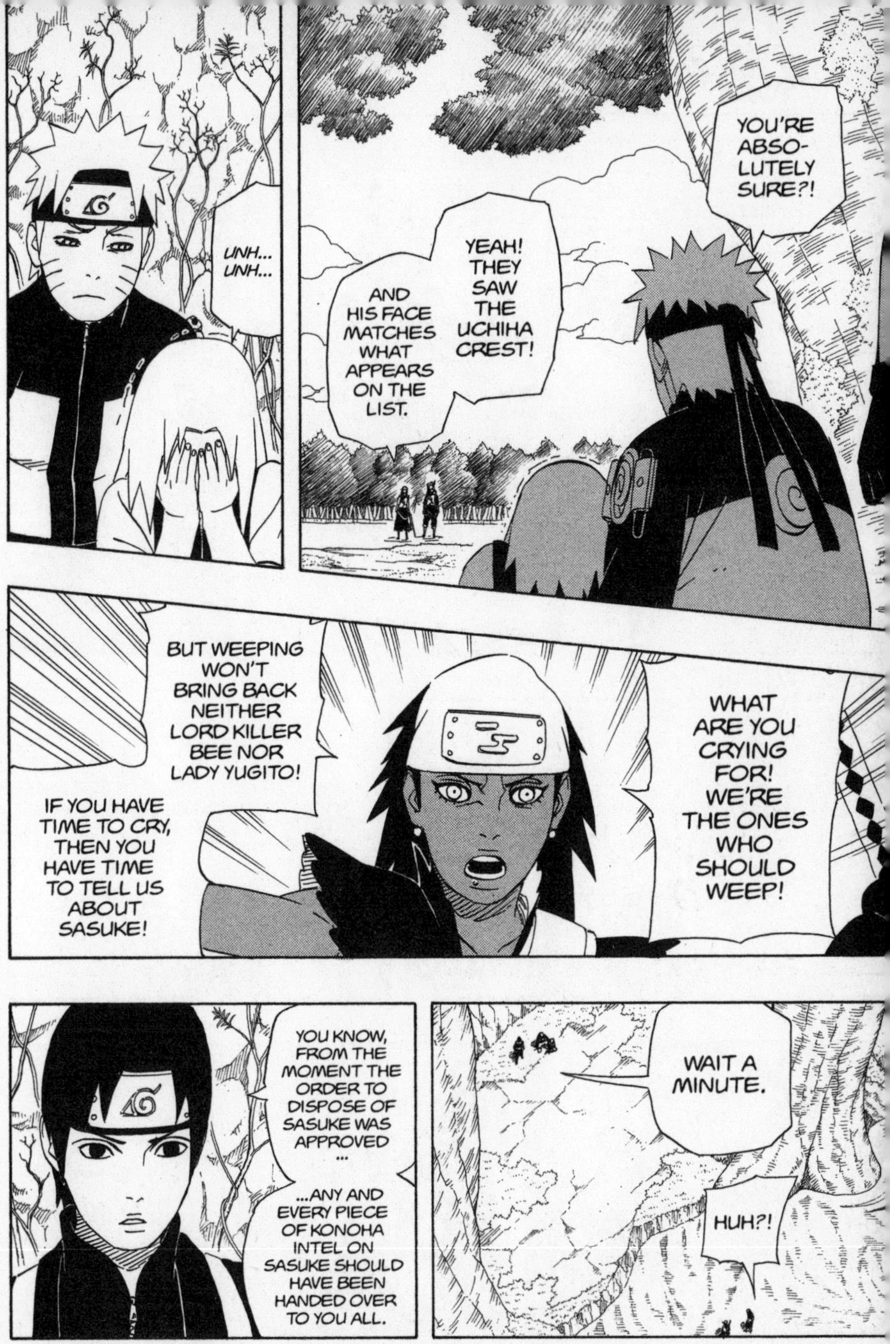

YOU'RE ABSO-LUTELY SURE?!
YEAH! THEY SAW THE UCHIHA CREST!
AND HIS FACE MATCHES WHAT APPEARS ON THE LIST.
UNH... UNH...
WHAT ARE YOU CRYING FOR! WE'RE THE ONES WHO SHOULD WEEP!
BUT WEEPING WON'T BRING BACK NEITHER LORD KILLER BEE NOR LADY YUGITO!
IF YOU HAVE TIME TO CRY, THEN YOU HAVE TIME TO TELL US ABOUT SASUKE!
WAIT A MINUTE.
HUH?!
YOU KNOW, FROM THE MOMENT THE ORDER TO DISPOSE OF SASUKE WAS APPROVED ...
...ANY AND EVERY PIECE OF KONOHA INTEL ON SASUKE SHOULD HAVE BEEN HANDED OVER TO YOU ALL.

READ THIS WAY

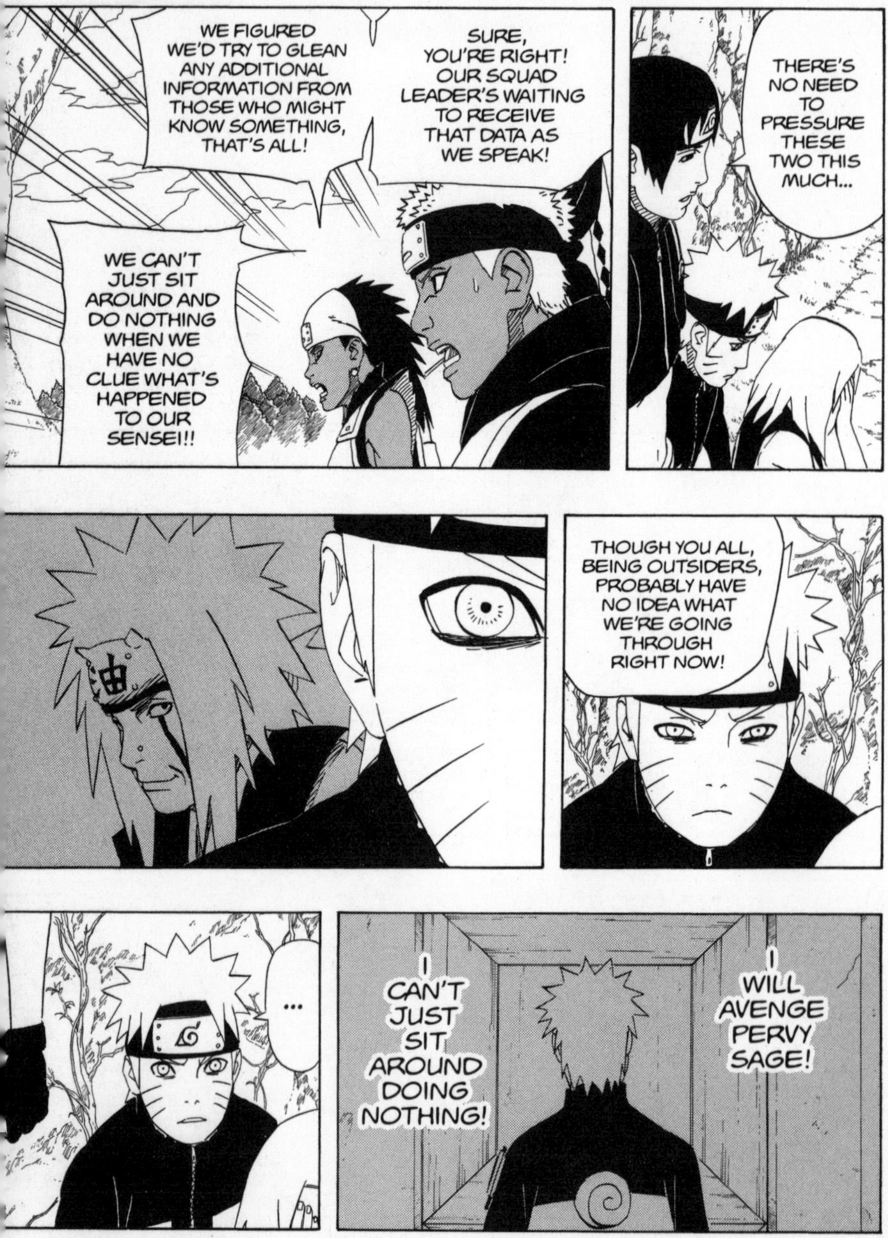
THERE'S NO NEED TO PRESSURE THESE TWO THIS MUCH...
SURE, YOU'RE RIGHT! OUR SQUAD LEADER'S WAITING TO RECEIVE THAT DATA AS WE SPEAK!
WE FIGURED WE'D TRY TO GLEAN ANY ADDITIONAL INFORMATION FROM THOSE WHO MIGHT KNOW SOMETHING, THAT'S ALL!
WE CAN'T JUST SIT AROUND AND DO NOTHING WHEN WE HAVE NO CLUE WHAT'S HAPPENED TO OUR SENSEI!!
THOUGH YOU ALL, BEING OUTSIDERS, PROBABLY HAVE NO IDEA WHAT WE'RE GOING THROUGH RIGHT NOW!
I WILL AVENGE PERVY SAGE!
I CAN'T JUST SIT AROUND DOING NOTHING!
...

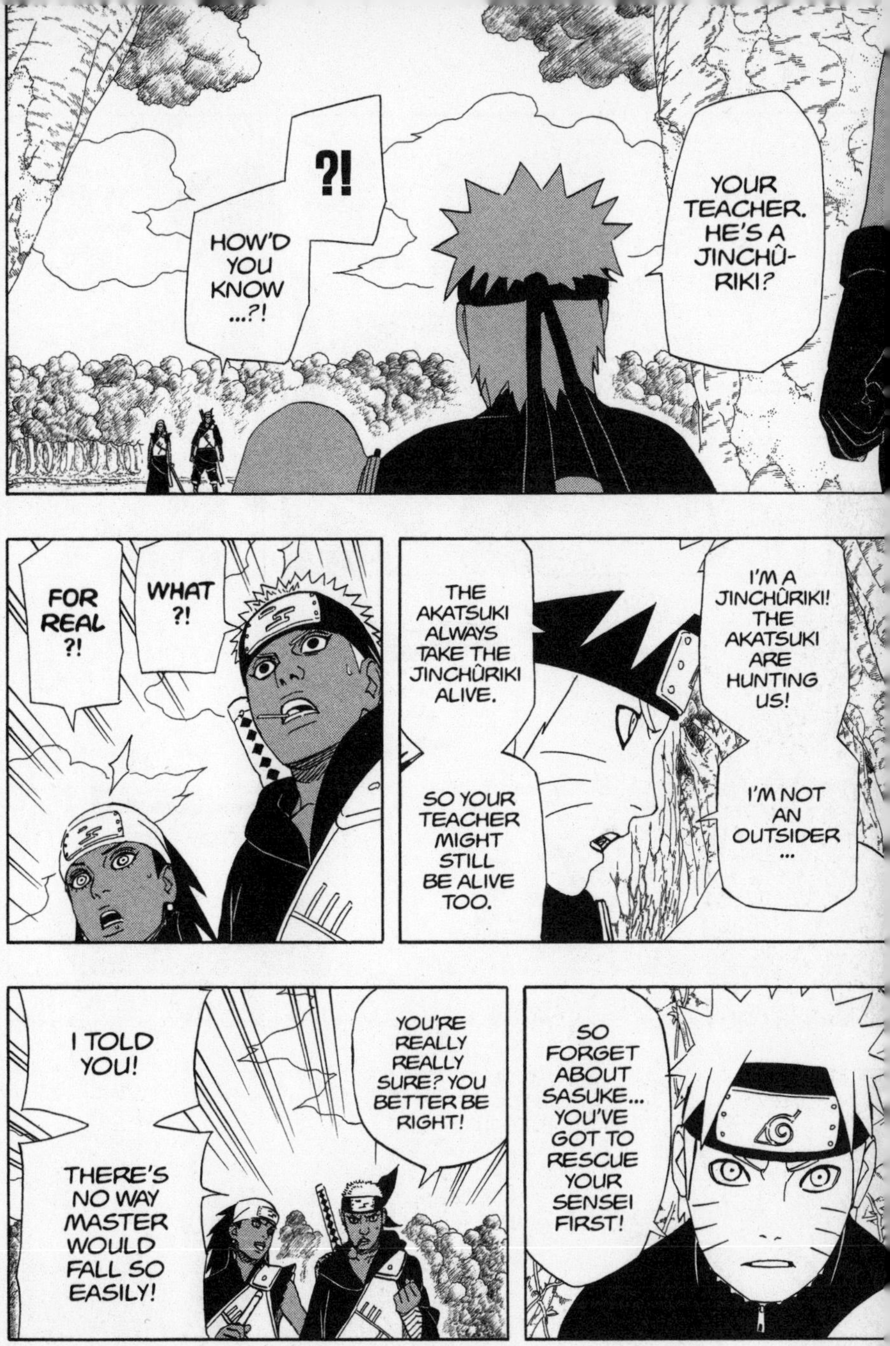
YOUR TEACHER. HE'S A JINCHÛ-RIKI?
?!
HOW'D YOU KNOW ...?!
I'M A JINCHÛRIKI! THE AKATSUKI ARE HUNTING US!
I'M NOT AN OUTSIDER ...
THE AKATSUKI ALWAYS TAKE THE JINCHÛRIKI ALIVE.
SO YOUR TEACHER MIGHT STILL BE ALIVE TOO.
WHAT ?!
FOR REAL ?!
SO FORGET ABOUT SASUKE... YOU'VE GOT TO RESCUE YOUR SENSEI FIRST!
YOU'RE REALLY REALLY SURE? YOU BETTER BE RIGHT!
I TOLD YOU!
THERE'S NO WAY MASTER WOULD FALL SO EASILY!

READ THIS WAY

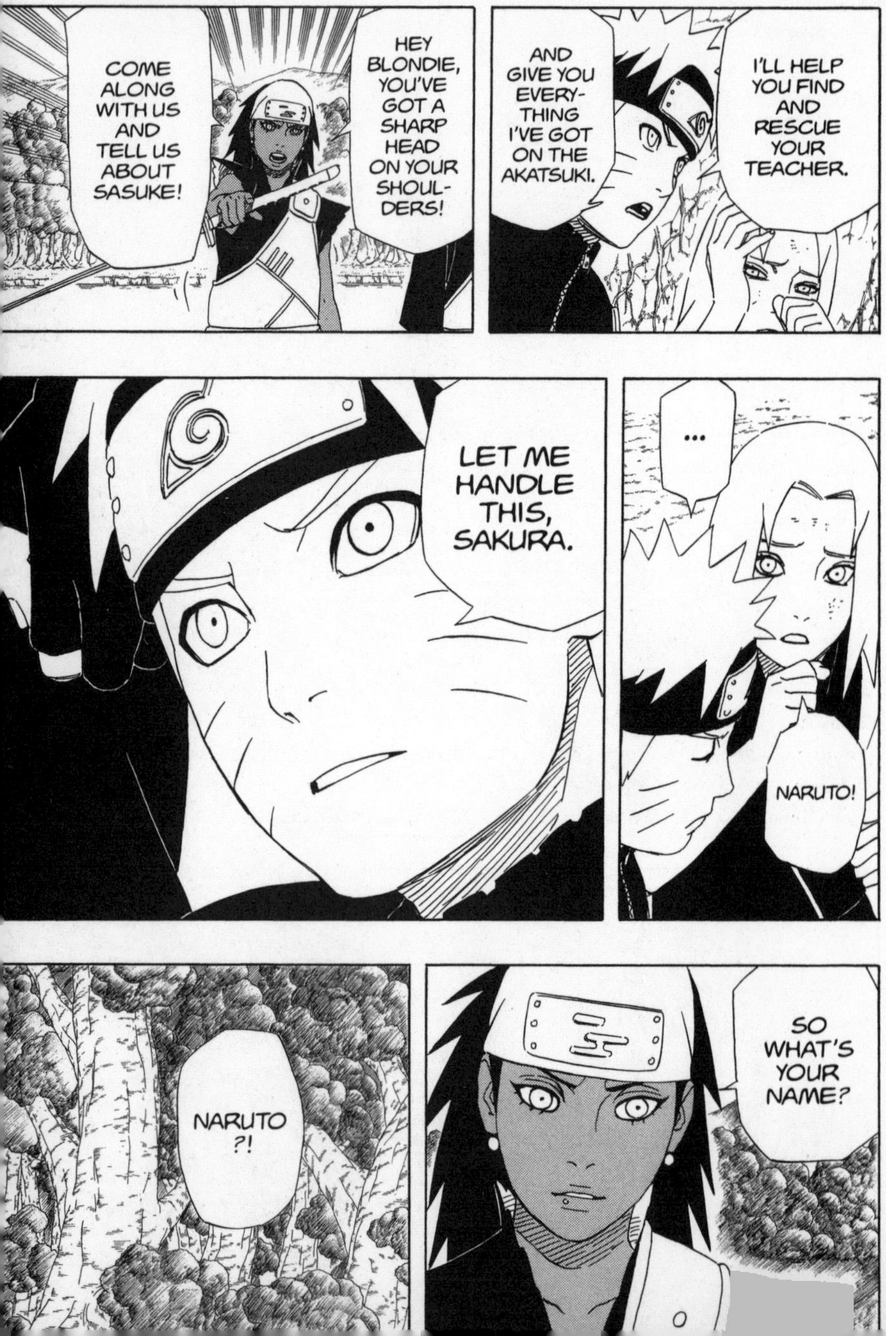
I'LL HELP YOU FIND AND RESCUE YOUR TEACHER.
AND GIVE YOU EVERY-THING I'VE GOT ON THE AKATSUKI.
HEY BLONDIE, YOU'VE GOT A SHARP HEAD ON YOUR SHOUL-DERS!
COME ALONG WITH US AND TELL US ABOUT SASUKE!
...
NARUTO!
LET ME HANDLE THIS, SAKURA.
SO WHAT'S YOUR NAME?
NARUTO ?!

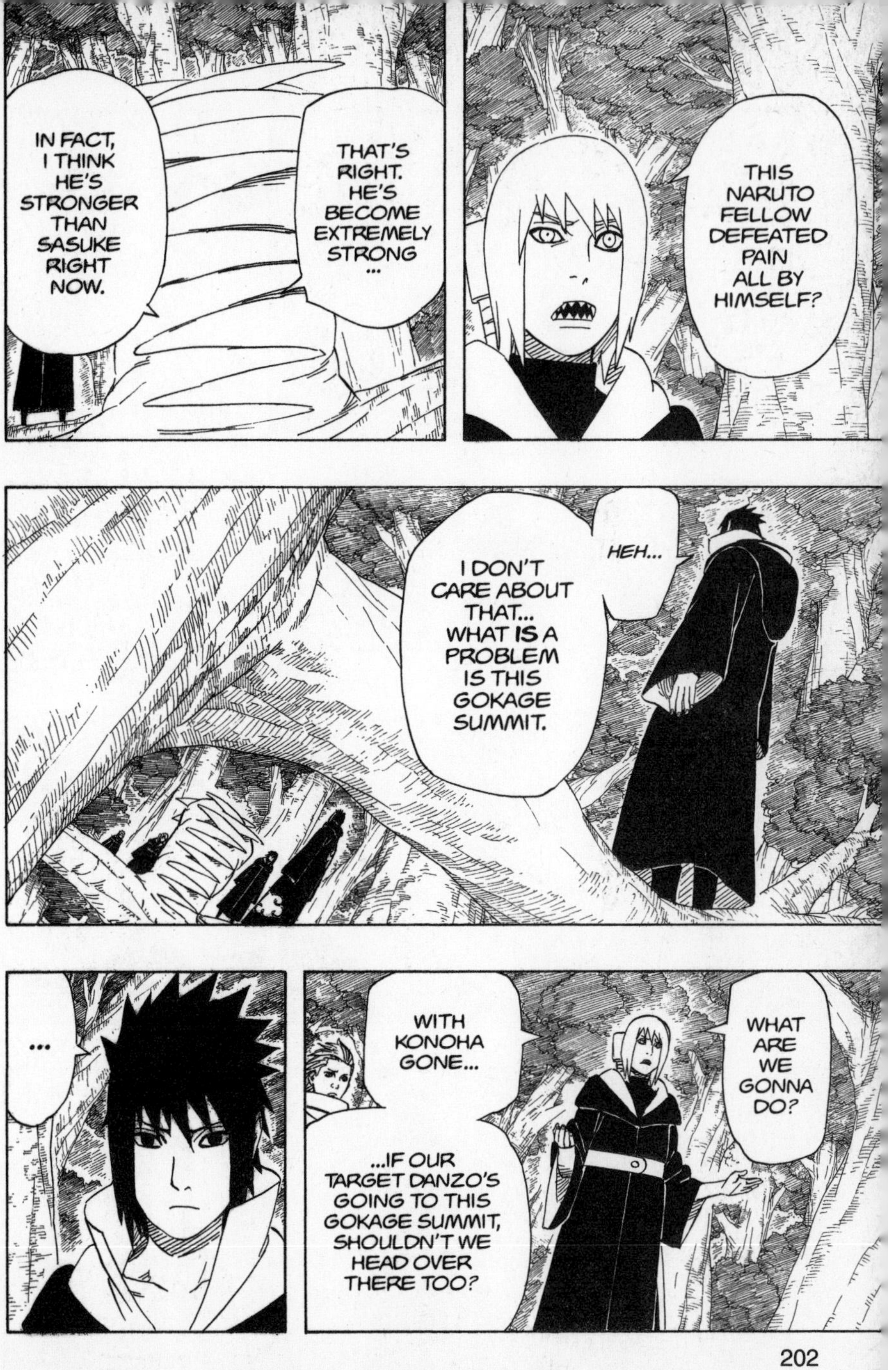
THIS NARUTO FELLOW DEFEATED PAIN ALL BY HIMSELF?
THAT'S RIGHT. HE'S BECOME EXTREMELY STRONG ...
IN FACT, I THINK HE'S STRONGER THAN SASUKE RIGHT NOW.
HEH...
I DON'T CARE ABOUT THAT... WHAT **IS** A PROBLEM IS THIS GOKAGE SUMMIT.
WHAT ARE WE GONNA DO?
WITH KONOHA GONE...
...IF OUR TARGET DANZO'S GOING TO THIS GOKAGE SUMMIT, SHOULDN'T WE HEAD OVER THERE TOO?
...

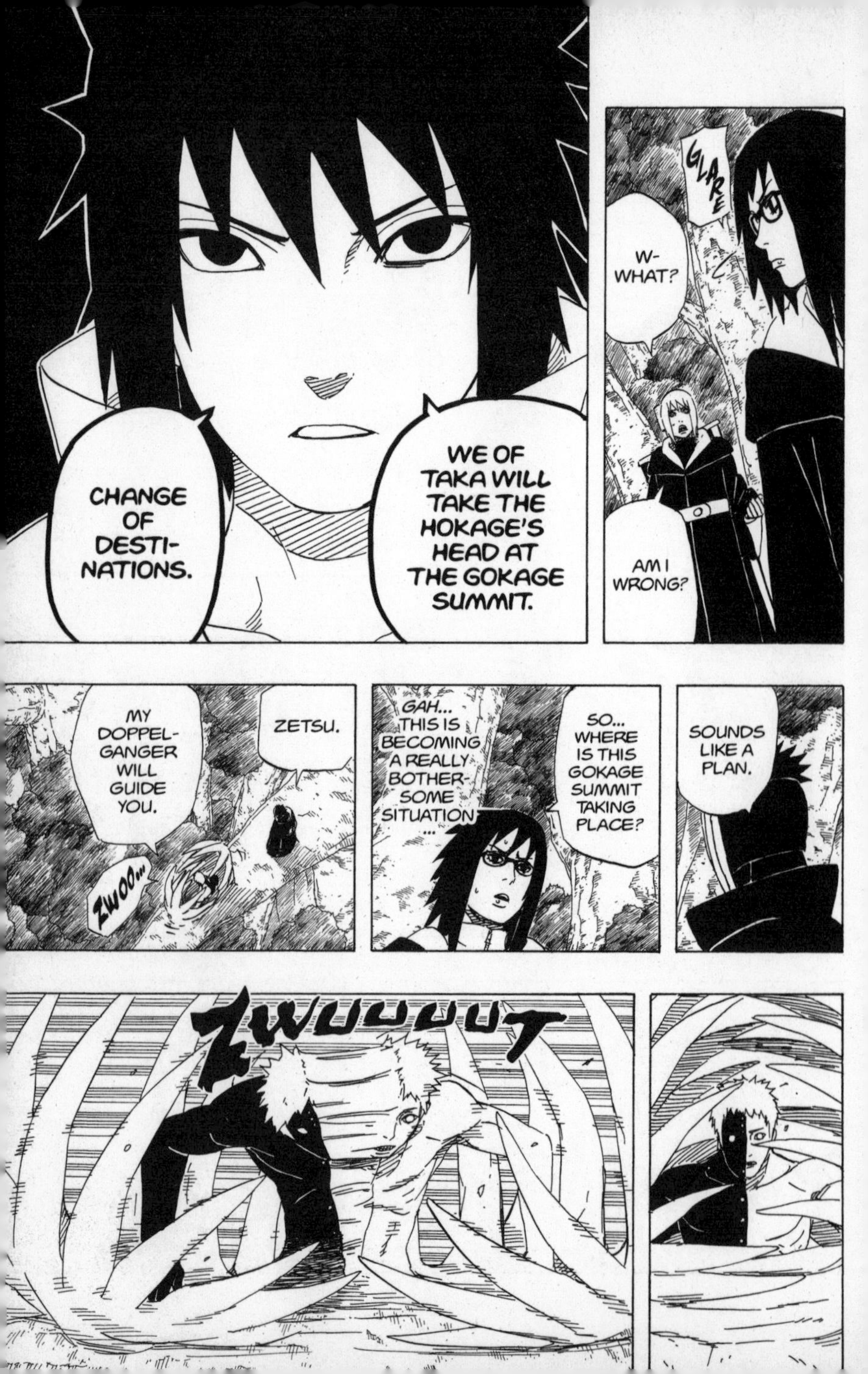
GLARE
W- WHAT?
AM I WRONG?
WE OF TAKA WILL TAKE THE HOKAGE'S HEAD AT THE GOKAGE SUMMIT.
CHANGE OF DESTI-NATIONS.
SOUNDS LIKE A PLAN.
SO... WHERE IS THIS GOKAGE SUMMIT TAKING PLACE?
GAH... THIS IS BECOMING A REALLY BOTHER-SOME SITUATION...
ZETSU.
MY DOPPEL-GANGER WILL GUIDE YOU.
ZWOO...
ZWUUUUUT

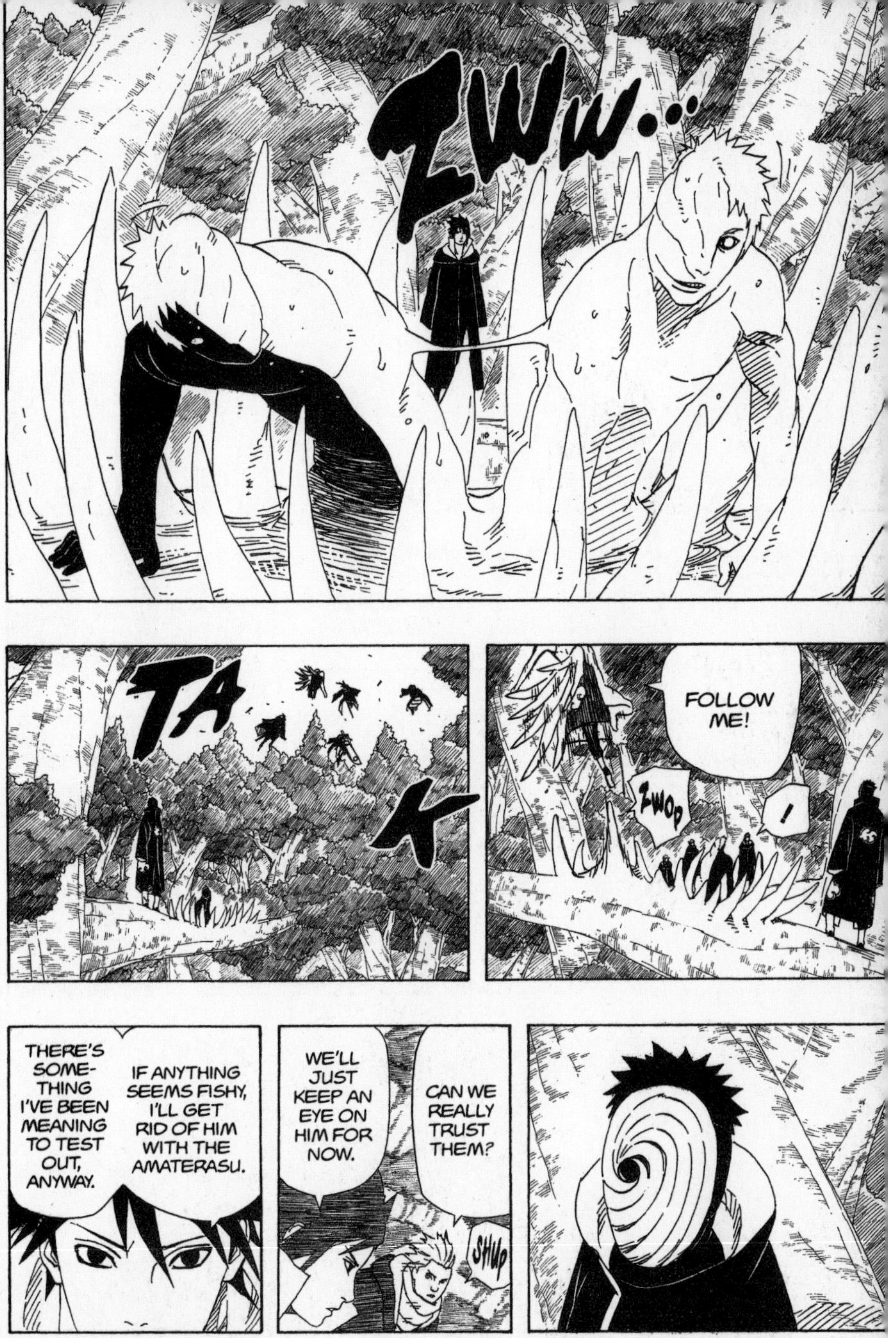
ZWW...
FOLLOW ME!
ZWOP
!
TAK
CAN WE REALLY TRUST THEM?
WE'LL JUST KEEP AN EYE ON HIM FOR NOW.
SHUP
IF ANYTHING SEEMS FISHY, I'LL GET RID OF HIM WITH THE AMATERASU.
THERE'S SOME-THING I'VE BEEN MEANING TO TEST OUT, ANYWAY.

READ THIS WAY

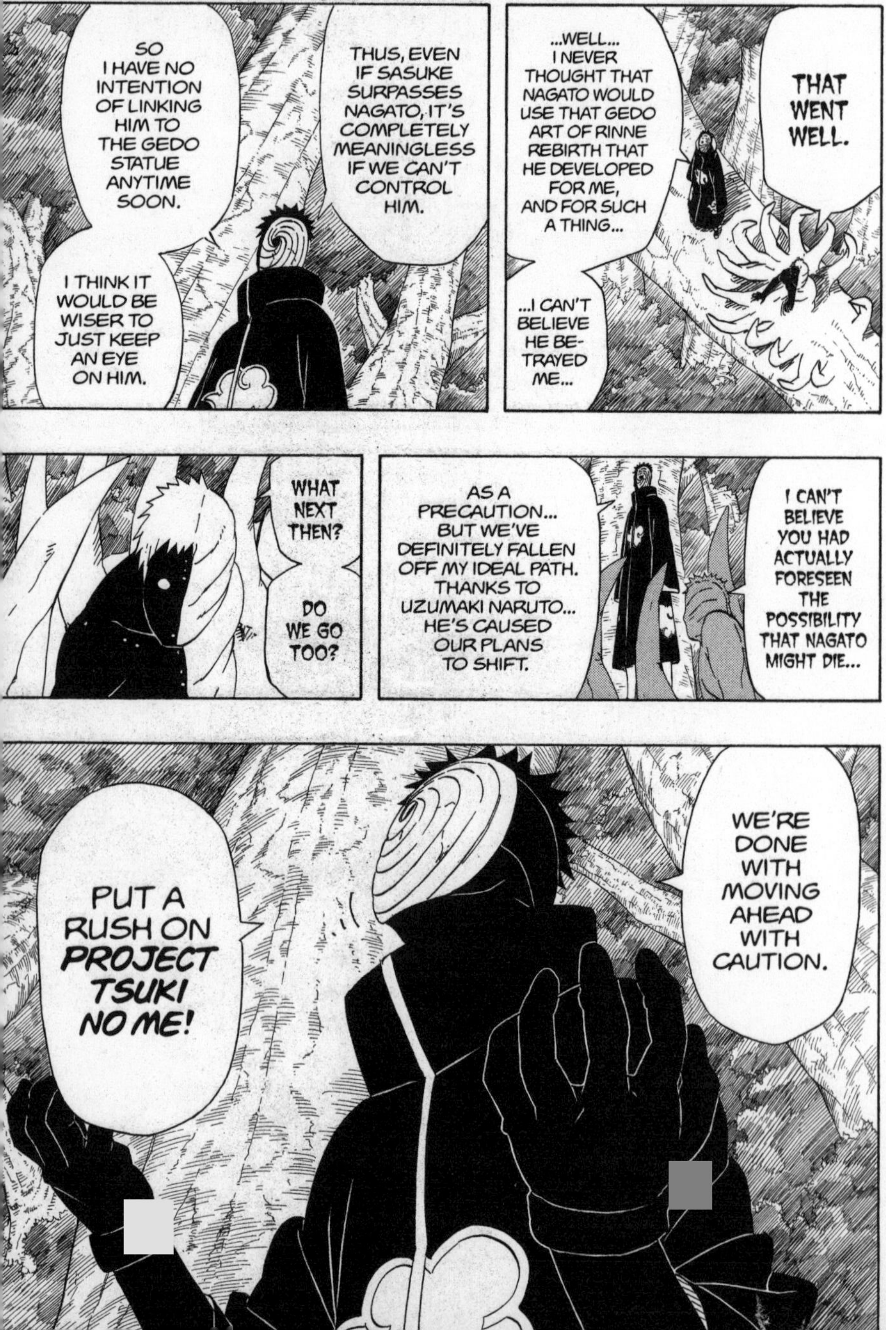
THAT WENT WELL.
...WELL... I NEVER THOUGHT THAT NAGATO WOULD USE THAT GEDO ART OF RINNE REBIRTH THAT HE DEVELOPED FOR ME, AND FOR SUCH A THING...
...I CAN'T BELIEVE HE BE-TRAYED ME...
THUS, EVEN IF SASUKE SURPASSES NAGATO, IT'S COMPLETELY MEANINGLESS IF WE CAN'T CONTROL HIM.
SO I HAVE NO INTENTION OF LINKING HIM TO THE GEDO STATUE ANYTIME SOON.
I THINK IT WOULD BE WISER TO JUST KEEP AN EYE ON HIM.
I CAN'T BELIEVE YOU HAD ACTUALLY FORESEEN THE POSSIBILITY THAT NAGATO MIGHT DIE...
AS A PRECAUTION... BUT WE'VE DEFINITELY FALLEN OFF MY IDEAL PATH. THANKS TO UZUMAKI NARUTO... HE'S CAUSED OUR PLANS TO SHIFT.
WHAT NEXT THEN?
DO WE GO TOO?
WE'RE DONE WITH MOVING AHEAD WITH CAUTION.
PUT A RUSH ON PROJECT TSUKI NO ME!

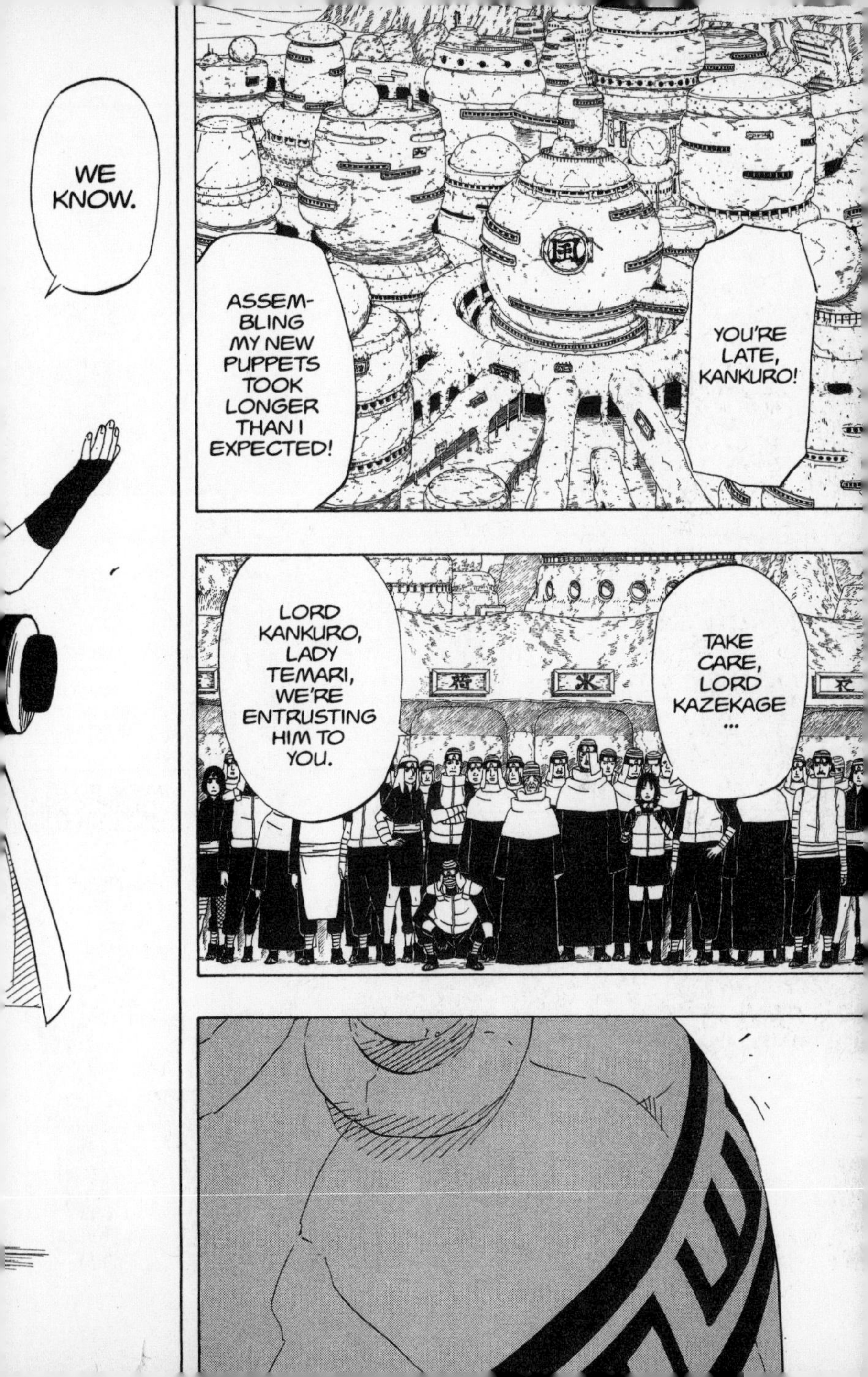
YOU'RE LATE, KANKURO!
ASSEM-BLING MY NEW PUPPETS TOOK LONGER THAN I EXPECTED!
TAKE CARE, LORD KAZEKAGE...
LORD KANKURO, LADY TEMARI, WE'RE ENTRUSTING HIM TO YOU.
WE KNOW.

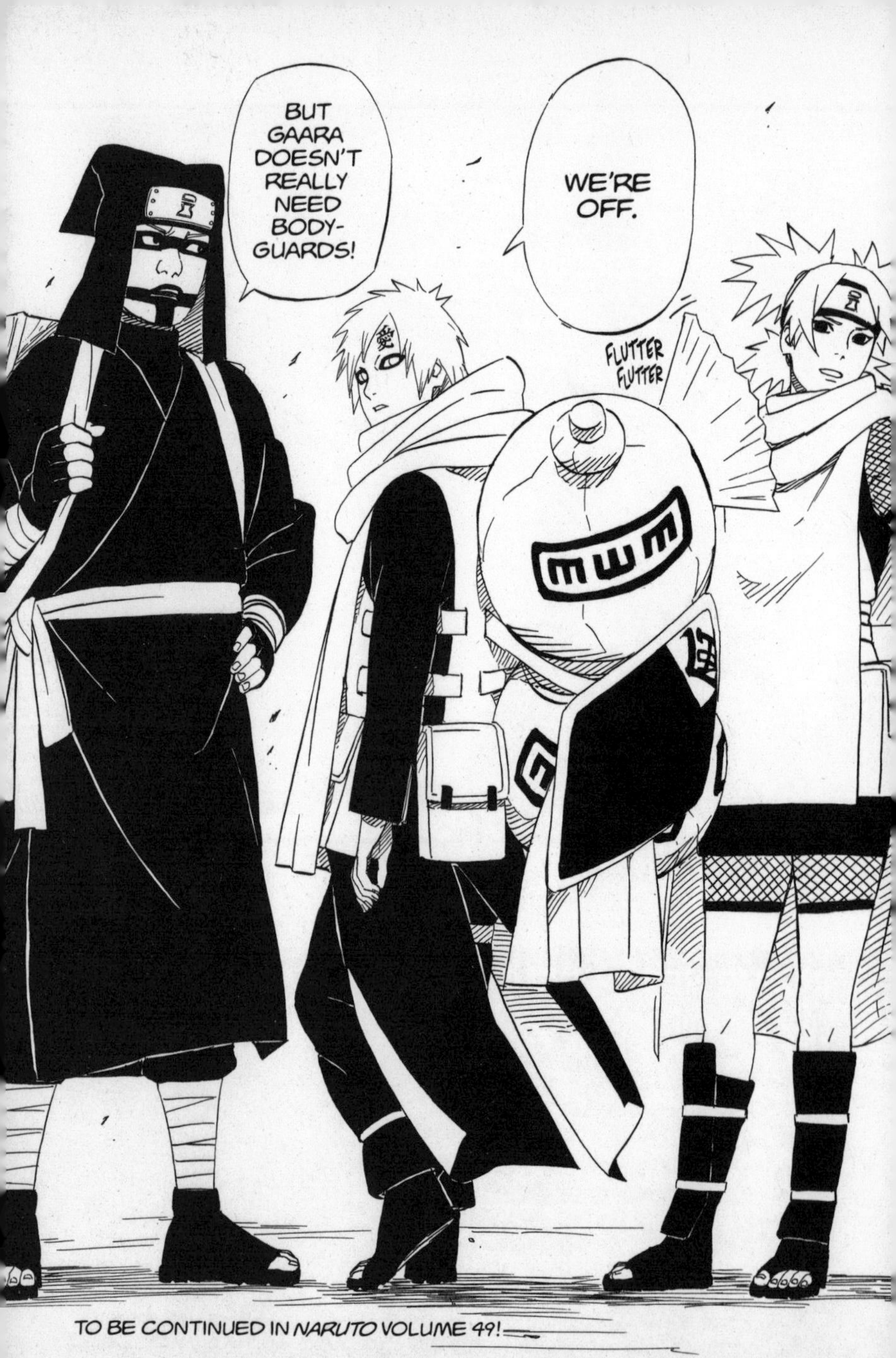
WE'RE OFF.
FLUTTER FLUTTER
BUT GAARA DOESN'T REALLY NEED BODY-GUARDS!

TO BE CONTINUED IN *NARUTO* VOLUME 49!

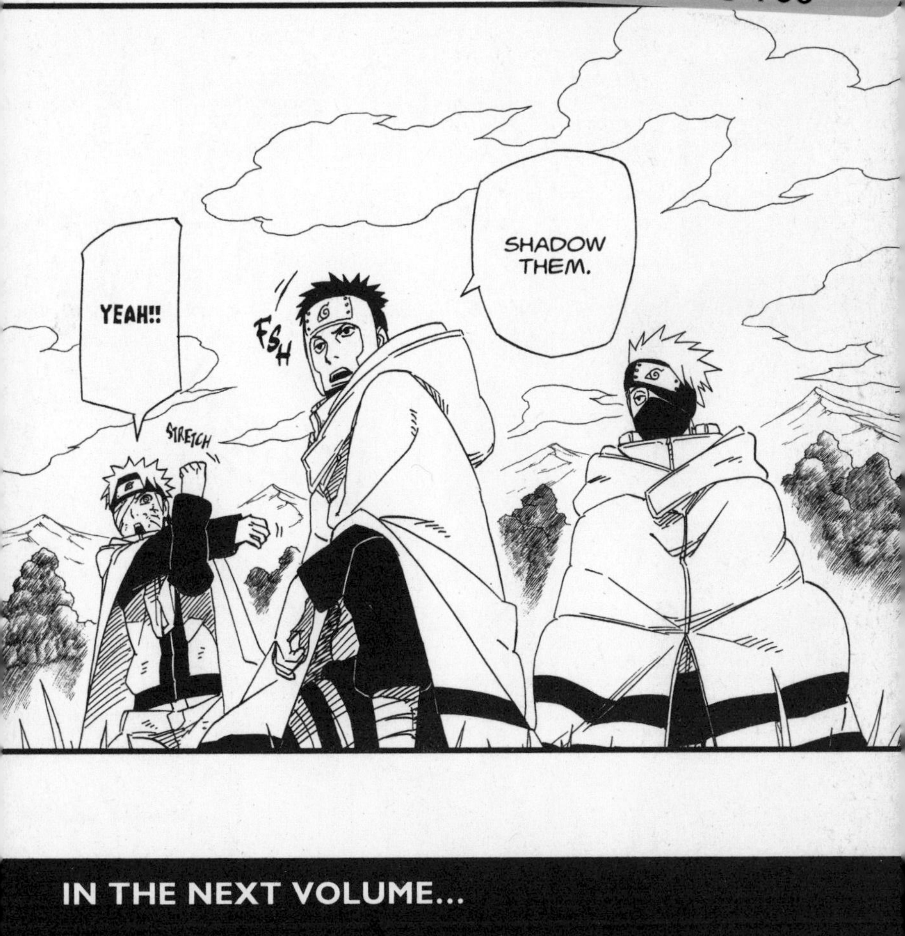
SHADOW THEM.
FSH
YEAH!!
STRETCH

IN THE NEXT VOLUME...

THE GOKAGE SUMMIT COMMENCES

As the five leaders of the strongest villages in the ninja world meet to discuss the fate of their universe—and how to deal with the ever-looming threat of the rogue organization, the Akatsuki—plans are made that will affect Naruto deeply. The new Hokage, leader of Naruto's village, is not afraid to make the final end move against Naruto's old pal Sasuke!

AVAILABLE OCTOBER 2010!
READ IT FIRST IN SHONEN JUMP MAGAZINE!